Ego Functions in Schizophrenics, Neurotics, and Normals: A Systematic Study of
Conceptual, Diagnostic, and Therapeutic Aspects
*by Leopold Bellak, Marvin Hurvich, and Helen A. Gediman*

Innovative Treatment Methods in Psychopathology
*edited by Karen S. Calhoun, Henry E. Adams, and Kevin M. Mitchell*

The Changing School Scene: Challenge to Psychology
*by Leah Gold Fein*

Troubled Children: Their Families, Schools, and Treatments
*by Leonore R. Love and Jaques W. Kaswan*

Research Strategies in Psychotherapy
*by Edward S. Bordin*

The Volunteer Subject
*by Robert Rosenthal and Ralph L. Rosnow*

Innovations in Client-Centered Therapy
*by David A. Wexler and Laura North Rice*

The Rorschach: A Comprehensive System
*by John E. Exner*

Theory and Practice in Behavior Therapy
*by Aubrey J. Yates*

Principles of Psychotherapy
*by Irving B. Weiner*

Psychoactive Drugs and Social Judgment: Theory and Research
*edited by Kenneth Hammond and C. R. B. Joyce*

Clinical Methods in Psychology
*edited by Irving B. Weiner*

Human Resources for Troubled Children
*by Werner I. Halpern and Stanley Kissel*

Hyperactivity
*by Dorothea M. Ross and Sheila A. Ross*

Heroin Addiction: Theory, Research, and Treatment
*by Jerome J. Platt and Christina Labate*

Children's Rights and the Mental Health Profession
*edited by Gerald P. Koocher*

The Role of the Father in Child Development
*edited by Michael E. Lamb*

THE ROLE OF THE FATHER
IN CHILD DEVELOPMENT

# THE ROLE OF THE FATHER
# IN CHILD DEVELOPMENT

*Edited by*

MICHAEL E. LAMB
*University of Wisconsin*
*Madison, Wisconsin*

A WILEY-INTERSCIENCE PUBLICATION

JOHN WILEY & SONS, New York • London • Sydney • Toronto

**Library of Congress Cataloging in Publication Data:**

Main entry under title:

The Role of the father in child development.

(Wiley series on personality processes)
"A Wiley-Interscience publication."
Includes bibliographies and index.
1.  Child development.  2.  Father and child.
I.  Lamb, Michael E., date [DNLM:  1.  Father-Child relations.  2.  Personality development.  3.  Child development. WS105 R746]

HQ772.R63        301.42'7        76-21778
ISBN 0-471-51172-2

Printed in the United States of America

10 9 8 7 6 5 4 3 2 1

# Contributors

HENRY B. BILLER, Department of Psychology, University of Rhode Island, Kingston, Rhode Island

ESTHER BLANK GREIF, Department of Psychology, Boston University, Boston, Massachusetts

MELVIN J. KONNER, Department of Anthropology, Harvard University, Cambridge, Massachusetts

MILTON KOTELCHUCK, Department of Psychology, University of Massachusetts, Boston, Massachusetts

MICHAEL E. LAMB, Department of Psychology, University of Wisconsin, Madison, Wisconsin

MICHAEL LEWIS, Infant Laboratory, Educational Testing Service, Princeton, New Jersey

VERONICA MACHTLINGER, Berlin

JOHN NASH, Department of Psychology, University of Hong Kong, Hong Kong

NORMA RADIN, School of Social Work, University of Michigan, Ann Arbor, Michigan

WILLIAM K. REDICAN, Department of Psychobiology and Physiology, Stanford Research Institute, Menlo Park, California

MARSHA WEINRAUB, Department of Psychology, Virginia Polytechnic and State University, Blacksburg, Virginia

MARY MAXWELL WEST, Department of Anthropology, Harvard University, Cambridge, Massachusetts

# Series Preface

This series of books is addressed to behavioral scientists interested in the nature of human personality. Its scope should prove pertinent to personality theorists and researchers as well as to clinicians concerned with applying an understanding of personality processes to the amelioration of emotional difficulties in living. To this end, the series provides a scholarly integration of theoretical formulations, empirical data, and practical recommendations.

Six major aspects of studying and learning about human personality can be designated: personality theory, personality structure and dynamics, personality development, personality assessment, personality change, and personality adjustment. In exploring these aspects of personality, the books in the series discuss a number of distinct but related subject areas: the nature and implications of various theories of personality; personality characteristics that account for consistencies and variations in human behavior; the emergence of personality processes in children and adolescents; the use of interviewing and testing procedures to evaluate individual differences in personality; efforts to modify personality styles through psychotherapy, counseling, behavior therapy, and other methods of influence; and patterns of abnormal personality functioning that impair individual competence.

IRVING B. WEINER

*Case Western Reserve University*
*Cleveland, Ohio*

# *Preface*

This volume was conceived in response to a belief that the field had reached a stage that demanded such a forum. On the one hand, a significant amount of data on various topics had been gathered, while on the other hand, the field was still in its infancy and required a synthesis of the available evidence to direct the way for future research. Previous attempts to synthesize the literature were less global in focus and had failed to reach a wide audience. Rather than attempt to synthesize the diverse and complex literature myself, it seemed preferable to permit persons who had been active in the area to share their expertise and knowledge. This volume is thus unique in its breadth of coverage and in the extent to which the persons writing the chapters have firsthand knowledge of the theoretical frameworks, the research and its problems, and the major questions—posed and unanswered.

Inspection of the Contents will give the reader an idea of the range of issues involved in attempts to define the role of the father in child development:

- What is the nature of father–child interaction?
- What influence does the father–child relationship have on sex-role, moral, and intellectual development?
- Within which theoretical frameworks can explanations be sought?
- What is the effect of growing up without a father?
- Is the nature of the father–child relationship culture-specific, or are there similarities from culture to culture, and from species to species?

Typically, the author of each chapter has reviewed the relevant conceptual frameworks and the empirical data bearing on the issue in an attempt both to evaluate existing hypotheses and to propose questions for future investigation. One chapter (9) presents detailed evidence from one study of parent–infant interaction; this is included because it demonstrates the type of detailed descriptive work that must be performed before we approach understanding of the process of sociopersonality development in infancy and childhood.

Our goals in the publication of this volume are threefold. First, we hope to redress the imbalanced focus on the mother's influence that has characterized much previous theorizing and research, by demonstrating that fathers, like mothers, have both direct and indirect influences on the psychological development of their offspring. Second, we hope to stimulate the interest of students, graduate and undergraduate, and our colleagues by presenting this synthesis of evidence relating to a complex issue. Finally, we hope that the conclusions we draw from the evidence will provoke interest among active researchers in a vastly underworked, poorly explored field.

Volumes that present a multifaceted approach to a specific issue often evoke misunderstanding about the motives of the authors. The presentation of numerous perspectives on the role of the father inevitably provokes speculation that the contributors are implying that fathers are the most important influences on child development. Clearly, such an argument would be absurd. Our intention is simply to show that fathers do, in fact, have an effect on the psychological development of their children—a fact that has been ignored altogether too often in past conceptualization.

My hope is that the net effect of this volume will be to stimulate, not simply research on father–child relations, but a radical reorientation in the manner in which we typically consider and research the processes of human development. Psychological development is complex, and the potential influences are multitudinous. Only when we come to appreciate the complexity are we likely to advance our understanding significantly. I believe that the family system, with its network of relationships and patterns of direct and indirect influence, plays the essential role in early sociopersonality development. When we come to conceive as significant, not only the mother–child, but also the father–child, father–mother, sibling–child, and sibling–parent relationships, I believe we will be on our way to understanding and explanation.

MICHAEL E. LAMB

*Madison, Wisconsin*
*July 1976*

# Contents

THE ROLE OF THE FATHER
IN CHILD DEVELOPMENT

# CHAPTER 1

# The Role of the Father: An Overview

MICHAEL E. LAMB

*University of Wisconsin-Madison*

This volume attempts to analyze critically our theoretical and empirical understanding of the contribution made by fathers to the socialization and social development of children. Subsequent chapters focus on specific areas in which fathers have been assumed to play an important role. This chapter reviews the different perspectives and attempts a synthesis of the notions deriving from several diverse viewpoints.

Recently both laymen and academics have shown an increasing interest in the role of the father in child development (Benson, 1968; Biller, 1971a, 1974d; Biller & Meridith, 1974; Dodson, 1974; Gilbert, 1975; Lamb, 1975a; Lynn, 1974; Shedd, 1975).

First, contemporary social development theorists, reflecting, no doubt, traditional cultural emphases (e.g., Briffault, 1927; Demos, 1974; Gorer, 1948; Sunley, 1955; cf. Westermarck, 1921), had increasingly stressed the role of the mother in the socialization of the child (Bowlby, 1969; Layman, 1961; Tallman, 1965; Williams, 1965). This was particularly true in considerations of infant social development—an issue to which I return later in this chapter. The focus on the mother–infant relationship was so unbalanced that several researchers were led to ask: Is it indeed true that the father is an almost irrelevant entity in the infant's social world?

A second reason for the ascendant interest in fathers and other family members relates to the disintegration of the family in contemporary Amer-

This chapter was written while the author was engaged in research supported by the Ecology of Human Development Program of the Foundation for Child Development. I am grateful to Thomas Achenbach, Urie Bronfenbrenner, and Sheila Huddleston for their helpful comments on earlier drafts of the manuscript.

Throughout the chapter the pronoun *it* will be used to refer to the child in an effort to avoid sexism. I do not intend to imply that children are inanimate or neuter.

ican society. Bronfenbrenner (1975b, 1975c) has dramatically illustrated the degree to which the ecology in which children are raised has been altered in recent years, and the rapidity and extensiveness of these changes have forced social scientists to consider the likely consequences. Unfortunately they find themselves knowing little about either the nature or the importance of the father–child relationship, the one most frequently disrupted (Bronfenbrenner, 1975c; Clausen, 1966; Herzog & Sudia, 1970; Wynn, 1964).

Finally researchers have been gathering extensive evidence suggesting that the infant, once assumed to be a passive and receptive partner in social interaction, is actually capable of playing a far more active role and that its sensory competence should not be underestimated. This fact, too, has led social scientists to question whether the infant's social world may not be far more complex than much of our theorizing has assumed. Perhaps then, infants form affective relationships to persons other than their mothers! The research discussed later in this chapter certainly suggests that infants relate extensively to both parents.

This chapter, then, attempts to summarize what we do know about the role the father plays in child development, and since (as the reader will anticipate on the basis of my introduction) there is much that we do not know, I attempt to identify issues toward which further investigation might profitably be directed. I also wish to draw attention to the dangers of over-specialization and the need to appreciate interdependencies. In the present context I am concerned with the tendency of researchers to focus on circumscribed stages of development while ignoring the need to see continuity in the life cycle. Accordingly one aim of this chapter is to search for this continuity, and I emphasize the need to see the father–infant, father–child, and father–adolescent relationships as different stages in the development of a continuous relationship between two persons.

## INFANCY

Almost without exception most theorists (Bijou & Baer, 1961; Bowlby, 1951, 1958, 1969, 1973; Freud, e.g., 1940; Kohlberg, 1966; Maccoby & Masters, 1970; Mowrer, 1950; Parsons, 1958; Sears, 1957; Winnicott, 1965), whatever their orientation, have assumed that the mother–infant relationship is unique and vastly more important than any contemporaneous, or indeed any subsequent, relationships (Lamb, 1975a). In fact Bowlby and Freud explicitly see the mother–infant relationship as the prototype of all later love relations, even though, as Schaffer (1971) writes: "Whether a child's first relationship is in any way the prototype of all future relationships we do not as yet know; the clinical material bearing on this point is hardly convincing" (p. 151).

For all except Bowlby the basis of this belief derives from the fact that the mother typically takes on the role of primary caretaker, so that the first affective relationship is presumed to develop from the continued association of the mother with the positive sensation of need gratification (Dollard & Miller, 1950). This *secondary drive hypothesis*, at least in its traditional form, lost adherents in the general fall from favor of Hull's (1943) drive reduction model of learning and was further weakened by Harlow's demonstration that infant monkeys prefer to cling to, and seek comfort from, soft terry-cloth mother surrogates rather than from wire surrogates that feed them (Harlow, 1961; Harlow & Zimmerman, 1959). Likewise Ainsworth (1963, 1967) and Schaffer and Emerson (1964) reported that many infants had strong attachments to persons who had little to do with their caretaking and physical gratification. In addition researchers have been unable to find consistent relationships between infantile gratification and later dependency behavior (Sears, Maccoby, & Levin, 1957; Sears, Whiting, Nowlis, & Sears, 1953).

Drawing on evidence such as this, the work of the ethologists on imprinting (Hinde, 1970; Lorenz, 1935; Sluckin, 1965), and his own previous research on the damaging effects of parental deprivation and institutionalization (Bowlby, 1944, 1951), Bowlby (1958, 1969) proposed instead a theory of attachment stressing the evolutionary advantage (survival value) of a bond between mother and infant leading the infant to strive to maintain proximity to the protective adult.

In the final analysis most theories assume that the mother is uniquely important in the child's life because she spends the most time with it and interacts most with it [1] This argument is unconvincing for several reasons.

[1] With the popularization of ethology, many psychologists have argued that females are biologically designed to be the primary socializers of infants (Bardwick, 1971; Bowlby, 1969; Kennell, Trause, & Klaus, 1975; Klaus, Trause, & Kennell, 1975; Leifer, Leiderman, Barnett, & Williams, 1972; Money & Tucker, 1975). Most of these arguments draw on evidence concerning the role of hormones in the establishment of maternal behavior in rats (Lamb, 1975e), and few even grant the possibility that the relevance of this research is questionable. The variability among rodents (e.g., rats vs. mice), the stereotypic nature of rodent parenting compared with the complexity of socialization and social interaction in human beings, the frequent incidence of "maternal behavior" in nulliparous male and female human beings, and the absence of any evidence suggesting that females are biologically designed (except for lactation) to play a primary role in socialization, or indeed that they perform this task more competently (L. Hoffman, 1974), combine to make the rat model totally inappropriate (cf. Bernal and Richards, 1973). Ford and Beach (1951) pointed out many years ago that the role of hormones in the display of sexual behavior decreased as

First, it exaggerates the extent of the interaction between a mother and her young children. The best evidence available suggests that, even when the mother is in the same room as the child, interaction is infrequent (Clarke-Stewart, 1973).[2] Similarly, in East Africa and Zambia, Goldberg (1972) and Leiderman and Leiderman (1974, 1975) note how minimal the social interaction is between mother and infant, even when the infant is being carried almost continually by its mother.

Second, empirical and theoretical considerations indicate that the amount of time spent together is a poor predictor of the quality of the infant's relationship with either mother or father (Feldman, 1973, 1974; Pederson & Robson, 1969; Schaffer & Emerson, 1964; but see Ainsworth, 1963). Perhaps the best evidence of this is the fact that extended, daily separations from mothers such as those demanded by day care attendance do not appear to disrupt the infant–mother attachment (Bronfenbrenner, 1975a; Caldwell, Wright, Honig & Tannenbaum, 1970; Doyle, 1975; Doyle & Somers, 1975; Feldman, 1973; Ragozin, 1975; Ramey & Mills, 1975; Ricciuti & Poresky, 1973; only Blehar, 1974, cites contradictory evidence), and there is no conceptual reason why the daily separations from a working father should be any more disruptive. Far more important are the quality of the interaction (Bossard & Bell, 1966; Pederson & Robson, 1969; Schaffer & Emerson, 1964) and the adult's sensitivity to the infant's signals (Ainsworth, Bell, & Stayton, 1971, 1974; Schaffer & Emerson, 1964): a few hours of pleasurable interaction may be far more conducive to the formation of strong and secure attachments than extensive hours of desultory and unstimulating cohabitation with a dissatisfied and harassed mother (Birnbaum, 1971; Yarrow, Scott, DeLeeuw, & Heinig,

---

one ascended the phylogenetic scale while cultural/learned factors increased in importance, and there is every reason to believe that, among human beings, societal prescriptions are *at least* as important in the regulation of parental behavior and are probably far more important. There is no reason to believe that hormones are either necessary or sufficient conditions for the display of human parental behavior.

Perhaps Daniel Lehrman, a pioneer in the attempts to explain the hormonal bases of parental behavior, was correct in his evaluation of the reason for the popularity of this type of thinking: "Concluding from these data that biology tells us that we are violating our inherent nature, in ways which are bound to be discordant, if the woman does not spend all her time caring for the baby while the man does important things like programming computers; and concluding that it is our biological nature that demands this kind of sex role differentiation—that it is a violation of natural selection and of Darwin's theories for a woman to feel as seriously about her work as a man— may be using what look like scientific considerations to justify our social prejudices (Lehrman, 1974, p. 194)."

[2] Fitzsimmons and Rowe (1971) and Stone (1970) reported vastly more maternal behavior, but they included in their estimates the amount of time spent in child-related activities that did not involve interpersonal interaction.

1962). As far as fathers are concerned, the findings of Gavron (1966) and of the Newsons (1963, 1968) show that most English fathers are highly accessible to their young children while at home. My research (Lamb, 1975b, 1975c, Chapter 9) and that of Pederson and Robson (1969) show that the interaction that at least some infants have with their fathers is enjoyable and marked by highly positive emotions on both sides. This may be critical in the formation of a strong infant–father relationship.

I am not implying that the mother–infant relationship is unimportant or that mothers never interact with their infants. My intention is simply to suggest that mother–infant interaction is not as extensive as many assume and that, in any event, the *extent* of interaction is probably unrelated to its *quality*, which appears to be the critical variable for both mothers and fathers. Clearly, there must be a minimal amount of interaction to allow an attachment to form, but beyond that, the quality appears unrelated to the extent of interaction. Many fathers, I hasten to add, do not interact either extensively or sensitively, but we must view this fact in the light of evidence, albeit from one small sample, that insecure attachments to mothers (resulting from insensitive interaction) are extremely common (Ainsworth & Bell, 1970; Ainsworth, Bell, & Stayton, 1971; Ainsworth & Wittig, 1969).

So strong have been the assumptions concerning the mother's pre-eminence in infancy that empirical investigations of them have been attempted only in the last few years. In an early study Schaffer and Emerson (1964) reported that infants protested separation from their mothers more often than from their fathers around 9 months of age, but later most infants protested separation from the two parents about equally. Perhaps because the technique of data collection (maternal reports) biased Schaffer and Emerson's findings, subsequent researchers have found that, when separation protest is the dependent measure, there is no demonstrable preference for either parent in the home or in the laboratory (Cohen & Campos, 1974; Kotelchuck, 1972, 1973; Kotelchuck, Zelazo, Kagan, & Spelke, 1975; Lamb, 1975e, 1976a; Ross, Kagan, Zelazo, & Kotelchuck, 1975; Spelke, Zelazo, Kagan & Kotelchuck, 1973). Indeed, some studies suggest that the intensity of greeting behavior may imply a preference for the father (Lamb, 1975e, 1976a). Even in the Schaffer and Emerson study, it should be noted how many infants were attached to their fathers from the beginning of attachment. All the evidence on this count, then, fails to substantiate Ainsworth's (1962) and Bowlby's (1969) notion of monotropy.

Further research using the frequency of attachment behaviors[3] (Ains-

[3] Separation protest is, of course, also an attachment behavior: The terminology used here is simply for clarity of exposition. By attachment behavior, I am referring here to the social behaviors displayed in an undisturbed free-play situation (Lamb, 1974).

worth, 1964; Bowlby, 1969) to assess preference has yielded contradictory evidence. Some studies report that 10- to 16-month-old infants prefer their mothers (Cohen & Campos, 1974; Lewis & Weinraub, 1974; Lewis, Weinraub, & Ban, 1972), but 2-year-old boys prefer their fathers, and girls prefer neither parent (Lamb, 1976a; Lewis et al., 1972). The preference of 1-year-old infants for their mothers may be influenced by the strangeness of the procedures and of the laboratory situation in which the infants were observed, particularly as even younger infants (7–8 months old) who prefer interaction with their fathers at home (Lamb, 1975b, 1975c, Chapter 9) prefer neither parent unequivocally in a structured laboratory setting (Lamb, 1975c, 1976b). Other evidence suggests that they behave differently in a strange situation (Lamb, 1976c), and it seems that on certain stressful occasions infants prefer to be near their mothers if both parents are present (Lamb, 1976d). When they do not have the choice, however, both 1- and 2-year-old children appear to organize their attachment and exploratory behaviors in the strange situation (Ainsworth, Blehar, Waters, & Wall, in preparation; Ainsworth & Wittig, 1969) in much the same way whether they are accompanied by their mothers or their fathers (Feldman & Ingham, 1975; Lamb, 1976d; Willemsen, Flaherty, Heaton, & Ritchey, 1974).

Pursuing a distinction drawn by Bretherton and Ainsworth (1974) between behaviors that can serve both the affiliative and attachment behavior systems and those that are likely to be restricted to intercourse with attachment figures, I noted that 8-month-old infants show no preference for either parent on the measures related to the attachment system but direct more affiliative-type behaviors to their fathers (Lamb, 1975b, see Chapter 9). This confirmed the suggestion that both parents are attachment figures but implied that fathers may simply be more fun to interact with (see, however, Keller, Montgomery, Moss, Sharp, & Wheeler, 1975).

Most of this research has attempted to answer this question: Are mothers preferred to fathers by young infants? The answer appears to be yes, although our evidence thus far is derived from a limited number of studies, mostly involving observations in laboratory settings. Note, furthermore, that these preferences are apparent in very specific circumstances in which the infant is distressed. In stress-free, natural situations, infants do not exhibit a preference for either parent.

We shall shortly consider the implication of this finding for the theories that have assumed that infants are uniquely attached, or "more attached" to their mothers than to anyone else. The revelant research certainly supports the notions that the infant's social world is far more complex than most have assumed and that, from the earliest age, the baby is likely to be influenced by, and reciprocally to influence, both directly and indirectly, at least both its parents and probably other relatives and friends as well (Lamb, in press; Weinraub, Brooks, & Lewis, 1976). The fact that infants form attachments to more than one person has clear survival value, as Mead (1962) points out, since the child then has insurance against loss of a parent.

## Maternal and Paternal Roles

The next issue to arise is perhaps even more crucial: If mothers and fathers are both important persons in the life of the infant, are they functionally distinguishable? There is widespread agreement that mothers and fathers play different roles in the socialization of older children (though this realization is apparently not universal, e.g., Miller & Swanson, 1958; Nowlis, 1952), but since fathers have been assumed to play no direct role with respect to infants and young children, there was little concern about the difference between maternal and paternal roles in infancy until recently (Lamb, 1975a).

Though the evidence on this score is limited, it indicates that differential parental roles exist in early infancy. A recent informal study by Biller (1974c) suggests one respect in which fathers and mothers interact differently with their infants. Whereas mothers were more likely to inhibit the child's exploration, Biller notes that fathers encouraged their babies' curiosity and urged them to attempt to solve cognitive and motoric challenges. He suggests that this fostered their sense of mastery over the environment.

A detailed observational study (see Chapter 9) specified the differentiating features more precisely. Whereas mothers engaged in more conventional and toy-mediated types of play, fathers initiated more physical (rough-and-tumble type) and idiosyncratic types of play. The infants in this study apparently preferred to play with their fathers, for they responded more positively when fathers initiated play than when their mothers did. The infants also preferred to be held by their fathers, which was not surprising, since the fathers were far more likely to pick them up to play with them, whereas the mothers most often picked them up to engage in caretaking activities.

Other evidence confirms the prominence of play in the infant–father interaction. Lamb (1976a) found that 2-year-old infants (particularly boys) were more likely to initiate play with their fathers than with their mothers when both were present, and were more likely to greet their fathers after a separation by trying to involve them in play. Likewise Lynn and Cross (1974) reported that, when given the choice between playing with their mothers or their fathers, boys of 2 years and older chose their fathers;

girls shifted from wanting their fathers to wanting their mothers between 2 and 4 years of age. These results are congruent with the findings of an earlier study of parental preferences (Ammons & Ammons, 1949).

The identification of the father with play is apparently acknowledged by the parents, too, for Fagot (1974) found that the parents of 2-year-old boys believed that the father's role involved playing with and providing role models for their sons. Significantly, parents of girls did not believe that mothers and fathers play differentiable roles. Because this is compatible with the finding that boys are more consistent in their preference for play with fathers, these findings may reflect different aspects of a cultural expectation that fathers should play a more active role in the socialization of their sons.

The early age at which parental emphasis on sex typing emerges is consistent with the argument that sex-role adoption may occur substantially earlier than the psychoanalytic theory would indicate. Money and his colleagues (Money & Ehrhardt, 1972; Money, Hampson, & Hampson, 1957; Hampson & Hampson, 1961) have assembled considerable evidence to suggest that sex-role adoption is accomplished by the age of 18 months; reassignment after this age commonly results in greater difficulty in adapting to the new role demands and in more severe socioemotional problems than earlier reassignment does. Others, too, have noted the early emergence of sex differences in interpersonal behavior (Brooks & Lewis, 1974; Goldberg & Lewis, 1969; Maccoby & Jacklin, 1973; Messer & Lewis, 1972), in the adoption of sexually appropriate roles in play (Greif, 1973), and in sex-role preferences (Hartup & Zook, 1960).

Clearly, of course, the mother also plays a role in this process (Goldberg & Lewis, 1969, Lewis, 1972b; Lewis & Weinraub, 1974; Moss, 1967). Mothers verbalize more to their daughters (Endsley, Garner, Odom, & Martin, 1975; Lewis, 1972a, 1975b; Moss, 1967) and encourage them in contact and proximity seeking, which they discourage in sons after the first 6 months (Goldberg & Lewis, 1969), during which boys tend to be crankier (Moss, 1967) and thereby demand more caretaking attention (Lewis, 1972a; Moss, 1967) from their mothers. Thus both parents play a part in encouraging sex-role-appropriate behavior in their infants, though the way each contributes may differ in some respects and be similar in others (Ban & Lewis, 1974; Lewis & Weinraub, 1974).

## Summary

I have dwelt at length on the research relating to infancy because I believe these data bear directly on the way we evaluate the older theories about the role of the father in child development. More specifically, it is usual to assume that the father–infant relationship is unimportant, or alternately, that before the child's third birthday, the father is merely an occasional mother substitute (Corter, 1974; Josselyn, 1956) or a source of emotional support for the mother (Bartemeier, 1953; Bowlby, 1951; Westley & Epstein, 1960). Thus role differentiation is perceived only along a quantitative rather than a qualitative dimension; most assume that mother and father roles per se are not yet delineated.

In contrast much of the evidence I have discussed suggests that many infants do form attachments to their fathers and that the father–infant and mother–infant relationships are qualitatively differentiable. Further research is needed to specify the distinctive aspects of the mother– and father–infant relationships and, subsequently, to determine what contributions fathers and mothers may be making to social development.

Many fathers do make themselves accessible to their infants, enjoy interacting with them, are responsive to their infant's signals, and become, therefore, salient and important figures in the social worlds of their babies —probably as important as their wives, even though the amount of time together may be relatively small. Although conclusive evidence is lacking, I believe that the infant who establishes close relationships with both parents has an advantage in the continuing process of socialization. Evidence bearing on this is reviewed in the next section.

Note, however, that many fathers are inaccessible to their infants; interact with them little, if at all; and are more apt to have a negative than a positive impact on their children's development, as should become clear in the following discussion of the father's contribution to child development and adjustment.

## THE FATHER AND OLDER CHILDREN: THEORETICAL PERSPECTIVES

### Psychoanalytic Theory

Probably the most influential characterization of the father–child relationship is the psychoanalytic theory of Sigmund Freud, who believed that both boys and girls formed their first and most important relationship with their mothers, though he did acknowledge that the infant pre-oedipally cathected and identified with both mother and father (Burlingham, 1973; Freud, [1905, 1939] 1948, 1950). At around 3 to 5 years of age, Freud proposed, the boy realized that his mother also loved his father, who was consequently seen as a rival for her affections. Further, the son became cognizant of the anatomical differences between the sexes, and assuming that girls once had penises, feared that his father might castrate him in retaliation, just as, presumably, his mother and other females were punished for their transgressions (Mullahy, 1948). To avert the possibility of this occurring, he repressed his affection for his mother and identified with his father (Freud, 1948). Not only is this supposed to diminish the father's aggression ("he would not castrate someone like him"), but also it is supposed to ensure the affection of the mother ("she will love me because she loves father and I am like father"). The identification with the father is crucial for the boy's sex-role adoption and also presages the formation of the superego, a prerequisite for the development of morality and moral behavior (Freud, 1909, 1923, 1924). The girl is supposed to undergo a somewhat analogous process, but because she lacks the boy's motive to identify (castration anxiety), the process is never as thoroughgoing as in boys, and consequently, the girl is believed to have a weaker superego than the boy (Freud, 1950).[4]

Other psychoanalysts (Meerloo, 1956, 1968; Von Der Heydt, 1964) have stressed the importance of the father in breaking the infantile, symbiotic mother–child relationship and thus "cutting the cord" between the two. This presumes, of course, the absence of an early father–infant relationship (Sullivan, 1953); indeed, insofar as this may involve the father in "feminine" interaction, Meerloo believes that the father's role in breaking the mother–child dyad may be rendered impossible by such a relationship. Though Jung (1949; Von Der Heydt, 1964) published a book on the father's role, his theory consistently placed greatest emphasis on the mother and on the archetypal representation of the father.

Mächtlinger, in her analysis of the father in psychoanalytic theory (Chapter 8), draws attention to the current trend toward an emphasis on the early years as crucial to personality development. Anna Freud and other contemporary theorists (e.g., Abelin, 1971, 1975) have discussed the roles of both parents in the early years of the child's life, and like the present author, they have been concerned with qualitative differences

---

[4] Helen Deutsch (1944) and most other analysts have followed Freud in this belief. In addition, there is evidence from researchers of different persuasions that indicates that females tend to be more conforming, while boys tend to be independent thinkers (Allen & Crutchfield, 1963; Bardwick, 1971; Douvan, 1957, 1960; Getzels & Walsh, 1958; Kagan, 1964; McGuire, 1961; Mussen, Rutherford, Harris, & Keasey, 1970; Rebelsky, Allinsmith, & Grinder, 1963). Mussen et al. (1970) suggested on the basis of such data that the morality of girls is developmentally more primitive: they claimed that, whereas 12-year-old boys evince moral relativism, female agemates are still at the level of moral realism (Piaget, 1932). The evidence is not, however, unequivocal. Indeed, if women are more expressive and empathic (Parsons & Bales, 1955) and empathy is fundamental to morality (Hogan, 1973), we might predict that women would be *more* moral. There is no unequivocal evidence of this either.

between the mother– and father–child relationships. Mächtlinger also notes the importance to psychoanalysis of seeing the father as important by virtue of his role within the family system. Empiricism has led most to an overly simplistic conceptualization of the father's role, whereas psychoanalysts have continually stressed both the dangers implicit in this and the complexity of the process of personality development.

## Parsons' Theory

Parsons (1954, 1958; Parsons & Bales, 1955), like Mowrer (1950), has proposed a theory of personality that involves an elaboration of Freud's theory of identification (Bronfenbrenner, 1960, 1961a). Parsons and Mowrer concur in depicting the child's early social world as consisting only of child and mother, but during the period in which Freud places the oedipal conflict, Parsons suggests that the mother–child subsystem is expanded to include the father. Before this stage, Parsons argues, the mother plays both an expressive (nurturant, empathic) and an instrumental (competence, achievement-focused) function in relation to the child. Hereafter, however, the father is established as the primary representative of the instrumental role, and the mother plays a more restricted expressive role. The functional dichotomy reflects not merely parental-role but more basic sex-role differences and reportedly characterizes sex-role differentiation in a variety of cultures (Stephens, 1963; Zelditch, 1955). Another dimension governing family structure is a *power* dimension, which, as Parsons predicted, differentiates parental from child roles (Emmerich, 1959b, 1961), though children apparently discriminate maternal and paternal roles along this dimension, too (Emmerich, 1959a, 1959b).

 Although research has failed to substantiate consistently the existence of sex differences on the *function* dimension as great as Parsons predicts— at least not among the American middle-class college students who serve as subjects in most research (see Maccoby & Jacklin, 1974 for a comprehensive review; Hartley, 1964, presents contradictory evidence), there is some evidence to suggest that this may be a useful way of differentiating parental roles (Emmerich, 1959b), and consequently, it merits more detailed consideration (see, for critiques, Black, 1961; Slater, 1961; and for similar notions, Lamb, 1975a; Meerloo, 1968; Stein, 1974).

 According to Parsons' formulation the father is seen by the child as representing an executive, action-oriented approach to the world. He is the primary link between the wider social system and the family system— an important aspect of Parsons' theory of action (Parsons & Shils, 1951), which seeks parallels, if not, as Baldwin (1961) labels them, "isomorphisms," between the family structure and the general social structure.

Thus the father would be the parent who introduces the child to the sex-role prescriptions of the wider world, encourages the acquisition of the competencies necessary for adaptation to the world, and represents and communicates the values and moralities of the social system. Evidently, although it is possible to relate the father's alleged "effects" to his instrumental function (Lynn, 1974), this is clearly not the only plausible explanation, and the theory is not formulated sufficiently precisely to be open to validation or rejection.

## Learning Theory

Most of the research conducted with older children has been within a learning theory framework. Although there is wider disagreement among learning theorists than is usually recognized, most would agree that learning and identification (imitation) are crucial aspects of preadolescent personality development (Mussen, 1967). Whereas both parents can, and do, engage in deliberate training, dispensing punishments and rewards in attempts to shape their children's behavior, most theorists stress that the father is the more punitive parent and thus is relatively more effective in the inhibition of antisocial and undesirable behaviors. Other researchers, most notably Bandura (Bandura, 1968; Bandura & Huston, 1961; Bandura & Walters, 1963), emphasize the importance of the learning that takes place without explicit reinforcement. Observational learning (modeling) is seen as the crucial process in the sex-role development of the young child, and thus the father's role in the development of the son's masculinity is of obvious importance. Lynn (1961, 1962, 1966, 1969) has, however, de-emphasized the father's role by arguing that boys "identify with the stereotype of the masculine role which the culture in general, not simply the father in particular spells out for them" (Lynn, 1959, p. 130).

Modeling of the father is obviously not vital for the sex-role development of his daughter. Most social learning theorists believe that he facilitates her femininity by rewarding dependent, flirtatious, and similarly "feminine" behavior and by discouraging "masculine" behavior (Lynn, 1974; cf. Deutsch, 1944). Thus whereas both deliberate training and modeling are stressed for the boy, only deliberate training is applicable to the girl. A reasonable prediction would be that the father has a greater impact on the sex-role development of his sons than of his daughters.

Modeling is not, however, restricted to sex-role learning. Thus both sons and daughters might be expected to imitate both mothers and fathers in at least some aspects of their behavior.

Clearly sex-role adoption has attracted the attention of most social learning metatheorists. In the subsequent section—Sex-Role Adoption—and in more detail in Biller's chapter (Chapter 3) on this topic, we evaluate the extent to which the research literature substantiates these theoretical propositions.

## REVIEW OF THE RESEARCH

In their chapters, Biller (Chapter 3) and Greif (Chapter 6) discuss the research conducted on sex-role adoption and moral development, respectively. It should be clear to the reader that theoretical considerations lead one to predict that the father's role in these two aspects of personality development should be substantial.

### Sex-Role Adoption

Most studies have focused on the father's role as a model, or identification figure, rather than as a socializing agent dispensing rewards and sanctions. Despite the emphasis placed on modeling and identification by psychoanalytically oriented and learning theorists, and the extensiveness of research in this area, the findings have been extraordinarily inconclusive and often contradictory.

With few exceptions (Gray, 1959; Hartup, 1962; Heilbrun, 1965; Sopchak, 1952, 1958) the modeling literature has failed to substantiate its fundamental hypothesis that masculine fathers will have masculine sons. In fact preadolescent boys are not more similar to their fathers than to their mothers (Hetherington, 1965; Hetherington & Brackbill, 1963; Lazowick, 1955; Lynn & Maaske, 1970; Sears, Rau, & Alpert, 1965), they do not perceive themselves as more similar to their fathers (Gray & Klaus, 1956; Kagan, Hosken, & Watson, 1961; Middleton & Putney, 1963), and the sex-role preferences of sons and fathers are uncorrelated (Angrilli, 1960; Mussen & Rutherford, 1963; Payne & Mussen, 1956). Indeed the only consistent correlate of paternal masculinity is the femininity of daughters (Heilbrun, 1965; Johnson, 1963; Mussen & Rutherford, 1963; Sears, Rau, & Alpert, 1965), and this correlation tends to support the notion of a role-complementation learning process similar to that discussed by Parsons. Although it is possible to argue that the methodological deficiencies of much of this research (see below) make any conclusion premature, it may seem parsimonious to state tentatively, along with Maccoby and Jacklin, "that modeling plays a minor role in the development of sex typed behavior" (1974, p. 300).

If modeling has yet to be proved an important precursor of sex-role learning, what of direct shaping or training? Though both parents probably participate in such training of both sons and daughters (Biller, 1968) and agree on sex-typing requirements (Emmerich, 1969), several studies have found that fathers are more concerned about sex typing (Bronfenbrenner, 1961c; Goodenough, 1957; Heilbrun, 1965; Sears, Maccoby & Levin, 1957; Tasch, 1955). Particularly in the middle class, however, fathers reportedly expect their wives to take primary responsibility for the raising of their daughters (Bronfenbrenner, 1961b; Kohn & Carroll, 1960) and so one might expect the fathers' influence on sons to be greater than on daughters.

Again the evidence is contradictory. There is disagreement about the association between paternal limit setting and filial masculinity: some studies have found a correlation (Altucher, 1957; Lefkowitz, 1962; Moulton, Burnstein, Liberty, & Altucher, 1966), but other have failed to replicate this (Biller, 1969a; Mussen & Distler, 1959, 1960; Mussen & Rutherford, 1963; Sears et al., 1965). Becker (1964) and Biller (1971a) have both pointed out, however, that it is important to consider the quality of the father–child relationship, not merely the father's masculinity or punitiveness. Bandura and Walters (1959) found, for example, that paternal punitiveness only enhanced masculinity when the father was also nurturant.

Modeling theorists would predict that the degree to which the son felt positively about his father would influence the degree to which he identified with his father. This prediction is supported by Bandura and Walters' findings. In addition warm, masculine fathers should have masculine sons, and indeed this has been shown in several studies (Biller & Borstelmann, 1967; Hetherington, 1967). But one important and consistent finding concerns the influence of a father who is warm and nurturant and participates extensively in childbearing. Such fathers have masculine sons (Anzimi, 1964; Bandura & Walters, 1959; Biller, 1969b; Distler, 1964; Freedheim, 1960; Kaplar, 1970; Moulton et al., 1966; Mussen, 1961; Mussen & Distler, 1959, 1960; Mussen & Rutherford, 1963; Payne & Mussen, 1956; P. Sears, 1953; Sears et al., 1957; Stoke, 1954) and feminine daughters (Johnson, 1963), regardless of their assessed masculinity or punitiveness. By contrast, when the father–child relationship is stressful, paternal and filial masculinity are negatively correlated (Bronson, 1959). This suggests strongly that we ought to examine the father–child relationship more closely, for the quality of this relationship appears more influential than the father's similarity to the caricatured masculinity or punitiveness that most studies have examined.

It is somewhat puzzling that, whereas common sense and theoretical considerations predict that fathers will have a greater influence on the sex-role development of sons than daughters, and despite the fact that male sex roles are defined earlier, more sharply, and more strictly (Brown, 1956, 1957a, 1958b; Cava & Rausch, 1952; Goodenough, 1957; Gray, 1957; Hacker, 1957; Lansky, 1967), there is greater consistency in the results of the few studies investigating feminine development. Deutsch (1944) had suggested that fathers enhanced the femininity of their daughters by rewarding "feminine" traits such as passivity and dependence with affection. This hypothesis, consistent with a role theory like Parsons', has been substantiated in several studies (Gardner, 1947; Heilbrun, 1965; Johnson, 1963; Landis, 1960; Mussen & Rutherford, 1963; Sears et al., 1965) and cited approvingly by other commentators (Biller & Weiss, 1970; Lynn, 1974). Again though, the crucial variable appears to be, not the masculinity of the father, but rather his warmth and the quality of the relationship with his daughter (Johnson, 1963).

*Father Absence.* From the studies reviewed thus far it seems that we can state only that an affectionate father–child relationship appears to facilitate the sex-role development of the children, though we are unable to be more specific about the outstanding characteristics of this relationship. The father-absence literature, reviewed more extensively by Biller in Chapter 3, does not permit us to be more specific either.

Boys raised without fathers are reported to be either less masculine in their sex-role preferences and behavior (Altus, 1958; Bach, 1946; Biller, 1969b, 1974b; Biller & Bahm, 1971; Burton & Whiting, 1960; Hetherington, 1966; Leichty, 1960; Lynn & Sawrey, 1959; Santrock, 1970a; P. Sears, 1951; R. Sears, Pintler, & P. Sears, 1946; Stoltz et al., 1954; Winch, 1949) or else to exhibit compensatory masculinity (Bartlett & Horrocks, 1958; Lynn & Sawrey, 1959; Pettigrew, 1964; Tiller, 1958, 1961; and perhaps McCord, McCord, & Thurber, 1962). Such boys have also been reported to have feminine (i.e., nonanalytic) cognitive styles (Altus, 1958; Barclay & Cusumano, 1967; Carlsmith, 1964, 1973; Milton, 1957; Nelson & Maccoby, 1966; Wohlford & Liberman, 1970).

Most studies suggest that father absence has its greatest effect on children who were separated from their fathers at a young age (Blaine, 1963; Blanchard & Biller, 1971; Carlsmith, 1964; Hetherington, 1966, 1972; Hetherington & Deur, 1971; Holman, 1953; Langner & Michael, 1963; Leichty, 1960; Santrock, 1970b). In girls, father absence is associated with difficulties in interacting with males (Hetherington, 1972; Jacobson & Ryder, 1969). It is interesting that father absence has its observable effects on girls in adolescence, even though, as with boys, early father absence is more debilitating. Nevertheless, perhaps because they have a role model present (Hetherington & Frankie, 1967; Mussen & Parker, 1965), girls are spared the harsher effects of father absence suffered by boys. The notion that girls raised without fathers reject their femininity (Jacobson & Ryder, 1969; Landy, Rosenberg, & Sutton-Smith, 1967) is controversial (Lynn & Sawrey, 1959; Santrock, 1970a, 1970b).

The presence of an alternative masculine model, for example, an older brother, may inhibit the effects of the father's absence to some degree (Brim, 1958; Koch, 1956; Rosenberg & Sutton-Smith, 1964; Santrock, 1970a; Sutton-Smith & Rosenberg, 1965; Wohlford, Santrock, Berger, & Liberman, 1971), though Biller (1968, 1971a) argues that the father is a superior role model. Nevertheless this illustrates the point that the effects of father absence cannot reasonably be determined without considering important ecological variables such as age at separation, the reason for the separation (Hetherington, 1972; Illsley & Thompson, 1961; Santrock & Wohlford, 1970), the family composition and structure, socioeconomic status and effects (Chilman & Sussman, 1964), the mother's behavior (Biller, 1970; Crain & Stamm, 1965), and the mother's reaction to the separation (Biller, 1969a; Biller & Bahm, 1971; Lerner, 1954; Pederson, 1966; Wylie & Delgado, 1959).

Although many of these studies (and the others discussed by Biller in Chapter 3) can be criticized for not taking these factors into account, sufficient studies have been done to permit a conclusion that father absence can be detrimental to the social adjustment of children, especially of sons.

*Implications of the Father-Absence Literature.* An important reason why we are as yet unable to specify the father's influence when he is present is that we have failed to take into account these same ecological variables. In effect we have been atttempting to characterize a role shorn of its contextual features. As I argue in a later section, these factors must be taken into account, not only because methodological requirements must be satisfied, but also because the role of father exists only in the context of a complex series of relationships within the family and in society at large.

In support of the importance of such factors several studies have shown that the extent to which the father is seen as the head of the household appears to influence the sex-role development of his son (Biller, 1969b; Freedheim, 1960; Hetherington, 1965; 1967; L. Hoffman, 1961; Kagan, 1958; Mussen & Distler, 1959). Correspondingly sex-role development may be retarded when the father plays a feminine role at home (Altucher, 1957; Bronfenbrenner, 1958). The greatest father–son similarity has been found in families in which the father dominates in interaction with his wife (Biller, 1969b; Hetherington, 1965; Hetherington & Brackbill, 1963; Hetherington & Frankie, 1967).

It is not only conceivable but likely that the failure to take such factors into account in other studies affected the results they obtained.

A second weakness in many of these studies relates to the techniques used to assess masculinity and similarity. The most popular means of assessing the child's identification and masculinity/femininity are doll play, projective tests, and paper-and-pencil questionnaires. Two decades ago Bronfenbrenner (1958) called attention to the methodological problems with research of this nature, but his suggestion for improvement has largely been ignored.

A further problem concerns the assessment of the parents' behavior or attitudes. It is rare indeed for the fathers to be interviewed directly (Tasch, 1952, 1955); most often, the children are asked to describe their parents' behavior, or alternately, the mothers are asked to describe their spouses and the father–child relationship. The former is more common. In most studies, then, there is a serious confounding, in that the sources of evidence about the child, the father, and their relationship are not independent. Our ability to draw inferences from such evidence is severely restricted. At best, most studies should be regarded as pilot investigations, preparing the way for methodologically and conceptually superior projects that, regrettably, have never been undertaken.

## Moral Development

Similar methodological problems have beset empirical investigations of the fathers' role in the moral development of their children. The development of conscience was ascribed by Freud to the formation of the superego following the oedipal crisis. This was probably the most influential factor in the theoretical instatement of the father as a major figure in moral development, even though the mechanisms postulated by the psychoanalysts can only be indirectly investigated. Parsons' theory would also attribute this role to the father because he is seen as the representative within the family of the values and standards of the society; without his mediation, the values would not be transmitted effectively. Unlike the psychoanalysts and Parsons, the cognitive developmental theorists do not see sexual identity and moral development as joint products of identification (Kohlberg, 1963, 1964, 1966, 1969) and do not place great emphasis on the father's role. Although the social learning theorists do stress the father's role via identification, M. Hoffman (1970b) concluded a review of the modeling literature by noting that "identification may have little bearing on moral development" (p. 317). Evidently, there is far less unanimity among theorists about the father's role in moral development than about his contribution to sex-role development.

The theoretical disagreements are paralleled by the inconclusiveness of the research literature. Martin Hoffman (1970b), in an authoritative review, noted that relationships between the child's morality and maternal behavior were more common than relationships between paternal behavior and the child's morality, and Holstein (1969) likewise found little father–child similarity in moral judgment but a significant mother–child similarity. Hoffman's research (M. Hoffman, 1966, 1970a, 1971a, 1971b; Hoffman & Saltzstein, 1967) showed, however, that fathers who had a positive approach to childrearing had sons who identified with them and displayed an internalized morality. This is consistent with other evidence suggesting that nurturant fathers (Rutherford & Mussen, 1968; Speece, 1967) and fathers who are more actively involved in caretaking in infancy (Speece, 1967) foster altruism and generosity (Livson, 1966, however, failed to find such a correlation). Weisbroth (1970) found that moral judgment in males was related to identification with both parents, whereas in females it was related only to identification with fathers.

Several studies have found that the father's reliance on love-oriented discipline is preferable, for this is more highly associated with morality than physical punitiveness is (MacKinnon, 1938; Moulton et al., 1966; Mussen & Distler, 1960). This implies that the psychoanalytic emphasis on the father's punitiveness may be misleading.

The literature indicates that delinquents are more likely to come from father-absent homes (Bacon, Child, & Barry, 1963; Bandura & Walters, 1959; Burton & Whiting, 1961; Glueck & Glueck, 1950, 1956; Gregory, 1965; Miller, 1958; Rohrer & Edmonson, 1960; Scarpitti, Murray, Dinitz, & Reckless, 1960; Siegman, 1966; Stephens, 1961), though father absence apparently has "no discernible effect on the conscience development of girls" (Hoffman, 1971a, p. 405, but see Clausen, 1961). Herzog and Sudia (1970, 1973) emphasize, however, the confounding in such studies of father absence with a host of socioeconomic problems that make it difficult to determine the father's direct effect. Support for the hypothesis that the father plays a role, as yet unspecified, in moral development can be drawn from the studies showing that delinquent sons come from homes where the father in antisocial, unempathic, and hostile (e.g., Andry, 1957, 1960, 1962; Bandura & Walters, 1959; Chinn, 1938; Crane, 1951; Glueck & Glueck, 1950, 1959; McCord, McCord, & Howard, 1961, 1963; Schaefer, 1965; Thrasher, 1927). Interestingly Andry found that poor father–child relationships were common antecedents of delinquency, even when there were apparently normal mother–child relationships. Hoffman (1971a) has proposed cautiously that "it appears that the effects of low identification with fathers who are present are quite similar though somewhat less pronounced than the effects of father absence" (p. 404). Perhaps the studies that attempted to correlate paternal characteristics with filial morality have had inconsistent results because of the nonindependence of the sources of evidence and the inadequacy of the assessment of paternal behavior. Future and more careful research will, it is hoped, clarify our knowledge of the father's role.

## The Father and Academic Performance

Apparently unaware of Parsons' notions, Osofsky (Osofsky & O'Connell, 1972; Osofsky & Oldfield, 1971) reported findings consonant with the Parsonian theory. In situations designed to elicit dependent and independent task-related behaviors from 5-year-old girls, fathers were consistently more likely to take an action-oriented role, and the mothers more often provided encouragement. The girls themselves exhibited "more task specificity with their fathers, and more interpersonal interaction with their mothers" (Osofsky & O'Connell, 1972, p. 167).

Meanwhile Radin (1972, 1973; Radin & Epstein, 1975; Jordan, Radin, & Epstein, 1975) postulated that, since boys with nurturant fathers should identify with their fathers more readily (Kagan, 1958; Mussen & Rutherford, 1963; Payne & Mussen, 1956; P. Sears, 1953), they might be expected to adopt the father's characteristics, for example, instrumental competence, that should foster intellectual functioning. The findings from a study of 4-year-old boys supported the hypothesis for middle-class but not for lower class boys. Further study showed that the correlation between paternal nurturance and the child's intellectual functioning was higher for boys than for girls (Jordan et al., 1975). An extensive study revealed that fathers did not directly facilitate intellectual performance in their daughters (Radin & Epstein, 1975): mixed messages characterized father–daughter interaction, and this appeared to retard intellectual performance. Paternal attitudes appeared to affect daughters indirectly, being mediated via the mothers (Epstein & Radin, 1975). Maternal nurturance was related to IQ for girls, but not for boys, in a lower class sample (Radin, 1974).

Though parental influences on cognitive development are poorly understood (Freeberg & Payne, 1967), there is a good deal of evidence (albeit correlational) that the father (Brenton, 1966) may exercise a strong influence over his son's intellectual development (cf. Lederer, 1964), and Biller's (1974c) recent study indicated that fathers may be facilitating cognitive development from infancy. Underachieving boys have inadequate relationships with their fathers, whom they regard as rejecting or hostile (Grunebaum, Hurwitz, Prentice, & Sperry, 1962; Hurley, 1967; Kimball, 1952), but high achievers want to be with their fathers more than low achievers do (Mutimer, Loughlin, & Powell, 1966) and perceive themselves as more like their fathers (Shaw & White, 1965). Observed (Solomon, 1969) and reported (Katz, 1967) paternal encouragement is correlated with achievement. Though this may not be true across all social classes (Kahl, 1953), a close father–child relationship and the characterization of the father as both dominant and democratic are associated with high achievement motivation (Bordua, 1960; Bowerman & Elder, 1964; Elder, 1962; Ellis & Lane, 1963; Gill & Spilka, 1962; L. Hoffman, 1961; Kahl, 1957) in both boys and girls, though particularly in boys (Norman, 1966; Werts, 1966), who are, in turn, less susceptible than girls to pressures to achieve exerted by their mothers (Kagan & Freeman, 1963). Further, salient fathers (Dreyer, 1975) are close father–son relationships (Bieri, 1960; Dyk & Witkin, 1965) are both associated with the adoption of a "masculine" (i.e., analytic) cognitive style.

*Father Absence.* In addition, one of the more consistently reported "effects" of father absence on boys is a deterioration of school performance (Bronfenbrenner, 1967; Deutsch, 1960; Deutsch & Brown, 1964) and intellectual capacity (Blanchard & Biller, 1971; Landy, Rosenberg, & Sutton-Smith, 1969; Lessing, Zagorin, & Nelson, 1970; Maxwell, 1961; Santrock, 1972; Sutton-Smith, Rosenberg, & Landy, 1968) accompanied by the absence of the analytic masculine cognitive style (Altus, 1958; Barclay & Cusumano, 1967; Carlsmith, 1964, 1973; Lessing et al., 1970; Nelsen & Maccoby, 1966) that the father should model. Some research has shown this to be true in lower class families as well, contrary to what one might have predicted from Radin's results (Blanchard & Biller, 1971; Deutsch & Brown, 1964; Santrock, 1972).

The findings are much less consistent for girls. Although father absence does not have the same debilitating effects as in boys (Lessing et al., 1970; Santrock, 1972; Sutton-Smith et al., 1968), there is evidence that paternal encouragement of intellectual performance is related to achievement (Crandall, Dewey, Katkovsky, & Preston, 1964) and that paternal rejection (Heilbrun, Harrell, & Gillard, 1965; Hurley, 1967) is detrimental to it. Further the zealous father (albeit nurturant) who believes strongly that his daughter should be feminine and who deprecates intellectual performance in women may thereby retard her cognitive capacity (Biller, 1974a, 1974d). This effect was suggested by Radin's findings (Radin & Epstein, 1975), though it was apparently absent in Osofsky's study.

The importance of fathers in fostering academic success, particularly in their sons, is clearly relevant to the attempts to improve intellectual performance in "deprived" children by intervention programs. Most of these children come from populations where father absence is particularly frequent (Bronfenbrenner, 1975c; Herzog & Sudia, 1970). Clearly it seems desirable to include fathers in efforts to involve parents in enrichment programs (Bronfenbrenner, 1974a; Fein, 1975; Scheinfeld, 1969) wherever possible, though stereotyping may hamper these efforts (Tuck, 1969).

Paternal rejection of a role in childrearing (Kohn & Carroll, 1960; Komarovsky, 1964) and the reinforcement by society and its institutions of such stereotypes may indeed be part of the problem.

## Adjustment and Interpersonal Interaction

The establishment of satisfying peer relationships (Leiderman, 1959; Lynn & Sawrey, 1959; Mitchell & Wilson, 1967; Stoltz et al., 1954; Tiller, 1957, 1958), general psychological adjustment, and later success in heterosexual relationships (Barclay, Stilwell, & Barclay, 1972; Hetherington, 1972; Holman, 1959; Palmer, 1960; Seplin, 1952; Winch, 1950) may also be facilitated by the presence of the father and by the warmth of the father–son relationship when he is present (Cox, 1962; Howells, 1969; Leiderman, 1959; Mussen, Bouterline-Young, Gaddini, & Morante, 1963; Rutherford & Mussen, 1968). Boys from mother-dominated homes have more difficulty in being accepted by peers (L. Hoffman, 1961). Paternal warmth is correlated with a boy's feeling of self-esteem (Coopersmith, 1967; Medinnus, 1965; Rosenberg, 1965; Sears, 1970) and his personality adjustment (Mussen, 1961; Mussen et al., 1963; Reuter & Biller, 1973; Slater, 1962; Warren, 1957). Nurturant fathers may, in addition, contribute greatly to the psychological adjustment of their daughters (Baumrind & Black, 1967; Fish & Biller, 1973) and facilitate their happiness in subsequent heterosexual relationships (Fisher, 1973; Lozoff, 1974). On the other hand, both disturbed father–child relationships (Becker, 1960; Becker, Peterson, Hellmer, Shoemaker, & Quay, 1959; Peterson, Becker, Hellmer, Shoemaker, & Quay, 1959; Peterson, Becker, Shoemaker, Luria, & Hellmer, 1961; Warren, 1957) and the failure to achieve same-sex identification (Lynn, 1961) may be pathogenic. Indeed they may be crucial in the etiology of homosexuality (Brown, 1957b, 1958a; Nash, 1965).

As in all the studies of "father effects," though, the mother– and father–child relationships are both part of a family system. A recent longitudinal study (Block, 1971; Block, Van der Lippe, & Block, 1973) demonstrated that the best adjusted adults were those who, in childhood, had warm relationships with effective mothers and fathers, in the context of a happy marital relationship.

## The Father–Child Relationship

Of the studies discussed in this section those of Osofsky and Radin are among the few in which the interaction between fathers and their children was directly observed while attempts were made to identify the distinctive and defining features of father–child interaction. A few other studies have

attempted to differentiate maternal and paternal roles by asking parents
how they would respond in particular situations (Atkinson & Endsley, in
press; Lambert, Yackley, & Hein, 1971; Marcus, 1975; Rothbart & Maccoby, 1966), but the vast majority of studies that have accorded the
father any explicit attention have relied on questionnaire and correlational
procedures from which they have inferred "father effects." Not only are
there methodological problems—most importantly, the facts that correlation of variables assessing synchronous events, attitudes, and/or recol-
lections cannot prove causality and that, in many cases, the sources of
information are indirect and are not independent[5]—but there is also the
conceptual question concerning the appropriateness of such research strategies. I have argued elsewhere (Lamb, 1975a) that the most important
question at this stage is not "what are the effects" but rather "the effects
of what." Until we have a better understanding of the father–child relationship, attempts to characterize its effects are probably premature.

Many of the studies reviewed here reported that the quality of the
relationship was perhaps more important than the father's punitiveness or
masculinity. As Mussen and Distler have noted, "from the child's point of
view, the significant factor seems to be the father's salience—his importance
in the child's life—rather than the particular technique he uses in dealing
with his child" (1959, p. 354). They found, moreover, that salient mother-
and father–child relationships had different outcomes, which suggests that
the relationships are differentiable, perhaps complimentary, and probably,
both important. Their study did not, however, help clarify what the differences were, and we are little closer today. I am unconvinced that terms
such as *masculinity, nurturance,* or *instrumental*, have unambiguous meanings or accurately depict the relationship between the child and either
parent. Careful observational studies, such as those of Osofsky and Radin
(ideally in the context of longitudinal projects considering at least both
parents), which permit the researcher to infer causality with some confidence, would, in the author's opinion, advance our understanding of the
father's role in child development far more than further studies in the
traditional mold.

## Summary

Despite the large number of studies conducted, the conclusions we can
draw with some confidence are few. As to sex-role development, the
father's masculinity and his status in the family are correlated with the

[5] There is good reason to question such research strategies. Eron, Banta, Walder, &
Laulicht (1961), for example, found little agreement between mothers and fathers on
their ratings of their children's behavior or on ratings of their own interaction with
the children.

masculinity of his sons and the femininity of his daughters. This association depends, however, on the fathers having sufficient interaction with their children, and, hence, the extent of the father's commitment in childrearing is crucial. Indeed one of the best established findings is that the masculinity of sons and the femininity of daughters are greatest when fathers are nurturant and participate extensively in childrearing. Thus the father's similarity to a caricatured stereotype of masculinity is far less influential than his involvement in what are often portrayed as female activities.

Psychoanalytic theorists have stressed the power and aggressiveness of the father in explaining identification (Defensive Identification: Fenichel, 1945). Learning theorists, whether or not they eschew the term *identification* and prefer to talk of *modeling,* predict that a child will be more likely to imitate a model about whom it feels positively than one of whom it is afraid. In general the evidence is consistent with the latter hypothesis. The most influential fathers appear to be those who take their role seriously and interact extensively with their children. Only in the context of such relationships does punitiveness seem to be a useful technique. Hence, in this respect, learning theory depicts identification and sex-role adoption better than psychoanalytic theory.

On the other hand the results of many studies have failed to support the learning theorists' predictions. For example, the demonstration that masculinity of the father is often uncorrelated with masculinity of the son (methodological problems notwithstanding) fails to validate a learning theory hypothesis that identification should involve behavioral similarity, but neither supports nor contradicts the Freudian postulation that identification refers to a motive or a process. "If the core of the concept of identification is a *motive* to become like another person, the presence of similarity is, at best, only a by-product rather than an essential feature of the phenomenon" (Bronfenbrenner, 1960, p. 29).

Parsons' theory is much more difficult to evaluate empirically because it is not formulated with sufficient precision to allow the investigator to formulate hypotheses that would not also be consistent with either the learning theory or psychoanalytic positions. The fact that so many studies have found paternal warmth to be crucial suggests that Parsons was incorrect in overstressing the instrumental function of the father while underrepresenting the importance of an expressive component to the relationship. On the other hand, Parsons' theory is best able to explain (learning a complementary role) the fact that more masculine fathers have more feminine daughters. It is conceivable, though, that such fathers engage in more extensive direct shaping and that the role theory explanation is gratuitous.

Parsons may, however, have the most parsimonious hypothesis concerning the father's role in moral development, though it is impossible at this stage to evaluate the predictive validity of any of the theories because of the inconclusiveness of the research in this area. If moral development is a product of early socialization in the family, developmental psychologists have had little success in specifying cause–effect relationships. The current negative results may reflect the inadequacies of research methodologies as much as the realities of the family's function.

As Radin notes in Chapter 7, there does appear to be a correlation between the warmth of the father–child relationship and the child's academic performance, and this is consistent with a learning theory prediction that the child who feels affection for the person modeling certain characteristics is more likely to identify and imitate these characteristics. There may, however, be tension in the father–daughter relationship that makes the girls less keen to model their fathers. This may be reinforced by explicit communications of disapproval about their displaying academic competence. Because female sex roles are currently in greatest transition, it was perhaps uncertainty about their daughters' present and future roles that rendered the fathers in Radin and Epstein's (1975) study ambivalent. If fathers are more concerned than mothers about sex typing, as research has indicated, this would explain why the ambivalence and tension are most marked in the father–child relationship.

In sum none of the theories is entirely consistent with the evidence, and all three appear to be correct in certain respects. It is not evident, moreover, that further research employing currently popular methodologies will ever be adequate to permit unambiguous refutation or validation of any theory.

The greatest problem with this body of research is, perhaps, that it is based almost exclusively on correlational strategies. Thus even if the other methodolgical problems—the nonindependence of sources of evidence, the dubious validity of many of the instruments used—were overcome, researchers would still be unable to specify either cause or effect. To test the hypothesis that characteristics of the father–child relationship are causal antecedents of certain aspects of the child's personality development, it will be necessary to use those correlational strategies that permit causal inferences, such as cross-lagged panel correlations, in the context of short- or long-term longitudinal studies. I have argued, here and elsewhere, that our discipline would best be served by a serious attempt to understand the nature of interaction within the family; reported "nurturance," "punitiveness," or "masculinity" are too vague, nonspecific, and subjective to be of predictive utility.

One problem underlying our inability to formulate a definitive specification of the father's role concerns the very definition of that role, which is currently being reevaluated, along with the traditional characterization of masculinity. Because of the recency of these changes in the cultural definitions of role-appropriate behavior, there is little one can say about the effect on the children. It is clear, though, that the participation of the father in childrearing is not seen as "unmasculine" by children, who indeed expect their fathers to be as influential and emotionally involved as mothers, even if the extent of their involvement (in terms of time) is substantially less (Bowerman & Elder, 1964; Dunn, 1960; Dyer & Urban, 1958; Hartley & Klein, 1959).

Much of the evidence reviewed has suggested that the father is the parent most concerned with the adoption of cultural values and traditional stereotypically defined sex roles.[6] It is plausible to assume that, if he were to favor more egalitarian sex roles, these, too, would be fostered, particularly if, by his own behavior, he showed that these were not incompatible with his own gender identification. There seems little reason to expect that the father's role in child development would be diminished by these developments; indeed, if they presaged a greater commitment to children by the many fathers currently uninvolved, one might predict that their importance would increase, and the scope of their influence would broaden.

## AN INTEGRATION OF THE EVIDENCE

Contrary to the findings of those studies that stressed the negative reactions of fathers to the pregnancy of their wives and the birth of their children (Arnstein, 1972; LeMasters, 1957; Leibenberg, 1967), and the limited amount of interaction between fathers and neonates (Rebelsky & Hanks, 1971), recent evidence shows that pregnancy (Soule, 1974) and childbirth (Colman & Colman, 1972; Cronenwett & Newmark, 1974; Greenberg & Morris, 1974) are exciting events for both parents and that fathers are active in interaction with their newborn infants, both when their wives are present and when they are absent (Parke & O'Leary, 1975; Parke, O'Leary, & West, 1972). This implies that more fathers should be allowed to participate in perinatal procedures (Cronenwett & Newmark, 1974) and interact with their young infants. Early (in-hospital) provision of opportunities for mothers to interact with their newborns appears to facilitate the formation of mother–infant bonds (Kennell, Jerauld, Wolfe, Chesler, Kreger, McAlpine, Steffa, & Klaus, 1974; Klaus, Jerauld, Kreger, McAlpine, Steffa, & Kennell, 1972; Leifer et al., 1972; Ringler, Kennell, Jarvella,

---

[6] This is not to deny, of course, that most societies have a variety of extrafamilial institutions that uphold the cultural stereotypes and values (Barry, Bacon, & Child, 1957; Mead, 1935, 1949).

Navojosky, & Klaus, 1975), and there is every reason to expect that similar acknowledgment of the fathers' involvement with infants would be beneficial (Caplan, 1959; Colman & Colman, 1972; Cronenwett & Newmark, 1974; Hines, 1971). The transition to parenthood marks the beginning of a new interpersonal situation for both parents (Murrell & Stachowiak, 1965). Unfortunately it is usual (though this may be changing) for hospitals to adopt practices that deprecate the father's role and encourage the belief that he is a superfluous appendage, whose value is limited to that of "provider" (Bowlby, 1951; Nash, 1965). Whereas society provides many supports for the young mother as she adopts a new role, there are few, if any, supports for the new father.

Subsequently, although mothers are almost universally assigned primary responsibility for the care of the infant (indeed this is how the role of mother is most clearly defined), the evidence I have reviewed indicates that most infants become attached to both parents in infancy. The important question relates to the nature of the mother– and father–infant relationships, rather than to quibbles about their existence or relative importance. Play appears to be the most prominent characteristic of the father–infant interaction, and caretaking is most outstanding in the mother–infant interaction. The mother maintains her association with caretaking responsibility as the child grows older (Bronfenbrenner, 1961b; Devereux, Bronfenbrenner, & Rodgers, 1969; Devereux, Bronfenbrenner, & Suci, 1962; Devereux, Shouval, Bronfenbrenner, Rodgers, Kav-Venaki, & Kiely, 1974; Kohn, 1959; Radke, 1946), but we know little about developmental changes in the definition of the father's role.

The research techniques and theoretical framework within which students of older children work differ so substantially from those employed in infancy research that attempts to link the role of the father in regard to the infant with his role vis-a-vis the older child must be regarded as speculative and heuristic, rather than definitive. Conceivably the infant constructs an expectation of its father as a person with whom interaction is pleasurable and stimulating. This enhances the child's desire to have commerce with the world in which its father immerses himself, and over which he exercises competence, and thus the child begins to explore the wider social system of which its father is the most accessible representative. As the more instrumental parent, the father also serves as the medium through which the values and role demands of the social system are encountered and internalized (Deutsch, 1944; Parsons & Bales, 1955).

Perhaps as a result of some form of oedipal conflict and its resolution or perhaps simply as a result of the child's growing awareness of the differences between the sexes (Kohlberg & Zigler, 1967) and the desire to be like the same-sex parent (Beier, 1953; Emmerich, 1959a; Gray & Klaus,

1956; Rau, 1960), the father is apparently the primary role model of the young boy, but only when the father–child relationship has been affectionate. Several studies have also found that an affectionate father–son relationship allows one to predict the son's masculinity regardless of the father's. This may mean that the father's satisfaction with his gender role, which is being observed by the child, is not being tapped by the measures of masculinity, which, at best, employ a stereotyped definition of masculinity. Several have argued that the father also plays a major role in the sex-role adoption of the young girl by encouraging feminine behavior and by providing a salient male figure whose behavior she learns to complement.

Similarly since it is mainly the father who represents to the child the values and precepts of the society, he not only should contribute an awareness of what the society regards as gender-appropriate behavior but also should foster and facilitate the adoption of the society's moral values. Researchers have, however, had difficulty in finding associations between childrearing practices and moral development (Hoffman, 1970b), though it is often reported that father absence is associated with delinquency or irregularities in moral development.

It would be inaccurate, however, to see the father as contributing only to sex-role and moral development. As the "instrumental" parent, and also as the major representative within the family of values in a society that lays great stress on academic achievement, it is predictable that the father would be concerned with the intellectual development of his offspring. Research findings indicate that this is indeed the case, fathers encouraging competence in their children (particularly sons) from infancy, though their ambivalence about cognitive competence in women may retard their daughters' development. Fathers, then, are undeniably playing an important role in child development (Murrell & Stachowiak, 1965; Mussen, 1973), and this role is qualitatively different from that of mothers. Further I would argue that the paternal role is important from very early in the child's life. Indeed, just as Bowlby and others argue that there may be a sensitive period in the formation of the mother–infant relationship, Nash 1954, 1965) has suggested that there may be an early, critical period during which the father–child relationship is most important. There are three sources of evidence for this assertion.

First, there is the evidence showing that many fathers interact extensively with their infants, that the type of interaction differs from that between mothers and infants, and that infants do not show consistent preferences for either parent. There can be little doubt that the father is often an important person in the life of the infant and young child.

Second, the severity of the effects of father absence is negatively correlated with the age of the child at the time of the separation. Perhaps this is because extrafamilial factors become increasingly important as the child grows older and thus compensate for the father's absence (Mischel, 1970).

Finally, Money and his colleagues have shown that sex-role assignment should be made before 18 months of age, indicating that, from early in its life, the child is made aware of the sex-appropriate manner in which it is expected to behave. Since fathers are more concerned than mothers about sex-role adoption, the father's role may be crucial from the first years of life.

The father's role is not limited to infancy. I would, however, argue that there is continuity from infancy to subsequent years that we would do well to appreciate. Further the sensitivity and warmth that are necessary attributes for the formation of parent–infant attachments, are the paternal characteristics most consistently associated with the personality development of older children.

## THE DEVALUATION OF THE FATHER

Social structure in our species has a complexity not matched in any other species. This demands a process of socialization that is equally complex, enduring, and multifaceted. It should not be surprising that such a process demands the participation of several persons. In Western society, primary responsibility for socialization devolves on the family system (Bronfenbrenner, 1975c; Clausen, 1966; Parsons & Bales, 1955). The family system itself has, however, been subjected to serve assaults in recent years. Bronfenbrenner (1975c) demonstrates forcefully that more and more marriages are being terminated by divorce, increasing numbers of children are being raised in single-parent families, and the family is being usurped as children become increasingly peer oriented (Condry & Siman, 1974). Increasingly children are being raised by substitute caretakers, rather than by parents (Bronfenbrenner, 1973, 1975c). Further there is less and less contact between children and the world of work, which contributes to the alienation in American society (Bronfenbrenner, 1972, 1974b). Presumably if indeed it is the father who should be the mediator between this world and the family subsystem, it is his role that is being inadequately filled.

It is still too early to evaluate the effects of some of these changes, but where research has been performed, the results are disturbing. There is every reason to believe that children raised in single-parent families will be at risk. The absence of a primary socializing agent (most often the father, as is attested by the figures Bronfenbrenner, 1975c, cites) is likely to have direct effects on the child and indirect effects mediated by the emotionally and economically strained (Herzog & Sudia, 1970) and often socially isolated (Hetherington, Cox, & Cox, 1975) remaining parent. Most profoundly disturbing is the fact that, whereas many societal practices are being discontinued, little attention is being given to constructing alternatives. The determination of the effects of discarding the traditional mechanisms of socialization, and the evaluation of feasible alternatives, are both urgent priorities for future research.

It is extremely important to remember that one of the most influential characteristics of the father–child relationship appears to be its warm and affectionate nature. There is also a presumption that the relationship should be enduring, rather than transitory. This implies that the provision of a succession of male models to father-absent boys (Lynn, 1974) is unlikely to fulfill the child's psychological needs. It is difficult to escape the implications that the enduring relationships within the family system are ideal and that, if this system is to be replaced, the alternatives are unlikely to be as simple as often implied.

Many social scientists believe, moreover, that, even in families in which the father is nominally present, his participation is often minimal (Biller, 1974d; Biller & Meridith, 1974; Lynn, 1974). Although I have been concerned in this essay with detailing the contributions that fathers make to their offsprings' development, it is regrettably true that many fathers have little to do with their children, interact minimally with them, and hence, make little positive contribution to their psychological development. As I have demonstrated, an inadequate father–child relationship may have detrimental effects. Perhaps then, it is important to emphasize not only the father's role in contemporary American society (for here it is typically devalued—Birdwhistell, 1957; Brenton, 1966; Foster, 1964; Kluckhorn, 1949; Rohrer & Edmondson, 1960) but also the potential power of the role. The widespread inadequate fulfillment of the role's demands is clearly not without its inevitable, and often quite serious, effects.

Social scientists have contributed, perhaps unwittingly, to the devaluation of the father's role. There is a peculiar tendency to infer sequentially that, because mothers are the primary caretakers, they are more important than fathers, and thus that they alone deserve investigation. This rapidly becomes translated into a belief that mothers are uniquely important. Fathers can hardly be expected to maintain a belief in their importance when they are continually being told of their irrelevance, other than as economic supporters of the family unit.

I will cite one particularly glaring example of this tendency. In a recent paper on early parent–neonate interaction, MacFarlane (1975) included a detailed narrative account of the mother's behavior. The record terminated with the terse notation "Baby given to father" (p. 11). By clear implication, any interaction or relationship with the father was as inconsequential as the obstetrical handling which preceeded the mother–infant sequence. This extraordinary prejudice on the part of professionals and researchers can scarcely facilitate the adjustment of young families to the responsibilities of parenthood.

## THE FATHER AND THE FAMILY SYSTEM

Although I have focused on the father's role in this essay, it should not be forgotten that the father's role is defined by his position within the family system. My thesis is not that the father is the *sole* important member of that system; rather, it is that the recent trend toward a denigration of his role is misguided. Both parents contribute to the psychological development of their offspring, and it is unlikely that their contributions are independent, although I have implied this in the present essay. Dyadic models, while simpler to conceptualize, seriously distort the psychological (and sociological) realities of the ecology in which children develop.

Within the family system there are numerous reciprocal relationships, role demands, and expectations. One of the legacies of the lengthy behaviorist domination of American psychology was the inculcation of a belief in overly simplistic stimulus-response association models in analyses of socialization. Only recently have psychologists again recognized the fact that the child is not simply a passive organism shaped by the social and physical environment. Rather, the child is an active contributor to the interaction: its characteristics modify the parents' behavior, it can initiate and terminate interaction, and it is capable, from an early age, of what might be considered remarkably sophisticated modes of relating to others (Bell, 1968, 1971; Harper, 1971; Lewis & Rosenblum, 1974; Osofsky, 1975; Rheingold, 1968; Stern, 1974, 1975; Yarrow, Waxler, & Scott, 1971). As Schaffer (1971) notes: "the basic characteristics of all interpersonal behavior is reciprocity" (p. 172). It is the active role of the child that makes sensitivity to signals so important in the establishment of the infant's relationships (Ainsworth et al., 1971, 1974; Schaffer, 1971; Schaffer & Emerson, 1964).

It should be remembered, too, that we are dealing with individuals with unique constitutions and histories. As Escalona (1969) points out, individual differences in the initial characteristics of interacting persons mean that the same stimulus can have varying effects on different individuals and, conversely, that the same effect can result from different stimulus situations.

Not only is the child affecting the behavior of its parents, but they are affecting each other as well as it (M. Hoffman, 1960; Yarrow, 1974). Each member of the family system is thus influencing and being influenced by every other member, both directly and indirectly. When there are siblings, for example, they not only interact with the child directly, becoming in the process profoundly salient aspects of the social environment (Sutton-Smith & Rosenberg, 1970), but they also affect the manner in which the parents interact with the child and press for sex typing (Elder & Bowerman, 1963; Koch, 1955; Lansky, 1964, 1967). The positive contribution of the father to the child's growth and development is comprehensible only within the context of this larger family system, and we would do well not to lose sight of this fundamental point (Burgess, 1926; Burgess & Locke, 1953; Handel, 1965).

In their chapter Lewis and Weinraub stress the indirect influence of the father upon his infant, insofar as this is mediated via the mother. With the exception of a recent study of Feiring (Feiring, 1976; Feiring and Taylor, 1976) these "second-order effects" have been all but ignored. Unfortunately, Feiring's research is seriously flawed—both methodologically and conceptually—and consequently is of purely heuristic significance. In addition, it is necessary to caution that because these authors overestimate the extent of mother–infant interaction and underestimate the extent of father–infant interaction, they imply that direct paternal influences upon the infant are negligible, which is probably not the case. It is certainly important that we come to recognize and accommodate the second-order effects in conceptualizations of socialization, though it is equally critical that we avoid embracing a doctrine in which second-order effects are stressed to the exclusion of first-order effects. In the absence of sound empirical investigations in the past, this area is certain to be a focus of extensive research in the future.

Several studies attest to the importance of the family unit in fostering the social development of the child (Schaefer, 1974). These range from studies showing the effects on the children of extensive family discord, hostile parental attitudes, and disagreements over details of childrearing practices and aspirations for the child's future (Baruch, 1937; Baruch & Wilcox, 1944; Coopersmith, 1967; Cottle, 1968; Elmer, 1967; Farber, 1962; Farber & McHale, 1959; Giovannoni & Billingsley, 1970; Gordon & Gordon, 1959; Graham & Rutter, 1973; M. Hoffman, 1960; Kauffman, 1961; Langner & Michael, 1963; Medinnus, 1963; Medinnus & Johnson, 1970; Nye, 1957; Putney & Middleton, 1960; Rutter, 1971, 1973, 1974; Van der Veen, 1965; Wyer, 1965) to studies showing the relatively subtle effects of the temporary absence of one parent on the other parent's attitude toward the child (Marsella, Dubanoski, & Mohs, 1974) and, for example, the enhancement of identification with their fathers in boys whose mothers feel positively about their husbands (Helper, 1955; Rau, 1960). There is also evidence that the child's attitudes toward an absent father are related to his mother's feelings about him (Bach, 1946; Biller, 1971b). Some researchers have noted that intimate family relationships depend on the nature of the mother–father relationship (Westley & Epstein, 1960) and that the perception of closeness to the father is the best indicator of family interaction (Landis, 1960). I have already discussed a number of studies that show how the father's status in the family influences the sex-role adoption of the children and their willingness or ability to display responsibility and leadership (Bronfenbrenner, 1961b).

Such studies indicate the limitations inherent in attempts to specify the father's effects: It is possible to do this only by recognizing the context in which the father and child are operating. The focus for our future investigation must be the family system, and our unit of analysis must be the interactional round. Further we cannot make profound advances in our understanding of social development by searching crudely for "father effects" using currently popular research techniques. We need to understand the patterns of interaction within the family, and then, within the framework of the family structure, understand the nature of the relationship within the father–child subsystem.

The challenge is not easy to meet: It demands a complete readjustment in the manner in which we customarily investigate socialization and social development. That the father–child relationship is important has been documented in this and subsequent chapters; that we know little about the relationship—the way in which the effects are mediated—should once more be underscored. The new focus should be motivated both by the realization of the relative fruitlessness of the socialization studies of the past decades (Caldwell, 1964; Zigler & Child, 1969) and by the appreciation of the complexity and multidimensionality of the process of integrating the child into the social world.

## A CONCLUDING NOTE

Throughout this chapter I have been concerned with demonstrating the importance of the father in the development of his children. In addition, many studies have demonstrated that the absence of a father can have serious consequences for the sex-role, moral, and intellectual development and personality adjustment of his children (see Biller, Chapter 3). This is true even where stringent attempts are made to control for the indirect effects—for example, on socioeconomic status—which went uncontrolled in many of the earlier studies (Herzog & Sudia, 1970, 1973).

As Biller (1974d; Biller & Meridith, 1974) and Lynn (1974) have recently pointed out, however, the presence of the father is no guarantee of adequate fathering. I have stressed frequently that the quality of the father–child relationship is more important a variable than the mere physical presence of the father. This is demonstrated by evidence showing the importance of a warm father–child relationship, established early in infancy, in fostering well-adjusted development, and conversely, by studies showing the retarding influence of a hostile, rejecting, or maladjusted father. Unfortunately the emphasis on the mother–child relationship by researchers has paralleled a devaluation of the father in society: childrearing and socialization are widely considered the "duty" of mothers (Favez-Boutonier, 1955; MacCalman, 1955; Métraux, 1955; Nash, 1965). Despite the belief of some (Bernhardt, 1957; Christopherson, 1956; Mogey, 1957; Nash, Chapter 2; Olsen, 1960) that social changes are affecting a change in the societal perception of the father's role, the changes are probably characteristic of a relatively small section of the population (e.g., Olsen, 1960).

Consequently the implications of this review are twofold. First, researchers must pay careful attention to the role of the father, particularly in early childhood when this seems most crucial. Second, society and its institutions must appreciate the importance of the father's role and encourage paternal participation in childrearing. All the evidence we have suggests that childrearing is most enjoyable, most enriching, and most successful when it is performed jointly by two parents, in the context of a secure marital relationship. This is a simple fact that we would be well advised not to ignore.

It is almost mandatory that literature reviews close with an appeal for further research. This field is clearly no exception. But what we need are not additional studies that apply a well-tried methodology to more refined questions. Particularly in the research on older children, it is the traditional methodology that is hampering our understanding. There have been numerous studies, but the questions remain unanswered (indeed, perhaps unasked) because of the inadequacy of the techniques, indirectness of the measures, and the nonindependence of the sources of evidence. Even where these problems are avoided, there remains the disadvantage that experimental rigor and control are often impossible, forcing a reliance on correlational procedures. Contrary to popular conviction this does not preclude causal analysis. Whereas it is true that correlations between simultaneous measures of two variables do not allow a researcher to draw causal conclusions (though this is exactly what has been done in most of the studies of sex-role adoption, moral development, and father absence), multivariate techniques such as path analysis, cross-lagged correlation, and multiple regression, used judiciously in longitudinal studies, permit the investigator to infer causality quite as justifiably as any experimentalist.

But before such techniques can be used wisely and productively, closer attention has to be paid to the antecedents as well as the consequents. I have argued before that the focus on the "father's role" and its "effects" is premature. What we need urgently are investigations that attempt to characterize the nature of father–child relationships. It is only when we have specified what appear to be important, salient, or common characteristics of their interaction that research on "effects" or consequences will be truly meaningful. Human relationships and the process of socialization are complex, but progress can come only when we acknowledge the complexity and deal with it directly.

Finally future researchers must attempt to deal directly with the complexity of the ecology of childhood and the multiplicity of the determinants of personality development. In the present context this means that we must acknowledge that the father–child relationship is but one in a network within and outside the family, that the father's role is defined in part by his relationship with the child's mother, and by corollary, that the child's perception of the father is influenced by its mother's attitudes toward him, and vice versa. Just as the trend toward the use of the terms *mother* and *parent* as synonmous underestimates the complexity of socialization, so the depiction of the father–child relationship as having "effects" in a vacuum is misleading.

My appeal, then, is not for much *more* research; it is for much *better* research: high-quality research that is methodologically and conceptually formalized so as both to ask and answer questions about the complex process and content of socialization and personality development.

## REFERENCES

Abelin, E. L. The role of the father in the separation–individuation process. In J. B. McDevitt & C. F. Settlage (Eds.), *Separation–Individuation*. New York: International Universities Press, 1971.

Abelin, E. L. Some further observations and comments on the earliest role of the father. *International Journal of Psychoanalysis,* 1975, **56**, 293–302.

Ainsworth, M. D. The effects of maternal deprivation: A review of findings and controversy in the context of research strategy. In *Deprivation of maternal care: A reassessment of its effects.* Geneva: WHO, 1962.

Ainsworth, M. D. The development of infant–mother attachment among the Ganda. In B. M. Foss (Ed.), *Determinants of infant behavior II*. London: Methuen, 1963.

Ainsworth, M. D. Patterns of attachment behavior shown by the infant in interaction with his mother. *Merrill-Palmer Quarterly*, 1964, **10**, 51–58.

Ainsworth, M. D. *Infancy in Uganda: Infant care and the growth of love*. Baltimore: Johns Hopkins Press, 1967.

Ainsworth, M. D., & Bell, S. M. Attachment, exploration and separation: Illustrated by the behavior of one-year-olds in a strange situation. *Child Development*, 1970, **41**, 49–67.

Ainsworth, M. D., Bell, S. M., & Stayton, D. J. Individual differences in strange situation behavior of one-year-olds. In H. R. Schaffer (Ed.), *The origins of human social relations*. London: Academic, 1971.

Ainsworth, M. D., Bell, S. M., & Stayton, D. J. Infant–mother attachment and social development: Socialization as a product of reciprocal responsiveness to signals. In M. P. M. Richards (Ed.), *The integration of a child into a social world*. Cambridge, England: Cambridge University Press, 1974.

Ainsworth, M. D., Blehar, M. C., Waters, E. C. & Wall, S. N. The strange situation. Monograph in preparation.

Ainsworth, M. D., & Wittig, B. A. Attachment and exploratory behavior of one-year-olds in a strange situation. In B. M. Foss (Ed.), *Determinants of infant behavior IV*. London: Methuen, 1969.

Allen, V. L., & Crutchfield, R. S. Generalization of experimentally reinforced conformity. *Journal of Abnormal and Social Psychology*, 1963, **67**, 326–333.

Altucher, N. Conflict in sex identification in boys. Unpublished doctoral dissertation, University of Michigan, 1957.

Altus, W. D. The broken home and factors of adjustment. *Psychological Reports*, 1958, **4**, 477.

Ammons, R. B., & Ammons, H. S. Parent preference in young children's doll-play interviews. *Journal of Abnormal and Social Psychology*, 1949, **44**, 490–505.

Andry, R. G. Faulty paternal– and maternal–child relationships, affection, and delinquency. *British Journal of Delinquency*, 1957, **8**, 34–48.

Andry, R. G. *Delinquency and parental pathology*. London: Methuen, 1960.

Andry, R. G. Paternal and maternal roles and delinquency. In *Deprivation of maternal care: A reassessment of its effects*. Geneva: WHO, 1962.

Angrilli, A. F. The psychosexual identification of pre-school boys. *Journal of Genetic Psychology*, 1960, **97**, 327–340.

Anzimi, C. Masculinity, femininity and perception of warmth and saliency in parent–son relationships. Unpublished doctoral dissertation, Michigan State University, 1964.

Arnstein, H. The crisis of becoming a father. *Sexual Behavior*, 1972, **2**, 42–48.

Atkinson, J., & Endsley, R. C. Influence of sex of child and parent on parental reactions to hypothetical parent–child situations. *Journal of Genetic Psychology*, in press.

Bach, G. R. Father-fantasies and father-typing in father-separated children. *Child Development*, 1946, **17**, 63–80.

Bacon, M. K., Child, I. L., & Barry, H. A cross-cultural study of correlates of crime. *Journal of Abnormal and Social Psychology*, 1963, **66**, 291–300.

Baldwin, A. The Parsonian theory of personality. In M. Black (Ed.), *The social theories of Talcott Parsons*. Englewood Cliffs, N.J.: Prentice-Hall, 1961.

Ban, P., & Lewis, M. Mothers and fathers, girls and boys: Attachment behavior in the one-year-old. *Merrill-Palmer Quarterly*, 1974, **20**, 195–204.

Bandura, A. Social-learning theory of identificatory process. In D. S. Goslin & D. C. Glass (Eds.), *Handbook of socialization theory and research*. Chicago: Rand McNally, 1968.

Bandura, A., & Huston, A. C. Identification as a process of incidental learning. *Journal of Abnormal and Social Psychology*, 1961, **63**, 311–318.

Bandura, A., & Walters, R. H. *Adolescent aggression: A study of the influence of child-rearing practices and family interrelationships*. New York: Ronald, 1959.

Bandura, A., & Walters, R. H. *Social learning and personality development*. New York: Holt, Rinehart, & Winston, 1963.

Barclay, A. G., & Cusumano, D. Father absence, cross-sex identity, and field-dependent behavior in male adolescents. *Child Development*, 1967, **38**, 243–250.

Barclay, J. R., Stilwell, W. E., & Barclay, L. K. The influence of parental occupation on social interaction measures of elementary school children. *Journal of Vocational Behavior*, 1972, **2**, 433–446.

Bardwick, J. M. *Psychology of women*. New York: Harper & Row, 1971.

Barry, H., Bacon, M. K., & Child, I. L. A cross-cultural survey of some sex differences in socialization. *Journal of Abnormal and Social Psychology*, 1957, **55**, 327–332.

Bartemeier, L. The contribution of the father to the mental health of the family. *American Journal of Psychiatry*, 1953, **110**, 277–280.

Bartlett, C. J., & Horrocks, J. E. A study of the needs status of adolescents from broken homes. *Journal of Genetic Psychology*, 1958, **93**, 153–159.

Baruch, D. A study of reported tension in interparental relationships as coexistent with behavior adjustment in young children. *Journal of Experimental Education*, 1937, **6**, 187–204.

Baruch, D., & Wilcox, A. J. A study of sex differences in preschool children's adjustment coexistent with interparental tensions. *Journal of Genetic Psychology*, 1944, **64**, 281–303.

Baumrind, D., & Black, A. E. Socialization practices associated with dimensions of competence in preschool boys and girls. *Child Development*, 1967, **38**, 291–327.

Becker, W. C. The relationship of factors in parental ratings of self and each other to the behavior of kindergarten children. *Journal of Consulting Psychology*, 1960, **24**, 507–527.

Becker, W. C. Consequences of different kinds of parental discipline. In M. L. Hoffman & L. W. Hoffman (Eds.), *Review of child development research I*. New York: Russell Sage Foundation, 1964.

Becker, W. C., Peterson, D. R., Hellmer, L. A., Shoemaker, D. J., & Quay, H. C. Factors in parental behavior and personality as related to problem behavior in children. *Journal of Consulting Psychology*, 1959, **23**, 107–118.

Beier, E. G. The parental identification of male and female college students. *Journal of Abnormal and Social Psychology*, 1953, **48**, 569–572.

Bell, R. Q. A reinterpretation of the direction of effects in studies of socialization. *Psychological Review*, 1968, **75**, 81–95.

Bell, R. Q. Stimulus control of parent or caretaker behavior by offspring. *Developmental Psychology*, 1971, **4**, 63–72.

Benson, L. *Fatherhood: A sociological perspective*. New York: Random House, 1968.

Bernal, J. F., & Richards, M. P. M. What can the zoologist tell us about human development? In S. A. Barnett (Ed.), *Ethology and development*. London: Heinemann, 1973.

Bernhardt, K. S. The father in the family. *Bulletin of the Institute for Child Study*, 1957, **19**, 2–4.

Bieri, J. Parental identification, acceptability, and authority, and within-sex differences in cognitive behavior. *Journal of Abnormal and Social Psychology*, 1960, **60**, 76–79.

Bijou, S. W., & Baer, D. M. *Child development I. A systematic and empirical theory*. New York: Appleton-Century-Crofts, 1961.

Biller, H. B. A multiaspect investigation of masculine development in kindergarten-age boys. *Genetic Psychology Monographs*, 1968, **76**, 89–139.

Biller, H. B. Father-absence, maternal encouragement, and sex-role development in kindergarten age boys. *Child Development*, 1969, **40**, 539–546 (a).

Biller, H. B. Father dominance and sex-role development in kindergarten age boys. *Developmental Psychology*, 1969, **1**, 87–94 (b).

Biller, H. B. Father absence and the personality development of the male child. *Developmental Psychology*, 1970, **2**, 181–201.

Biller, H. B. *Father, child, and sex role*. Lexington, Mass.: Heath, 1971 (a).

Biller, H. B. The mother-child relationship and the father-absent boy's personality development. *Merrill-Palmer Quarterly*, 1971, **17**, 227–241 (b).

Biller, H. B. Paternal and sex-role factors in cognitive and academic functioning. In J. K. Cole & R. Dienstbier (Eds.), *Nebraska symposium on motivation*. Lincoln: University of Nebraska Press, 1974 (a).

Biller, H. B. Paternal deprivation, cognitive functioning, and the feminized classroom. In A. Davids (Ed.), *Child personality and psychopathology: Current topics*. New York: Wiley, 1974 (b).

Biller, H. B. The father–infant relationship: Some naturalistic observations. Unpublished manuscript, University of Rhode Island, 1974 (c).

Biller, H. B. *Paternal deprivation: Family, school, sexuality and society*. Lexington, Mass.: Heath, 1974 (d).

Biller, H. B., & Bahm, R. M. Father absence, perceived maternal behavior, and masculinity of self-control among junior high school boys. *Developmental Psychology*, 1971, **4**, 178–181.

Biller, H. B., & Borstelmann, L. J. Masculine development: An integrative review. *Merrill-Palmer Quarterly*, 1967, **13**, 253–294.

Biller, H. B., & Meridith, D. L. *Father power*. New York: David McKay, 1974.

Biller, H. B., & Weiss, S. D. The father–daughter relationship and the personality development of the female. *Journal of Genetic Psychology*, 1970, **116**, 79–93.

Birdwhistell, R. L. Is there an ideal father? *Child Study*, 1957, **34**, 29–33.

Birnbaum, J. A. Life patterns, personality style, and self-esteem in gifted family-oriented and career-committed women. Unpublished doctoral dissertation, University of Michigan, 1971.

Black, M. (Ed.) *The social theories of Talcott Parsons*. Englewood Cliffs, N.J.: Prentice Hall, 1961.

Blaine, G. B. The children of divorce. *The Atlantic,* 1963 (March), 98–101.

Blanchard, R. W., & Biller, H. B. Father availability and academic performance among third grade boys. *Developmental Psychology*, 1971, **4**, 301–305.

Blehar, M. C. Anxious attachment and defensive reactions associated with day care. *Child Development*, 1974, **45**, 683–692.

Block, J. *Lives through time*. Berkeley: Bancroft, 1971.

Block, J., Van der Lippe, A., & Block, J. D. Sex role and socialization: Some personality concomitants and environmental antecedents. *Journal of Consulting and Clinical Psychology*, 1973, **41**, 321–341.

Bordua, D. J. Educational aspirations and parental stress on college. *Social Forces*, 1960, **38**, 262–269.

Bossard, J. H., & Boll, E. S. *The sociology of child development*. New York: Harper & Row, 1966.

Bowerman, C. E., & Elder, G. H. Variations in adolescent perception of family power structure. *American Sociological Review*, 1964, **29**, 551–567.

Bowlby, J. Forty-four juvenile thieves: Their characters and home life. *International Journal of Psychoanalysis*, 1944, **25**, 107–128.

Bowlby, J. *Maternal care and mental health.* Geneva: WHO, 1951.

Bowlby, J. The nature of the child's tie to his mother. *International Journal of Psychoanalysis,* 1958, **39,** 350–375.

Bowlby, J. *Attachment and Loss.* Vol. 1. *Attachment.* New York: Basic Books, 1969.

Bowlby, J. *Attachment and Loss.* Vol. 2. *Separation: Anxiety and anger.* New York: Basic Books, 1973.

Brenton, M. *The American male.* New York: Howard McCann Inc., 1966.

Bretherton, I., & Ainsworth, M. D. Responses of one-year-olds to a stranger in a strange situation. In M. Lewis & L. A. Rosenblum (Eds.), *The origins of fear.* New York: Wiley, 1974.

Briffault, R. *The mothers.* New York: MacMillan, 1927.

Brim, O. G. Family structure and sex role learning by children. *Sociometry,* 1958, **21,** 1–16.

Bronfenbrenner, U. The study of identification through interpersonal perception. In R. Tagiuri & L. Petrullo (Eds.), *Person perception and interpersonal behavior.* Stanford: Stanford University Press, 1958.

Bronfenbrenner, U. Freudian theories of identification and their derivatives. *Child Development,* 1960, **31,** 15–40.

Bronfenbrenner, U. Parsons' theory of identification. In M. Black (Ed.), *The social theories of Talcott Parsons.* Englewood Cliffs, N.J.: Prentice Hall, 1961 (a).

Bronfenbrenner, U. Some familial antecedants of responsibility and leadership in adolescents. In L. Petrullo & B. M. Bass (Eds.), *Leadership and interpersonal behavior.* New York: Holt, Rinehart, & Winston, 1961 (b).

Bronfenbrenner, U. The changing American child. *Journal of Social Issues,* 1961, **17,** 6–18 (c).

Bronfenbrenner, U. The psychological costs of quality and inequality in education. *Child Development,* 1967, **38,** 909–925.

Bronfenbrenner, U. The roots of alienation. In U. Bronfenbrenner (Ed.), *Influences on human development.* Hinsdale, Ill.: Dryden, 1972.

Bronfenbrenner, U. Who cares for America's children? In F. Rebelsky & L. Dorman (Eds.), *Child development and behavior* (2nd ed.). New York: Knopf, 1973.

Bronfenbrenner, U. *Is early intervention effective?* Washington, D.C.: U.S. Department of Health, Education, & Welfare, Office of Child Development, 1974 (a).

Bronfenbrenner, U. The origins of alienation. *Scientific American,* 1974, **23,** 53–61 (b).

Bronfenbrenner, U. Research on the effects of day care. Unpublished manuscript, Cornell University, 1975 (a).

Bronfenbrenner, U. Social change: The challenge to research and policy. Paper presented to the Society for Research in Child Development, Denver, April, 1975 (b).

Bronfenbrenner, U. Who cares for America's children? Unpublished manuscript, Cornell University, 1975 (c).

Bronson, W. C. Dimensions of ego and infantile identification. *Journal of Personality*, 1959, **27**, 532–545.

Brooks, J., & Lewis, M. Attachment behavior in thirteen-month-old opposite-sex twins. *Child Development*, 1974, **45**, 243–247.

Brown, D. G. Sex role preference in young children. *Psychological Monographs*, 1956, **70**, 1–19.

Brown, D. G. Masculinity–femininity development in children. *Journal of Consulting Psychology*, 1957, **21**, 197–203 (a).

Brown, D. G. The development of sex role inversion and homosexuality. *Journal of Pediatrics*, 1957, **50**, 613–619 (b).

Brown, D. G. Inversion and homosexuality. *American Journal of Orthopsychiatry*, 1958, **28**, 424–429 (a).

Brown, D. G. Sex role development in a changing culture. *Psychological Bulletin*, 1958, **55**, 232–242(b).

Burgess, E. S. The family as a unity of interacting personalities. *The Family*, 1926, **7**, 3–9.

Burgess, E. W., & Locke, H. J. *The family*. New York: American Book Co., 1953.

Burlingham, D. The pre-oedipal infant–father relationship. *Psychoanalytic Study of the Child*, 1973, **28**, 23–47.

Burton, R., & Whiting, J. W. M. The absent father: Effects on the developing child. Paper presented to the American Psychological Association, Chicago, September, 1960.

Burton, R. V., & Whiting, J. W. M. The absent father and cross-sex identity. *Merrill-Palmer Quarterly*, 1961, **7**, 85–95.

Caldwell, B. M. The effects of infant care. In M. L. Hoffman & L. W. Hoffman (Eds.), *Review of child development research I*. New York: Russell Sage Foundation, 1964.

Caldwell, B. M., Wright, C. M., Honig, A. S., & Tannenbaum, J. Infant day care and attachment. *American Journal of Orthopsychiatry*, 1970, **40**, 397–412.

Caplan, G. *Concepts of mental health and consultation*. Washington, D.C.: U.S. Department of Health, Education, & Welfare, 1959.

Carlsmith, L. Effect of early father-absence on scholastic aptitude. *Harvard Educational Review*, 1964, **34**, 3–21.

Carlsmith, L. Some personality characteristics of boys separated from their fathers during World War II. *Ethos*, 1973, **1**, 466–477.

Cava, E. L., & Rausch, H. L. Identification and the adolescent boy's perception of his father. *Journal of Abnormal and Social Psychology*, 1952, **47**, 855–856.

Chilman, L., & Sussman, M. B. Poverty in the United States in the mid-sixties. *Journal of Marriage and the Family*, 1964, **26**, 391–395.

Chinn, W. L. A brief survey of nearly 1000 juvenile delinquents. *British Journal of Educational Psychology*, 1938, **8**, 78–85.

Christopherson, V. A. An investigation of patriarchal authority in the Mormon family. *Marriage and Family Living*, 1956, **18**, 328–333.

Clarke-Stewart, K. A. Interactions between mothers and their young children: Characteristics and consequences. *Monographs of the Society for Research in Child Development*, 1973, **38** (Serial No. 153).

Clausen, J. A. Drug addiction. In R. K. Merton & R. A. Nisbet (Eds.), *Contemporary social problems*. New York: Harcourt, Brace, & World, 1961.

Clausen, J. A. Family structure, socialization, and personality. In L. W. Hoffman & M. L. Hoffman (Eds.), *Review of child development research II*. New York: Russell Sage Foundation, 1966.

Cohen, L. J., & Campos, J. J. Father, mother, and stranger as elicitors of attachment behaviors in infancy. *Developmental Psychology*, 1974, **10**, 146–154.

Colman, A. D., & Colman, L. *Pregnancy: The psychological experience*. New York: Herder & Herder, 1972.

Condry, J. C., & Siman, M. A. Characteristics of peer- and adult-oriented children. *Journal of Marriage and the Family*, 1974, **36**, 543–554.

Coopersmith, S. *The antecedents of self-esteem*. San Francisco: Freeman, 1967.

Corter, C. Infant attachments. In B. M. Foss (Ed.), *New perspectives in child development*. Harmondsworth, England: Penguin, 1974.

Cottle, T. J. Father perceptions, sex role identity and the prediction of school performance. *Education and Psychological Measurement*, 1968, **28**, 861–886.

Cox, F. N. An assessment of children's attitudes towards parent figures. *Child Development*, 1962, **33**, 821–830.

Crain, A. J., & Stamm, C. S. Intermittent absence of fathers and children's perceptions of parents. *Journal of Marriage and the Family*, 1965, **27**, 344–347.

Crandall, V. J., Dewey, R., Katkovsky, W., & Preston, A. Parents' attitudes and behaviors and grade school children's academic achievements. *Journal of Genetic Psychology*, 1964, **104**, 53–66.

Crane, A. R. A note on preadolescent gangs. *Australian Journal of Psychology*, 1951, **3**, 43–46.

Cronenwett, L. R., & Newmark, L. L. Fathers' responses to childbirth. *Nursing Research*, 1974, **23**, 210–217

Demos, J. The American family in past time. *American Scholar*, 1974, **43**, 422–446.

Deutsch, H. *The psychology of women.* Vol. I. New York: Grune & Stratton, 1944.

Deutsch, M. Minority group and class status as related to social and personality factors in scholastic achievement. *Monographs of the Society for Applied Anthropology*, 1960, **2**, 1–32.

Deutsch, M., & Brown, B. Social influences in Negro–white intelligence differences. *Journal of Social Issues*, 1964, **20**, 24–35.

Devereux, E. C., Bronfenbrenner, U., & Rodgers, R. R. Child-rearing in England and the United States: A cross-cultural comparison. *Journal of Marriage and the Family*, 1969, **32**, 257–270.

Devereux, E. C., Bronfenbrenner, U., & Suci, G. Patterns of parent behavior in the United States of America and the Federal Republic of Germany: A cross-cultural comparison. *International Social Science Journal*, 1962, **14**, 488–506.

Devereux, E. C., Shouval, R., Bronfenbrenner, U., Rodgers, R. R., Kav-Venaki, S., & Kiely, E. Socialization practises of parents, teachers, and peers in Israel: The kibbutz versus the city. *Child Development*, 1974, **45**, 269–282.

Distler, L. S. Patterns of parental identification: An examination of three theories. Unpublished doctoral dissertation, University of California, Berkeley, 1964.

Dodson, F. *How to father.* Los Angeles: Nash, 1974.

Dollard, J., & Miller, N. E. *Personality and psychotherapy.* New York: McGraw-Hill, 1950.

Douvan, E. Independence and identity in adolescence. *Children,* 1957, **4**, 180–190.

Douvan, E. Sex differences in adolescent character processes. *Merrill-Palmer Quarterly*, 1960, **6**, 203–211.

Doyle, A. B. Infant development in day care. *Developmental Psychology*, 1975, **11**, 655–656.

Doyle, A. B., & Somers, K. The effect of group and individual day care on infant development. Paper presented to the Canadian Psychological Association, Quebec, June, 1975.

Dreyer, A. S. Family interaction: Situation and cross-sex effects. Paper presented to the Society for Research in Child Development, Denver, April, 1975.

Dunn, M. S. Marriage role expectations of adolescents. *Marriage and Family Living*, 1960, **22**, 99–104.

Dyer, W. G., & Urban, D. The institutionalization of equalitarian family norms. *Marriage and Family Living*, 1958, **20**, 53–58.

Dyk, R. B., & Witkin, H. A. Family experiences related to the development of differentiation in children. *Child Development*, 1965, **36**, 21–55.

Elder, G. H. *Adolescent achievement and mobility aspirations.* Chapel Hill, N.C.: University of North Carolina, 1962.

Elder, G. H., & Bowerman, C. E. Family structure and child-rearing patterns: The effect of family size and sex composition. *American Sociological Review,* 1963, **28,** 891–905.

Ellis, R. A., & Lane, W. C. Structural supports for upward mobility. *American Sociological Review,* 1963, **28,** 743–756.

Elmer, E. *Children in jeopardy: A study of abused minors and their families.* Pittsburgh: University of Pittsburgh Press, 1967.

Emmerich, W. Parental identification in young children. *Genetic Psychology Monographs,* 1959, **60,** 257–308 (a).

Emmerich, W. Young children's discrimination of parent and child roles. *Child Development,* 1959, **30,** 403–419 (b).

Emmerich, W. Family role concepts of children ages six to ten. *Child Development,* 1961, **32,** 609–624.

Emmerich, W. The parental role: A functional cognitive approach. *Monographs of the Society for Research in Child Development,* 1969, **34** (Serial No. 132).

Endsley, R. C., Garner, A. R., Odom, A. H., & Martin, M. J. Interrelationships among selected maternal behaviors and preschool children's verbal and nonverbal curiosity behavior. Paper presented to the Society for Research in Child Development, Denver, April, 1975.

Epstein, A. S., & Radin, N. Paternal questionnaire data, observational data, and child performance. Unpublished manuscript, University of Michigan, 1975.

Eron, L. D., Banta, T. J., Walder, L. D., & Laulicht, J. H. Comparison of data obtained from mothers and fathers on child rearing practices and their relation to child aggression. *Child Development,* 1961, **32,** 457–472.

Escalona, S. K. *The roots of individuality.* London: Tavistock, 1969.

Fagot, B. I. Sex differences in toddler's behavior and parental reaction. *Developmental Psychology,* 1974, **10,** 554–558.

Farber, B. Marital integration as a factor in parent–child relations. *Child Development,* 1962, **33,** 1–14.

Farber, B., & McHale, J. L. Marital integration and parents' agreement on satisfaction with their child's behavior. *Marriage and Family Living,* 1959, **21,** 65–69.

Favex-Boutonier, J. Child development patterns in France. In K. Soddy (Ed.), *Mental health and infant development,* Vol. 1. London: Routledge & Kegan Paul, 1955.

Fein, G. G. (Chpsn.) Three models for parent education: The parent–child development centers. Symposium presented at the Society for Research in Child Development, Denver, April, 1975.

Feiring, C. The preliminary development of a social systems model of early infant-mother attachment. Paper presented to the Eastern Psychological Association, New York, April 1976.

Feiring, C., & Taylor, J. The influence of the infant and secondary parent on maternal behavior: Toward a social systems view of infant attachment. Unpublished manuscript, University of Pittsburgh, 1976.

Feldman, S. S. Some possible antecedents of attachment behavior in two-year-old children. Unpublished manuscript, Stanford University, 1973.

Feldman, S. S. The impact of day care on one aspect of children's social-emotional behavior. Paper presented to the American Association for the Advancement of Science, San Francisco, February 1974.

Feldman, S. S., & Ingham, M. E. Attachment behavior: A validation study in two age groups. *Child Development*, 1975, **46**, 319–330.

Fenichel, O. *The psychoanalytic theory of neurosis.* New York: Norton, 1945.

Fish, K. D., & Biller, H. B. Perceived childhood paternal relationships and college females' personal adjustment. *Adolescence*, 1973, **8**, 415–420.

Fisher, S. F. *The female orgasm: Psychology, physiology, fantasy.* New York: Basic Books, 1973.

Fitzsimmons, J. J., & Rowe, M. P. A study in child care, 1970–1971. Cambridge, Mass.: ABT Associates, 1971.

Ford, C., & Beach, F. A. *Patterns of sexual behavior.* New York: Harper, 1951.

Foster, J. E. Father images: Television and ideal. *Journal of Marriage and the Family*, 1964, **26**, 353–355.

Freeberg, N. E., & Payne, D. T. Parental influence on cognitive development in early childhood: A review. *Child Development*, 1967, **38**, 65–87.

Freedheim, D. K. An investigation of masculinity and parental role patterns. Unpublished doctoral dissertation, Duke University, 1960.

Freud, S. *Three essays on the theory of sexuality* (1905). New York: Avon, 1962.

Freud, S. Analysis of a phobia in a five-year-old boy (1909). In *The sexual enlightenment of children.* New York: Collier, 1963.

Freud, S. *The ego and the id* (1923). New York: Norton, 1962.

Freud, S. The passing of the oedipus complex. In *Collected Papers,* Vol. 2. London: Hogarth, 1924.

Freud, S. Moses and monotheism (1939). *The Standard Edition,* Vol. 23. London: Hogarth, 1964.

Freud, S. *An outline of psychoanalysis* (1940). New York: Norton, 1940.

Freud, S. *Group psychology and the analysis of the ego.* London: Hogarth, 1948.

Freud, S. Some psychological consequences of the anatomical distinction between the sexes. In *Collected Papers,* Vol. 5. London: Hogarth, 1950.

Gardner, L. P. An analysis of children's attitudes towards fathers. *Journal of Genetic Psychology*, 1947, **70**, 3–28.

Gavron, H. *The captive wife: Conflicts of housebound mothers.* London: Routledge & Kegan Paul, 1966.

Getzels, J. W., & Walsh, J. J. The method of paired direct and projective questionnaires in the study of attitude structure and socialization. *Psychological Monographs,* 1958, **72** (Whole No. 454).

Gilbert, S. D. *What's a father for?* New York: Parents' Magazine Press, 1975.

Gill, L. J., & Spilka, B. Some nonintellectual correlates of academic achievement among Mexican–American secondary school students. *Journal of Educational Psychology,* 1962, **53**, 144–149.

Giovannoni, J. M., & Billingsley, A. Child neglect among the poor: A study of parental adequacy in three ethnic groups. *Child Welfare,* 1970, **49**, 196–204.

Glueck, S., & Glueck, E. *Unraveling juvenile delinquency.* New York: Commonwealth Fund, 1950.

Glueck, S., & Glueck, E. T. *Physique and delinquency.* New York: Harper, 1956.

Glueck, S., & Glueck, E. *Predicting delinquency and crime.* Cambridge, Mass.: Harvard University Press, 1959.

Goldberg, S. Infant care and growth in urban Zambia. *Human Development,* 1972, **15**, 77–89.

Goldberg, S., & Lewis, M. Play behavior in the year-old infant: Early sex differences. *Child Development,* 1969, **40**, 21–31.

Goodenough, E. W. Interest in persons as an aspect of sex difference in the early years. *Genetic Psychology Monographs,* 1957, **55**, 287–323.

Gordon, R. S., & Gordon, K. Social factors in the prediction and treatment of emotional disorders of pregnancy. *American Journal of Obstetrics & Gynecology,* 1959, **77**, 1074–1083.

Gorer, G. *The American people: A study of national character.* New York: Norton, 1948.

Graham, P., & Rutter, M. Psychiatric disorder in the young adolescent: A follow-up study. *Proceedings of the Royal Society of Medicine,* 1973, **66**, 1226–1229.

Gray, S. Masculinity–femininity in relation to anxiety and social acceptance. *Child Development,* 1957, **28**, 203–214.

Gray, S. Perceived similarity to parents and adjustment. *Child Development,* 1959, **30**, 91–107.

Gray, S. W., & Klaus, R. The assessment of parental identification. *Genetic Psychology Monographs,* 1956, **54**, 81–114.

Greenberg, M., & Morris, N. Engrossment: The newborn's impact upon the father. *American Journal of Orthopsychiatry,* 1974, **44**, 520–531.

Gregory, I. Anterospective data following childhood loss of a parent. I. Delinquency and high school dropout. *Archives of General Psychiatry,* 1965, **13**, 99–109.

Greif, E. B. A study of role-playing in preschool children. Unpublished doctoral dissertation, Johns Hopkins University, 1973.

Grunebaum, M. G., Hurwitz, I., Prentice, N. M., & Sperry, B. M. Fathers of sons with primary neurotic learning inhibition. *American Journal of Orthopsychiatry*, 1962, **32**, 462–473.

Hacker, H. M. The new burdens of masculinity. *Marriage and Family Living*, 1957, **19**, 227–233.

Hampson, J. L., & Hampson, J. G. The ontogenesis of sexual behavior in man. In W. C. Young (Ed.), *Sex and internal secretions* (ed. 3), Baltimore: Williams & Wilkins, 1961.

Handel, G. Psychological study of whole families. *Psychological Bulletin*, 1965, **63**, 19–41.

Harlow, H. F. The development of affectional patterns in infant monkeys. In B. M. Foss (Ed.), *Determinants of infant behavior I*. London: Methuen, 1961.

Harlow, H. F., & Zimmerman, R. R. Affectional responses in the infant monkey. *Science*, 1959, **130**, 421.

Harper, L. V. The young as a source of stimuli controlling caretaking behavior. *Developmental Psychology*, 1971, **4**, 73–85.

Hartley, R. E. Sex role identification: A symposium. A developmental view of female sex role definition and identification. *Merrill-Palmer Quarterly*, 1964, **10**, 3–16.

Hartley, R. E., & Klein, A. Sex role concepts among elementary-school-age girls. *Marriage and Family Living*, 1959, **21**, 59–64.

Hartup, W. W. Some correlates of parental imitation in young children. *Child Development*, 1962, **33**, 85–97.

Hartup, W. W., & Zook, E. A. Sex role preference in three- and four-year-old children. *Journal of Consulting Psychology*, 1960, **24**, 420–426.

Heilbrun, A. B. An empirical test of the modelling theory of sex-role learning. *Child Development*, 1965, **36**, 789–799.

Heilbrun, A. B. Parent identification and filial sex-role behavior: The importance of biological context. In J. K. Cole & R. Dienstbier (Eds.), *Nebraska Symposium on Motivation*. Lincoln: University of Nebraska Press, 1974.

Heilbrun, A. B., Harrell, S. N., & Gillard, B. J. Perceived identification of late adolescents and level of adjustment: The importance of parent-model attributes, ordinal position, and sex of child. *Journal of Genetic Psychology*, 1965, **107**, 49–59.

Helper, M. M. Learning theory and the self-concept. *Journal of Abnormal and Social Psychology*, 1955, **51**, 184–194.

Herzog, E., & Sudia, C. *Boys in fatherless families*. Washington, D.C.: U.S. Department of Health, Education, & Welfare, 1970.

Herzog, E. & Sudia, C. Children in fatherless families. In B. M. Caldwell &

H. N. Ricciuti (Eds.), *Review of child development research III*. Chicago: University of Chicago Press, 1973.

Hetherington, E. M. A developmental study of the effects of sex of the dominant parent on sex-role preference, identification, and imitation in children. *Journal of Personality and Social Psychology*, 1965, **2**, 188–194.

Hetherington, E. M. Effects of paternal absence on sex-typed behaviors in Negro and white preadolescent males. *Journal of Personality and Social Psychology*, 1966, **4**, 87–91.

Hetherington, E. M. The effects of familial variables on sex typing, on parent-child similarity, and on imitation in children. In J. P. Hill (Ed.), *Minnesota Symposia on Child Psychology I*. Minneapolis: University of Minnesota Press, 1967.

Hetherington, E. M. Effects of father-absence on personality development in adolescent daughters. *Developmental Psychology*, 1972, **7**, 313–326.

Hetherington, E. M., & Brackbill, Y. Etiology and covariation of obstinacy, orderliness, and parsimony in young children. *Child Development*, 1963, **34**, 919–943.

Hetherington, E. M., Cox, M., & Cox, R. Beyond father absence: Conceptualization of effects of divorce. Paper presented to the Society for Research in Child Development, Denver, April, 1975.

Hetherington, E. M., & Deur, J. L. The effects of father absence on child development. *Young Children*, 1971, 233–248.

Hetherington, E. M., & Frankie, G. Effects of parental dominance, warmth, and conflict on imitation in children. *Journal of Personality and Social Psychology*, 1967, **6**, 119–125.

Hinde, R. A. *Animal behavior: A synthesis of ethology and comparative psychology*. New York: McGraw-Hill, 1970.

Hines, J. D. Father: The forgotten man. *Nursing Forum*, 1971, **10**, 176–200.

Hoffman, L. W. The father's role in the family and the child's peer-group adjustment. *Merrill-Palmer Quarterly*, 1961, **7**, 97–105.

Hoffman, L. W. Effects of maternal employment on the child: A review of the research. *Developmental Psychology*, 1974, **10**, 204–228.

Hoffman, L. W., & Lippitt, R. The measurement of family life variables. In P. H. Mussen (Ed.), *Handbook of research methods in child development*. New York: Wiley, 1960.

Hoffman, M. L. Power assertion by the parent and its impact on the child. *Child Development*, 1960, **31**, 129–143.

Hoffman, M. L. Paternal practices and the development of internal social control. Paper presented to the Society for Research in Child Development, Bowling Green, Ohio, 1966.

Hoffman, M. L. Conscience, personality, and socialization technique. *Human Development*, 1970, **13**, 90–126 (a).

Hoffman, M. L. Moral development. In P. H. Mussen (Ed.), *Carmichael's manual of child psychology* (3rd ed.), Vol. 2. New York: Wiley, 1970 (b).

Hoffman, M. L. Father absence and conscience development. *Developmental Psychology*, 1971, **4**, 400–406 (a).

Hoffman, M. L. Identification and conscience development. *Child Development*, 1971, **42**, 1071–1082 (b).

Hoffman, M. L., & Saltzstein, H. D. Parent discipline and the child's moral development. *Journal of Personality and Social Psychology*, 1967, **5**, 45–57.

Hogan, R. Moral conduct and moral character: A psychological perspective. *Psychological Bulletin*, 1973, **79**, 217–232.

Holman, P. Some factors in the etiology of maladjustment in children. *Journal of Mental Science*, 1953, **99**, 654–688.

Holman, P. The etiology of maladjustment in children. *Journal of Mental Science*, 1959, **99**, 654–688.

Holstein, C. B. Parental consensus and interaction in relation to the child's moral development. Unpublished doctoral dissertation, University of California, Berkeley, 1969.

Howells, J. G. Fathering. In J. G. Howells (Ed.), *Modern perspectives in international child psychiatry*. Edinburgh: Oliver & Boyd, 1969.

Hull, C. L. *Principles of behavior*. New York: Appleton-Century-Crofts, 1943.

Hurley, J. R. Parental malevolence and children's intelligence. *Journal of Consulting Psychology*, 1967, **31**, 199–204.

Illsley, R., & Thompson, B. Women from broken homes. *Sociological Review*, 1961, **9**, 27–54.

Jacobson, G., & Ryder, R. G. Parental loss and some characteristics of the early marriage relationship. *American Journal of Orthopsychiatry*, 1969, **39**, 779–787.

Johnson, M. M. Sex role learning in the nuclear family. *Child Development*, 1963, **34**, 315–333.

Jordan, B. E., Radin, N., & Epstein, A. Paternal behavior and intellectual functioning in preschool boys and girls. *Developmental Psychology*, 1975, **11**, 407–408.

Josselyn, I. M. Cultural forces, motherliness, and fatherliness. *American Journal of Orthopsychiatry*, 1956, **25**, 264–271.

Jung, C. G. *The significance of the father in the destiny of the individual*. Zurich: Rascher, 1949.

Kagan, J. The concept of identification. *Psychological Review*, 1958, **65**, 295–305.

Kagan, J. Acquisition and significance of sex-typing and sex-role identity. In M. L. Hoffman & L. W. Hoffman (Eds.), *Review of child development research I*. New York: Russell Sage Foundation, 1964.

Kagan, J., & Freeman, M. Relation of childhood intelligence, maternal behaviors, and social class to behavior during adolescence. *Child Development,* 1963, **34,** 899–911.

Kagan, J., Hosken, B., & Watson, S. Child's symbolic conceptualization of parents. *Child Development,* 1961, **32,** 625–636.

Kahl, J. A. Educational and occupational aspirations of "common man" boys. *American Educational Review,* 1953, **23,** 186–203.

Kahl, J. A. *The American class structure.* New York: Holt, Rinehart, & Winston, 1957.

Kanin, E. T. Male aggression in dating—courtship relations. *American Journal of Sociology,* 1957, **63,** 197–204.

Kaplar, J. E. Creativity, sex-role preference, and perception of parents in fifth-grade boys. Unpublished doctoral dissertation, University of Massachusetts, 1970.

Katz, I. Socialization of academic motivation in minority group children. In D. Levine (Ed.), *Nebraska Symposium on Motivation.* Lincoln: University of Nebraska Press, 1967.

Kauffman, J. H. Interpersonal relations in traditional and emergent families among midwest Mennonites. *Marriage and Family Living,* 1961, **23,** 247–252.

Keller, H. R., Montgomery, B., Moss, J., Sharp, J. & Wheeler, J. Differential parental effects among one-year-old infants in a stranger and separation situation. Paper presented to the Society for Research in Child Development, Denver, April 1975.

Kennell, J. H., Jerauld, R., Wolfe, H., Chesler, D., Kreger, N. C., McAlpine, W., Steffa, M., & Klaus, M. H. Maternal behavior one year after early and extended post-partum contact. *Developmental Medicine and Child Neurology,* 1974, **16,** 172–179.

Kennell, J. H., Trause, M. A., & Klaus, M. H. Evidence for a sensitive period in the human mother. Unpublished manuscript, Case Western Reserve University, 1975.

Kimball, B. The sentence completion technique in a study of scholastic under-achievement. *Journal of Consulting Psychology,* 1952, **16,** 353–358.

Klaus, M. H., Jerauld, R., Kreger, N. C., McAlpine, W., Steffa, M., & Kennell, J. H. Maternal attachment: Importance of the first post-partum days. *New England Journal of Medicine,* 1972, **286,** 460–463.

Klaus, M., Trause, M. A., & Kennell, J. H. Human maternal behavior following delivery: Is this species-specific? Unpublished manuscript, Case Western Reserve University, 1975.

Kluckhorn, C. *Mirror for man.* New York: McGraw-Hill, 1949.

Koch, H. L. Some personality correlates of sex, sibling position and sex of siblings among five- and six-year-old children. *Genetic Psychology Monographs,* 1955, **52,** 3–50.

Koch, H. L. Sissiness and tomboyishness in relation to sibling characteristics. *Journal of Genetic Psychology*, 1956, **88**, 231–244.

Kohlberg, L. Moral development and identification. In H. W. Stevenson (Ed.), *Child psychology*. Chicago: University of Chicago Press, 1963.

Kohlberg, L. The development of moral character and ideology. In M. L. Hoffman & L. W. Hoffman (Eds.), *Review of child development research I*. New York: Russell Sage Foundation, 1964.

Kohlberg, L. A cognitive-developmental analysis of children's sex-role concepts and attitudes. In E. E. Maccoby (Ed.), *The development of sex differences*. Stanford: Stanford University Press, 1966.

Kohlberg, L. Stage and sequence: The cognitive-developmental approach to socialization. In D. A. Goslin (Ed.), *Handbook of socialization theory and research*. Chicago: Rand McNally, 1969.

Kohlberg, L., & Zigler, E. The impact of cognitive maturity on the development of sex-role attitudes in the years 4 to 8. *Genetic Psychology Monographs*, 1967, **75**, 89–165.

Kohn, M. L. Social class and the exercise of parental authority. *American Sociological Review*, 1959, **24**, 352–366.

Kohn, M. L., & Carroll, E. E. Social class and the allocation of parental responsibilities. *Sociometry*, 1960, **23**, 372–392.

Komarovsky, M. *Blue-collar marriage*. New York: Random House, 1964.

Kotelchuck, M. The nature of the child's tie to his father. Unpublished doctoral dissertation, Harvard University, 1972.

Kotelchuck, M. The nature of the child's tie to his father. Paper presented to the Society for Research in Child Development, Philadelphia, April 1973.

Kotelchuck, M., Zelazo, P., Kagan, J., & Spelke, E. Infant reaction to parental separations when left with familiar and unfamiliar adults. *Journal of Genetic Psychology*, 1975, **126**, 255–262.

Lamb, M. E. A defense of the concept of attachment. *Human Development*, 1974, **17**, 376–385.

Lamb, M. E. Fathers: Forgotten contributors to child development. *Human Development*, 1975, **18**, 245–266 (a).

Lamb, M. E. Infant attachment to mothers and fathers. Paper presented to the Society for Research in Child Development, Denver, April 1975 (b).

Lamb, M. E. Infants, fathers, and mother: Interaction at eight months of age in the home and in the laboratory. Paper presented to the Eastern Psychological Association, New York, April 1975 (c).

Lamb, M. E. Physiological mechanisms in the control of maternal behavior in rats: A review. *Psychological Bulletin*, 1975, **82**, 104–119 (d).

Lamb, M. E. Separation and reunion behaviors as criteria of attachment to mothers and fathers. Unpublished manuscript, Yale University, 1975 (e).

Lamb, M. E. Interactions between two-year-olds and their mothers and fathers. *Psychological Reports*, 1976, **38**, 447–450 (a).

Lamb, M. E. Parent–infant interaction in eight-month-olds. *Child Psychiatry and Human Development*, 1976, **7**, in press (b).

Lamb, M. E. Proximity-seeking attachment behaviors: A critical review of the literature. *Genetic Psychology Monographs*, 1976, **93**, 63–89 (c).

Lamb, M. E. Twelve-month-olds and their parents: Interaction in a laboratory playroom. *Developmental Psychology*, 1976, **12**, 237–244 (d).

Lamb, M. E. A re-examination of the infant social world. *Human Development*, in press.

Lambert, W. E., Yackley, A., & Hein, R. M. Child training values of English–Canadian and French–Canadian parents. *Canadian Journal of Behavioral Science*, 1971, **3**, 217–236.

Landis, P. H. Research on teen-age dating. *Marriage and Family Living*, 1960, **22**, 266–267.

Landy, F., Rosenberg, B. G., & Sutton-Smith, B. The effect of limited father-absence on the cognitive and emotional development of children. Paper presented to the Mid-Western Psychological Association, Chicago, May 1967.

Landy, F., Rosenberg, B. G., & Sutton-Smith, B. The effect of limited father-absence on cognitive development. *Child Development*, 1969, **40**, 941–944.

Langner, T. S., & Michael, S. T. *Life stress and mental health*. New York: Free Press, 1963.

Lansky, L. M. The family structure also affects the model: Sex-role identification in parents of preschool children. *Merrill-Palmer Quarterly*, 1964, **10**, 39–40.

Lansky, L. M. The family structure also affects the model: Sex-role attitudes in parents of preschool children. *Merrill-Palmer Quarterly*, 1967, **13**, 139–150.

Layman, E. M. Discussion: Symposium: Father influence in the family. *Merrill-Palmer Quarterly*, 1961, **7**, 107–111.

Lazowick, L. M. On the nature of identification. *Journal of Abnormal and Social Psychology*, 1955, **51**, 175–183.

Lederer, W. Dragons, delinquents, and destiny. *Psychological Issues*, 1964, **4** (Whole No. 3).

Lefkowitz, M. M. Some relationships between sex role preference of children and other parent and child variables. *Psychological Reports*, 1962, **10**, 43–53.

Lehrman, D. S. Can psychiatrists use ethology? In N. F. White (Ed.), *Ethology and psychiatry*. Toronto: University of Toronto Press, 1974.

Leichty, M. The absence of the father during early childhood and its effect upon the Oedipal situation as reflected in young adults. *Merrill-Palmer Quarterly*, 1960, **6**, 212–217.

Leiderman, G. F. Effect of parental relationships and child-training practices on boys' interactions with peers. *Acta Psychologia*, 1959, **15**, 469.

Leiderman, P. H., & Leiderman, G. F. Familial influences on infant development in an East African agricultural community. In E. J. Anthony & C. Koupernik (Eds.), *The child in his family: Children at a psychiatric risk*. New York: Wiley, 1974.

Leiderman, P. H., & Leiderman, G. F. Affective and cognitive consequences of polymatric infant care in the East African Highlands. In A. D. Pick (Ed.), *Minnesota symposia on child psychology*, Vol. 8. Minneapolis: University of Minnesota Press, 1975.

Leifer, A. D., Leiderman, P. H. Barnett, C. R., & Williams, J. A. Effects of mother–infant separation on maternal attachment behavior. *Child Development*, 1972, **43**, 1203–1218.

LeMasters, E. E. Parenthood as crisis. *Marriage and Family Living*, 1957, **19**, 352–355.

Lerner, S. H. Effects of desertion on family life. *Social Casework*, 1954, **35**, 3–8.

Lessing, E. E., Zagorin, S. W., & Nelson, D. WISC subtest and IQ score correlates of father absence. *Journal of Genetic Psychology*, 1970, **67**, 181–195.

Lewis, M. Parents and children: Sex role development. *School Review*, 1972, **80**, 229–240 (a).

Lewis, M. State as an infant–environment interaction: An analysis of mother–infant interaction as a function of sex. *Merril-Palmer Quarterly*, 1972, **18**, 95–121 (b).

Lewis, M., & Rosenblum, L. A. (Eds.) *The effect of the infant on its caregiver*. New York: Wiley, 1974.

Lewis, M., & Weinraub, M. Sex of parent x sex of child: Socioemotional development. In R. Richart, R. Friedman, & R. Vande Wiele (Eds.), *Sex differences in behavior*. New York: Wiley, 1974.

Lewis, M., Weinraub, M., & Ban, P. Mothers and fathers, girls and boys: Attachment behavior in the first two years of life. *Educational Testing Service Research Bulletin*, Princeton, N.J., 1972.

Liebenberg, B. Expectant fathers. *American Journal of Orthopsychiatry*, 1967, **37**, 358–359.

Livson, N. Parental behavior and children's involvement with their parents. *Journal of Genetic Psychology*, 1966, **109**, 173–194.

Lorenz, K. Companions as factors in the bird's environment (1935). In *Studies in animal and human behavior*. Cambridge, Mass.: Harvard University Press, 1970.

Lozoff, M. M. Fathers and autonomy in women. In R. B. Kundsin (Ed.), *Women and success*. New York: Morrow, 1974.

Lynn, D. B. A note on sex differences in the development of masculine and feminine identification. *Psychological Review*, 1959, **66**, 126–135.

Lynn, D. B. Sex differences in identification development. *Sociometry*, 1961, **24**, 372–383.

Lynn, D. B. Sex role and parental identification. *Child Development*, 1962, **33**, 555–564.

Lynn, D. B. The process of learning parental and sex-role identification. *Journal of Marriage and the Family*, 1966, **28**, 466–470.

Lynn, D. B. *Parental and sex-role identification: A theoretical formulation.* Berkeley: McCutchan Publishing Corp., 1969.

Lynn, D. B. *The Father: His role in child development.* Monterery, Calif.: Brooks/Cole, 1974.

Lynn, D. B., & Cross, A. R. Parent preference of preschool children. *Journal of Marriage and the Family*, 1974, **36**, 555–559.

Lynn, D. B., & Maaske, M. Imitation versus similarity: Child to parent. Paper presented to the Western Psychological Association, Los Angeles, April 1970.

Lynn, D. B., & Sawrey, W. L. The effects of father-absence on Norwegian boys and girls. *Journal of Abnormal and Social Psychology*, 1959, **59**, 258–262.

MacCalman, D. R. Background to child development patterns in the United Kingdom. In K. Soddy (Ed.), *Mental health and infant development*, Vol. 1. London: Routledge & Kegan Paul, 1955.

Maccoby, E. E., & Jacklin, C. N. Stress, activity, and proximity seeking: Sex differences in the year-old child. *Child Development*, 1973, **44**, 34–42.

Maccoby, E. E., & Jacklin, C. N. *The psychology of sex differences.* Stanford: Stanford University Press, 1974.

Maccoby, E. E., & Masters, J. C. Attachment and dependency. In P. H. Mussen (Ed.), *Carmichael's manual of child psychology* (3rd ed.), Vol. 2. New York: Wiley, 1970.

MacFarlane, A. The first hours, and the smile. In R. Levin (Ed.), *Child alive!* New York: Anchor-Doubleday, 1975.

MacKinnon, D. W. Violations of prohibitions. In H. A. Murray (Ed.), *Explorations in personality.* New York: Oxford University Press, 1938.

Marcus, R. F. The child as elicitor of parental sanctions for independent and dependent behavior: A simulation of parent–child interaction. *Developmental Psychology*, 1975, **11**, 443–452.

Marsella, A. J., Dubanoski, R. A., & Mohs, K. The effects of father presence and absence upon maternal attitudes. *Journal of Genetic Psychology*, 1974, **125**, 257–263.

Maxwell, A. E. Discrepancies between the pattern of abilities for normal and neurotic children. *Journal of Mental Science*, 1961, **107**, 300–307.

McCord, W., McCord, J., & Howard, A. Familial correlates of aggression in nondelinquent male children. *Journal of Abnormal and Social Psychology*, 1961, **62**, 79–93.

McCord, W., McCord, J., & Howard, A. Family interaction as antecedent to the direction of male aggressiveness. *Journal of Abnormal and Social Psychology*, 1963, **66**, 239–242.

McCord, J., McCord, W., & Thurber, E. Some effects of paternal absence on male children. *Journal of Abnormal and Social Psychology*, 1962, **64**, 361–369.

McGuire, C. Sex role and community-variability in test performances. *Journal of Educational Psychology*, 1961, **52**, 61–73.

Mead, M. *Sex and temperament in three primitive societies.* New York: Morrow, 1935.

Mead, M. *Male and female.* New York: Morrow, 1949.

Mead, M. A cultural anthropologist's approach to maternal deprivation. In *Deprivation of maternal care: A reassessment of its effects.* Geneva: WHO, 1962.

Medinnus, G. N. The relation between inter-parent agreement and several child measures. *Journal of Genetic Psychology*, 1963, **102**, 139–144.

Medinnus, G. N. Delinquents' perception of their parents. *Journal of Consulting Psychology*, 1965, **29**, 5–19.

Medinnus, G. N., & Johnson, T. M. Parental perceptions of kindergarten children. *Journal of Educational Research*, 1970, **63**, 370–381.

Meerloo, J. A. M. The father cuts the cord. *American Journal of Psychotherapy*, 1956, **10**, 471–480.

Meerloo, J. A. M. The psychological role of the father: The father cuts the cord. *Child and Family*, 1968, 102–114.

Messer, S. B., & Lewis, M. Social class and sex differences in the attachment and play behavior of the one-year-old infant. *Merrill-Palmer Quarterly*, 1972, **18**, 295–306.

Métraux, R. Parents and children: An analysis of contemporary German child-care and youth guidance literature. In M. Mead & M. Wolfenstein (Eds.), *Childhood in contemporary culture.* Chicago: University of Chicago Press, 1955.

Middleton, R., & Putney, S. Political expression of adolescent rebellion. *American Journal of Sociology*, 1963, **68**, 527–535.

Miller, D. R., & Swanson, G. E. *The changing American parent.* New York: Wiley, 1958.

Miller, W. B. Lower class culture as a generating milieu of gang delinquency. *Journal of Social Issues*, 1958, **14**, 5–19.

Milton, G. A. The effects of sex-role identification upon problem solving skills. *Journal of Abnormal and Social Psychology*, 1957, **55**, 208–212.

Mischel, W. Sex typing and socialization. In P. H. Mussen (Ed.), *Carmichael's manual of child psychology* (3rd ed.), Vol. 2. New York: Wiley, 1970.

Mitchell, D., & Wilson, W. Relationship of father-absence to masculinity and popularity of delinquent boys. *Psychological Reports*, 1967, **20**, 1173–1174.

Mogey, J. M. A century of declining paternal authority. *Marriage and Family Living*, 1957, **19**, 234–239.

Money, J., & Ehrhardt, A. A. *Man and woman: Boy and girl*. Baltimore: Johns Hopkins Press, 1972.

Money, J., Hampson, J. G., & Hampson, J. L. Imprinting and the establishment of gender role. *Archives of Neurology and Psychiatry*, 1957, **77**, 333–336.

Money, J., & Tucker, P. *Sexual signatures*. Boston: Little Brown, 1975.

Moss, H. A. Sex, age, and state as determinants of mother–infant interaction. *Merrill-Palmer Quarterly*, 1967, **13**, 19–36.

Moulton, P. W., Burnstein, E., Liberty, D., & Altucher, N. The patterning of parental affection and dominance as a determinant of guilt and sex-typing. *Journal of Personality and Social Psychology*, 1966, **4**, 363–365.

Mowrer, O. H. Identification: A link between learning theory and psychotherapy. In *Learning theory and personality dynamics*. New York: Ronald, 1950.

Mullahy, P. *Oedipus: Myth and complex*. New York: Hermitage, 1948.

Murrell, S. A., & Stachowiak, J. G. The family group: Development, structure and therapy. *Journal of Marriage and the Family*, 1965, **27**, 13–18.

Mussen, P. H. Some antecedents and consequences of masculine sex-typing in adolescent boys. *Psychological Monographs*, 1961, **75** (Whole No. 506).

Mussen, P. H. Early socialization: Learning and identification. In T. M. Newcomb (Ed.), *New directions in psychology III*. New York: Holt, Rinehart, & Winston, 1967.

Mussen, P. H. *The psychological development of the child*. New York: Prentice-Hall, 1973.

Mussen, P. H., Bouterline Young, H., Gaddini, R., & Morante, L. The influence of father–son relationships on adolescent personality and attitudes. *Journal of Child Psychology and Psychiatry*, 1963, **4**, 3–16.

Mussen, P. H., & Distler, L. Masculinity, identification, and father–son relationships. *Journal of Abnormal and Social Psychology*, 1959, **59**, 350–356.

Mussen, P. H., & Distler, L. Child rearing antecedents of masculine identification in kindergarten boys. *Child Development*, 1960, **31**, 89–100.

Mussen, P. H., & Parker, A. L. Mother nurturance and the girl's incidental imitative learning. *Journal of Personality and Social Psychology*, 1965, **2**, 94–97.

Mussen, P. H., & Rutherford, E. Parent–child relation and parental personality in relation to young children's sex-role preferences. *Child Development*, 1963, **34**, 589–607.

Mussen, P. H., Rutherford, E., Harris, S., & Keasey, C. B. Honesty and altruism among preadolescents. *Developmental Psychology*, 1970, **3**, 169–194.

Mutimer, D., Loughlin, L., & Powell, M. Some differences in the family relationships of achieving and underachieving readers. *Journal of Genetic Psychology*, 1966, **109**, 67–74.

Nash, J. Critical periods in human development. *Bulletin of the Maritime Psychological Association*, 1954, 18–22.

Nash, J. The father in contemporary culture and current psychological literature. *Child Development*, 1965, **36**, 261–297.

Nelsen, E. A., & Maccoby, E. E. The relationship between social development and differential abilities on the Scholastic Aptitude Test, *Merrill-Palmer Quarterly*, 1966, **12**, 269–289.

Newson, J., & Newson, E. *Pattern of infant care in an urban community*. London: Allen & Unwin, 1963.

Newson, J., & Newson, E. *Four years old in an urban community*. London: Allen & Unwin, 1968.

Norman, C. D. The interpersonal values of parents of achieving and non-achieving gifted children. *Journal of Psychology*, 1966, **64**, 49–57.

Nowlis, V. The search for significant concepts in a study of parent–child relationships. *American Journal of Orthopsychiatry*, 1952, **22**, 286–299.

Nye, F. I. Child adjustment in broken and unbroken homes. *Marriage and Family Living*, 1957, **19**, 356–361.

Olsen, M. E. Distribution of family responsibilities and social stratification. *Marriage and Family Living*, 1960, **22**, 60–65.

Osgood, C., Suci, G., & Tannenbaum, P. H. *The measurement of meaning*. Urbana: University of Illinois Press, 1957.

Osofsky, J. D. Neonatal characteristics and directional effects in mother–infant interaction. Paper presented to the Society for Research in Child Development, Denver, April 1975.

Osofsky, J. D., & O'Connell, E. J. Parent–child interaction: Daughters' effects upon mothers' and fathers' behaviors. *Developmental Psychology*, 1972, **7**, 157–168.

Osofsky, J. D., & Oldfield, S. Children's effects upon parental behavior: Mothers' and fathers' responses to dependent and independent child behaviors. Paper presented to the American Psychological Association, Washington, D.C., August 1971.

Palmer, R. C. Behavior problems of children in Navy Officers' families. *Social Casework*, 1960, **41**, 177–184.

Parke, R. D., & O'Leary, S. Father–mother–infant interaction in the newborn period: Some findings, some observations, and some unresolved issues. In K. F. Riegel & J. Meacham (Eds.), *The developing individual in a changing world*. Vol. 2. *Social and environmental issues*. The Hague: Mouton, 1975.

Parke, R. D., O'Leary, S., & West, S. Mother–father–newborn interaction: Effects of maternal medication, labor, and sex of infant. *Proceedings of the 80th Annual Convention of the American Psychological Association,* 1972, 85–86.

Parsons, T. The father symbol: An appraisal in the light of psychoanalytic and sociological theory. In L. Bryson, L. Kinkelstein, R. M. MacIver, & R. McKeon (Eds.), *Symbols and values.* New York: Harper & Row, 1954.

Parsons, T. Social structure and the development of personality: Freud's contribution to the integration of psychology and sociology. *Psychiatry,* 1958, **21,** 321–340.

Parsons, T., & Bales, R. F. *Family, socialization, and interaction process.* Glencoe, Ill.: Free Press, 1955.

Parsons, T., & Shils, E. A. (Eds.) *Towards a general theory of action.* Cambridge, Mass.: Harvard University Press, 1951.

Payne, D. E., & Mussen, P. H. Parent–child relations and father identification among adolescent boys. *Journal of Abnormal and Social Psychology,* 1956, **52,** 358–362.

Pederson, F. A. Relationship between father absence and emotional disturbance in male military dependents. *Merrill-Palmer Quarterly,* 1966, **12,** 321–333.

Pederson, F. A., & Robson, K. S. Father participation in infancy. *American Journal of Orthopsychiatry,* 1969, **39,** 466–472.

Peterson, D. R., Becker, W. C., Shoemaker, D. J., Luria, Z., & Hellmer, L. A. Child behavior problems and parental attitudes. *Child Development,* 1961, **32,** 131–162.

Peterson, D. R., Becker, W. C., Hellmer, L. A., Shoemaker, D. J., & Quay, H. C. Parental attitudes and child development. *Child Development,* 1959, **30,** 119–130.

Pettigrew, T. F. *A profile of the Negro American.* Princeton, N.J.: Van Nostrand, 1964.

Piaget, J. *The moral judgment of the child.* New York: Harcourt Brace, 1932.

Putney, S., & Middleton, R. Effect of husband–wife interaction on the strictness of attitudes towards child rearing. *Marriage and Family Living,* 1960, **22,** 171–173.

Radin, N. Father–child interaction and the intellectual functioning of four-year-old boys. *Developmental Psychology,* 1972, **6,** 353–361.

Radin, N. Observed paternal behaviors as antecedents of intellectual functioning in young boys. *Developmental Psychology,* 1973, **8,** 369–376.

Radin, N. Observed maternal behavior with four-year-old boys and girls in lower class families. *Child Development,* 1974, **45,** 1126–1131.

Radin, N., & Epstein, A. Observed paternal behavior and the intellectual functioning of preschool boys and girls. Paper presented to the Society for Research in Child Development, Denver, April 1975.

Radke, M. J. The relation of parental authority to children's behavior and attitudes. *University of Minnesota Institute of Child Welfare Monograph,* 1946, No. 22.

Ragozin, A. Attachment in day care children: Field and laboratory findings. Paper presented to the Society for Research in Child Development, Denver, April 1975.

Ramey, C. T., & Mills, P. J. Mother–infant interaction patterns as a function of rearing conditions. Paper presented to the Society for Research in Child Development, Denver, April 1975.

Rau, L. Parental antecedents of identification. *Merrill-Palmer Quarterly*, 1960, **6**, 77–82.

Rebelsky, F. G., Allinsmith, W. A., & Grinder, R. Sex differences in children's use of fantasy confession and their relation to temptation. *Child Development*, 1963, **34**, 955–962.

Rebelsky, F., & Hanks, C. Fathers' verbal interaction with infants in the first three months of life. *Child Development*, 1971, **42**, 63–68.

Reuter, M. W., & Biller, H. B. Perceived paternal nurturance–availability and personality adjustment among college males. *Journal of Consulting and Clinical Psychology*, 1973, **40**, 339–342.

Rheingold, H. L. The social and socializing infant. In D. A. Goslin (Ed.), *Handbook of socialization theory and research*. Chicago: Rand McNally, 1968.

Ringler, N. M., Kennell, J. H., Jarvella, R., Navojosky, B. J., & Klaus, M. H. Mother-to-child speech at 2 years—effects of early postnatal contact. *Journal of Pediatrics*, 1975, **86**, 141–144.

Ricciuti, H. N., & Poresky, R. H. Development of attachment to caregivers in an infant nursery during the first year of life. Paper presented to the Society for Research in Child Development, Philadelphia, March, 1973.

Rohrer, J. H., & Edmonson, M. S. (Eds.) *The eighth generation*. New York: Harper, 1960.

Rosenberg, B. G., & Sutton-Smith, B. Ordinal position and sex role identification. *Genetic Psychology Monographs*, 1964, **70**, 297–328.

Rosenberg, M. *Society and the adolescent self-image*. Princeton, N.J.: Princeton University Press, 1965.

Ross, G., Kagan, J., Zelazo, P., & Kotelchuck, M. Separation protest in infants in home and laboratory. *Developmental Psychology*, 1975, **11**, 256–257.

Rothbart, M. K., & Maccoby, E. E. Parents' differential reactions to sons and daughters. *Journal of Personality and Social Psychology*, 1966, **4**, 237–243.

Rutherford, E. E., & Mussen, P. H. Generosity in nursery school boys. *Child Development*, 1968, **39**, 755–765.

Rutter, M. Parent–child separation: Psychological effects on the children. *Journal of Child Psychology and Psychiatry*, 1971, **12**, 233–260.

Rutter, M. Why are London children so disturbed? *Proceedings of the Royal Society of Medicine*, 1973, **66**, 1221–1225.

Rutter, M. Epidemiological strategies and psychiatric concepts in research on the vulnerable child. In E. J. Anthony & C. Koupernik (Eds.), *The child in his family: Children at psychiatric risk,* Vol. 3. New York: Wiley, 1974.

Santrock, J. W. Paternal absence, sex typing, and identification. *Developmental Psychology,* 1970, **2,** 264–272 (a).

Santrock, J. W. Influence of onset and type of paternal absence on the first four Eriksonian developmental crises. *Developmental Psychology,* 1970, **3,** 273–274 (b).

Santrock, J. W. Relation of type and onset of father–absence to cognitive development. *Child Development,* 1972, **43,** 455–469.

Santrock, J. W., & Wohlford, P. Effects of father-absence: Influence of the reason for and the onset of the absence. Paper presented to the American Psychological Association, August 1970.

Scarpitti, F. R., Murray, E., Dinitz, S., & Reckless, W. C. The "good" boy in a high delinquency area: Four years later. *American Sociological Review,* 1960, **25,** 555–558.

Schaefer, E. S. Children's reports of parental behavior: An inventory. *Child Development,* 1965, **36,** 413–424.

Schaefer, E. S. The ecology of child development: Implications for research and the professions. Paper presented to the American Psychological Association, New Orleans, August 1974.

Schaffer, H. R. *The growth of sociability.* Harmondsworth: England: Penguin, 1971.

Schaffer, H. R., & Emerson, P. E. The development of social attachments in infancy. *Monographs of the Society for Research in Child Development,* 1964, **29** (Serial No. 94).

Scheinfeld, D. R. On developing developmental families. Paper presented at Head Start Research Seminar No. 5, Washington D.C., January 1969.

Sears, P. S. Doll play aggression in normal young children: Influence of sex, age, sibling status, father's absence. *Psychological Monographs,* 1951, **65,** No. 6.

Sears, P. S. Childrearing factors related to the playing of sex-typed roles. *American Psychologist,* 1953, **8,** 431 (Abstract).

Sears, R. R. Identification as a form of behavioral development. In D. R. Harris (Ed.), *The concept of development.* Minneapolis: University of Minnesota Press, 1957.

Sears, R. R. Relation of early socialization experiences to self-concepts and gender role in middle childhood. *Child Development,* 1970, **41,** 267–289.

Sears, R. R., Maccoby, E. E., & Levin, H. *Patterns of child rearing.* Evanston, Ill.: Row Peterson, 1957.

Sears, R. R., Pintler, M. H., & Sears, P. S. The effect of father separation on preschool children's doll play aggression. *Child Development,* 1946, **17,** 219–243.

Sears, R. R., Rau, L. & Alpert, R. *Identification and child rearing.* Stanford: Stanford University Press, 1965.

Sears, R. R., Whiting, J. W. M., Nowlis, V., & Sears, P. S. Some child-rearing antecedents of aggression and dependency in young children. *Genetic Psychology Monographs*, 1953, **47**, 135–236.

Seder, J. A. The origin of differences in extent of independence in children: Developmental factors in perceptual field dependence. Unpublished bachelor's thesis, Radcliffe College, 1957. [Cited by Dyk, R. B., & Witkin, H. A. Family Experience related to the development of differentiation in children. *Child Development*, 1965, **36**, 21–55.]

Seplin, C. D. A study of the influence of the father's absence for military service. *Smith College Studies in Social Work*, 1952, **22**, 123–124.

Shaw, M. C., & White, D. L. The relationship between child–parent identification and academic underachievement. *Journal of Clinical Psychology*, 1965, **21**, 10–13.

Shedd, C. *Smart dads I know.* New York: Sheed & Ward, 1975.

Siegman, A. W. Father-absence during childhood and antisocial behavior. *Journal of Abnormal Psychology*, 1966, **71**, 71–74.

Slater, P. E. Parental role differentiation. *American Journal of Sociology*, 1961, **67**, 296–311.

Slater, P. E. Parental behavior and the personality of the child. *Journal of Genetic Psychology*, 1962, **101**, 53–68.

Sluckin, W. *Imprinting and early learning.* London: Methuen, 1965.

Solomon, D. The generality of children's achievement-related behavior. *Journal of Genetic Psychology*, 1969, **114**, 109–125.

Sopchak, A. L. Parental identification and tendencies toward disorders as measured by the MMPI. *Journal of Abnormal and Social Psychology*, 1952, **47**, 159–165.

Sopchak, A. L. Spearman correlations between MMPI scores of college students and their parents. *Journal of Consulting Psychology*, 1958, **22**, 207–209.

Soule, A. B. The pregnant couple. Paper presented to the American Psychological Association, New Orleans, August 1974.

Speece, B. A. Altruism in the elementary school. Unpublished doctoral dissertation, University of Nebraska Teachers College, 1967.

Spelke, E., Zelazo, P., Kagan, J., & Kotelchuck, M. Father interaction and separation protest. *Developmental Psychology*, 1973, **9**, 83–90.

Stein, E. V. Fathering: Fact or fable? *The Journal of Pastoral Care*, 1974, **28**, 23–25.

Stephens, W. N. Judgment by social workers on boys and mothers in fatherless families. *Journal of Genetic Psychology*, 1961, **99**, 59–64.

Stephens, W. N. *The family in cross-cultural perspective.* New York: Holt, Rinehart, & Winston, 1963.

Stern, D. N. Mother and infant at play: The dyadic interaction involving facial, vocal, and gaze behaviors. In M. Lewis & L. A. Rosenblum (Eds.), *The effect of the infant on its caregiver*. New York: Wiley, 1974.

Stern, D. N. Infant regulation of maternal play behavior and/or maternal regulation of infant play behavior. Paper presented to the Society for Research in Child Development, Denver, April 1975.

Stoke, S. M. An inquiry into the concept of identification. In W. E. Martin & C. B. Stendler (Eds.), *Readings in child development*. New York: Harcourt, Brace, & World, 1954.

Stoltz, L. M. and colleagues. *Father relations of war-born children*. Stanford: Stanford University Press, 1954.

Stone, P. J. Child care in 12 countries. Paper delivered at the World Congress of Sociology, Varna, Bulgaria, 1970.

Sullivan, H. S. *The interpersonal theory of psychiatry*. New York: Norton, 1953.

Sunley, R. Early nineteenth-century American literature on child rearing. In M. Mead & M. Wolfenstein (Eds.), *Childhood in contemporary cultures*. Chicago: University of Chicago Press, 1955.

Sutton-Smith, B., & Rosenberg, B. G. Age changes in the effects of ordinal position on sex-role identification. *Journal of Genetic Psychology*, 1965, **107**, 61–73.

Sutton-Smith, B., & Rosenberg, B. G. *The sibling*. New York: Holt, Rinehart, & Winston, 1970.

Sutton-Smith, B., Rosenberg, B. G., & Landy, F. Father-absence effects in families of different sibling compositions. *Child Development*, 1968, **38**, 1213–1221.

Tallman, I. Spousal role differentiation and the socialization of severely retarded children. *Journal of Marriage and the Family*, 1965, **27**, 37–42.

Tasch, R. J. The role of the father in the family. *Journal of Experimental Education*, 1952, **20**, 319–361.

Tasch, R. J. Interpersonal perceptions of fathers and mothers. *Journal of Genetic Psychology*, 1955, **87**, 59–65.

Thrasher, F. M. *The gang*. Chicago: University of Chicago Press, 1927.

Tiller, P. O. Father absence and personality development of children in sailor families. Part II. In N. Anderson (Ed)., *Studies of the Family*, Vol. 2. Gottingen: Vandenhoeck & Ruprecht, 1957.

Tiller, P. O. Father-absence and personality development of children in sailor families. *Nordisk Psyckologi's Monograph Series*, 1958, **9**, 1–48.

Tiller, P. O. *Father separation and adolescence*. Oslo: Institute for Social Research, 1961.

Tuck, S. A model for working with black fathers. *Institute for Juvenile Research: Research Report*, 1969, **6** (Whole No. 11).

Van der Veen, F. The parent's concept of the family unit and child adjustment. *Journal of Counseling Psychology*, 1965, **12**, 196–200.

Von Der Heydt, V. The role of the father in early mental development. *British Journal of Medical Psychology*, 1964, **37**, 123–131.

Warren, W. Conduct disorders in children. *British Journal of Delinquency*, 1957, **1**, 164.

Weinraub, M., Brooks, J., & Lewis, M. The social network: A reconsideration of the concept of attachment. *Human Development*, 1976, in press.

Weisbroth, S. P. Moral judgment, sex, and parental identification in adults. *Developmental Psychology*, 1970, **2**, 396–402.

Werts, C. E. Social class and initial career choice of college freshman. *Sociology of Education*, 1966, **39**, 74–85.

Westermarck, E. A. *The history of human marriage*. New York: MacMillan, 1921.

Westley, W. A., & Epstein, N. G. Parental interaction as related to the emotional health of children. *Social Problems*, 1960, **8**, 87–92.

Willemsen, E., Flaherty, D., Heaton, C., & Ritchey, G. Attachment behavior of one-year-olds as a function of mother vs. father, sex of child, session, and toys. *Genetic Psychology Monographs*, 1974, **90**, 305–324.

Williams, R. M. *American society* (2nd ed.). New York: Knopf, 1965.

Winch, R. F. The relation between the loss of a parent and progress in courtship. *Journal of Social Psychology*, 1949, **29**, 51–56.

Winch, R. F. Some data bearing on the oedipal hypothesis. *Journal of Abnormal and Social Psychology*, 1950, **45**, 481–489.

Winnicott, D. W. *The maturational process and the facilitating environment*. London: Hogarth, 1965.

Wohlford, P., & Liberman, D. Effect of father absence on personal time, field independence, and anxiety. Paper presented to the American Psychological Association, August 1970.

Wohlford, P., Santrock, J. W., Berger, S. E., & Liberman, D. Older brothers' influence on sex-typed, aggressive, and dependent behavior in father-absent children. *Developmental Psychology*, 1971, **4**, 124–134.

Wyer, R. S. Effect of child-rearing attitudes and behavior on children's responses to hypothetical social situations. *Journal of Personality and Social Psychology*, 1965, **2**, 480–486.

Wylie, H. L., & Delgado, R. A. Pattern of mother–son relationship involving the absence of the father. *American Journal of Orthopsychiatry*, 1959, **29**, 644–649.

Wynn, M. *Fatherless families*. London: Michael Joseph, 1964.

Yarrow, L. J. (Chmn.) Parents and infants: An interactive network. Symposium presented at the American Psychological Association Convention, New Orleans, August 1974.

Yarrow, M. R., Scott, P., DeLeeuw, L., & Heinig, C. Child rearing in families of working and non-working mothers. *Sociometry*, 1962, **25**, 122–140.

Yarrow, M. R., Waxler, C. Z., & Scott, P. M. Child effects on adult behavior. *Developmental Psychology*, 1971, **5**, 300–311.

Zelditch, M. Role differentiation in the nuclear family: A comparative study. In T. Parsons & R. F. Bales (Eds.), *Family, socialization, and interactional processes*. Glencoe, Ill.: Free Press, 1955.

Zigler, E., & Child, I. L. Socialization. In G. Lindzey & E. Aronson (Eds.), *Handbook of social psychology* (2nd ed.) Reading, Mass.: Addison-Wesley, 1969.

## CHAPTER 2

# Historical and Social Changes in the Perception of the Role of the Father

JOHN NASH

*University of Hong Kong*

The purpose of this volume is, in the editor's words, "to analyze critically our theoretical and empirical understanding of the contribution made by fathers to the socialization and social development of children" (p. 1).

In this chapter I attempt to give an overview of some of the new directions in research on this topic. This purpose is a little complicated in that many of the people who have produced this recent research are themselves contributors, and I risk, therefore, overlap with their chapters. Consequently, I refer to their work in only enough detail to illustrate these new directions. I also suggest some areas in which there are lacunae in the research.

In 1965 I published an article making what I have since come to recognize as an unwarranted assumption. In that article (Nash, 1965) I drew attention to the poverty of research data on fathers and assumed that this neglect of the father by developmental psychologists reflected a lack of interest by the culture in fathers and by fathers in their role. This latter assumption is the more suspect—because of the real and evident lack of interest in fathers by psychologists and others, we have no data on what fathers in the 1950s or 1960s, or earlier, really thought about their role.

Whatever the facts about the past, there appears to be little doubt that there has been an increase in public paternal activity (or "male care"). It can probably be fairly claimed that today there is a greater openness about male care than was evident a generation ago.

I had hoped to trace this topic back to prehistory by an evolutionary approach, but the data available to me are inadequate for any comprehensive treatment. Among vertebrates the first instance of "fathering" is in the stickleback (Tinbergen, 1953). The male fish prepares a nest in which one or more females are induced to lay eggs, which the male then fertilizes. He protects and oxygenates the eggs and guards the young after hatching. The females take no further part in the productive process after laying the eggs.

In many avian species nest building is a joint activity, usually in a territory "won" and defended by the male. Both incubation and feeding of the fledgelings are commonly shared activities.

Among mammals the male generally takes little part in the care of offspring. I have personally witnessed male mice engaged in nest building *before* parturition of the mate. Perhaps they were imitating the female, though the activity was not invariably simultaneous, but I can find no reference to this in the literature.

In primates the first reference to such behaviors is in the prosimian species *tupaia* (tree shrew). In this species the male builds the nest before the birth, a behavior unique among mammals (Martin, 1966). The female is a rather neglectful mother, suckling the young only at long intervals (Rosen, 1974). Indeed Rosen uses this behavior of the female, atypical of primates, to reinforce the argument that tree shrews are not primates.

Research at the University of California, Davis, by Mitchell and his coworkers (1974) demonstrated that adult male rhesus monkeys caged with an infant show male care (a term Mitchell prefers to paternal behavior), grooming and cuddling the infant. This type of behavior has not been observed in rhesus monkeys in feral conditions. Observations by Harlow showed that isolation-reared females are markedly abnormal in infant care, commonly battering infants. Mitchell's experiments showed that, though isolate males differed from socially reared ones in infant handling, they did not ill-treat the infants. They did show markedly higher rates of cuddling than the normally reared males.

If one takes a broader view of the primates and reviews a wider range of species, it does appear that male care is in fact a fairly common phenomenon, at least in the monkeys (Mitchell, 1975). This distinguishes primates from other mammals, though why the great apes are apparently deficient in this regard is an interesting question.

The chimpanzee male is a poor father, generally absenting himself from the "family" (Van Lawick-Goodall, 1971). The male orangutan is also a reluctant father (Rosen, 1974). The gorilla is somewhat more paternal, indulging in a little play with the young (Fossey, 1970).

On the whole, fatherhood in the social sense is a peculiarly human characteristic, though instances of male–infant interaction are to be found at various phylogenetic levels (see Chapter 11). Just how social fatherhood evolved in man is unknown, though the family as a social institution apparently has a very long history. Frazer's (1915) notion in *The Golden Bough* of promiscuous groups of human beings mating indiscriminately and bringing up children communally has little support either from comparative or anthropological data.

My mandate, as implied by the title of this chapter, is to speculate about changes in the perception of the father's role, and this places me in the role of historian, who must often speculate about why events happen. Historians of social changes, rarely having available the kinds of data that psychologists as scientists consider adequate, have to rely instead on direct evidence, such as eyewitness anecdotes of incidents that illustrate social attitudes and portrayals of life by writers of diaries, novels, or poems. The soundness and relevance of such data can only be subjectively evaluated.

This task may become easier with the emergence of a specialized branch of psychology (or of history) having its own journals (see references—Psychohistory).

Since observations of social phenomena by trained observers are a very recent development confined almost entirely to the lifetime of most of the readers of this volume, I have very little information about the past against which to measure change. Even today, attitudes toward fathers are often inferred rather than documented by direct study.

Thus I am going to suggest something not susceptible to proof, as scientists understand proof. It is that Western family structures have their origins in the Roman concept of the *paterfamilias* as absolute head of the family. Roman law did not form the basis of all later European legal systems (British law, for example, is case law and is not in any strong sense derived from the Romans). The basic concept of *paterfamilias* passed, however, into custom and usage, if not into law, in Britain and Europe, and Britain supplied the American colonists not only with its language but also with much of its culture.

Remnants of this concept were preserved in Germany, Denmark, and other parts of Europe in the custom of "kneeing" (Onians, 1954), in which the father accepted the newborn child as his and a member of the family by placing it on his knees.

## THE FATHER IN HISTORICAL TIMES

The nature of childrearing in historical times is not easy to deduce. It was not until the 18th century that Rousseau challenged the idea of the child as a miniature adult; until that time few people thought it necessary to distinguish children as a special group of people. Even the extensive history of children by Aries (1962/1973) gave few data on patterns of fathering (and little about mothering). It is more a social history of children as part of the economic system than a history of childrearing practices. Further data are provided in the series of papers edited by de Mause (1975).

Such data as we have relate mainly to families of position and wealth. For instance, there are the celebrated letters of the 4th Earl of Chesterfield, written from 1737 on to his natural son Philip, as a guide to affairs of the world (i.e., the world of diplomacy and aristocracy). His son was then a young man, and Chesterton has described the letters, later bound into a large volume, as the best book on education ever written. Unfortunately, it throws little light on the early father–child relationship, though we do learn from it of an 18th century aristocratic father's concern for his boy, but how general such concern was at that time is not revealed.

On more humble families of the time we have even fewer data, though poverty was doubtless a modifying influence on family life for most people of the time. At that period Britain and most of Europe were agrarian, having a domestic economy with the sex division of labor that typifies primitive societies.

We do have this fragment from the poor men's poet (Robert Burns' "The Cotter's Saturday Night," 1785, slightly translated):

> The' expectant wee things, toddlin' stagger through
> To meet their dad, wi' [flickering] noise an' glee. . . .
> The lisping infant prattling on his knee,
> Does a' his weary [anxiety] and care beguile.
> And makes him quite forget his labour and his toil.

Whether this is true to life or poetic licence is difficult to know, but Burns did tend to realism. The cotter was, of course, an agrarian worker.

A notable feature of the numerous pictures of schoolrooms from medieval times on is the birch rod—apparently an essential item of pedagogical equipment. Whether this instrument was a feature of childrearing in the family is not recorded, though one might suspect that it was.

Of the 19th century, Samuel Butler (*The Way of All Flesh*, published posthumously in 1903, though written in the 19th century and set in that period, tells us:

It must be remembered that at the beginning of the nineteenth century the relations between parents and children were still far from satisfactory. The violent type of father, as described by Fielding, Richardson, Smollett and Sheridan, is now hardly . . . likely to find a place in literature . . . , but the type was much too persistent not to have been drawn from nature closely. The parents in Miss Austen's novels are less like savage wild beasts than those of her predecessors, but she evidently looks upon them with suspicion, and an uneasy feeling that *Le père de famille est capable de tout* makes itself sufficiently apparent throughout the greater part of her writings. In the Elizabethan time the relations between parents and children seem on the whole to have been more kindly. The fathers and the sons are for the most part friends in Shakespeare, nor does the evil appear to have reached its full abomination till a long course of Puritanism had familiarised men's minds with Jewish ideals as those which we should endeavour to reproduce in our everyday life. What precedents did not Abraham, Jephthah and Jonadab the son of Recham offer? How easy was it to quote and follow them in an age when few reasonable men or women doubted that every syllable of the Old Testament was taken down verbatim from the mouth of God. Moreover, Puritanism restricted natural pleasures; it substituted the Jeremiad for the Paean, and it forgot that the poor abuses of all times want countenance (1903, pp. 31–32).

The hero of the book is the Rev. Pontifex, himself reared by his father in the old tradition, who applies these techniques to his son, which Butler rebukes as inconsistent with his calling.

## WESTERN RELIGION AND THE FATHER

It is worthwhile to examine Butler's contention that the Judeo-Christian tradition has influenced our conceptions of fathers.

Christianity is distinguished by the concept of "God the Father" (Kee, 1971), in contrast to one other major religion, Buddhism, which has little reference to God. Buddhists do not worship the Buddha but endeavor to follow his teachings, which emphasize self-knowledge and self-discipline. Unlike Jesus or Mohammed, Gautama (the Buddha) made no claim to represent God to man. He made no promise of a Heaven elsewhere, nor, significantly, did he warn of a Hell, though a concept of Hell entered later Buddhist teaching. Heaven is here on earth in nirvana, the state of self-knowledge and self-discipline. Hell is failure to attain this state.

The Old Testament God described himself (Deuteronomy 5): "I the Lord thy God am a jealous God, visiting the iniquities of the fathers upon the children . . . ," though he did promise mercy to those who paid due homage.

Although Jesus, like Gautama, emphasized love in his teachings, the vengeful God of Wrath occupied the attention of the Puritan preachers Butler mentions, who backed up their denunciations of the iniquitous with threats of hellfire.

These fire brand preachers had, in fact, thoroughly misunderstood the essence of Jesus' teaching, which was in keeping with the more liberal

Judaism of his time that was replacing the old God of terrible vengeance with a more fatherly concept (E. Kvan, 1975). The hellfire Puritan preachers were so much in sympathy with the sterner aspects of the old Jewish God that they missed entirely the love of God represented to men by Jesus. Fond as they were of Paul in his more condemnatory moods (especially where sins of the flesh were concerned), they missed completely his emphatic words on love in Corinthians 13, and too many of their captive audiences lacked the critical capacity to recognize the inconsistency. Some special groups, like the Quakers, saw things differently.

In this context, it is not difficult to believe that the example of this irascible, punitive Father God, thundered every Sunday to an overawed congregation, was mirrored in the conduct of temporal fathers, especially in an age when, as Butler stated, the majority of people accepted the doctrines of these preachers. The wrathful Father God and the powerful *paterfamilias* were compatible concepts reinforcing one another and may well provide a historical background to concepts of the father's role in our culture.

A testable hypothesis does converge from this discussion. Although Buddhism is widely practiced throughout the East, the country that could fairly be said to be most strongly Buddhist is Thailand, where by tradition men are supposed to spend at least some period of their lives as monks, and in fact 80% of young men (including the heir to the throne) take the saffron robes for a period. I could not name the most typically Christian country, but a comparative study of perceptions of the role of the father in Thailand and Christendom might be very revealing. The casual observations I have been able to make suggest that the Thai role is indeed in contrast to the Christian one.

An attempt to analyse religions in terms of patrism and matrism has been made by Rattray Taylor (1965). Patrist religions are those with a father God and are the roots of patriarchal organizations in societies practicing them. The converse is not entirely true of matrist religions. Rattray Taylor is mainly concerned with the influence of religion and culture on attitudes to sex, but his book contains much of interest to the present discussion and tends to support Butler's contentions, the basic religion of our society being patrist (though with matrist periods that appear to account for the confusion of sexual attitudes in our society).

Unfortunately Rattray Taylor bases his analysis on psychoanalytic theory and, in my opinion, shows the inadequacy of this framework. This may not be a serious failure, for historical trends are not susceptible to the kinds of hypothesis testing that a more scientific theory might generate. Despite this weakness, his scholarly review does bring together a great deal of interesting material. It is probably the only kind of data ever likely to be available to us.

## NOVELS AS SOURCES OF DATA

Of the novelists Butler mentions, Richardson's life spanned the 17th and 18th centuries, though most of his writing was done in the latter. Fielding, Smollett, Austen, and Sheridan all lived in the 18th century and presumably represent it.

Edmund Gosse's *Father and Son* (1907/1965) is often considered a portrayal of 19th century life. Though it gives insights into certain facets of life in that century, it is more an account of an obsessive-compulsive father's relation with his child than a description of typical father–son relations in the 19th century.

As Mazlish (1975) has pointed out, the 19th century autobiography of John Stuart Mill, which devotes considerable space to his father James Mill, is extraordinary in making no reference whatsoever to his mother and possibly reflects the heavy patrism of the period.

*Dombey and Son* (1847), by Dickens, presents a dismal picture of a cold, proud, and ambitious father using his son to fulfill his own needs (at the same time neglecting his daughter Florence) and again should be viewed more as a case history than as typical of the 19th century.

Dickens' own childhood was a parable on the effect of social forces on family life, and this is probably the major lesson a developmental psychologist can learn from it. As is well known, *David Copperfield* is an autobiographical novel that illustrates the impact of social forces on children. It tells us more about mother–child relationships than about fathers, and in describing David's early relations with his widowed mother, Dickens anticipates Freud. In this novel we encounter Mr. Wickfield's morbid (but apparently harmless) relationship with his daughter Agnes.

Obviously, sorting out Dickens' view on father–child relationships would involve a long, painstaking analysis, with no statistics adequate to handle the data. How typical he was of his time is controversial, but in the absence of developmental psychologists, novelists are almost our only source of data.

A happier picture of 19th century fathers is presented by Rolt (1957) in his biography of the engineers Brunel, father and son. This was, indeed, a 19th century family flowing with warmth.

As a kind of antifather theme from North America we have Frances Burnett's highly sentimental *Little Lord Fauntleroy* (1886), which as the best-seller of its time, probably reflected public sentiment and perhaps reinforced it. The theme is well summed up in the widowed mother's words on hearing her son has inherited a peerage in England and is to be separated from her:

"Oh," she said, "will he have to be taken away from me? We love each other so much! He is such a happiness to me! He is all I have. I have tried to be a good mother to him." And her sweet young voice trembled, and the tears rushed to her eyes. "You do not know what he has been to me!" she said.

It appears from the popularity of the book (at least among parents) that this was regarded as an ideal relationship, despite its pre-Freudian oedipal overtones. Fauntleroy, a model child, reciprocated these sentiments. He must have been truly hated by children required to emulate this nauseous model.

Today's children have few child models in literature or in cinema. About the only one that comes readily to mind is implicit in Robin's relation to Superman, which had slight overtones of pederasty. There have been a few children's television series such as "The Partridge Family" (in which Mr. Partridge was a nonentity if he existed at all) and "The Brady Bunch" (which did indeed have a father). Modern children's literature (and its visual counterparts) appears rather lacking in either father or mother figures.

## CHILDREN IN ART

Some rather novel data are provided by Finger (1975), who studied paintings of children made by 34 artists from the Middle Ages to the present time. Finger's goal was to determine if infants were held more commonly on the left or the right side, since, according to the Salk hypothesis, there should be a preference for the left, which enables the child better to hear the soothing heartbeat. Of the 649 pictures, 55% showed the child being held to the left. Too few paintings of males holding infants were found for statistical analysis, but no preference was detectable. A point neglected here is that a right-handed mother more frequently holds a child in circumstances where she needs her right hand free for other activities, whereas a father in our culture is likely to hold a child only when having nothing else to do.

It would appear that, in the perception of Western artists (mostly European), men do not hold babies. A large proportion of the earlier pictures depicted the Madonna and Child. The neglect of Joseph in the religious thought of the Church is perhaps of significance to the present topic.

# THE INDUSTRIAL REVOLUTION AND FAMILY LIFE

With the coming of the Industrial Revolution the Western family gradually changed from the cooperative economy of the extended family that characterized most households in agricultural or pastoral societies to the nuclear family with the father as supporter and breadwinner and the mother as childrearer.

After the first, disruptive impact of the Revolution on family life, new concepts of the family began to emerge.

## Child Labor Laws and Compulsory Education

Legislation affecting the physical disposition of children has also had an impact on childrearing. Before the Industrial Revolution, children (at least in working-class families) typically participated in the economic activities of their parents and, hence, knew what their parents did all day. If the father was a tradesman, the children (and sons in particular) assisted in his trade. In the early years of the Industrial Revolution children worked in factories, though not necessarily alongside their parents.

The net result of the Revolution was a disruption of family life for most of the population. Both parents and children worked such long hours that exhausted sleep and hasty meals must have been among the only activities shared in the home.

As various labor laws removed children from the factories and shortened working hours for women, the new family pattern of the absent, working father became established. But the advent of compulsory education again removed children from the family for much of the day (and re-created the working mother).

Most children had (and have) little or no idea how the father spent (and spends) his day at that mysterious activity called "work." Though not yet a widespread phenomenon or an accepted one, there are some indications of children's gaining access to places of employment. Bronfenbrenner (1974) mentions a newspaper that, as an experiment, admitted groups of schoolchildren, who actually took part in various stages of production, but such experiments are infrequent. My own father was a printer, and I frequently visited the works (his employers apparently raising no objection), and so the smells and clatter of the pressroom were quite familiar to me. My school in England did organize visits to various local industries, though the primary object was to teach how things were made rather than to give insight into the adult working world, though this was an incidental result.

The establishment of regular visits by children to parental places of work as a recognized custom could greatly improve parent–child under-standing. Bronfenbrenner sees the absence of knowledge or experience by children of their fathers' work role as a major source of alienation between the generations.

### The Protestant Ethic and Family Structure

In North America the early colonists faced hardships in establishing them-selves in the new land, and from this developed the so-called "protestant ethic" of diligent work,[1] a corollary of which was that the man of the house worked hard to support the family, and his role as supporter excused him from direct concern with domestic matters. Indeed he was almost ex-pected to absent himself from the family to perform this duty. In rural communities interaction with sons began only when they were old enough to join the father in his labors. In most instances, fathers saw little of their daughters, who spent their time with the mother.

In urban groups, as the Industrial Revolution reached North America, the same ethic kept the father in the factory or office for long hours, and no domestic duties were expected of him. The same ethic also appeared in Europe.

Today there are important social changes, notably a shorter working day and week, that remove this reason for being an absentee father. More-over, greater job security has relieved men of the fear of unemployment's causing inability to meet their commitments as breadwinners. Freed from this burden, husbands have become more relaxed and less driven by the Protestant ethic, becoming able and willing to take a more domestic role (Yankelovich, 1974). Further pressure for a sharing of domestic duties, including child care, has resulted from the accelerated entry of women into the labor force.

## SOME OBSERVATIONS ON THE MODERN FATHER

Though I can find little concrete evidence to support my conclusion, I believe there has been a widespread reappraisal of the male role in childrearing. Recently, Schaffer and Emerson (1964) have shown that

[1] The quotation marks are used to indicate that this is a poor term if it implies that only Protestants work hard. It had some validity in the early pioneer days of the American colonies, when British Protestants heavily outnumbered other religious and ethnic groups. Work is not a specifically religious virtue or the prerogative of any one ethnic group.

"monotropy" (attachment to one person) is not as predictable as Bowlby (1958) had suggested. Children attach to both parents, and these researchers found that, in about one-third of the infants, the primary attachment was to the father.

Further, in the reappraisal of Bowlby's thesis on maternal deprivation, Rutter (1972) points to the obvious: "Children have fathers too" (p. 125). Bowlby had not denied this, but he had relegated the father's role to that of breadwinner and emotional supporter of the mother.

In the view of Bronfenbrenner (1961) fathers are taking a more nurturant role in childrearing and are becoming more child centered. A number of writers characterize North American child-rearing practices as child centered, which suggests that fathers are becoming acculturated in this regard.

### The Father and Gender Identity in Boys

A fairly large volume of literature has concerned itself with the father's role in the sex-role development of the boy.

Much of this literature is reviewed by Biller in Chapter 3, and so the purpose of this chapter is not to discuss such studies in any detail but to consider them insofar as they throw light on change of perspective. That the same names (such as Biller and Sutton-Smith) reappear gives the impression that a fairly limited number of psychologists are interested in this question. Whether this indicates that psychologists in general are satisfied that the father's role in male gender identity is fully established is not clear.

My 1965 article dealt mainly with the matricentric nature of psychologists' accounts of the childrearing process. I noted that many workers equated parent with mothers in discussing family influences on childrearing, that numerous studies purporting to study family influences in fact studied only mothers, and that, if they collected any data on fathers, it was commonly secondhand through the mother. A recent exception is a report by Solomon et al. (1969), who, in a study of achievement-related behaviors of Negro parents, did directly study fathers (in fact their design required the simultaneous presence of both parents and the child).

### The Father and Femininity

One historical trend that can be detected in the psychological literature is the increased interest of nonpsychoanalytic theorists in the father's place in the sex-role development of girls. This is not, of course, an idea peculiar to the present; it is implicit in Freud's theorizing. Although most of

Freud's publications are of the 20th century, it would be fair to say that his thinking is representative of the late 19th century. In particular, the oedipus complex, central to his theorizing on the role of the father, dates from about 1897 (Jones, 1953).

In a paper delivered in 1967 I outlined the father's role in the development of sex differences, with particular reference to the development of femininity in daughters. This theme was later taken up by Biller (1971).

Kundsin (1974), who reviewed the biographies of successful professional women, shows how their fathers influenced the advancement of their self-image and ability to achieve.

Studies of the effects of father absence have been said to show an element of sexism in that more attention has been given to effects on boys than on girls (Herzog and Sudia, 1973). Dickens, in *Dombey and Son*, recognizes a daughter's need for a father's love. We read this of Florence (who was also motherless) watching other children at play:

Ah! how to gain it! [her father's love] How to know the charm in its beginning! There were daughters here, who rose up in the morning, and lay down to rest at night, possessed of fathers' hearts already. They had no repulse to overcome, no coldness to dread, no frown to smooth away. As the morning advanced, and the windows opened one by one, and the dew began to move upon the flowers and grass, and youthful feet began to move upon the lawn, Florence, glancing round at the bright faces, thought what was there she could learn from these children? It was too late to learn from them; each could approach her father fearlessly, and put up her lips to meet the ready kiss, and wind her arms about the neck that bent down to caress her. She could not begin by being so bold. Oh! could it be that there was less and less hope as she studied more and more!

A few pages later, Dickens emphasizes Florence's position by portraying a poor workingman's affection for his ugly, misshapen daughter (also apparently motherless).

### The Father and Cognitive Development

Another line of research has opened up recently that provides a sign of renewed scientific interest in fathers. Cognitive development has long been of interest to psychologists, but now fathers are being considered as factors in the development of intellectual functioning in preschool children (Radin and Epstein, 1975). Although parents have been considered in a number of previous studies (parent usually meaning mother), this emphasis on the father is a fresh approach. Since Norma Radin will be contributing her own chapter, I need do no more here than to note this sign of the times.

**The Father in the Clinic**

In recent years a number of studies have concerned themselves with the father as either patient or agent in the psychiatric clinic. This is a new phenomenon; an extensive search of the literature I made in 1965 disclosed only a few substantive articles on the topic.

Lacoursiere (1972a) points out that, though an extensive literature on mental illness is associated with motherhood, exploration of the mental health of fathers is only now developing. In a bibliography of 49 items, only 14 predate the past decade, and most of the earlier references treat the topic only superficially.

Lacoursiere concludes, on the basis of his own experience at the Menninger Clinic and the recent literature, that reactions to fatherhood are to be considered seriously by mental health workers. He also cites evidence that psychiatric disturbance in the father can be a precipitating factor in postpartum psychosis in the mother, and he further suggests that unrecognized mental disturbance in the father could be a factor in the "battered-baby syndrome."

Adverse effects of pregnancy on the mental health of the mother is a widely recognized indication for abortion, and Lacoursiere (1972b) suggests that therapeutic abortion might also be considered when the pregnancy induces mental illness in the father.

The role of the father in the etiology of schizophrenic illness is discussed in a psychoanalytic framework by Erichsen (1973), though psychoanalytic studies of the father are no novelty. Perhaps it is a relief from the "schizophrenogenic mother" to have this study of the schizophrenogenic father. Like many analysts, Erichsen concentrates on the "bad" father.

The involvement of the father in child guidance clinics is discussed by Strean (1962), though he concentrates largely on fathers who themselves need treatment. Adler's hypothesis that "uncertainty of one's sexual role, and of one's masculinity ranks high among the causes of neurosis and psychosis" has been examined by Biller (1973), who confirms it in general terms, though certain details of the causal links need to be explored.

**Father–Infant Relations**

A recent innovation in child study is the investigation of father–infant interactions. Though establishing precedence may not be important, except in a historical sense (and this chapter is historical and hence chronological), the earliest such study appears to be that of Pedersen and Robson (1969).

These authors studied the families of 45 infants (21 male, 24 female), all firstborn. The families were all described as middle-class, the mean educational level of the fathers being 3 years of college. The authors apologetically admit that most of the data on the fathers were collected from the mothers but justify this on the grounds that theirs was a pilot study, noting that further work will require direct observations of the fathers.

They used a total of eight measures of paternal behavior, and although these are by no means the only possible ones, they do provide a guideline for future research. In the context of this chapter, variable 8, "overall availability," is of particular interest. The group studied had a mean of 26 hours per week (range 5–47 hours) in the home during the infants' usual waking hours. As the authors point out, this provides an appreciable opportunity for interaction. The study also points to some differences in the quality of interactions between different fathers and children, another point for further investigation. This is, of course, what we must expect. Temperamental differences in the members of the dyads would prevent uniformity of interaction.

This sample suggests that there is a cultural shift, at least among well-educated middle-class men, toward greater participation in baby care (though in the absence of any comparable data on previous generations, this shift can only be inferred). Unfortunately, the paper does not provide enough details of the mode of selection of the families studied to permit judgment of what sampling biases may have been involved. (The selection was made prenatally from participants in what is described as a larger longitudinal study.)

The next study appears to be that of Rebelsky and Hanks (1971), who reported the extent of verbal interactions of fathers with children in early infancy. Like the previous one, this study arose from a larger study of infant vocalization. Ten normal babies were monitored for a 24-hour period at 2-week intervals from 2 weeks to 3 months.

Fathers spent relatively (sic) little time daily in vocal interaction with infants (mean number of interactions 2.7, mean time 37.7 seconds), though this finding is a little ambiguous, because mothers' interactions were not reported. Other studies have, however, shown mothers to increase vocalizations during this period, whereas in this study fathers showed a decrease in vocalization.

As with many other studies (including the Pedersen and Robson one) fathers showed differential interactions between male and female children, vocalizing less with the latter. It would be interesting to know the developmental consequences of this. Although, on the average, girls are more verbal than boys, as with most sex differences, the overlap is considerable. Are the more verbal boys, who exceed the female norm, the outcome of highly vocal early paternal interactions, or is this trait independent of early parental (father and mother) vocal interactions? It appears from other studies (e.g., Fagot, 1974) that, in the later preschool period, both parents interact verbally more with girls than with boys, and so there is apparently a developmental point at which fathers reverse this tendency to reduce vocal interaction with girls—presumably the point at which the girls start speech may be critical.

Lamb's investigations have shown that 8-month-old infants at home responded more positively to contact with fathers than with mothers, the difference appearing to be related to differences in the modes of handling of the two parents. Mothers handled mainly to perform routine care functions, whereas fathers more frequently handled in play (Lamb, 1975b and Chapter 9).

A noteworthy innovation in methodology is provided by Parke and O'Leary (1975), who studied father–mother–infant interactions. Studying the triad is clearly preferable to studying either of the dyads. As these authors point out, the presence of the other parent may facilitate the activity of the partner, and their results tend to support this assumption, though in some respects the mothers were inhibitory, in the sense that in her absence the fathers were more likely to touch and rock the infant. Similarly, the mothers interacted less in the presence of the fathers.

In other contexts I have objected to the implication in many studies that "parent" and "mother" are synonymous (Nash, 1965). Equally, we should recognize that the term *parent* implies both mother and father, who should be regarded as a mutually interactive unit.

## The Father in the Delivery Room

Through the *couvade*, or simulated pregnancy and ritual parturition by the father, is a well-known phenomenon among primitive peoples, it has until recently had no parallel in our own society. Today there are signs of a move toward institutionalized participation of the father in childbirth. But, because the literature is sparse, I must confine my remarks here largely to anecdote and personal experience.

In 1953 I was present at the birth of my firstborn. This was in Edinburgh and was, so far as I could discover, the first known instance of the father's being present at a birth in the modern history of that city. (In earlier times, of course, a father might deliver his wife of his own child, though more usually a midwife performed this function.) In Britain at the time in question, the National Health Service encouraged home confinements as a means of economizing on hospital facilities, the physician being aided by a trained midwife, who brought portable equipment to the home.

This circumstance facilitated my presence, though it was a new experience for the somewhat dubious physician. In 1956, at Saint John, New Brunswick, Canada, I was not permitted to attend the birth of my second child (largely, I gather, at the insistence of the hospital's nursing staff, though the physician was willing). In Fredericton, New Brunswick, a colleague (whose wife was herself a physician) was likewise refused permission. In 1958 I attended the birth of my third child in University Hospital, Saskatoon. This was regarded as somewhat innovative (the fact that I was chief psychologist at the hospital no doubt aided).

I also know of fathers in attendance at confinements in places as far-flung as Sydney, Australia, and Hong Kong, and it appears to be becoming a more widely accepted procedure, though I have been unable to uncover any statistics on the topic. Parke and O'Leary (1975) mention that, of the 19 fathers in their study (at University Hospital, Madison, Wisconsin), 18 had been present at the birth.

Medical objections appear to have been based on the assumption that fathers would become upset at some inconvenient point, though the extent to which this is justified is unsubstantiated. Sterility is another, probably false issue, arising perhaps from the prevalence of puerperal fever in the past, usually carried by physician or midwife from previous confinements.

The customary absence of modern fathers from childbirth is probably due mainly to the curious myth that parturition is a medical emergency requiring the facilities of an operating room. It occasionally is, of course, but only in a minority of cases, and these are usually predictable.

Many primitive societies also have a mythology that excludes the father (or other males) from presence at a birth, but there are welcome signs that the mystique surrounding parturition created by the medical profession is breaking down. Childbirth is becoming a shared experience in which the parents are the principal participants, with medical people as attendants.

A number of relevant questions arise, for which answers have yet to be given. Fathers who choose to be present at birth are probably a highly selected group, and one might suppose that they are particularly accepting of the father role. Subsequent father–child interactions are likely to be favorably biased by this, and so one cannot claim that presence at birth facilitates this relationship. I would modestly hesitate to suggest that birth-present fathers are necessarily "good" fathers, though I would maintain that presence suggests some commitment to the role of father.

A similar problem exists in assessing the effects on the marriage. Couples who agree to share this experience are doubtless a selected group, already close rather than rendered thus by the event.

On the whole I can see no logical reason for arguing that paternal presence at delivery is a "good" thing in improving paternal relationships, because at this point in history, expectant fathers who opt for it are already biased as accepting fathers. Parke and O'Leary (1975) think otherwise, arguing that presence at the delivery is likely to increase fathers' involvement with the infant, though I would see their sample as a biased one of already committed fathers. If, however, the father's presence becomes widespread and incorporated into social custom, it may in the future become an important experience to more reluctant fathers and strengthen the concept of paternity.

From discussions with expectant mothers I know that not all women express a desire for their husband's presence at the birth, but I have insufficient evidence to give an opinion on what this really indicates about the marriage or the mother's attitude to the paternal role. This is another issue that merits further inquiry.

Though we lack data concerning the father's presence at the actual delivery, there are some data on the father's reactions to neonates. Greenberg and Morris (1974) found that fathers report the birth of a child to be a highly significant event, though it seems hardly necessary to prove that by solemn data. But it is worth commenting that hospital practice allows the father only a carefully sterilized glance at his child through a plate glass window—a modern barbarism that should be eradicated, in my opinion. Hospitals, as traditionally conceived by the medical profession, are not suitable entrances into the family and the world.

## CHILDREARING AND WOMEN'S LIBERATION

This topic cannot be evaded, even if it may be diplomatic to do so. I am too well aware that, regardless of what a male writes on this topic, and irrespective of the care he takes in his choice of terms, there will be an outcry. I can only attempt to be honest and fair in my discussion.

Women's liberation is frequently accused of being against motherhood, on the grounds that motherhood interferes with the pursuit of a career. But a recent study of university students by Eagley and Anderson (1974) traces the attitude more to a concern about world population, since a sample of liberated women were quite willing to adopt children. On the other hand, a meeting of women students at Oxford University in March 1975 (reported in *South China Morning Post*, March 5, 1975) denounced the family as an institution to repress women. It becomes, therefore, a little difficult to decide what the facts are. It could be that United States and British liberationists differ on this or that the Eagley and Anderson evidence is more scientific and accurate. I personally agree with Gilder (1975) that women's liberation has been an antimotherhood movement.

Several writers, including Mead and Simone de Beauvoir (see Rosaldo and Lamphere, 1974) have pointed out that, in many cultures, activities in which men engage assume enhanced value. The converse is also true. The medical profession in Russia is said to have lost prestige because of (or coincident with) the heavy preponderance of women in its ranks. In Sweden, crane operation lost status when labor shortages brought in women operators (see Feedback, 1975).

If this is true, then the increased participation of men in childrearing may be expected to enhance its prestige. At least one human society regards childcare as the man's concern—the Manus of New Guinea (Mead 1930)—child care enjoys there an important position (Mead 1935). At the age of 1 year the child is transferred from the care of the mother to that of the father, who feeds and bathes it, plays with it, and sleeps with it at night. He may also take it to the men's "clubhouse," which no women may enter.

A major tenet of Gilder's argument is what he calls the "male imperative," which feminists threaten. This has two aspects: first, the mystique of the job with male companionship, and second, the role of supporter and provider.

A man's job may serve as a male sanctum, but Gilder presents no concrete data (except that of Bednarik, 1970) to show that most men in fact view their job this way. The job itself is often unrewarding and tedious, but on invasion by females, he maintains, it becomes intolerable. There are no data regarding the threat to the provider role, but given the decay of the "Protestant ethic," one might predict that this is less an imperative than in the past.

At many points in his argument Gilder appeals to the concept of the "aggressive male" innately inclined to fight to defend his masculinity. In another context I have argued against this concept (Dawson and Nash, 1976), which is also criticized by Lewis and Towers (1973).

## THE FUTURE FOR THE FAMILY

It is plain that the family in Western society, and perhaps throughout the world, is at a crucial point in its history. Despite the findings mentioned earlier, Gilder (1975) agrees with the Oxford ladies where North American feminists are concerned. Their aim is indeed, he claims, to free women from the hindrances of childrearing.

The family has been an extraordinarily viable institution. Its greatest challenge was probably the Industrial Revolution. Having survived that, it will probably survive the women's liberation movement also.

My own observation, unsupported by statistical data, is that there has been a steady reawakening of the possibilities of fatherhood as a satisfying life role that predates women's liberation. In 1956 I wrote an article in the popular Canadian magazine *McLeans* under the title "It's Time Father Got Back into the Family." The feedback I received was convincing that a considerable number of men were thinking that way too. The women's movement could, I suppose, be dated from Germaine Greer's *The Female Eunuch* (1971) or perhaps Betty Frieden's *The Feminine Mystique* (1963), though Margaret Mead and Simone de Beauvoir doubtless prepared the way.

It is difficult to chart a history of "father revival." English and Foster produced a book called *Fathers are Parents Too* (1953), and Ostrovsky later wrote a book pleading for more male influence in schools (1959), but neither of these had the popular success of Greer's or Frieden's book. The antimotherhood movement has been much more vocal, and although I cannot document this accurately, I believe that the women's movement happened to come at a time when a quieter change was occurring in men, who were discovering the satisfactions of fatherhood to be greater than those of career success. The father role was in process of reevaluation, though the social forces behind this rethinking are difficult to identify.

Men have discovered the emptiness of life at the top, something women have yet to discover, and have been finding the alternative satisfactions of life as father. The disillusionment with the role of aggressive provider that society had imposed on men was possibly a factor.

Since society does not possess either the technology or the willingness to dispense with mothers, the family as a mother–father–child triad will probably continue. Moreover, if my hypothesis about father–daughter relationships is correct, the present generation of girls brought up by warm fathers will lack the corrosive bitterness evident in the more strident liberationists, who are, I propose, the product of inadequate father–child relationships.

If my other thesis concerning the influence of religious thought on the concept of the father is correct, then the death of the "wrathful God" theology may have played a part in ameliorating present-day perceptions of the father. Disbelief in this God may be part of the general climate of opinion influencing modern thinking on fathers.

## CONCLUSION

Because of the paucity of reliable records of childrearing practices in times past, the historical factors leading up to present perceptions of the father's role in childrearing are not readily documented, and a good deal of conjecture is needed in attempting to describe them. (Indeed, even in 1976, statements about how society in general perceives fathers, or how fathers themselves perceive their role, are to a large degree conjectural, though a body of factual data is growing.) A review does show a growing interest in fathers by researchers in various disciplines.

The increased interest in fathers by psychologists, or by others to whom the label "child care experts" can be applied, has no necessary correlation with what laymen fathers have been thinking or doing about their role.

It appears to me that what this "expert" inquiry has revealed is that, spontaneously, and probably quite independently of what the "experts" have said on the topic, an increasing number of men have discovered the father role. In an earlier section I made some suggestions about the possible historical factors in this development.

Alternatively, there may have existed among men in general a greater consciousness of the paternal role than "experts"—their perceptions modified by theoretical blinkers, especially those created by psychoanalytic theories—have been aware of. After all, it is difficult to believe that men have for generations been accepting the responsibilities and tribulations of fatherhood without some expectation of reward in that role.

The father as a "forgotten contributor to child development" is discussed by Lamb (1975a), and at the conclusion of that paper he warns of the possible consequences of our ignorance—that social scientists are unable to offer the kinds of guidance to a society in transition that might be expected of them.

With the changes evident in the family at the present, it is necessary to have accurate data on which this guidance can be based. Research on fathers is, therefore, of considerable social importance at this point in history.

## REFERENCES

Adler, A., *Praxis und Theorie der Individualpsychologie* (4th ed.) München, Bergmann, 1930.

Aries, P. [*Centuries of childhood.*] Harmondsworth, England: Penguin, 1973, (Originally published, 1962.)

Bednarik, P. *The male in crisis.* New York: Knopf, 1970.

Biller, H. B. *Father, child, and sex role.* Lexington, Mass.: Heath, 1971.

Biller, H. B. Sex-role uncertainty and psychopathology. *Journal of Individual Psychology*, 1973, **29**, 24–25.

Bowlby, J. The nature of the child's tie to his mother. *International Journal of Psychoanalysis*, 1958, **39**, 350–373.

Bronfenbrenner, U. The changing American child—a speculative analysis. *Merrill-Palmer Quarterly*, 1961, **7**, 73–84.

Bronfenbrenner, U. The origins of alienation. *Scientific American*, 1974, **231**, 53–61.

Butler, S. *The way of all flesh*. London: Collins, 1903.

Chesterfield, 4th Earl of. Manuscript in British Museum Library, dated 1737.

Dawson, J. L. M., & Nash, J. *Human ecology*. In preparation, 1976.

de Mause, L. *History of childhood*. New York: Harper and Row, 1975.

Dickens, C. Dombey and son (1847).

Dickens, C. David Copperfield (1849).

Eagley A. H. & Anderson, P. Sex role and attitudinal correlates of desired family size. *Journal of Applied Social Psychology*, 1974, **4**, 151–164.

English, O. S., & Foster, C. J. *Fathers are parents too*. London: George Allen and Unwin, 1953.

Erichsen, F. The fathers of schizophrenics. *Psychotherapy and Medical Psychology*, 1973, **23**, 130–140.

Fagot, B. Sex differences in toddlers' behavior and parental reaction. *Developmental Psychology*, 1974, **10**, 554–558.

"Feedback": Men take fright when women move in. *New Scientist*, 1975, **65**, 228.

Finger, D. Child-holding patterns in western art. *Child Development*, 1975, **46**, 267–271.

Fossey, D. Making friends with mountain gorillas. *National Geographic*, 1970, **137**, 48–67.

Frazer, Sir J. G. *The golden bough* (3rd ed.). London: Macmillan, 1915.

Frieden, B. *The feminine mystique*. New York: Dell, 1963.

Gilder, G. F. *Sexual suicide*, New York: Bantam, 1975.

Gosse, E. [*Father and son*] (W. Irvine, Ed.). Cambridge, England: Riverside, 1965. (Originally published, 1907.)

Greenberg, M., & Morris, N. Engrossment: The newborn's impact upon the father. *American Journal of Orthopsychiatry*, 1974, **44**, 520–531.

Greer, G. *The female eunuch*. New York: McGraw-Hill, 1971.

Herzog, E., & Sudia, C. E. Children in fatherless families. In B. M. Caldwell & H. N. Ricciuti (Eds.), *Review of child development research, 3*. Chicago: University of Chicago Press, 1973.

Jones, E. [*Sigmund Freud: Life and Works*]. Harmondsworth, England: Penguin, 1964. (Originally published, 1953.)

Kee, A. *The way of transcendance*. Harmondsworth, England: Penguin, 1971.

Kundsin, R. B. *Women and success: The anatomy of achievement*. New York: Morrow, 1974.

Kvan, Rev. E. Personal communication, 1975.

Lacoursiere, R. B. Fatherhood and mental illness: A review and new material. *Psychiatric Quarterly*, 1972, **46**, 109–124 (a).

Lacoursiere, R. B. The mental health of the prospective father: A new indication for therapeutic abortion. *Bulletin of the Menninger Clinic*, 1972, **36**, 645–649 (b).

Lamb, M. Fathers: Forgotten contributors to child development. *Human Development*, 1975, **18**, 245–266 (a).

Lamb, M. Infant attachment to mothers and fathers. Paper presented to the Society for Research in Child Development, Denver, April 1975 (b).

Lewis, J., & Towers, B. *Naked ape or homo sapiens*. New York: Mentor, 1973.

Martin, R. D. Tree shrews: Unique reproductive mechanism of systematic importance. *Science*, 1966, **152**, 1402–1404.

Mazlish, B. The changing face of Oedipus: Fathers and sons in modern times. *The Columbia Forum*, 1975 (winter), pp. 18–27.

Mead, M. Social organization in Manua. *Bernice P. Bishop Museum Bulletin*, 1930, Vol. 76.

Mead, M. *Sex and temperament in three primitive societies*. London: Routledge and Kegan Paul, 1935.

Mitchell, G. Parental behavior in non-human primates. In J. Money & H. Musaph (Eds.), *Handbook of sexology*. Amsterdam: Elsevier, 1975.

Mitchell, G., Redican, W. K., & Gomber, J. Males can raise babies, too. *Psychology Today*, April 1974, pp. 64–68.

Nash, J. The father in contemporary culture and current psychological literature. *Child Development*, 1965, **36**, 261–297.

Onians, R. B. *The origins of European thought*. Cambridge, England: University Press, 1954.

Ostrovsky, E. S. *Father to the child*. New York: Putnam's, 1959.

Parke, R. D., & O'Leary, S. Father–mother–infant interaction in the newborn period: Some findings, some observations, and some unresolved issues. In K. Riegel & J. Meacham (Eds.), *The developing individual in a changing world, II. Social and environmental issues*. The Hague: Mouton, 1975.

Pedersen, F. A., & Robson, K. S. Father participation in infancy. *American Journal of Orthopsychiatry*, 1969, **39**, 466–472.

Psychohistory, Journal of (Lloyd de Mause, Ed.), 2315 Broadway, New York, N.Y. 10024.

Radin, N., & Epstein, A. Observed paternal behavior and the intellectual functioning of preschool boys and girls. Paper presented at the meeting of the Society for Research in Child Development, Denver, April 1975.

Rattray Taylor, G. *Sex in history*. London: Panther, 1965.

Rebelsky, F., & Hanks, C. Fathers' verbal interaction with infants in the first three months of life. *Child Development*, 171, **42**, 63–68.

Rolt, L. T. C. *Isambard Kingdom Brunel*. London: Longman Green, 1957.

Rosaldo, M. Z., & Lamphere, D. (Eds.). *Women, culture and society.* Stanford, Calif.: Stanford University Press, 1974.

Rosen, S. I. *Introduction to the primates.* Englewood Cliffs, N.J.: Prentice-Hall, 1974.

Rutter, M. *Maternal deprivation reassessed.* Harmondsworth, England: Penguin, 1972.

Schaffer, H. R., & Emerson, P. E. The development of social attachments in infancy. *Monographs of the Society for Research in Child Development,* 1964, **29** (Whole No. 94).

Solomon, D., Parelius, R. J., & Busse, T. V. Dimensions of achievement-related behavior among lower-class Negro parents. *Genetic Psychology Monographs,* 1969, **79,** 173-190.

Strean, H. S. A means of involving fathers in family treatment: Guidance groups for fathers. *American Journal of Orthopsychiatry,* 1962, **32,** 719-725.

Sutton-Smith, B., Rosenberg, B. G., & Landy, F. Father absence effects in families of different sibling compositions. *Child Development,* 1968, **39,** 1213-1221.

Tinbergen, N. *Social behavior in animals.* London: Methuen, 1953.

Van Lawick-Goodall, J. *In the shadow of man.* Boston: Houghton Mifflin, 1971.

Yankelovich, D. Changing attitudes towards work. *Dialogue,* 1974, **7,** 3-13.

# CHAPTER 3

# The Father and Personality Development: Paternal Deprivation and Sex-Role Development

HENRY B. BILLER

*University of Rhode Island*

This chapter emphasizes the important contribution that fathers can make to the sex-role and personality development of their children. Data are reviewed that show that nurturant, competent, and available fathers positively influence their sons' and daughters' psychological functioning, whereas various forms of paternal deprivation are often related to difficulties in children's emotional, cognitive, and interpersonal development. This chapter is based on my more extensive discussions of the impact of the father on child development (Biller, 1971a, 1974c).

The focus in this chapter is on reviewing and integrating empirical studies; the reader who wishes a more theoretical perspective on the father's role in personality development, including a discussion of the various theories of identification, should consult other sources (e.g., Biller, 1971a, 1974c; Lynn, 1974). The first section of this chapter reviews research linking the quality of the father–child relationship with the boy's sex-role development, and the second section describes data pertaining to the effects of father absence on the boy's sex-role development. The third section is an analysis of the influence of adequate and inadquate fathering on various facets of the boy's personal and social adjustment. The fourth section concentrates on the influence of the father–daughter relationship on the girl's emotional and interpersonal functioning. The final section is a brief overview of practical implications for coping with paternal deprivation.

Throughout this chapter it is emphasized that variations in paternal influence do not take place in a vacuum. Factors such as the child's constitutional characteristics and developmental status, the quality of the mother–child and father–mother relationships, the family's sociocultural background, and the availability of surrogate models are frequently discussed. Unfortunately, most investigators have not systematically considered the potential interactions of paternal influence with factors such as the quality of the mother–child relationship or the child's constitutionally based individuality, and the methodological shortcomings of previous research are often noted.

## THE FATHER AND MASCULINE DEVELOPMENT

This section discusses how various dimensions of paternal behavior may influence the boy's masculine development. Research on the effects of paternal masculinity, nurturance, limit setting, and power is reviewed, and methodological issues are considered.

### Paternal Masculinity

There are data indicating that the quality of the father–son relationship is a more important influence on the boy's masculine development than the amount of time the father spends at home (Biller, 1968a, 1971a). A crucial factor in this development is the degree to which his father exhibits masculine behavior in family interactions. Imitation of the father directly enhances the boy's masculine development only if the father displays masculine behavior in the presence of his son.

When the father consistently adopts a mother-like role, it is likely that his son will be relatively low in masculinity. Bronfenbrenner (1958), reanalyzing data originally collected by Lansky (1956), found that adolescent boys low in masculinity of interests often came from homes in which the father played a traditionally feminine role. The fathers of these boys took over activities such as cooking and household chores and generally did not participate in family decision making or limitsetting. Bronfenbrenner also described the findings of a study by Altucher (1957) in which adolescent boys with low masculine interests "were likely to come from families in which there was little role differentiation in household activities, and in which the mother, rather than the father, tended to dominate in the setting of limits for the child" (p. 120). What seemed to inhibit the boy's masculine development was not the father's participation in some traditionally feminine activities in the home per se (e.g., helping with the housework), but the father's passivity in family interactions and decision making and/or a relative parental role reversal.

I found a strong relationship between kindergarten-age boys' masculinity and the degree to which they perceived their fathers as making family decisions. On measures of sex-role orientation (masculinity–femininity of self-concept), sex-role preference (masculinity–femininity of interests and attitudes), and sex-role adoption (masculinity–femininity of social and environmental interaction), a high level of perceived decision making by the father was associated with strongly masculine behavior. Perception of the father's status in decision making was particularly highly correlated with sex-role orientation. Perceived competence of the father was most related to sex-role orientation, although it was also significantly related to preference and adoption (Biller, 1969a). Other studies have also suggested a positive association between the son's masculinity and his perception of his father's masculinity (Heilbrun, 1965b, 1974; Kagan, 1958; Rychlak & Legerski, 1967).

Even though they consistently show a relationship between father's and son's masculinity, the studies cited above share a common methodological shortcoming. Measurement of father's and son's masculinity was generally not independent, both assessments usually being deduced from the son's responses. It could be argued that such evidence is not a sufficient basis on which to conclude that father's and son's masculinity are related. For example, an alternative explanation is that masculine sons tend to see their fathers as highly masculine, regardless of their father's actual masculinity. A boy may appear similar to his father and yet have learned his masculine behavior, not from him, but from his peer group. As Bronfenbrenner (1958) pointed out, the boy's perceived similarity to his father is not necessarily a measure of his identification with his father. Father son similarity may be just a reflection of exposure to a common social environment.

In a methodologically superior study Hetherington (1965) evaluated the relative dominance of parents by placing them in an actual decision-making situation. She found that masculinity of preschool-age and preadolescent boys' projective sex-role behavior (IT scale) was positively related to paternal dominance. She discovered, moreover, a general tendency for both similarity between father and son and the extent of filial imitation of fathers to be higher in father-dominant than in mother-dominant homes (Hetherington, 1965; Hetherington & Brackbill, 1963; Hetherington & Frankie, 1967).

Using essentially the same parental interaction procedure as Hetherington, I found that father dominance in father–mother interaction was positively related to kindergarten-age boys' sex-role orientations, preferences, and adoptions (Biller, 1969a). However, father dominance in parental interaction showed weaker relationships with sex-role development than the boy's perception of father dominance did. The boy's behavior seems to be much determined by his particular perception of family interactions, and it may be that his view of the father is the most accurate measure. The boy's perception of his father can also be influenced by his mother's behavior. In father–mother interactions some mothers encouraged their husbands to make decisions, and others appeared to prevent their husbands from serving as adequate models by constantly competing with them for the decision-making role.

Other analyses of the data suggested the complex influences of family interactions on the boy's sex-role development. Several of the boys low in masculinity had fathers who were dominant in interaction with their wives and generally seemed masculine. These fathers also appeared, however, to be controlling and restrictive of their son's behavior. For instance, this type of dominant father punished his son for disagreeing with him. Masculine development is facilitated when the father is a competent masculine model and allows and encourages the boy to be dominant. Such paternal behavior is particularly important in development of sex-role adoption. In families in which the mother and father were competing for the decision-making function, boys were often very restricted. It seems that, in some families, when the mother does not allow her husband to be influential in family decisions, he is more apt to attempt to dominate his son in a restrictive and controlling manner.

It is the father's sex-role adoption in family interactions that is crucial and not the degree of masculine behavior he exhibits outside the home. Many fathers have masculine interests and are masculine in their peer and work relationships but are very ineffectual in their interactions with their wives and children. The stereotype of the masculine, hard-working father whose primary activity at home is lying on the couch, watching television, or sleeping is an all too accurate description of many fathers. If the father is not consistently involved in family functioning, it is much harder for his son to learn to be appropriately assertive, active, independent, and competent.

## Paternal Nurturance

In general, paternal nurturance refers to the father's affectionate, attentive encouragement of his child. Such behavior may or may not be manifested in the caretaking or protective activities that appear more common in descriptions of maternal nurturance. At this point the focus is on paternal nurturance and masculine development; the influence of paternal nurturance on other dimensions of development is discussed in other sections of this chapter.

In a study of elementary school-age children Bronson (1959) reported findings indicating that both the father's masculinity and the quality of the father–son relationship have to be taken into account. The father's behavior and the father–child relationship were assessed from interviews of the fathers and family history data. The masculinity of toy preferences of boys who had chronically stressful relationships with their fathers was negatively associated with the fathers' masculinity. Boys who had undemonstrative, frustrating, and critical fathers seemed to reject them as models. In contrast, where the father–son relationship was nonstressful (father warm, affectionate, and supportive), the masculinity of boys' toy preferences was positively correlated to fathers' masculinity. Masculine development is facilitated when the father is both masculine and nurturant.

There is other evidence that a warm, affectionate father–son relationship can strengthen the boy's masculine development. In a study by Pauline Sears (1953), preschool boys who assumed the father role in doll play activities (used the father doll with high frequency) tended to have warm, affectionate fathers. Mussen and Distler (1959) studied the structured doll play of kindergarten boys. Their results revealed that boys who scored high in masculinity of projective sex-role responses perceived fathers as more warm and nurturant than boys with low masculinity scores did. Using the same methodology, Mussen and Rutherford (1963) reported similar findings for first-grade boys. Studying kindergarten-age boys, I found that perceived paternal nurturance was related to a fantasy game measure of sex-role orientation (Biller, 1969a).

According to maternal interview data collected by Mussen and Distler (1960), the high masculine boys described in their earlier (1959) article had more affectionate relationships with their fathers than the low masculine boys did. Interviews with the boys' mothers also indicated a trend for the fathers of the high masculine boys to take care of their sons more often, as well as to have more responsibility for family childrearing practices. Many researchers have also found evidence suggesting that paternal nurturance is related to older boys' masculinity and/or similarity to their fathers (Bandura & Walters, 1959; Bronson, 1959; Distler, 1964; Mussen, 1961; Payne & Mussen, 1956).

## Paternal Limit Setting

Findings suggesting a relationship between paternal limit setting and masculine development have been presented by several researchers. Lefkowitz's (1962) findings revealed that third and fourth-grade boys who made at least some feminine toy choices had fathers who took less part in setting limits for them than fathers of boys who made completely masculine toy choices did. In Altucher's (1957) study, more adolescent boys who scored high in masculinity of interests than boys who scored low said their fathers set limits for them. Moulton, Burnstein, Liberty, and Altucher (1966) reported a similar association in male college students, but Distler (1964) did not. Other investigators have reported findings linking paternal discipline with various forms of aggressive behavior in boys (Eron, Walder, Toigo, & Lefkowitz, 1963; Kagan, 1958; Levin & Sears, 1956).

The implication of such data is that boys often learn to be aggressive and masculine by modeling themselves after their fathers, the disciplinary situation being particularly relevant. Others factors may be operating to produce a relationship between paternal limit setting and boys' aggressive behavior. Boys may be aggressive as a function of the frustration engendered by severe paternal punitiveness. Furthermore global ratings of aggression and other complex personality traits should be viewed with some degree of caution. For example, not all forms of aggression are culturally accepted as appropriate for boys; assertiveness in play and an active physical stance in interactions with peers seem appropriate, but tattling on other children and fighting with girls seem inappropriate (e.g., Biller & Borstelmann, 1967; Shortell & Biller, 1970).

In any case, findings about the influence of paternal limit setting are inconsistent. In Mussen and Distler's (1959) study, the kindergarten boys who manifested highly masculine projective sex-role responses perceived their fathers as somewhat more punitive and threatening in structured doll play situations than boys low in masculinity did. Mussen and Rutherford (1963) found a similar trend for first-grade boys. But in both studies, perceived nurturance of father was found to be much more related to high masculine preferences. In addition Mussen and Distler (1960) ascertained nothing to indicate that the fathers of the high masculine kindergarten boys actually punished them more than the fathers of the low masculine boys did. In my study with kindergarten-age boys, perceived paternal limit setting was slightly related to a measure of sex-role orientation but not to measures of sex-role preference or adoption (Biller, 1969a). Sears, Rau, and Alpert (1965) did not find a consistent relationship between interview measures of paternal limit setting and preschool boys' masculinity.

The adolescent boys with high masculine interests in Mussen's study (1961) described fathers as nonpunitive and nonrestrictive in their TAT stories. Some of the discrepancy between this study and the Mussen and Distler (1959) and Mussen and Rutherford (1963) studies may be due to age differences. For example, by adolescence, a father who earlier was perceived as threatening because of his "awesome size" may be less threatening when his son becomes similar in size and strength. During adolescence the father is also less likely to use physical means of punishment and more likely to set limits verbally. A related point is that limit setting is not necessarily performed in a punitive context.

When the father plays a significant part in setting limits, the boy's attachment to his father and masculine development are facilitated *only* if there is an already established affectionate father–son relationship. If the father is not nurturant, and is punitive, the boy is likely to display a low level of father imitation. Bandura and Walters (1959) found that adolescent boys who had highly punitive and generally nonnurturant and nonrewarding fathers exhibited relatively low father preference and little perception of themselves as acting and thinking like their fathers.

## Paternal Power

Mussen and Distler (1959) found that boys with highly masculine projective sex-role behavior perceived their fathers as more "powerful" than boys low in masculinity did. When perceived nurturance and perceived punitiveness scores were combined, the difference between the masculine and nonmasculine boys was particularly clear-cut. Mussen and Rutherford (1963) reported similar results for first-grade boys, but the relationship was not as strong. Freedheim's (1960) data suggested that the father's total salience to the child and overall involvement in family decision making is the best predictor of the elementary school boy's masculinity (Freedheim & Borstelmann, 1963). In my study with kindergarten-age boys, the overall amount of perceived father influence was much more important than the perception of the father as dominant in a particular area of family or parent–child functioning (Biller, 1969a).

Parent perception and sex-role research with college students have also yielded results that are in line with formulations stressing the importance of the total father–son relationship. Distler (1964) found that college males who described themselves as strongly masculine on an adjective check list viewed their fathers as high in nurturance, limit setting, and competence; in other words, as very powerful. In a study by Moulton et al. (1966), college males with the most masculine sex-role preferences (modified version of Gough's Femininity Scale) reported that their fathers were high in affection and the dominant disciplinarians in their families.

Bronfenbrenner (1961) found that the development of leadership, responsibility, and social maturity in adolescent males is closely associated with a father–son relationship that not only is nurturant but also includes a strong component of paternal limit setting. A study by Reuter and me, discussed in more detail in a later section, also suggests the importance of evaluating both the quality and quantity of paternal behavior (Reuter & Biller, 1973). The combination of at least moderate paternal availability with at least moderate nurturance was associated with positive personal adjustment among male college students.

## Methodological Issues

The bulk of the research on father–child relationships and personality development can be criticized because of methodological deficiencies and/or limited generality. In most investigations the father's behavior is not directly assessed, and maternal or child reports of paternal behavior are used. In many of the studies the sources of evidence about parental behavior and the child's behavior are not independent, leading to problems of interpretation. For example, in many studies children are asked to describe both their own and their parents' behavior. More studies in which there is an assessment of the amount of consistency among observer ratings of familial interactions and children's and parents' perceptions of parent–child relationships should be done. In addition, procedures that allow observers, parents and children to rate each family member independently should be compared to those in which instructions call for comparative ratings of family members. One goal of such investigations would be to examine which type or types of measures are most related to specific dimensions of children's personality functioning (Biller, 1971a, 1974c).

Most of the studies on the father–child relationship and personality development have been correlational. Often the child's perception of his father or some report of the father's behavior is linked to a measure of the child's personality development. For instance, when significant correlations are found between the degree to which a boy perceives his father as nurturant and the boy's masculinity, it is usually assumed that paternal nurturance has been an antecedent of masculine development. But fathers may become nurturant and accepting when their sons are masculine and rejecting when their sons are unmasculine. Longitudinal research would be particularly helpful in determining the extent to which certain paternal behaviors precede or determine particular dimensions of children's behavior. Careful observations of families in various environmental settings could be especially revealing.

## FATHER ABSENCE AND MASCULINE DEVELOPMENT

Many researchers have speculated that the primary effects of father absence are manifested by deficits and/or abnormalities in the boy's sex-role development (Biller, 1970, 1971a). In this section, research findings on this relationship are discussed. A comparison of the sex-role development of father-absent and father-present boys suggests some of the ways in which fathering and paternal deprivation influence personality development.

**Sex-Typed Behavior**

Most of the early studies dealing with the effects of father absence were done with children whose fathers were or had been absent because of military service during World War II. The Sears conducted a pioneering investigation of the effects of father absence on 3- to 5-year-old boys (Sears, 1951). Each child was given an opportunity to play with a standardized set of doll play equipment, and the investigators recorded his behavior. Compared to the father-present boys, the father-absent boys were less aggressive and also had less sex-role differentiation in their doll play activity. For example, their play contained less emphasis on the maleness of the father and boy dolls (Sears, Pintler, & Sears, 1946). Bach (1946) used a similar procedure to study the effects of father absence on 6- to 10-year-old children. As in the Sears' study father-absent boys were less aggressive in doll play than father-present boys were. Bach observed that "the father-separated children produced an idealistic and feminine fantasy picture of the father when compared to the control children who elaborated the father's aggressive tendencies" (p. 79).

In a very thorough investigation Stoltz et al. (1954) gathered data concerning 4- to 8-year-old children who, for approximately the first 2 years of their lives, had been separated from their fathers. Interviews revealed that the boys were generally perceived by their fathers as "sissies." Careful observation of these boys supported this view. The boys were less assertively aggressive and independent in their peer relations than boys who had not been separated from their fathers. They were more often observed to be very submissive or to react with immature hostility, and they were actually more aggressive in doll play than boys who had not been separated from their fathers. However, the facts that the fathers were present in the home at the time of this study and that the father–child relationships were stressful make it difficult to speculate about what influence father absence per se had on the children's personality development.

Paternal employment can be related to frequent father absence. In a very extensive investigation Tiller (1958) and Lynn and Sawrey (1959) studied Norwegian children aged 8 to 9½ whose fathers were sailors absent at least 9 months a year. They compared these children with a matched group of children whose fathers had jobs that did not require them to be separated from their families. The boys' responses to projective tests, and interviews with their mothers, demonstrated that father separation was associated with compensatory masculinity (the boys behaving at times in an exaggerated masculine manner, at other times in a highly feminine manner). The father-separated boys appeared to be much less secure in their masculinity than the control group boys did. Consistent with the findings of Bach (1946) and Sears (1951) the father-separated boys were less aggressive in doll play than the control group.

Several investigators have attempted to assess differences between father-absent and father-present boys in terms of their human figure drawings. Phelan (1964) assumed that boys who drew a female when asked to draw a person had failed to make a shift from an initial identification with the mother to one with the father. In her study there was a higher rate of father absence among elementary school-age boys who drew a female first as compared to those who drew a male first. An additional analysis of some of my (1968a) data with kindergarten-age children revealed that father-absent boys were less likely to draw a male first or to differentiate clearly their male and female drawings, particularly if they became father absent before the age of 4.

Burton (1972) asked 8- to 15-year-old Caribbean children to draw human figures. His evidence suggested that father absence during the first 2 years of life was associated with relatively unmasculine self-concepts for boys. Compared to father-present boys, boys who had been father-absent during their first 2 years of life (and did not subsequently have a permanent father figure) less often drew a male first and drew males shorter. They also generally drew males shorter than they drew females.

Clear-cut relationships between father absence and figure drawings have not, however, been consistently found with older children. A problem with many of the studies concerned with figure drawings is that there is no presentation of specific information regarding length and age of onset of father absence (e.g., Donini, 1967; Lawton & Sechrest, 1962).

## Developmental Stages

The quality of the early father–child attachment is an important factor in the child's sex-role and personality development. The degree and quality of the father's involvement, even in the first year of life, have much influence on the child's behavior (Biller, 1974c).

Father absence before the age of 4 or 5 appears to have a retarding effect on masculine development. Hetherington (1966) reported that 9- to 12-year-old boys whose fathers had been absent since before their 4th birthdays manifested less masculine projective sex-role behavior and were rated by male recreation directors as more dependent on their peers, less aggressive, and as engaging in fewer physical contact games than father-present boys were. There were, however, no consistent differences on the sex-role measures when the father-present boys were compared with boys who had become father absent after the age of 4.

I found that father-absent 5-year-old boys had less masculine sex-role orientations (fantasy game measure) and sex-role preferences (game choice) than father-present boys did (Biller, 1969b). Moreover the boys who became father absent before the age of 4 had significantly less masculine sex-role orientations than those who became father absent in their 5th year. In an investigation Bahm and I conducted with junior high school boys, those who became father absent before the age of 5 appeared less masculine on an adjective check list measure of masculinity of self-concept than those who were father present did (Biller & Bahm, 1971).

Many other studies suggest that early father absence retards the young boy's development of independence and other masculine behaviors (e.g., Green, 1974; Leichty, 1960; Santrock, 1970b; Stendler, 1954). There is also cross-cultural evidence indicating that early father absence is often associated with sex-role conflicts among males in other societies (e.g., Burton, 1972; Burton & Whiting, 1961; Rogers & Long, 1968; Stephens, 1962; Whiting, Kluckhohn, & Anthony, 1958).

A study of lower class fifth-grade boys by Santrock (1970b) revealed that boys who became father absent before the age of 2 were more handicapped in several dimensions of personality development than boys were who became father absent at a later age. For example, these boys were found to be less trusting and less industrious and to have more feelings of inferiority than boys who became father absent between the ages of 3 to 5. Other evidence is consistent with the supposition that early father absence is associated with a heightened susceptibility to a variety of psychological problems (Biller, 1971a, 1974c). Studies relating to the effects of the timing of father absence on various dimensions of personality development are reviewed in later sections of this chapter.

## Different Aspects of Sex-Role Development

As the findings relating to developmental status have suggested, different aspects of sex-role may not be affected in the same way by father absence. It is common for young father-absent children to seek intensely the attention of older males. Because of deprivation effects father-absent children often have a strong motivation to imitate and please potential father figures. Father-absent boys may strive to appear masculine in some facets of their behavior while continuing to behave in an unmasculine or feminine manner in others. For example, a paternally deprived boy may be exposed only to females who encourage passivity and dependency in the first 4 or 5 years of his life, but later there may be much peer and societal pressure for him to behave in a masculine manner. Demands for masculine behavior may not become apparent to the boy until he reaches school age or even adolescence, but in any case under such conditions his sex-role preference and/or sex-role adoption may differ from his basic sex-role orientation (Biller & Borstelmann, 1967).

Barclay and Cusumano (1967) did not find any differences between father-present and father-absent adolescent males on a measure of sex-role preference (Gough Femininity Scale). However, the father-absent males were more field dependent on Witkin's rod and frame test. The investigators conceptualized the field dependence–field independence dimension as reflecting underlying sex-role orientation. In a study I did with lower class, 6-year-old children, father-absent boys were significantly less masculine than father-present boys on a measure of projective sex-role behavior used to assess sex-role orientation. The two groups were not, however, consistently different in their direct sex-role preferences (the toys and games they said they liked) or teachers' ratings of sex-role adoption (Biller, 1968b). Even though the father-absent boys had significantly fewer masculine game preferences, differences were most clear-cut in responses to the sex-role orientation procedure. No consistent differences were apparent with respect to the sex-role adoption measure.

If it can be assumed that attending college is more typical of middle-class than of lower class adolescents, an investigation by Altus (1958) involving college students suggests that father-absent, middle-class boys remain relatively low in masculinity of sex-role preference throughout adolescence. Father-absent and father-present male freshmen at the University of California were compared. Father absence was due to divorce, but no data on the age of onset of father absence were reported. The father-absent group scored significantly higher on the masculinity–femininity scale of the MMPI, indicating less masculinity of interests and attitudes. In contrast an examination of data from several other studies suggests that, particularly by adolescence, there is relatively little difference among lower-class father-present and father-absent boys with respect to many facets of sex-role awareness, preference, and adoption (e.g., Barclay & Cusumano, 1967; D'Andrade, 1962; Greenstein, 1966; McCord, McCord, & Thurber, 1962; Miller, 1961; Mitchell & Wilson, 1967; Tiller, 1961).

## Surrogate Models

Paternal absence or paternal inadequacy does not rule out the possible presence of other male models. A brother, uncle, grandfather, or male boarder may ensure that the boy has much interactions with a competent adult male. An important role can be played by male neighbors and teachers. Male teachers, particularly, may influence father-absent boys (Biller, 1974a, 1974b, 1974c; Lee & Wolinsky, 1973).

The child may even learn some masculine behaviors by patterning himself after a movie or television star, an athlete, a fictional hero, and so forth. Freud and Burlingham (1944) described how a fatherless, 2-year-old boy developed a fantasy role model. Bob's mother had told him about a 9-year-old boy whom he referred to as "Big Bobby," and thereafter Bob actively used Big Bobby as a masculine model, attempting physical feats that he thought Big Bobby could perform. Bob perceived Big Bobby as physically superior to everyone else.

Some investigators have found that masculinity is related to the general amount of contact boys have with adult males. Nash (1965) studied a group of Scottish orphans who went to live in cottages run by married couples, in which they thus had masculine models. Even though less masculine (in terms of a variety of sex-role measures) than boys raised in a typical family setting, they were more masculine than a group of orphans brought up entirely by women. Similarly, Steimel (1960) reported that adolescent boys who were high (compared to those who were low) in masculinity of interests on both the MMPI and Strong Vocational Interest Blank recalled more childhood experiences with older males. In terms of maternal interview data Santrock (1970a) found that father-absent boys with a father substitute were significantly less dependent than father-absent boys with no father substitute.

*Siblings.* Older brothers can be very important masculine models for children. Thus paternal deprivation may have a very different effect on a 5-year-old boy who is an only child than on one who has two older brothers who were not themselves paternally deprived in early childhood. Obviously many other variables have to be considered, including the frequency and quality of interactions among siblings. A problem with many of the sibling studies is that they consider only the presence or absence of a particular type of sibling. This is somewhat analogous to studies that take into account only whether a child is father present or father absent (Biller, 1974c).

Interestingly, in two-child, father-absent families, there is some evidence that boys with brothers suffer less of a deficit in academic aptitude than boys with sisters do (Sutton-Smith, Rosenberg, & Landy, 1968). In Santrock's (1970a) study father-absent boys with only older male siblings appeared more masculine (on a maternal interview measure of sex-role behavior) than father-absent boys with only older female siblings. In an extension of Santrock's investigation, Wohlford, Santrock, Berger, &

Liberman (1971) found that father-absent children with older brothers appeared less dependent than those without older brothers on both doll play and maternal interview measures. The presence or absence of older female siblings was not, however, related to the sex-role measures and did not affect the older brother's influence. The 5-year-old boys in the Sears investigations appeared to be less influenced by father absence than the 3- or 4-year-old boys did (Sears, 1951); an examination of the Sears' data indicates that the 5-year-old boys had more siblings than the younger children did. Unfortunately no details are given regarding the sex and age of siblings, but it is possible that the older children had more male siblings, a circumstance that could thereby have lessened the effects of father absence (Biller & Borstelmann, 1967).

Although the presence of male siblings may lessen the effects of father absence, data from one of my investigations imply that the presence of a father is generally a much more important factor in masculine development than the presence of an older brother is (Biller, 1968a).

*Peers.* The masculine role models provided by the peer group can be particularly influential for the paternally deprived boy. In a social class or subculture in which instrumental aggression and physical prowess are very important as a means of achieving peer acceptance, many father-absent boys are likely to emulate their masculine peers. Peer models seem especially important in lower class neighborhoods. Miller (1958) emphasized the centrality of traits such as toughness and independence in the value system of lower class adolescents. Lower class boys respect aggressiveness more than middle-class boys do, and one of the types of boys they most admire is the aggressive, belligerent youngster who earns their respect because of his toughness and strength (Pope, 1953).

During the elementary school years, and in some cases even earlier, peer group pressure for masculine behavior begins to have an effect on most paternally deprived boys. In some family situations emotional and instrumental dependency on the mother is so strong that peer influences do not have an effect or are delayed until adolescence. Because of certain physical handicaps such as lack of strength or coordination, it may be relatively impossible for a boy to interact successfully with a masculine-striving peer group.

On the other hand the physically well-equipped boy may find it relatively easy to gain acceptance from his peers. Many paternally deprived boys behave in a generally effective and masculine manner. For example, an additional case study analysis of some of the 5-year-old boys in my (1968a, 1969b) studies has demonstrated that father-absent boys who are relatively mesomorphic are less likely to be retarded in their sex-role development than father-absent boys with unmasculine physiques are. A boy's physique has an important stimulus value because of the expectations and reinforcements it elicits from others, and it may, along with correlated constitutional factors, predispose him toward success or failure in particular types of activities. The influence of the child's anatomical, temperamental, and cognitive predispositions on parental and peer behavior must be taken into account when one evaluates the effects of father absence (Biller, 1974c).

## Methodological Issues

In addition to the obvious theoretical and practical relevance of studying the effects of father absence, a possible methodological justification is that father absence is a naturalistic manipulation. It can be argued that father absence must be an antecedent rather than a consequence of certain behaviors in children. However, a general problem with studies comparing father-absent and father-present children is that investigators have usually treated both types of children as if they represented homogeneous groups. There has been a lack of concern for the meaning of these two conditions. For example, there have been few attempts to ensure that a group of consistently father-absent boys is compared with a group of boys who have a high level and quality of father availability.

Most researchers have treated father absence in an overly simplistic fashion. In many studies variables such as type, length, and age of onset of father absence have not been specified. Potentially important variables such as the child's sex, intelligence, constitutional characteristics, birth order, relationship with his mother, and sociocultural background, as well as availability of father surrogates, are often not taken into account, either in subject matching or in data analysis. When careful matching procedures are followed, more clear-cut findings seem to emerge (e.g., Biller, 1969b, 1971a; Blanchard & Biller, 1971; Hetherington, 1966).

Investigators have made inferences about the effects of father absence and variations in paternal behavior on sex-role development and the identification process, but measurement of hypothesized dependent variables has often been indirect or included only a very narrow range of behaviors. Data on a limited measure of masculinity have frequently been used to make inferences about overall patterns of identification and sex-role development; multidimensional assessment procedures are needed if we are to gain a clearer understanding of the influence of father absence on the child's sex-role development (Biller, 1968a, 1971a).

## THE FATHER AND COGNITIVE FUNCTIONING

A number of studies have investigated the association between inadequate father–son relationships or father-absence and academic difficulties among boys. These studies clearly bear on the discussion of the father's influence on personality development, but because they are discussed by Norma Radin in Chapter 7, they are not considered here.

## PERSONAL AND SOCIAL ADJUSTMENT

This section comprises a discussion of the influence of the father–child relationship and paternal deprivation on self-concept, anxiety, impulsiveness, moral development, delinquent behavior, interpersonal relations, and psychopathology.

### Self-Esteem and Personal Adjustment

A number of investigations have revealed an association between self-esteem and various facets of paternal behavior. The father's interest and consistent participation seem to contribute strongly to the development of the child's self-confidence and self-esteem. Sears (1970) found a relationship between mother-reported paternal warmth and a questionnaire measure of six-grade boys' self-esteem. Medinnus (1965a) reported that college students' self-esteem was positively related to paternal love and negatively related to paternal rejection and neglect. Mussen, Young, Gaddini, & Morante (1963) presented data showing that adolescent boys with unaffectionate relationships with their fathers were particularly likely to feel rejected and unhappy.

In Coopersmith's (1967) study of elementary school boys, paternal involvement in limit setting was associated with high self-esteem. In contrast boys with low self-esteem were much more likely to be punished exclusively by their mothers. Coopersmith also noted that boys who were able to confide in their fathers were likely to have high self-esteem. Rosenberg's (1965) results suggested that the early father–child relationship is particularly important for the child's self-esteem. Among adolescents those who were father absent had lower self-esteem than those who were father present, especially when father absence had begun in early childhood.

Slater (1962) examined the relationship between college men's personality characteristics and their perceptions of their parents. Students who scored high on questionnaire measures of ego strength and social competence were likely to perceive their fathers as affectionate and emotionally supportive. In contrast, students who responded in a manner suggesting low ego strength, impulsiveness, and social introversion were liable to see their fathers as being inhibiting in their demands and discipline. Paternal involvement was positively associated with the son's responsivity toward others.

Reuter and I studied the relationship between various combinations of perceived paternal nurturance–availability and college males' personal adjustment (Reuter & Biller, 1973). A family background questionnaire was designed to assess perceptions of father–child relationships and the amount of time the father spent at home when the subjects were children. The personal adjustment scale of Gough and Heilbrun's Adjective Check List and the socialization scale of the California Psychological Inventory were employed as measures of personality adjustment. High paternal nurturance combined with at least moderate paternal availability, and high paternal availability combined with at least moderate paternal nurturance were related to high scores on the personality adjustment measures. A male who has frequent opportunities to observe a nurturant father can imitate his behavior and develop positive personality characteristics. The father who is both relatively nurturant and relatively available may have a more nearly adequate personality adjustment than other types of fathers.

In contrast high paternal nurturance combined with low paternal availability, and high paternal availability combined with low paternal nurturance were associated with relatively poor scores on the personality adjustment measures. The boy with a highly nurturant but seldom-home father may feel quite frustrated that his father is not home more often and/or may find it difficult to imitate such an elusive figure. Males who reported that their fathers had been home much of the time but gave them little attention seemed to be especially handicapped in their psychological functioning. The unnurturant father is an inadequate model, and his consistent presence appears to be a detriment to the boy's personality functioning. To put it another way, the boy with an unnurturant father may be better off if his father is not very available. This is consistent with evidence suggesting that father-absent boys often have better personality adjustments than boys with passive, ineffectual fathers (Biller 1971a, 1974c).

## Anxiety and Maladjustment

The results of many other investigations have suggested that low perceived similarity to the father is related to anxiety and maladjustment among males. Cava and Rausch (1952) had adolescent boys fill out a vocational interest test for themselves and then as they thought their fathers would do it. Boys having low perceived similarity to the father generally scored high in castration anxiety as measured by projective test responses. Sopchak (1952) had college students fill out the MMPI for themselves and as they thought their parents would. Men who perceived themselves as dissimilar to their fathers were more likely to be anxious and maladjusted in their MMPI responses. Lazowick (1955) found that the more the son perceived himself to be similar to his father on a personality inventory, the lower his score was likely to be on an anxiety scale. In Helper's (1955) study there was a positive relationship between perceived similarity to the father and peer acceptance.

Gray (1959), studying fifth through eighth graders, reported a positive association between boys' perceived similarity to fathers and peer ratings of adjustment. Lockwood and Guerney's (1962) study revealed that fathers as well as their adolescent sons were likely to perceive strong father–son similarity when the son scored high on an adjustment inventory. In David's (1968) study there was an association between low perceived similarity to the father and low ego strength among both college males and females. Barry and I, studying college males, found that individuals who were masculine in their sex-role orientations and preferences perceived themselves to be more similar to their fathers and had more nearly adequate personality adjustments than those with other sex-role patterns did (Biller & Barry, 1971).

Inadequate fathering is often associated with a high level of anxiety and maladjustment in children. The paternally deprived child's insecurity in his interpersonal relationships can contribute to feelings of anxiety and low self-esteem. In addition the paternally deprived child may experience much anxiety because of an overly intense relationship with his mother (Biller, 1971a, 1971b). The father-absent child, in particular, is likely to encounter economic insecurity and, depending on the reason for paternal absence, may be concerned with his father's well-being. Feelings of being different may also increase his anxiety and perception of being inadequate (Biller, 1974c).

Stolz et al. (1954) reported that 4- to 8-year-old children, whose fathers were away on military service during their first few years of life, were more anxious than children whose fathers had been consistently present. Previously father-separated children were observed to be more anxious with peers and adults in story completion sessions when the situation involved the father, and in maternal reports of the seriousness and number of fears. The fathers were not absent at the time of the study but were having stressful relationships with their children. In a study of nursery school children Koch (1961) found that father-absent children (eight boys and three girls) exhibited more anxiety on a projective test than a matched group from intact families did. The father-absent children more often selected unhappy faces for the central child depicted in various situations.

McCord et al. (1962), analyzing social workers' observations of 10- to 15-year-old, lower class boys, concluded that father-absent boys manifested more anxiety about sex than a matched group of father-present boys, although the difference in the amount of general fearfulness was insignificant. In a retrospective study Stephens (1961) asked social workers about their experiences with father-absent boys. These boys were described as being more effeminate and anxious about sex than father-present boys were. Leichty (1960) did not find any evidence that father absence during early childhood was associated with castration anxiety in college males, although some of her findings did suggest that it was related to anxiety about heterosexual relationships.

Chronic anxiety and poor adjustment seem uncommon among boys who have solid identifications with their fathers (Lynn, 1969, 1974; Schoeppe, Haggard, & Havighurst, 1953). There is much evidence suggesting that males who perceive themselves as being similar to their fathers, particularly when their fathers are masculine, are likely to be relatively free of serious psychological difficulties (Biller & Barry, 1971; Cava & Rausch, 1952; David, 1968; Heilbrun, 1962; Heilbrun & Fromme, 1965; Helper, 1955; Lockwood & Guerney, 1962; Lazowick, 1955; Sopchak, 1952).

Some very extensive longitudinal data underscore the importance of both the father's behavior and the father–mother relationship in the personality adjustment of the child. In general, Block (1971) found that males who achieved a successful emotional and interpersonal adjustment in adulthood had both fathers and mothers who were highly involved and responsible in their upbringing. In contrast poorly adjusted adult males had fathers who were typically uninvolved in childrearing and mothers who tended to have a neurotic adjustment.

In a related investigation Block, von der Lippe, and Block (1973) reported that well-socialized and successful adult males were likely to have had highly involved fathers and to have come from homes where their parents had compatible relationships. In contrast adult males who were relatively low in socialization skills and personal adjustment were likely to have grown up in homes in which the parents were incompatible and in which the fathers were either uninvolved or weak and neurotic.

## Impulsive and Antisocial Behavior

Mischel conducted a series of studies on the antecedents and correlates of impulse control in Caribbean children (e.g., Mischel, 1961c). In an earlier phase of his research Mischel (1958) discovered that 7- to 9-year-old black West Indian children chose immediate gratification significantly more frequently than white West Indian children did. The differences between the black and white children appeared to be related to the greater incidence of father absence among the black children. Studying 8- and 9-year-old children, Mischel (1961b) found that father-absent children showed a stronger preference for immediate gratification than father-present children did. Father-absent children, for instance, more often chose a small candy for immediate consumption rather than wait a week for a large candy bar.

Mischel (1958) speculated that father absence interferes with the young child's development of trust of other people. It is also possible that many young, father-absent children trust adult females but not adult males; in Mischel's research an adult male offered the choice between immediate and delayed gratification. The young, father-absent child may learn to be secure in the presence of his mother and generalize this trust to other females, but a basis for trusting adult males may be lacking.

When Mischel (1961b) studied 11- to 14-year-old children, he did not find an association between father absence and preference for immediate gratification. Perhaps, as Mischel suggested, as the father-absent child grows older, his wider experience helps him to develop a trust of others beyond those in his immediate family. With added experience most father-absent children may learn to trust males. In addition, according to Mischel, many of the older, father-absent children may have been without their fathers for a relatively brief period. The older, paternally deprived children may have been father present during the age period most crucial to the development of trust. In Mischel's studies the criterion of father absence was simply whether or not the father was living at home, and there was no measure of duration of father absence. In research with fifth-grade boys, Santrock (1970b) found that father absence beginning in the first 2 years of life was more disruptive to the development of trust than that during the ages of 3 to 5.

Santrock and Wohlford (1970) studied delay of gratification among fifth-grade boys. They found that boys who were father absent because of divorce, as compared to those who were father absent because of death, had more difficulty in delaying gratification. The former group more often chose an immediately available small candy bar rather than wait till the next day for a much larger one. Boys who became father separated before the age of 2 or between the ages of 6 to 9 were more likely to choose the immediate reward than those who were separated from their fathers between the ages of 3 to 5.

There is also some evidence that individuals who have been father absent during childhood are likely to have difficulties making long-term job commitments. Studying Peace Corps volunteers, Suedfield (1967) discovered that those who were father absent during childhood were much more likely not to complete their scheduled overseas tours than those who had not been father absent. Premature terminations were associated with problems of adjustment and conduct and included some psychiatrically based decisions. Other research suggests a relationship between father absence in childhood and frequent job terminations in adulthood (Gay & Tonge, 1967; Hall & Tonge, 1963).

*Moral Development and Self-Control.* Paternal dominance in discipline when combined with a high level of paternal affection is strongly associated with male children's sensitivity to their moral transgressions (Moulton et al., 1966). The father who can set limits firmly and can also be affectionate and responsive to his child's needs seems to be a particularly good model for interpersonal sensitivity and moral development. Holstein (1972) found that morally mature adolescents were likely to have warm, nurturant, and highly moral fathers.

Hoffman (1971a) reported data on the conscience development of seventh-grade children. Father-absent boys consistently scored lower than father-present boys on a variety of indices of morality. They scored lower on measures of internal moral judgment, guilt following transgressions, acceptance of blame, moral values, and rule conformity. In addition they were rated as higher in aggression by their teachers, a ranking that may also reflect difficulties in self-control. Although there were generally not clear-cut differences on the measures that Hoffman had used, Santrock (1975) found that, among elementary school boys, those who were father absent were consistently rated by their teachers as having a lower level of moral maturity than those who were father present.

Hoffman (1971a, 1971b) also found that weak father identification among father-present boys was more related to less than adequate conscience development than strong father identification was. Father identification was determined by responses to questions involving the person the boy felt most similar to, most admired, and most wanted to resemble when he grew up. Among the seventh graders that Hoffman studied, boys with strong father identifications scored higher on the measures of internal moral judgment, moral values, and conformity to rules than boys with low father identifications did.

The quality of the father–child relationship seems to have particular influence on whether the child takes responsibility for his own actions or acts as if his behavior is controlled by external forces. Children who have a warm relationship with a competent father who can constructively set limits for them are much more likely to develop a realistic internal locus of control. Increasingly, attention is being paid to the familial ante-cedents of variations in locus of control among children (e.g., Davis & Phares, 1969; MacDonald, 1971; Nowicki & Segal, 1974).

A number of clinicians, including Aichorn (1935) and Lederer (1964), have speculated about inadequacies in the self-control and conscience development of the father-absent boy. In his experience as a psychothera-pist Meerloo (1956) found that a lack of accurate time perception, often associated with difficulties in self-control, is common among father-absent individuals. In a study of elementary-school children in a Cuban section of Miami, Wohlford and Liberman (1970) reported that father-absent children had less well-developed future time perspective than father-present children did. Tolor, Brannigan, and Murphy (1970) investigated the relationship between perceived psychological distance from the father and future perspective among college students. Students who perceived themselves as distant from their fathers were less able to extend them-selves into a future time perspective than students who felt close to their fathers.

Meerloo (1956) assumed that the father represents social order and that his adherence to time schedules gives the child an important lesson in social functioning. The paternally deprived boy may find it very difficult to follow the rules of society. Antisocial acts are often impulsive as well as aggressive, and there is evidence that inability to delay gratification is associated with inaccurate time perception, lack of social responsibility, low achievement motivation, and juvenile delinquency (e.g., Mischel, 1961a, 1961c).

The father-absent boy often lacks a model from whom to learn to delay gratification and to control his aggressive and destructive impulses. A boy who has experienced paternal deprivation may have particular difficulty in respecting and communicating with adult males in positions of authority. Douvan and Adelson (1966) observed much rebelliousness against adult authority figures and particularly a rejection of men among adolescent, father-absent boys. (It is interesting to contrast such a reaction to the continual seeking of male adults among many young father-absent children—perhaps there has been a disillusionment process.)

The boy whose father has set limits for him in a nurturant and realistic manner is better able to set limits for himself. There is also some evidence that perceived similarity to the father is related to positive relationships with authority figures (Bieri & Lobeck, 1959). Investigators have found that boys who receive appropriate and consistent discipline from their fathers are less liable to commit delinquent acts, even if they are gang members (Glueck & Glueck, 1950; Stanfield, 1966).

*Delinquency.* Antisocial behavior among children and adolescents can have many different etiologies, but paternal deprivation is a frequent contributing factor. Many researchers have noted that father absence is more common among delinquent than nondelinquent boys. Studying adolescents, Glueck and Glueck (1950) reported that more than two-fifths of the delinquent boys were father absent as compared with less than one-fourth of a matched nondelinquent group. McCord et al. (1962) found that the lower class, father-absent boys in their study committed more felonies than the father-present group did, although the rates of gang delinquency were not different. Gregory (1965a) listed a large number of investigations linking father absence with delinquent behavior and also detected a strong association between these variables in his study of high school students.

Early father absence has a particularly strong association with delinquency among males. Siegman (1966) analyzed medical students' responses to an anonymous questionnaire about their childhood experiences. He compared the responses of students who had been without a father for at least 1 year during their first few years of life with those of students who had been continuously father present. The father-absent group admitted to a greater degree of antisocial behavior during childhood. Anderson (1968) found that a history of early father absence was much more frequent among boys committed to a training school. He also discovered that father-absent nondelinquents had a much higher rate of father substitution (stepfather, father surrogate, etc.) between the ages of 4 to 7 than father-absent delinquents did. Kelly and Baer (1969) studied the recidivism rate among male delinquents. Compared to a 12% rate among father-present males, they found a 39% recidivism rate among males who had become father absent before the age of 6. However, boys who became father absent after the age of 6 had only a 10% recidivism rate.

Miller (1958) argued that most lower class boys suffer from paternal deprivation and that their antisocial behavior is often an attempt to prove they are masculine. Bacon, Child, and Barry (1963), in a cross-cultural study, found that father availability was negatively related to the amount of theft and personal crime. Degree of father availability was defined in terms of family structure. Societies with a predominantly monogamous nuclear family structure tended to be rated low in the amount of theft and personal crime, whereas societies with a polygamous mother–child family structure tended to be rated high in both theft and personal crime. Following Miller's hypothesis, these investigators suggested that such antisocial behavior was a reaction against a female-based household and an attempted assertion of masculinity. A large number of psychiatric referrals with the complaint of aggressive acting-out are made by mothers of preadolescent and adolescent father-absent boys, and clinical data suggest that sex-role conflicts are frequent in such boys (e.g., MacDonald, 1938; Wylie & Delgado, 1959).

Herzog and Sudia (1970) cited much evidence demonstrating that lack of general family cohesiveness and supervision, rather than father absence per se, is the most significant factor associated with juvenile delinquency. Many familial and nonfamilial factors have to be considered, and in only some cases is father absence directly linked to delinquent behavior. For example, boys in father-absent families who have a positive relationship with their mothers seem to be less liable to become delinquent than boys in father-present families who have inadequate fathers (Biller, 1971a, 1974c; McCord et al., 1962).

Father-present juvenile delinquents appear to have very poor relationships with their fathers. Bach and Bremer (1947) reported that pre-adolescent delinquent boys produced significantly fewer father fantasies on projective tests than a nondelinquent control group did. The delinquents portrayed fathers as lacking in affection and empathy. Similarly Andry (1962) found that delinquents characterized their fathers as glum, uncommunicative, and as employing unreasonable punishment and little praise. Father–son communication was particularly poor.

Andry's findings are consistent with those of Bandura and Walters (1959), who reported that the relationship between delinquent sons and fathers is marked by rejection, hostility, and antagonism. McCord, McCord, and Howard (1963) found that a deviant, aggressive father in the context of general parental neglect and punitiveness was strongly related to juvenile delinquency. Medinnus (1965b) obtained data suggesting a very high frequency of negative father–child relationships among delinquent boys. The delinquent adolescent boys in Medinnus's study perceived their fathers as much more rejecting and neglecting than their mothers.

Schaefer's (1965) data also revealed the particularly negative way delinquent boys often perceive their fathers. Compared to nondelinquent boys they viewed their fathers as laxer in discipline, more neglecting, and generally less involved. Surprisingly the delinquents described their mothers as more positive and loving than the nondelinquents did. Gregory (1965a) found, moreover, a higher rate of delinquency among boys living with their mothers after father loss than among boys living with fathers after mother loss. Such data suggest that paternal deprivation is more of a factor in the development of delinquency than maternal deprivation is.

There is considerable evidence that father-present delinquents are likely to have inadequate fathers who themselves have difficulties in impulse control. Jenkins (1968) found that the fathers of delinquent children seen at a child guidance clinic were frequently described as rigid, controlling, and prone to alcoholism. McCord et al. (1963) reported that criminal behavior in adulthood was often found among men whose fathers had been criminals, alcoholics, and/or extremely abusive to their families. Other researchers have also presented data suggesting a link between paternal inadequacy and delinquent behavior (Glueck & Glueck, 1950; Rosenthal, Ni, Finkelstein, & Berkwits, 1962).

Boys who commit delinquent acts by themselves appear to have poorer relationships with their fathers than boys do who commit delinquent acts with other gang members (Brigham, Ricketts, & Johnson, 1967). On the other hand boys who have positive relationships with their fathers are likely to engage in constructive and prosocial gang behavior (Crane, 1955; Thrasher, 1927). Such findings indicate that the quality of fathering a boy receives greatly influences his peer relationships.

## Interpersonal Relationships

The father–infant relationship can have much impact on the child's subsequent relationships with others. For example, infants who have little contact with their fathers are more likely to experience greater anxiety on separation from their mothers and more negative reactions to strangers (Biller, 1974c; Spelke, Zelazo, Kagan, & Kotelchuck, 1973). The way the father interacts with the child presents a particularly potent modeling situation that the child is apt to generalize to his relationships with others.

Paternal deprivation can severely interfere with the development of successful peer relationships. The observations by Stolz et al. (1954), as well as mothers' and fathers' reports, indicate that 4- to 8-year-old children who had been father absent for the first few years of life had poorer peer relationships than children who had not been father absent. The Norwegian, father-separated boys in Tiller's (1958) investigation were judged to have less nearly adequate peer relationships than boys who were not father separated. Other investigators have reported that continuously father-absent boys are less popular and have less satisfying peer relationships than father-present boys do (e.g., Leiderman, 1953; Miller, 1961; Mitchell & Wilson, 1967).

Paternally deprived boys are often handicapped in their peer relationships because they lack a secure masculine orientation. Sex-appropriate behavior is very important in the formation of friendships among elementary school children. For instance, Tuddenham (1951, 1952) found that the most popular boys in the first grade were those who were considered by their peers to be good sports, good at games, daring, not bashful, and "real boys." Gray (1957, 1959) reported similar results for fifth- to eighth-grade boys. In addition boys who were rated high in popularity perceived themselves as more similar to their fathers than boys who were rated low (Gray, 1959).

A positive father–son relationship gives the boy a basis for successful peer interactions. Rutherford and Mussen (1968) reported evidence showing that nursery school boys who perceive their fathers as warm and nurturant are likely to be generous with other children. Fourth-grade boys in Leiderman's (1953, 1959) study who had high acceptance among their peers had warmer relationships with their fathers than those with low peer acceptance did. Payne and Mussen (1956) found that adolescent boys who were similar to their fathers in responses to the California Psychological Inventory were rated as more friendly by their teachers than boys who had responses markedly different from their fathers.

A study by Mussen et al (1963) also revealed that positive father–son relationships were associated with successful peer interactions and self-confidence among adolescent males. Studying high school boys, Helper (1955) found that boys who perceived themselves as similar to their fathers were likely to be highly accepted by their peers. Lois Hoffman's (1961) results demonstrated that boys from mother-dominant homes had much more difficulty in their peer relationships than boys from father-dominant homes did. Maternal dominance was associated with impulsiveness and an inability to influence peers. On the other hand self-confidence, assertiveness, and overall competence in peer group interaction were related to warm father–son relationships.

For boys the presence of a masculine father, a positive father–son relationship, generally sex-appropriate behavior, and popularity with peers are strongly related. The absence of a warm, affectionate relationship with an adult male, during which mutual enjoyment of sex-typed interests and activities takes place, can seriously interfere with the boy's social development (Biller, 1971a, 1947c).

*Sexual and Marriage Relationships.* A positive father–child relationship can greatly facilitate the boy's security in interacting with females. The boy who has developed a positive masculine self-image has much more confidence in heterosexual interactions. Considerable evidence indicates that the male's adjustment to marriage is related to his relationship with his father and his parents' marital relationship (Barry, 1970).

Difficulty in forming lasting heterosexual relationships often appears to be linked to paternal deprivation. Andrews and Cristensen's (1951) data suggested that college students whose parents had been divorced were likely to have frequent but unstable courtship relationships. Winch (1949, 1950) found that father absence among college males was negatively related to degree of courtship behavior (defined as closeness to marriage). He also reported that a high level of emotional attachment to the mother was negatively related to the degree of courtship behavior. In their interview study Hilgard, Neuman, and Fisk (1960) detected that many men whose fathers had died when they were children continued to be very dependent on their mothers, if their mothers did not remarry. For example, only 1 of the 10 men whose mothers did not remarry seemed to manifest a fair degree of independence in his marital relationship.

Jacobson and Ryder (1969) did an exploratory interview study with young marrieds who suffered the death of a parent before marriage. Husbands losing a father before the age of 12 had a high rate of marriage difficulty. Husbands, father absent early in life, were described as immature and as lacking interpersonal competence. Participation in feminine-type domestic activities and low sexual activity were commonly reported for this group. In general their marriages were relatively devoid of closeness and intimacy. In contrast, when the husbands had lost a father after the age of 12, they were more likely to be involved in positive marriage relationships.

Other researchers have reported evidence showing that individuals who have experienced father absence because of a broken home in childhood are more likely to have their own marriages end in divorce or separation (Landis, 1965; Rohrer & Edmonson, 1960). In many of these situations there is probably a strong modeling effect: children see parents attempting to solve their marital conflicts by ending a marriage and are more likely to behave in a similar fashion themselves. Research by Pettigrew (1964) with lower class blacks is consistent with the supposition that father-absent males frequently have difficulty in their heterosexual relationships. Compared to father-present males, these males were "more likely to be single or divorced—another manifestation of their disturbed sexual identification" (p. 420).

*Homosexuality.* Although no systematic studies have been made of the rates of homosexuality among father-absent males, some investigators have suggested that these males are more prone than father-present males to become homosexual. Both West (1959) and O'Connor (1964) reported that homosexual males more often than neurotic males had histories of long periods of father absence during childhood. The paternally deprived boy's search for a father figure can often be involved in the development of homosexual relationships.

West (1967) presents an excellent review of data pertaining to the antecedents of male homosexuality: Males who as children are father absent or have ineffectual fathers and are involved in an intense, close-binding relationship with their mothers seem particularly prone to develop a homosexual pattern of behavior. A close-binding, sexualized, mother–son relationship seems more common in father-absent than in father-present homes and may, along with related factors, lessen the probability of the boy's entering into meaningful heterosexual relationships. Homosexuals in a significant proportion were discouraged by their mothers during childhood from participating in masculine activities and were often reinforced for feminine behavior (e.g., Bieber et al., 1962; Gundlach, 1969).

There is much evidence that male homosexuals do not develop strong attachments to their fathers. Chang and Block (1960) compared a group of relatively well-adjusted male homosexuals with a heterosexual control group. They found that the homosexuals reported stronger identifications with their mothers and weaker identifications with their fathers. A study by Nash and Hayes (1965) suggests that male homosexuals who take a passive, feminine role in sexual affairs have a particularly weak identification with their fathers and a strong one with their mothers.

Both Bieber et al. (1962) and Evans (1969) found that more fathers of homosexuals than fathers of heterosexuals were described as detached and hostile. Mothers of homosexuals were depicted as closely bound with their sons and relatively uninvolved with their husbands. Bené (1965) reported that more male homosexuals than heterosexuals perceived their fathers as weak and were hostile toward them. Similarly studies by Apperson and McAdoo (1968) and Saghir and Robbins (1973) suggested a pattern of very negative father–child relations during the childhoods of male homosexuals.

A particularly extensive study of the family backgrounds of homosexuals was conducted by Thompson, Schwartz, McCandless, and Edwards (1973). College-age, well-educated homosexuals were recruited through their friends, and their family backgrounds and childhood activities were compared with those of a control group. Homosexual men described very little interaction with their fathers and a relative lack of acceptance by their fathers during their childhoods. The homosexuals generally viewed their fathers as weak, hostile, and rejecting. In general Thompson et al. found the classic male homosexual pattern of paternal deprivation coupled with an overintense mother–child relationship and early avoidance of masculine activities.

Heterosexuals as well as homosexuals who avoided masculine activities in childhood reported more distance from both their fathers and men in general. It may be that the major difference between these homosexuals and heterosexuals was their adolescent sexual experience. For example, opportunities for positive heterosexual relationships may have been more readily available for some of the boys. More homosexuals than heterosexuals described themselves as frail or clumsy during childhood; again there may be mediating constitutional factors in the development of some cases of homosexuality. The data fit well with a hypothesis suggesting that early paternal deprivation makes the individual more vulnerable to certain influences in later development. The particular form of adjustment the paternally deprived male makes is determined by a complex interaction of factors (Biller, 1974c).

## Psychopathology

Much data relating paternal deprivation and childhood maladjustment have already been reviewed. The investigations discussed in this section have generally focused on clinically diagnosed individuals. In most of the studies discussed previously the individuals were grouped according to their test responses, behavior in specific situations, and/or in terms of ratings made by others; they were not clinically diagnosed as having some form of psychopathology and were not being treated at a clinic or hospital. Individuals who are clinically labeled are not, of course, necessarily more psychologically impaired than individuals who have not been clinically diagnosed. Much of the time the major difference is that so-called mentally disturbed individuals have simply come into contact with a mental health facility.

The Becker and Peterson research group has conducted extensive studies to ascertain the association between parental behaviors and specific types of clinically diagnosed psychological disturbance among 6- to 12-year-old children (Becker, Peterson, Hellmer, Shoemaker, & Quay, 1959; Becker, Peterson, Luria, Shoemaker, & Hellmer, 1962; Peterson, Becker, Hellmer, Shoemaker, & Quay, 1959). Children who had conduct problems (problems in impulse control and/or aggressiveness) frequently had dictatorial and controlling fathers. Children who had personality problems (shy, oversensitive, low self-concept) frequently had insensitive and dictatorial fathers.

Block (1969) also attempted to distinguish between the parental characteristics of children in different diagnostic groupings. Although Block's findings were not specifically consistent with the Becker and Peterson studies, a picture of paternal inadequacy as a major factor in childhood psychopathology again emerged. Liverant (1959) found that fathers of disturbed children responded in a much more negative fashion on the MMPI than fathers of nondisturbed children did. The responses of the fathers of disturbed children showed that they were impulsive, anxious, depressed, and concerned with bodily complaints.

*Father-absence.* Garbower (1959), studying children from Navy families, found that those seen for psychiatric problems had more frequent and lengthy periods of father absence than a nondisturbed comparison group did. The fathers of the disturbed children also seemed less sensitive to the effects of their being away from their families. Pedersen (1966) also studied military families. Although he discovered a similar amount of father absence among 11- to 15-year-old boys, irrespective of whether they were referred for psychiatric help, he did find the degree of their psychopathology highly associated with the amount of father absence they had experienced.

Trunnell (1968), studying children at an outpatient clinic, learned that severity of psychopathology varied with the length of father absence and the age of onset of the absence. The longer the absence and the younger the child at the onset of his absence, the more serious the psychopathology. Oltman and Friedman (1967) found particularly high rates of father absence in childhood among adults who had chronically disturbed personalities and inadequate moral development. In addition they found above-average rates of father absence among neurotics and drug addicts. Rosenberg (1969) also reported extremely high rates of frequent father absence in childhood among young alcoholics and drug addicts. Maternal dominance combined with father absence or inadequacy is common in the histories of drug addicts (Chein, Gerrard, Lee, & Rosenfeld, 1964; Wood & Duffy, 1966).

There is a high rate of father loss among patients hospitalized for attempting to commit suicide (e.g., Gay & Tonge, 1967; Robins, Schmidt, & O'Neal, 1957). Other evidence shows that individuals who have been father absent are more likely to exhibit, to a pathological degree, feelings of loss and depressed behavior (e.g., Beck, Sehti, & Tuthill, 1963; Haworth, 1964; Hill & Price, 1967; Keeler, 1954; Travis, 1933).

Brown (1961) and Beck et al. (1963) observed that paternal absence before the age of 4 was highly associated with depression, but other studies have implied that loss of father between the ages of 10 and 14 may also be particularly predisposing to depression (Dennehy, 1966; Hill & Price, 1967). Loss of father due to death may be more strongly related to chronically depressed behavior than is loss of father due to other factors. Methodological flaws, notably the lack of careful controls, limit research concerning father absence and depressed behavior to an heuristic value. For instance, many of the subjects suffering from paternal loss have frequently also had a history of institutionalization.

Brill and Liston (1966) reported that loss of father due to death in childhood was not unusually high among mental patients. However, the frequency of loss of father due to divorce or separation in childhood was much higher for individuals suffering from neurosis, psychosis, or personality disorders than for a number of different comparison groups. Con-

sistent with Brill and Liston's data, father absence due to divorce, separation, or desertion has also been found to be more highly associated with
delinquency (Goode, 1961), maladjustment (Baggett, 1967), low self-
esteem and sexual acting-out (Hetherington, 1972), and cognitive deficits
(Santrock, 1972). Other researchers who have reported that rates of father
absence in childhood are higher among adult patients classified as neurotic
or schizophrenic than among the general population have not done systematic analyses of reason for father absence (e.g., Da Silva, 1963; Ingham,
1949; Madow & Hardy, 1947; Norton, 1952; Oltman, McGarry, &
Friedman, 1952; Wahl, 1954, 1956).

   Gregory (1958, 1965b), critically evaluating many of the relevant
studies, emphasized some of the methodological pitfalls in comparisons
involving the relative incidence of mental illness among father-present and
father-absent individuals. Lack of consideration of the possible effects of
socioeconomic status is a major shortcoming of most of the studies. Cobliner (1963) reported some provocative observations suggesting that father
absence is more apt to be related to serious psychological disturbance in
lower class, as compared to middle-class, individuals. Middle-class families,
particularly with respect to the mother–child relation, may have more
psychological as well as economic resources with which to cope with
paternal deprivation (Biller, 1971a, 1971b, 1974c).

   *Family Interaction Patterns.* Some of the most intriguing, as well as
methodologically sound, studies have provided observations of family
functioning in standardized problem-solving situations. Mishler and Waxler (1968) and Schuham (1970) learned that high paternal involvement in
decision making is uncommon in families in which there is a severely disturbed son. In families with nondisturbed sons, the fathers were most
often the ascendant figures, and mutually acceptable decisions were much
more common (Schuham, 1970).

   In his observational study Alkire (1969) noted that fathers usually dominated in families with normal adolescents but mothers dominated in
families with disturbed adolescents. Other research on interactions among
disturbed families has pointed out several subtypes of inappropriate fathering (McPherson, 1970). Paternal hostility toward the child and mother
and lack of open communication among family members were very common. Leighton, Stollak, and Ferguson (1971) compared the interactions
of families that had disturbed children. In general, fathers in normal
families were in a dominant position and their role was accepted by family
members. In contrast clinic families were usually dominated by mothers,
even though the rest of the family was opposed to and uncomfortable with
this arrangement. Maternal dominance has been associated with a varied
array of psychopathological problems, especially among males (e.g.,

Alkire, 1969; Chein et al., 1964; Gassner & Murray, 1969; Lidz, Parker, & Cornelison, 1956; Schuham, 1970; Westley and Epstein, 1970).

Many investigators have, however, found evidence indicating that overly dominant fathers can have just as negative an effect on their child's development as overly dominant mothers can. Researchers have reported much data relating arbitrary paternal power assertion and overcontrol to poor adjustment and psychopathology among children (e.g., Ferreira, Winter, & Poindexter, 1966; Rubenstein & Levitt, 1957; Trapp & Kausler, 1958).

The degree of husband–wife dominance may not be a particularly good indication of degree of paternal deprivation, except where there is extreme maternal dominance. Extreme paternal dominance, which is indicative of inadequate fathering, squelches the development of independence and competence in the child as much as extreme maternal dominance does.

Adequate personality development seems to be facilitated in families in which the father clearly represents a positive masculine role and the mother a positive feminine role. Kayton, and I (1971) studied matched groups of nondisturbed, neurotic, paranoid schizophrenic, and nonparanoid schizophrenic adult males. We discovered that the nondisturbed subjects perceived their parents as exhibiting sex-appropriate behaviors to a greater extent than the disturbed subjects did. A smaller proportion of individuals in the disturbed groups viewed their fathers as possessing masculine–instrumental traits, and particularly among the schizophrenic groups, their mothers as having feminine–expressive characteristics. Severely disturbed behavior is often associated with difficulties and/or abnormalities in sex-role development (e.g., Biller, 1973; Biller & Poey, 1969; Heilbrun, 1974; Kayton & Biller, 1972; McClelland & Watt, 1968).

*Types of Paternal Deprivation.* Some data suggest that boys from father-absent homes are in many cases less retarded in their personality development than boys from intact, maternally dominated homes are (Biller, 1968a; Reuter & Biller, 1973). In Nye's (1957) study children from broken homes had better family adjustments and lower rates of anti-social behavior and psychosomatic illness than children from unhappy, unbroken homes had. Other research has also suggested that a child may function more nearly adequately in a father-absent home than in one in which there is an inappropriate husband–wife relationship (e.g., Benson, 1968; Landis, 1962).

Father-absent children may be more influenced by factors outside the home than children from intact but unhappy and/or maternally dominated homes are. Some children may be particularly affected by attention from an adult male because of their intense feelings of paternal deprivatino. Children with inadequate fathers often become resigned to their situation. For example, the father-present, but maternally dominated, child is liable to develop a view of men as ineffectual, especially if his father is continually being controlled by his mother. In contrast the father-absent child may develop a much more flexible view of adult male behavior.

Research described in this section and in other sections points out that inadequate fathering and/or father absence predisposes children toward certain developmental deficits. There are, however, many paternally deprived children who are generally well-adjusted. Such children should be more carefully studied, to determine why they differ from less well-adjusted, paternally deprived children. Investigators should consider both the type of child maladjustment and the type of family inadequacy.

On the other hand extremely severe psychopathology such as autism or childhood schizophrenia does not develop simply as a function of disturbed parent–child relationships. The child's genetic and/or constitutional predispositions play an important part in determining the severity of his psychopathology as well as the quality of parent–child interactions. Most children are handicapped if they have experienced paternal deprivation or inadequacy, and they are likely to have much difficulty in their emotional and interpersonal development. But in the great majority of cases insufficient or inappropriate fathering (and/or mothering) per se does not account for children who are unable to develop basic communication skills and to form interpersonal attachments. For example, the child's neurological malfunctioning or extreme temperamentally related hypersensitivity or hyposensitivity can make it very difficult for the parent to respond in a positive manner. In some cases constitutionally atypical children contribute to the development of psychopathology in their parents (Biller, 1974c).

## THE FATHER AND FEMALE PERSONALITY DEVELOPMENT

In this section data are reviewed that show that the father–daughter relationship has important effects on the female's personality development. The influences of variations in fathering and of paternal deprivation with respect to the girl's emotional development and social and sexual interactions are emphasized.

### Feminine Development

There has been a marked tendency to define femininity in negative terms and/or as the opposite of masculinity; for instance, a stress on passivity and dependency (e.g., Salzman, 1967). Traditional femininity has often been negatively associated with adjustment (Bardwick, 1971; Johnson, 1963). But since a focus of the present discussion is on ways in which the father can facilitate his daughter's personality development, it is relevant to analyze elements of femininity that are related to psychological adjustment rather than maladjustment. It is meaningful to define feminine behavior in positive terms; for example, femininity in social interaction can be related to skill in interpersonal communication, expressiveness, warmth, and sensitivity to the needs of others (Biller, 1971a; Biller & Weiss, 1970).

Femininity, according to the present definition, is based on a positive feeling about being a female and a particular patterning of interpersonal behavior. Whether or not a woman enjoys housework or chooses a career should not be used as the ultimate criterion in assessing her femininity. Women who possess both positive feminine and positive masculine characteristics and secure sex-role orientations are most able to actualize their potential. Women who have pride in their femininity and are independent and assertive as well as nurturant and sensitive are likely to achieve interpersonal and creative fulfillment (Biller, 1971a, 1974c; Biller & Meredith, 1974).

The girl's feminine development is much influenced by how the father differentiates his "masculine" role from her "feminine" role and what type of behavior he considers appropriate for his daughter. Mussen and Rutherford (1963) found that fathers of highly feminine girls encouraged their daughters more in sex-typed activities than fathers of unfeminine girls did. These investigators suggested that masculine fathers who actively encourage and appreciate femininity in girls are particularly able to facilitate their daughter's sex-role development. Similarly, in their study with nursery school children, Sears et al. (1965) reported a significant correlation between girls' femininity and their fathers' expectations of their participation in feminine activities.

In an examination of the familial antecedents of sex-role behavior Heilbrun (1965b) concluded that fathers are more proficient than mothers in differentiating between their male and female children. He emphasized that "fathers are more capable of responding expressively than mothers are of acting instrumentally . . . that fathers systematically vary their sex role as they relate to male and female offspring" (p. 796). He found that daughters who perceive themselves as feminine, as well as sons who perceive themselves as masculine, are likely to view their fathers as masculine.

Goodenough's (1957) results support the view that fathers influence their children's sex-role development more than mothers do. Focusing on the influence of the parents in determining the social interests of nursery school children, she learned that ". . . the father has a greater interest in sex differences than the mother and hence exerts stronger influence in general sex-typing" (p. 321); for example, there was much more paternal encouragement for girls to develop skills in social interaction. Much paternal emphasis on sex-role differentiation was also noted in a study by Aberle and Naegele (1952). Differences in parent–child interactions are a function of the sex of the child as well as of the sex of the parent (e.g., Bronfenbrenner, 1961; Papenek, 1969; Sutton-Smith & Rosenberg, 1970; Rothbart & Maccoby, 1966).

Tasch (1952, 1955), interviewing fathers of boys and girls to learn about their conceptions of the paternal role, reported much evidence of paternal differentiation in terms of sex of child. Fathers viewed their daughters as more delicate and sensitive than their sons. Fathers used physical punishment more frequently with their sons than with their daughters. Fathers tended to define household tasks in terms of their sex-appropriateness. For example, they expected girls to iron and wash clothes and baby-sit for siblings, while boys were expected to be responsible for taking out the garbage and helping their fathers in activities involving mechanical and physical competence. Unfortunately fathers often have rigid sex-role sterotypes, and in their zeal to "feminize" females, they actively discourage the development of intellectual and physical competence in their daughters (Biller & Meredith, 1974).

Nevertheless the child is not merely a passive recipient of familial and sociocultural influences. As has been stressed in earlier sections of this chapter, the child's constitutional predispositions can play a very important part in influencing parent–child and environmental interactions. For example, the young girl who is temperamentally responsive to social interaction and is very attractive may make it especially easy for her father to encourage her positive feminine development. Similarly, if the girl facially and physically resembles a highly feminine mother, the father is likely to treat her as a female. On the other hand, the girl who is physically large and unattractive may be perceived as unfeminine by her father. The father may reject his daughter if she does not fit his conception of the physical characteristics of femininity. If the father does not have a son, and his daughter is particularly vigorous and well-coordinated, he may tend to treat her as if she were a boy (Biller, 1971a, 1974c).

## Personal and Social Adjustment

When the father is not involved in the family, his daughter is likely to have problems in her sex-role and personality development. Hoffman (1961) found that girls from mother-dominant homes had difficulty relating to males and were disliked by boys. Hetherington (1965) did not, however, find a clear-cut association between parental dominance and girl's sex-role preferences, although girls with dominant fathers were much more likely to imitate them and to be similar to them than girls with dominant mothers were. Other studies are also consistent with the supposition that paternal dominance is a less influential factor for girls than it is for boys (Biller, 1969c; Hetherington & Frankie, 1967).

My results suggested that the girls' feminine development is facilitated if the mother is seen as a generally salient controller of resources (Biller, 1969c). Kindergarten-age girls perceived their fathers as more competent and more as decision makers, their mothers more as limit setters, and both parents as similar in nurturance. I found a subgroup of girls whose femininity scores were low and who perceived their mothers as relatively high as decision makers and limit setters but as quite low in nurturance and competence. In most cases at least a moderate level of paternal involvement in decision making seemed important in the girl's feminine development.

Zung and I reported data suggesting that very strong maternal control and dominance hampers girls' as well as boys' personality development (Biller & Zung, 1972). We noted that high maternal control and intrusiveness was associated with sex-role conflict and anxiety among elementary school girls. For girls the optimal level of paternal dominance may be moderate, allowing the mother to be viewed also as a "salient controller of resources" but in a general context of paternal involvement. It is important that the girl perceive her father as competent and as appreciating her behavior, even if she does not perceive him as the dominant parent.

An investigation by Fish and myself (1973) suggests that the father plays a particularly important role in the girl's personality adjustment. College females' perceptions of their relationships with their fathers during childhood were assessed by means of an extensive family background questionnaire. Subjects who perceived their fathers as having been very nurturant and positively interested in them scored high on the Adjective Check List personal adjustment scale. In contrast subjects who perceived their fathers as having been rejecting scored very low on the personal adjustment measure. Findings from other investigations have also pointed to the influence of positive paternal involvement in the girl's interpersonal adjustment (e.g., Baumrind & Black, 1967; Torgoff & Dreyer, 1961).

Block's (1971) analysis of data collected from the Berkeley Longitudinal Study highlights the importance of both the father–daughter and father–mother relationships in the quality of the female's personality functioning. For example, the females who were the best adjusted as adults grew up in homes with two positively involved parents. Their mothers were described as affectionate, personable, and resourceful and their fathers as warm, competent, and firm. A second group of relatively well-adjusted females came from homes with extremely bright, capable, and ambitious mothers but rather passive yet warm fathers. In contrast poorly adjusted females were likely to have been reared in homes where either one or both parents were very inadequate. Even though they represented a wide range of personality adaptations, the poorly adjusted women were likely to have come from homes where there was little opportunity to view a positive father–mother relationship.

The most well-adjusted females in the longitudinal study by Block et al. (1973) tended to come from homes where both parents had been positively involved with them. Their fathers were described as warm and accepting, and their mothers appeared to be oriented toward rationality, achievement, and intellectual attainment. A variety of complex family patterns emerged among the less well-adjusted females, but it was clear that few if any had family backgrounds marked by a combination of a compatible father–mother relationship and a positively involved father.

## Marital and Sexual Adjustment

Many women choose to pursue a full-time career rather than marriage because of very realistic factors, such as self-fulfillment and economic need. The choice of a career is sometimes, however, motivated by a fearful avoidance of marriage. Unmarried career women often have much underlying sex-role conflict (Levin, 1966). In Rushing's (1964) study with adolescents, girls who reported satisfactory relationships with their fathers were less likely to give priority to a career than those were who had unsatisfactory relationships with their fathers. When a girl is continually frustrated in her interactions with her father, she may develop a negative attitude toward close relationships with men and marriage. White (1959) compared the self-concepts and familial backgrounds of women whose interests focused on marriage and childrearing with those whose interests revolved around a career. More of the women interested in marriage appeared to have close relationships with both parents and to be comfortable in their self-concepts. More of the women interested in careers came from homes in which the father had died or in which there was inadequate parent–child communication.

Of course, one problem with such studies is that they do not include a group of women interested both in careers and in marriage and childrearing. Women who can comfortably pursue their occupational interests and develop their intellectual competence as well as be successful wives and mothers are more likely to have come from homes in which both parents were positively involved.

Findings from a study by Block et al. (1973) suggest how difficult it is for a female to get the necessary family support to develop into a well-rounded, secure, and competent adult. It is striking that few fathers tended to be adequately involved with their daughters and to encourage both a positive feminine self-concept and instrumental competence. Again many of these problems seem associated with our overly rigid sex typing and negative definition of feminine behavior. Gradually increasing flexibility in sex roles should lead to more and more women having a positive, feminine self-concept as well as a wide range of competencies and a successful, fufilling career (Biller & Meredith, 1974).

Other data reveal the significant consequences that the father–daughter relationship can have on marriage. In Winch's (1949, 1950) questionnaire study of college students females who had long-term romantic attachments (who appeared near marriage) reported closer relationships with their fathers than females who did not have serious heterosexual involvements. Luckey (1960) reported that women who were satisfied with their marriages perceived their husbands as more similar to their fathers than women who were not satisfied in their marriages. The female's ability to have a successful marriage is increased when she has experienced a warm, affectionate relationship with a father who has encouraged her positive feminine development. In questionnaire studies with female students we found a strong association between the students' perceived relationships with their fathers during childhood and their marital adjustments. Divorce, separation, and unhappy marriages were much higher among women reporting that they had been father absent or had had poor or very infrequent interactions with their fathers (Biller, 1974c).

Fisher (1973) presented evidence that paternal deprivation in early childhood is associated with infrequent orgasms among married women. He and his co-workers studied the sexual feelings and fantasies of almost 300 middle-class married women. The women were well-educated volunteers, most of them married to graduate students and in their early and middle 20s. An extensive array of assessment procedures, including interviews, questionnaires, and projective techniques, was used. The limited representativeness of Fisher's sample could be questioned, but his results do seem very consistent with other data about the father's general impact on the female's sexual development.

A central theme emerging from the low-orgasmic women was their lack of meaningful relationships with their fathers. There was a high incidence of early loss and of frequent separation from the father among the low-orgasmic group. These women were more preoccupied with fear of loss of control than high-orgasmic women were, and this was associated with their lack of security and lack of trust in their fathers during childhood. They more often saw themselves as lacking dependable relationships with their fathers.

Questionnaire data revealed that the lower a woman's orgasmic capacity, the more likely she was to report that her father treated her in a laissez-faire manner. Low-orgasmic women described uninvolved fathers who did not have well-defined expectations or rules for their daughters. They also described much physical and psychological father absence during early childhood. In contrast high-orgasmic women were more likely to perceive their fathers as having had definite and demanding expectations and a concern for their enforcement. Fisher continually emphasized that his findings reveal that the father is much more important in the development of orgasmic adequacy in females than the mother is.

Inappropriate and/or inadequate fathering is a major factor in the development of homosexuality in females as well as in males. Bené (1965) reported that female homosexuals felt their fathers were weak and incompetent. The homosexual women were more hostile toward and afraid of their fathers than the heterosexual women were. Kaye et al. (1967), analyzing background data on homosexual women in psychoanalysis, discovered that the fathers of the homosexual women (as compared to the fathers of women in a heterosexual control group) tended to be puritanical, exploitative, and feared by their daughters as well as possessive and infantalizing. They also presented evidence that female homosexuality is associated with rejection of femininity early in life. In another study lesbians described their fathers as less involved and affectionate than heterosexual women did (Gundlach & Reiss, 1968). In general the lesbians described their fathers as acting like strangers toward them. Other researchers have also found that girls who feel devalued and rejected by their fathers are more likely to become homosexual than girls are whose fathers are warm and accepting (e.g., Hamilton, 1929; West, 1967).

College-age, well-educated female homosexuals were recruited by their friends in a study by Thompson et al. (1973). Compared to a control group of female heterosexuals, the female homosexuals indicated that they were less accepting of their fathers and their femininity during early childhood. There was also some evidence that they perceived their fathers as more detached, weak, and hostile toward them. In general, available research has suggested that inadequate fathering is more of a factor in the development of female homosexuality than inadequate mothering is. Note also the general similarity in negative father–child relations among female and male homosexuals. Paternal deprivation makes the individual more vulnerable to difficulties in sexual development, but again it is only one of many factors that determine the type of adjustment an adult will make (Biller, 1974c).

## Father Absence

Some data suggest that females are less affected by father absence than males are (e.g., Bach, 1946; Lessing, Zagorin, & Nelson, 1970; Lynn & Sawrey, 1959; Santrock, 1972; Winch, 1950). There is, however, other research supporting the conclusion that girls are at least as much influenced in their social and heterosexual development by father absence as boys are (e.g., Biller, 1971a, 1974c; Biller & Weiss, 1970; Hetherington, 1972). The extent and direction of the differential impact of father absence on males and females probably varies with respect to which dimensions of personality development are considered.

Father absence can interfere with the girl's feminine development and her overall heterosexual adjustment. In Seward's (1945) study women who rejected the feminine role of wife and mother were more likely to come from broken homes than women were who accepted these roles. White (1959) reported similar data. Landy, Rosenberg, and Sutton-Smith's (1967) results also suggest that, among college females, father absence during adolescence is sometimes associated with a rejection of feminine interests. Although she studied father-present females, Fish's (1969) data also seem relevant. College females who reported that their fathers spent more time with them during their childhood had less feminine self-concepts than those did who reported moderate or high father availability. Anthropological evidence also suggests that low father availability is associated with sex-role conflicts for girls as well as boys (Brown, 1963; Stephens, 1962).

In Jacobson and Ryder's (1969) interview study many women who had been father–absent early in life complained of difficulties in achieving satisfactory sexual relationships with their husbands. Lack of opportunity to observe meaningful male–female relationships in childhood can make it much more difficult for the father-absent female to develop the interpersonal skills necessary for adequate heterosexual adjustment. Case studies of father-absent girls are often filled with details of problems (particularly sexual ones) in interactions with males (e.g., Leonard, 1966; Neubauer, 1960).

Other findings suggest, however, that father-absent girls are not usually inhibited in their development of sex-typed interests or perceptions of the incentive value of the feminine role (Hetherington, 1972; Lynn & Sawrey, 1959; Santrock, 1970a). In fact, in a study with disadvantaged black children, Santrock (1970a) found a tendency for father-absent girls to be more feminine on a doll play sex-role measure than father-present girls were; a very high level of femininity may be associated with a rigid sex-role development that devalues males and masculine activities. In many cases father absence seems to have more effect on the girl's ability to function in interpersonal and heterosexual relationships than it does on her sex-role preference.

The father-absent girl may have difficulty in dealing with her aggressive impulses. In their study of doll play behavior, Sears et al. (1946) found "no indication that the girls are more frustrated when the father is present; on the contrary, his absence is associated with greater aggression, especially self-aggression" (p. 240). These investigators speculated that a high degree of aggressive doll play may be a function of the father-absent girl's conflict with her mother. In a clinical study Heckel (1963) observed frequent school maladjustment, excessive sexual interest, and social acting-out behavior in five fatherless preadolescent girls. Other investigators have also detected a high incidence of delinquent behavior among lower class father-absent girls (Monahan, 1957; Toby, 1957). Such acting-out behavior may manifest frustration associated with the girl's unsuccessful attempts to find a meaningful relationship with an adult male. Father absence appears to increase the probability that a girl will experience difficulties in interpersonal adjustment. Many studies referred to in previous sections suggested that father-absent children are likely to have emotional and social problems, but one difficulty in interpreting many of them is that they do not differentiate between boys and girls in data analyses.

The devaluation of maleness and masculinity, so prevalent in paternally deprived, matrifocal families, adversely affects many girls as well as boys (Biller, 1974c). Children in lower class families often do not have opportunities to interact with adequate fathers. In lower class families father–daughter relationships are generally inadequate. The father may be very punitive and express little affection toward his daughter (Elder & Bowerman, 1963). Many investigators have observed that lower class girls develop derogatory attitudes toward males in families in which the father is absent or ineffectual (e.g., Pettigrew, 1964; Rohrer & Edmonson, 1960).

The downgrading of males in terms of their seeming social and economic irresponsibility is common among lower class black families. Negative attitudes toward males are transmitted by mothers, grandmothers, and other significant females and, unfortunately, are often strengthened by the child's observation of or involvement in, destructive male–female relationships. Paternal deprivation and devaluation of the male role are major factors in the lower class females' frequent difficulties in interacting with their male relatives, boyfriends, husbands, and children. Maternally based households seem to become like family heirlooms—passed from generation to generation (Moynihan, 1965; Rohrer & Edmonson, 1960).

The most nearly comprehensive and the best controlled study of father absence and the girl's development was conducted by Hetherington (1972).

Her subjects were adolescent, lower middle-class girls (ages 13 to 17) who regularly attended a community recreation center. She was particularly interested in the possible differential effects of father absence due to divorce or death of the father. She compared three groups of girls: those whose fathers were absent because of divorce and who had had no contact with them since the divorce, those whose fathers were absent because of death, and those with both parents living at home. She was careful to control for sibling variables (all the girls were firstborns without brothers), and none of the father-absent children had any adult males living in their homes after separation from the father.

The most striking observation was that both groups of father-absent girls had great difficulty in interacting comfortably with men and male peers. Hetherington discovered that the difficulties were manifested differently for the daughters of divorcees than for the daughters of widows. The daughters of widows tended to be extremely shy and timid in interacting with males. Although their behavior was very different, both of the father-absent groups reported that they were very insecure with males. In contrast all three groups of girls generally appeared to have appropriate interactions with their mothers and with female adults and peers. One of the exceptions was that the father-absent girls seemed more dependent on women, an observation consistent with Lynn and Sawrey's (1959) findings of increased mother dependency among father-separated girls.

Observations at the recreation center revealed that, compared with the other girls, daughters of divorcées sought more attention from men and tried to be near and have physical contacts with male peers. On the other hand, the daughters of widows avoided proximity to males and much preferred to be with females. Compared to other girls the daughters of widows reported less heterosexual activity, the daughters of divorcées, more.

With male interviewers the daughters of widows sat as far away as possible, whereas the daughters of divorcées tended to sit as close as possible. (The girls from intact families generally sat at an intermediate distance.) Daughters of widows also showed avoidance behavior in their postures during interactions with male interviewers; they often sat stiffly upright, leaned backward, kept their legs together, and showed little eye contact. In contrast the daughters of divorcées tended to sprawl in their chairs, have an open leg posture, lean slightly forward, and exhibit much eye contact and smiling. Nelsen and Vangen (1971) also found that, among lower class eighth-grade black girls, those who were father absent because of divorce or separation were more precocious in their dating behavior and in their knowledge of sex than father-present girls were. They speculated that when the father is in the home he is an important limit setter for the girl's sexual behavior and that when he is absent there is a great decrease in parental control.

Hetherington generally noted that girls had the most difficulties in their heterosexual interactions when their father absence began before the age of 5. Early father separation was usually more associated with inappropriate behavior with males than father absence after the age of 5 was, although differences were not significant for every measure. Early father absence was also associated with more maternal overprotection than father absence after the age of 5 was. Other evidence indicates that early father absence is more associated with maternal overprotection than father absence beginning later in the child's life is (e.g., Biller, 1969b; Biller & Bahm, 1971).

Additional data in Hetherington's study emphasize the importance of taking into account the context of, and reason for, father absence. Daughters of widows recalled more positive relationships with their fathers and described them as warmer and more competent than daughters of divorcées did. The divorced mothers also painted a very negative picture of their marriages and ex-husbands. Daughters of divorcées were quite low in self-esteem, but daughters of widows did not differ significantly in their self-esteem from daughters from father-present homes. Nevertheless both groups of father-absent girls had less feelings of control over their lives and more anxiety than father-present girls did.

## Inadequate Fathering

The father–mother interaction can have much impact on the child's personality development. Family stability and cohesiveness help to provide a positive atmosphere for the developing child. An inadequate father is often also an inadequate husband. The father may influence his daughter's personality development indirectly in terms of his relationship with his wife. If the father meets his wife's needs, she may, in turn, be able to interact more adequately with her children. Bartemeier (1953) emphasized that the wife's capacity for appropriately nurturing her children, and her general psychological adjustment, are much influenced by her relationship with her husband. A number of investigations have suggested that a warm and nurturant mother–daughter relationship is important in positive feminine development (e.g., Hetherington, 1965; Hetherington & Frankie, 1967; Mussen & Parker, 1965; Mussen & Rutherford, 1963).

Inadequate fathering or mothering is frequently a reflection of difficulties in the husband–wife relationship, difficulties that may be particularly apparent in the husband's and wife's inability to provide one another adequately with affection and sexual satisfaction. The parents' interpersonal problems are usually reflected in their interactions with their children and in their children's adjustment. For example, clinical studies have revealed that difficulties in parental sexual adjustment, combined with overrestrictive parental attitudes, are often associated with incestuous and acting-out behavior among adolescent females (e.g., Kaufman, Peck & Tagiuri, 1954; Robey, Rosenwald, Snell, & Lee, 1964).

Severe marital conflict can have a disorganizing effect on both paternal and maternal behavior. Baruch and Wilcox's (1944) results showed that marital conflict negatively influences the personality development of both boys and girls. Some of their data implied that girls can be even more handicapped than boys. Girls may suffer more because of their interpersonal sensitivity. Some research points out that familial factors seem to have more impact on girls' than on boys' personality development (Lynn, 1969, 1974).

*Father Imitation.* Sopchak (1952) and Lazowick (1955) presented data supporting the proposition that inadequate fathering is related to the development of psychological problems among females. Lazowick (1955) noted that lack of identification with the father was related to a high degree of manifest anxiety among undergraduate women. Sopchak (1952) also studied college students and reported that:

Women with tendencies toward abnormality as measured by the MMPI show a lack of identification with their fathers. . . . Masculine women identify with their fathers less than feminine women . . . and identification with the father is more important in producing normal adjustment than is identification with the mother (pp. 164–165).

The well-adjusted female's identification with her father seems to involve understanding and empathizing with the father rather than rejecting her basic femininity and wishing she were a male. A positive father identification may also include the sharing of many paternal values and attitudes, as long as there is no interference with the girl's development of a feminine self-concept and an expressive mode of social interaction (Biller, 1971a; Biller & Weiss, 1970).

Wright and Tuska (1966) compared college women who rated themselves as very feminine with those who rated themselves as only slightly feminine, or masculine. The highly feminine women had more favorable conceptions of their fathers, whereas the unfeminine women seemed to have engaged in more imitation of their fathers' masculine behaviors. The investigators speculated that the masculine women coped with frustrating relationships with their mothers by imitating their fathers, whereas the feminine women adopted expressive role behavior by imitating their mothers' interactions with their fathers.

Poffenberger (1959) described some of the adverse effects of paternal rejection on the child's self-concept and general attitude toward life. Case studies illustrate how fathers who do not accept their daughters' femininity can have very destructive effects on their daughters' personality development (e.g., Neubauer, 1960; West, 1967). The father who wants his daughter to be the son he never had, or the father who cannot cope with feminine behavior, may compulsively reinforce his daughter's rejection of her femininity. Difficulties in the husband–wife relationship that center around sexual interactions are particularly common in such families.

If she receives adequate fathering, the probability of a girl's compulsively imitating the father's behaviors and/or spurning her femininity seems high only if the mother is cold and rejecting or if she is somehow unable to express acceptance, warmth, and nurturance toward her daughter (Biller, 1971a). When the father plays an active and competent masculine role in the family, his daughter is likely to imitate his non-sextyped positive attributes and develop a broad, adaptive cognitive and interpersonal behavioral repertoire. If the father is inadequate, his daughter may be generally limited in her social experience and not be able to develop fully her intellectual and interpersonal competence. These speculations appear to integrate and make more intelligible the results of a number of diverse studies (e.g., Beier & Ratzeburg, 1953; Carpenter & Eisenberg, 1935; Gray, 1959; Mussen & Rutherford, 1963).

Some data indicate that the father–daughter relationship may influence a girl's cognitive and academic functioning. For example, father-absent girls have sometimes been found to perform more poorly on intelligence and achievement tests than father-present girls. On the other hand, high paternal expectations in the context of a positive father–daughter relationship have been found to facilitate the girl's development of independence, assertiveness, and other personality characteristics that can help her maximize her intellectual and career success (Biller, 1974c; Biller & Meredith, 1974; Crandall, Dewey, Katkovsky, & Preston, 1964).

*Severe Psychopathology.* Paternal inadequacy can be a factor in the development of severe psychopathology in the female as well as in the male child. Unfortunately many of the studies examining the influence of paternal deprivation on childhood psychopathology reviewed earlier did not include female children or did not take the sex of the child into account in data analyses. There is, however, some research that focuses on—or specifically includes—females.

In their extensive studies Lidz et al. (1956) reported a high incidence of inadequate fathering for female as well as male schizophrenics. The fathers of the schizophrenic females were frequently observed to be in severe conflict with their wives, to contradict their wives' decisions, and to degrade their wives in front of their daughters. These fathers made rigid and unrealistic demands on their wives. Similarly such fathers were insensitive to their daughters' needs to develop an independent self-concept. The fathers of the schizophrenic females made attempts to manipulate and mold their daughters in terms of their own unrealistic needs. Females who formed an allegiance with a disturbed father, frequently in reaction to rejection by an unloving mother, seemed most likely to become psychotic.

Hamilton and Wahl (1948) found that almost 75% of the hospitalized schizophrenic women they studied had experienced some inadequacy of fathering in childhood. Prolonged father absence, paternal rejection, and paternal abuse were very common. Baker and Holzworth (1961) compared a group of male and female adolescents hospitalized for psychological disturbances with a group who were successful in their interpersonal and school adjustments. The fathers of the hospitalized group were more likely to have had social histories involving court convictions and excessive drinking than the fathers of the successful adolescents were.

Variations in sociocultural background may, however, be a primary factor contributing to such findings. For example, both criminal convictions and commitment to state hospitals are more frequent for lower class than for middle-class individuals. The general economic and social deprivation that lower class children experience seems to exacerbate the effects of paternal deprivation.

Severe psychopathology is also often related to the child's constitutional predispositions and does not usually develop simply as a function of disturbed parent–child relationships. For example, the girl who is temperamentally unresponsive to affection may negatively reinforce her father's attempts to form a positive relationship with her. Similarly, if a little girl is extremely hyperactive and aggressive, it may be very difficult for her father to relate to her.

## PRACTICAL IMPLICATIONS

In discussing the influence of the father on sex role and personality development I have summarized a massive body of relevant research and have put forth a great many interpretations, generalizations, and speculations. This final section is a brief attempt to look at what is being done, or could be done, to counteract and prevent paternal deprivation.

## Therapy

Since paternally deprived individuals are overrepresented among individuals with psychological problems, it is not surprising that they are found in abundance in the case reports of psychotherapists. Despite the lack of controlled research, there are many illuminating descriptions of how psychotherapists have attempted to help father-absent or inadequately fathered children (e.g., Crumley & Blumenthal, 1973; Forrest, 1966; Green, 1974; Meerloo, 1956; Neubauer, 1960; Wylie & Delgado, 1959).

Unfortunately the emphasis on the mother–child relationship in most child psychotherapy has usually obscured the father's role, even when the father is an integral part of the family. The father should be encouraged to participate in the assessment and treatment of the child's problem. In many cases the father's participation can be made a condition for helping the family. The importance of the father to the family and his potential for positively affecting his child should be stressed in making such demands. Even if the child's problems do not stem from inadequate fathering, the father's active involvement may do much to improve the situation. If a child has been paternally deprived, a family difficulty may provide the opportunity for getting the father more integrated into the family (Biller & Meredith, 1974). It is striking how many well-meaning fathers are relatively peripheral members of their families. Many difficulties that children and mothers experience can be quickly remedied or mitigated if ways in which the father can become a more active participant are clearly communicated to the family. Much of the success of family therapy is due to the inclusion of the father (e.g., Ackerman, 1966; Forrest, 1969; Green, 1974; Haley & Hoffman, 1967).

A child's problems, if not directly a result of family interactions, can be exacerbated by the family's reaction to them. Treating the father, mother, child, and other relevant family members as a group allows the therapist to observe both strengths and difficulties in family interactions. Valuable time can be saved and a more accurate understanding achieved by observing family behavior directly rather than by inferring how the family interacts from comments made separately by the child or his parents.

The application of modeling and related behavior modification techniques, such as those described by Bandura (1969), is a particularly meaningful course to explore in individual, group, and family therapy with paternally deprived children. The probability of successful treatment can be greatly increased if knowledge about positive fathering is integrated into the psychotherapy process. For example, the therapist can demonstrate appropriate paternal behaviors in his interactions with the family; however, the therapist must be careful to support the father's strengths and not undermine his effectiveness by unwittingly competing with him.

The therapist can explicitly model ways in which a father can communicate to his wife and his children. Having both a male and female therapist provides even more explicit examples of appropriate male–female interactions for the family to observe. Role-playing for family members is very helpful in teaching and reinforcing effective behavior patterns. Of course, any attempt to modify the family's functioning should take into account their previous modes of interaction and their sociocultural background. It is important that the family's environment be considered in treatment. Observing and modifying the family's behavior is often more meaningful when it is done in their own home rather than in the therapist's office (Biller, 1974c).

## Father Substitutes

The availability of father surrogates is important for father-present children with inadequate fathers, as well as for father-absent children. Many paternally deprived children have very effective father surrogates in their own families or find an adequate role model among teachers or older peers. Older, well-adjusted boys can be very salient and influential models for younger, paternally deprived children. When it is impossible or impractical to deal with the child's father, therapists can strengthen their impact on the father-absent or paternally disadvantaged child by also working with the child's actual or potential father surrogate. This could be accomplished by consultation, but engaging the father surrogate and child in joint sessions (or in groups with other children and father surrogates) can be even more beneficial.

The Gluecks (1950) reported that many delinquent boys who form a close relationship with a father surrogate resolve their antisocial tendencies. Similarly Trenaman (1952) observed that young men who had been chronically delinquent while serving in the British Army improved as a function of their relationships with father surrogates. A father-absent child may be particularly responsive to a male therapist or role model because of his motivation for male companionship. Rexford (1964), in describing the treatment of young antisocial children, noted that therapists are more likely to be successful with father-absent boys than with boys who have strongly identified with an emotionally disturbed, criminal, or generally inadequate father.

There are many organizations, including Big Brothers, YMCA, Boy Scouts, athletic teams, camps, churches, and settlement houses, that provide paternally deprived children with meaningful father surrogates. Additional professional consultation and more community support (especially more father surrogates) would allow these organizations to be of even greater benefit to many more children.

Available research points out that, even in the first few years of life, the child's personality development can be very much influenced by the degree and type of involvement of a father or father surrogate. Group settings such as day care centers can be used as vehicles to provide father surrogates for many children (both boys and girls). The facilities of organizations such as Big Brothers and the YMCA could also be used to help younger children.

## Community Mental Health

Children confined to institutions are especially in need of warm relationships with competent father surrogates. Institutionalized children, including the orphaned or emotionally disturbed, can benefit from a larger proportion of interaction with adult males. For example, Nash's (1965) data suggest that having institutionalized children live in a situation in which they are cared for and supervised by a husband–wife team is beneficial for their sex-role development. Many of the same variables involved in children's social learning and imitation within the family setting are important to consider in an analysis of the impact of child care workers in residential settings (Portnoy, Biller, & Davids, 1972).

Fathers, mothers, and father surrogates can be made more aware of the significance of the father in child development through education and the mass media (Biller & Meredith, 1972, 1974). Explicit advantages such as financial and other support for fathers remaining with their families, in contrast to the current rewarding of father absence by many welfare departments, might do much to keep some families intact and to reconstitute other families. Tuck (1971) described a fascinating community program that led to the greater involvement of lower class fathers with their children and neighborhood.

Preventive programs can focus on families that seem to have a high risk of becoming father absent. Systematic techniques can be developed to determine the potential consequences of father absence for a family where separation or divorce is being contemplated. There are many families in which both the parents and the children would benefit from divorce. When the divorce process is taking place, more consideration should be given to whether all or some of the children might benefit from remaining with their father. It is usually easier to find mother surrogates (e.g., grandmothers, housekeepers) then to find father surrogates. It is also relevant to consider potential paternal effectiveness in placing children with adoptive or foster parents (Biller & Meredith, 1974).

The mother in the paternally deprived family must not be neglected. For example, the mother's reaction to husband absence may greatly influence the extent to which father absence or lack of father availability affects her children. She is often in need of psychological as well as social and economic support. Mental health professionals have outlined many useful techniques for helping mothers and children in fatherless families (e.g., Baker, Cove, Fagen, Fischer, & Janda, 1968; Despert, 1957; Hill, 1949; Jones, 1963; Klein, 1973; Lerner, 1954; McDermott, 1968; Wylie & Delgado, 1959).

In a pilot project one of the central goals of a welfare mother's group was to help husbandless mothers deal constructively with their social and familial problems (Biller & Smith, 1972). Pollak (1970) discussed the frequent interpersonal and sexual problems of parents without partners and gave some excellent suggestions for helping such parents cope with their concerns. Education and therapeutic groups such as "Parents without Partners" can be very meaningful for the wifeless father as well as the husbandless mother (e.g., Egelson & Frank, 1961; Freudenthal, 1959; Schlesinger, 1966).

A significant dimension of community mental health efforts, in terms of both prevention and treatment, should be supplying father surrogates to groups of paternally deprived children; far-reaching community, state, and government programs are needed. A vast number of children do not have consistent and meaningful contact with adult males. This very serious situation must be remedied if all our children are to take full advantage of their growing social and educational opportunities (Biller, 1970, 1971a).

## Educational Implications

Our educational system could do much to mitigate the effects of paternal deprivation if more male teachers were available, particularly in nursery school, kindergarten, and the early elementary school grades. Competent and interpersonally able male teachers can facilitate the cognitive development of many children as well as contribute to their general social functioning (Biller, 1974a; Ostrovsky, 1959).

Greater incentives are needed to encourage more males to become teachers of young children. There must be more freedom and autonomy to innovate as well as greater financial rewards. We must make both men and women aware of the impact that males can have even in the early years of child development.

The remedy for the feminized classroom is not just having more male teachers per se, but giving men and women a more nearly equal distribution of the responsibilities and decisions related to education. As Sexton (1969) suggests both boys and girls might be better off if there were more women in top administrative positions as well as more men in the classroom. As in the family situation children can profit much from opportunities of seeing males and females interact in a cooperative, creative manner. Men and women in the classroom could help each other understand better the different socialization experiences of males and females and contribute to a lessening of sex-role stereotypes (Biller, 1974a, 1974b).

Even if significantly more male teachers are not immediately available, our school system could better use existing personnel. Many of the males who teach in the upper elementary school grades, junior high, and high school could also be very effective with younger children. Again we need to emphasize the importance of males' interacting with young children (as well as with older children). Programs could also be planned so that male teachers could spend some of their time with a wider range of children, particularly in tasks where they had much skill and enthusiasm. Perhaps their responsibilities could be concentrated on father-deprived children. In addition other males, such as older students or retired men, might be encouraged to participate in educating young children.

There is a general need to make our schools more a part of the community and to invite greater participation, especially from fathers. Men in the community could be invited to talk about and demonstrate their work. Participants could include members of various professions, skilled craftsmen and technicians, politicians, and athletes. Of course it is also important to have women in various occupations come to the school and describe their activities. Both boys and girls need to become aware that women can be successful in "traditionally masculine" fields (Biller & Meredith, 1974).

Further advances are needed in the development of educational and training programs for parents and prospective parents. Gordon's (1970) *Parent Effectiveness Training* is probably the best example of a successful parent education program designed to improve parent–child relationships. There have not, however, been systematic programs especially developed to include issues particularly relevant to fathers. Unfortunately most parent education programs focus on mothers, and relatively few fathers participate. Meredith and I have written a book, *Father Power*, that we hope will stimulate parent education programs to deal with issues in regard to the father–child and father–mother relationships (Biller & Meredith, 1974).

## REFERENCES

Aberle, D. F., & Naegele, F. D. Middle-class fathers' occupational role and attitude toward children. *American Journal of Orthopsychiatry*, 1952, **22**, 366–378.

Ackerman, N. W. *Treating the troubled family*. New York: Basic Books, 1966.

Aichorn, A. *Wayward youth*. New York: Viking, 1935.

Alkire, A. A. Social power and communication within families of disturbed and nondisturbed preadolescents. *Journal of Personality and Social Psychology*, 1969, **13**, 335–349.

Altucher, N. Conflict in sex identification in boys. Unpublished doctoral dissertation, University of Michigan, 1957.

Altus, W. D. The broken home and factors of adjustment. *Psychological Reports*, 1958, **4**, 477.

Anderson, R. E. Where's dad? Paternal deprivation and delinquency. *Archives of General Psychiatry*, 1968, **18**, 641–649.

Andrews, R. O., & Christensen, H. T. Relationship of absence of a parent to courtship status: A repeat study. *American Sociological Review*, 1951, **16**, 541–544.

Andry, R. G. Paternal and maternal roles in delinquency. In *Deprivation of maternal care* (Public Health Paper No. 14). Geneva: World Health Organization, 1962, pp. 31–43.

Apperson, L. B., & McAdoo, W. G., Jr. Parental factors in the childhood of homosexuals. *Journal of Abnormal Psychology*, 1968, **73**, 201–206.

Bach, G. R. Father-fantasies and father typing in father-separated children. *Child Development*, 1946, **17**, 63–80.

Bach, G. R., & Bremer, G. Projective father fantasies of preadolescent, delinquent children. *Journal of Psychology*, 1947, **24**, 3–17.

Bacon, M. K., Child, I. L., & Barry, H. A cross-cultural study of correlates of crime. *Journal of Abnormal and Social Psychology*, 1963, **66**, 291–300.

Baggett, A. T. The effect of early loss of father upon the personality of boys and girls in late adolescence. *Dissertation Abstracts*, 1967, **28** (1-B), 356–357.

Baker, J. W., & Holzworth, A. Social histories of successful and unsuccessful children. *Child Development*, 1961, **32**, 135–149.

Baker, S. L., Cove, L. A., Fagen, S. A., Fischer, E. G., & Janda, E. J. Impact of father-absence: III. Problems of family reintegration following prolonged father-absence. Paper presented at the meeting of the American Orthopsychiatric Association, Washington, D.C., March 1968.

Bandura, A. *Principles of behavior modification.* New York: Holt, Rinehart and Winston, 1969.

Bandura, A., & Walters, R. H. *Adolescent aggression: A study of the influence of child-rearing practices and family interrelationships.* New York: Ronald Press, 1959.

Barclay, A. G., & Cusumano, D. Father-absence, cross-sex identity, and field-dependent behavior in male adolescents. *Child Development,* 1967, **38,** 243–250.

Bardwick, J. M. *Psychology of women.* New York: Harper and Row, 1971.

Barry, W. A. Marriage research and conflict: An integrative review. *Psychological Bulletin,* 1970, **73,** 41–55.

Bartemeier, L. The contribution of the father to the mental health of the family. *American Journal of Psychiatry,* 1953, **110,** 277–280.

Baruch, D. W., & Wilcox, J. A. A study of sex differences in preschool children's adjustment coexistent with interparental tensions. *Journal of Genetic Psychology,* 1944, **61,** 281–303.

Baumrind, D., & Black, A. E. Socialization practices associated with dimensions of competence in preschool boys and girls. *Child Development,* 1967, **38,** 291–327.

Beck, A. T., Sehti, B. B., & Tuthill, R. W. Childhood bereavement and adult depression. *Archives of General Psychiatry,* 1963, **9,** 295–302.

Becker, W. C., Peterson, D. R., Hellmer, L. A., Shoemaker, D. J., & Quay, H. D. Factors in parental behavior and personality as related to problem behavior in children. *Journal of Consulting Psychology,* 1959, **23,** 107–118.

Becker, W. C., Peterson, D. R., Luria, Z., Shoemaker, D. S., & Hellmer, L. A. Relations of factors derived from parent interview ratings to behavior problems of five-year-olds. *Child Development,* 1962, **33,** 509–535.

Beier, E. G., & Ratzeburg, F. The parental identifications of male and female college students. *Journal of Abnormal and Social Psychology,* 1953, **48,** 569–572.

Bené, E. On the genesis of female homosexuality. *British Journal of Psychiatry,* 1965, **3,** 815–821.

Benson, L. *Fatherhood: A sociological perspective.* New York: Random House, 1968.

Bieber, I. et al. *Homosexuality: A psychoanalytic study.* New York: Basic Books, 1962.

Bieri, J., & Lobeck, R. Acceptance of authority and parental identification. *Journal of Personality,* 1959, **27,** 74–87.

Biller, H. B. A multiaspect investigation of masculine development in kindergarten-age boys. *Genetic Psychology Monographs,* 1968, **76,** 89–139 (a).

Biller, H. B. A note on father-absence and masculine development in young lower-class Negro and white boys. *Child Development*, 1968, **39**, 1003–1006 (b).

Biller, H. B. Father dominance and sex-role development in kindergarten-age boys. *Developmental Psychology*, 1969, **1**, 87–94 (a).

Biller, H. B. Father-absence, maternal encouragement, and sex-role development in kindergarten-age boys. *Child Development*, 1969, **40**, 539–546 (b).

Biller, H. B. Maternal salience and feminine development in young girls. *Proceedings of the 77th Annual Convention of the American Psychological Association*, 1969, **4**, 259–260 (c).

Biller, H. B. Father-absence and the personality development of the male child. *Developmental Psychology*, 1970, **2**, 181–201.

Biller, H. B. *Father, child, and sex role*, Lexington, Mass.: D. C. Heath and Company, 1971 (a).

Biller, H. B. The mother–child relationship and the father-absent boy's personality development. *Merrill-Palmer Quarterly*, 1971, **17**, 227–241 (b).

Biller, H. B. Sex-role uncertainty and psychopathology. *Journal of Individual Psychology*, 1973, **29**, 24–25.

Biller, H. B. Paternal and sex-role factors in cognitive and academic functioning. In J. K. Cole & R. Dienstbier (Eds.), *Nebraska Symposium on Motivation, 1973*, Lincoln: University of Nebraska Press, 1974, 83–123 (a).

Biller, H. B. Paternal deprivation, cognitive functioning, and the feminized classroom. In A. Davids (Ed.), *Child personality and psychopathology: Current topics.* New York: Wiley, 1974, pp. 11–52 (b).

Biller, H. B. *Paternal deprivation.* Lexington, Mass.: D. C. Heath and Company, 1974 (c).

Biller, H. B., & Bahm, R. M. Father-absence, perceived maternal behavior, and masculinity of self-concept among junior high school boys. *Developmental Psychology*, 1971, **4**, 178–181.

Biller, H. B., & Barry, W. Sex-role patterns, paternal similarity, and personality adjustment in college males. *Developmental Psychology*, 1971, **4**, 107.

Biller, H. B., & Borstelmann, L. J. Masculine development: An integrative review. *Merrill-Palmer Quarterly*, 1967, **13**, 253–294.

Biller, H. B., & Meredith, D. L. The invisible American father. *Sexual Behavior*, 1972, **2** (7), 16–22.

Biller, H. B., & Meredith, D. L. *Father power.* New York: David McKay, 1974.

Biller, H. B., & Poey, K. An exploratory comparison of sex-role related behavior in schizophrenics and nonschizophrenics. *Developmental Psychology*, 1969, **1**, 629.

Biller, H. B., & Smith, A. E. An AFDC mothers group: An exploratory effort in community mental health. *Family Coordinator*, 1972, **21**, 287–290.

Biller, H. B., & Weiss, S. The father–daughter relationship and the personality development of the female. *Journal of Genetic Psychology*, 1970, **114**, 79–93.

Biller, H. B., & Zung, B. Perceived maternal control, anxiety, and opposite sex-role preference among elementary school girls. *Journal of Psychology*, 1972, **81**, 85–88.

Blanchard, R. W., & Biller, H. B. Father availability and academic performance among third-grade boys. *Developmental Psychology*, 1971, **4**, 301–305.

Block, J. Parents of schizophrenic, neurotic, asthmatic, and congenitally ill children: A comparative study. *Archives of General Psychiatry*, 1969, **20**, 659 674.

Block, J. *Lives through time*, Berkeley: Bancroft Books, 1971.

Block, J., von der Lippe, A., & Block, J. H. Sex-role and socialization: Some personality concomitants and environmental antecedents. *Journal of Consulting and Clinical Psychology*, 1973, **41**, 321–341.

Brigham, J. C., Ricketts, J. L., & Johnson, R. C. Reported maternal and paternal behaviors of solitary and social delinquents. *Journal of Consulting Psychology*, 1967, **31**, 420–422.

Brill, N. Q., & Liston, E. H. Parental loss in adults with emotional disorders. *Archives of General Psychiatry*, 1966, **14**, 307–314.

Bronfenbrenner, U. The study of identification through interpersonal perception. In R. Tagiuri & L. Petrullo (Eds.), *Person perception and interpersonal behavior*. Stanford: Stanford University Press, 1958, 110–130.

Bronfenbrenner, U. Some familial antecedents of responsibility and leadership in adolescents. In L. Petrullo & B. M. Bass (Eds.), *Leadership and interpersonal behavior*. New York: Holt, Rinehart, and Winston, 1961, 239–272.

Bronson, W. C. Dimensions of ego and infantile identification. *Journal of Personality*, 1959, **27**, 532–545.

Brown, F. Depression and childhood bereavement. *Journal of Mental Science*, 1961, **107**, 754–777.

Brown, J. K. A cross-cultural study of female initiation rites. *American Anthropologist*, 1963, **65**, 837–853.

Burton, R. V. Cross-sex identity in Barbados. *Developmental Psychology*, 1972, **6**, 365–374.

Burton, R. V., & Whiting, J. W. M. The absent father and cross-sex identity. *Merrill-Palmer Quarterly*, 1961, **7**, 85–95.

Carpenter J., & Eisenberg, P. Some relations between family background and personality. *Journal of Psychology*, 1935, **6**, 115–136.

Cava, E. L., & Rausch, H. L. Identification and the adolescent boy's perception of his father. *Journal of Abnormal and Social Psychology*, 1952, **47**, 855–856.

Chang, J., & Block, J. A study of identification in male homosexuals. *Journal of Consulting Psychology*, 1960, **24**, 307–310.

Chein, I., Gerrard, D. L., Lee, B. S., & Rosenfeld, E. *The road to H.* New York: Basic Books, 1964.

Cobliner, W. G. Social factors in mental disorders: A contribution to the etiology of mental illness. *Genetic Psychology Monographs*, 1963, **67**, 151–215.

Coopersmith, S. *The antecedents of self-esteem.* San Francisco: W. H. Freeman, 1967.

Crandall, V. J., Dewey, R., Katkovsky, W., & Preston, A. Parents' attitudes and behaviors and grade-school children's academic achievements. *Journal of Genetic Psychology*, 1964, **104**, 53–66.

Crane, A. R. Preadolescent gangs: A sociopsychological interpretation. *Journal of Genetic Psychology*, 1955, **86**, 275–279.

Crumley, F. E., & Blumenthal, D. S. Children's reactions to temporary loss of the father. *American Journal of Psychiatry*, 1973, **130**, 778–782.

D'Andrade, R. G. Father-absence and cross-sex identification. Unpublished doctoral dissertation, Harvard University, 1962.

Da Silva, G. The role of the father with chronic schizophrenic patients. *Journal of the Canadian Psychiatric Association*, 1963, **8**, 190–203.

David, K. H. Ego-strength, sex differences, and description of self, ideal, and parents. *Journal of General Psychology*, 1968, **79**, 79–81.

Davis, W. C., & Phares, E. Parental antecedents of internal–external control of reinforcement. *Psychological Reports*, 1969, **24**, 427–436.

Dennehy, C. Childhood bereavement and psychiatric illness. *British Journal of Psychiatry*, 1966, **112**, 1049–1069.

Despert, I. J. The fatherless family. *Child Study*, 1957, **34**, 22–28.

Distler, L. S. Patterns of parental identification: An examination of three theories. Unpublished doctoral dissertation, University of California, Berkeley, 1964.

Donini, G. P. An evaluation of sex-role identification among father-absent and father-present boys. *Psychology*, 1967, **4**, 13–16.

Douvan, E., & Adelson, J. *The adolescent experience.* New York: Wiley, 1966.

Egelson, J., & Frank, J. F. *Parents without partners.* New York: Dutton, 1961.

Elder, G. H., Jr., & Bowerman, C. E. Family structure and child-rearing patterns: The effect of family size and sex composition. *American Sociological Review*, 1963, **28**, 891–905.

Eron, L. D., Walder, L. O., Toigo, R., & Lefkowitz, M. M. Social class, parental punishment for aggression, and child aggression. *Child Development*, 1963, **34**, 849–867.

Evans, R. B. Childhood parental relationship of homosexual men. *Journal of Consulting and Clinical Psychology*, 1969, **33**, 129–135.

Ferreira, A. J., Winter, W. D., & Poindexter, E. J. Some interactional variables in normal and abnormal families. *Family Process,* 1966, **5,** 60–75.

Fish, K. D. Paternal availability, family role-structure, maternal employment, and personality development in late adolescent females. Unpublished doctoral dissertation, University of Massachusetts, 1969.

Fish, K. D., & Biller, H. B. Perceived childhood paternal relationships and college females' personal adjustment. *Adolescence,* 1973, **8,** 415–420.

Fisher, S. F. *The female organism: Psychology, physiology, fantasy.* New York: Basic Books, 1973.

Forrest, T. Paternal roots of female character development. *Contemporary Psychoanalyst,* 1966, **3,** 21–28.

Forrest, T. The paternal roots of male character development. *The Psychoanalytic Review,* 1967, **54,** 81–99.

Forrest, T. Treatment of the father in family therapy. *Family Process,* 1969, **8,** 106–117.

Freedheim, D. K. An investigation of masculinity and parental role patterns. Unpublished doctoral dissertation, Duke University, 1960.

Freedheim, D. K., & Borstelmann, L. J. An investigation of masculinity and parental role-patterns. *American Psychologist,* 1963, **18,** 339. (Abstract)

Freud, A., & Burlingham, D. T. *Infants without families.* New York: International University Press, 1944.

Freudenthal, K. Problems of the one-parent family. *Social Work,* 1959, **4,** 44–48.

Garbower, G. *Behavior problems of children in Navy officers' families: As related to social conditions of Navy family life.* Washington, D.C.: Catholic University Press, 1959.

Gassner, S., & Murray, E. J. Dominance and conflict in the interactions between parents of normal and neurotic children. *Journal of Abnormal Psychology,* 1969, **74,** 33–41.

Gay, M. J., & Tonge, W. L. The late effects of loss of parents in childhood. *British Journal of Psychiatry,* 1967, **113,** 753–759.

Glueck, S., & Glueck, E. *Unravelling juvenile delinquency.* Cambridge, Mass.: Harvard University Press, 1950.

Goode, W. Family disorganization. In R. K. Merton & R. A. Nisbet (Eds.), *Contemporary social problems.* New York: Harcourt, Brace, and World, 1961.

Goodenough, E. W. Interest in persons as an aspect of sex differences in the early years. *Genetic Psychology Monographs,* 1957, **55,** 287–323.

Gordon, T. *Parent effectiveness training.* New York: Peter Wyden, 1970.

Gray, S. W. Masculinity–femininity in relation to anxiety and social acceptance. *Child Development,* 1957, **28,** 203–214.

Gray, S. W. Perceived similarity to parents and adjustment. *Child Development,* 1959, **30,** 91–107.

Green, R. *Sexual identity conflict in children and adults.* New York: Basic Books, 1974.

Greenstein, J. F. Father characteristics and sex-typing. *Journal of Personality and Social Psychology,* 1966, **3**, 271–277.

Gregory, I. Studies of parental deprivation in psychiatric patients. *American Journal of Psychiatry,* 1958, **115**, 432–442.

Gregory, I. Anterospective data following childhood loss of a parent: I. Delinquency and high school dropout. *Archives of General Psychiatry,* 1965, **13**, 99–109 (a).

Gregory, I. Anterospective data following childhood loss of a parent: II. Pathology, performance, and potential among college students. *Archives of General Psychiatry,* 1965, **13**, 110–120 (b).

Gundlach, R. H. Childhood parental relationships and the establishment of gender roles of homosexuals. *Journal of Consulting and Clinical Psychology,* 1969, **33**, 136–139.

Gundlach, R. H., & Riess, B. F. Self and sexual identity in the female: A study of female homosexuals. In B. F. Riess (Ed.), *New directions in mental health.* New York: Grune and Stratton, 1968.

Haley, J., & Hoffman, L. *Techniques of family therapy.* New York: Basic Books, 1967.

Hall, P., & Tonge, W. L. Long-standing continuous unemployment in male patients with psychiatric symptoms. *British Journal of Preventive and Social Medicine,* 1963, **17**, 191–196.

Hamilton, C. V. *A research in marriage.* New York: Boni, 1929.

Hamilton, D. M., & Wahl, J. G. The hospital treatment of dementia praecox. *American Journal of Psychiatry,* 1948, **104**, 346–352.

Haworth, M. R. Parental loss in children as reflected in projective responses. *Journal of Projective Techniques,* 1964, **28**, 31–35.

Heckel, R. V. The effects of fatherlessness on the preadolescent female. *Mental Hygiene,* 1963, **47**, 69–73.

Heilbrun, A. B. Parental identification and college adjustment. *Psychological Reports,* 1962, **10**, 853–854.

Heilbrun, A. B. The measurement of identification. *Child Development,* 1965, **36**, 111–127 (a).

Heilbrun, A. B. An empirical test of the modeling theory of sex-role learning. *Child Development,* 1965, **36**, 789–799 (b).

Heilbrun, A. B. Parent identification and filial sex-role behavior: The importance of biological context. In J. C. Cole & R. Dienstbier (Eds.), *Nebraska Symposium on Motivation, 1973.* Lincoln: University of Nebraska Press, 1974. Pp. 125–194.

Heilbrun, A. B., & Fromme, D. K. Parental identification of late adolescents and level of adjustment: The importance of parent-model attributes, ordinal position, and sex of child. *Journal of Genetic Psychology*, 1965, **107**, 49–59.

Helper, M. M. Learning theory and the self-concept. *Journal of Abnormal and Social Psychology*, 1955, **51**, 184–194.

Herzog, E., & Sudia, C. E. *Boys in fatherless families.* Washington, D.C.: Office of Child Development, 1970.

Hetherington, E. M. A developmental study of the effects of sex of the dominant parent on sex-role preference, identification, and imitation in children. *Journal of Personality and Social Psychology*, 1965, **2**, 188–194.

Hetherington, E. M. Effects of paternal absence on sex-typed behaviors in Negro and white preadolescent males. *Journal of Personality and Social Psychology*, 1966, **4**, 87–91.

Hetherington, E. M. Effects of father-absence on personality development in adolescent daughters. *Developmental Psychology*, 1972, **7**, 313–326.

Hetherington, E. M., & Brackbill, Y. Etiology and covariation of obstinacy, orderliness, and parsimony in young children. *Child Development*, 1963, **34**, 919–943.

Hetherington, E. M., & Frankie, G. Effects of parental dominance, warmth, and conflict on imitation in children. *Journal of Personality and Social Psychology*, 1967, **6**, 119–125.

Hilgard, J. R., Neuman, M. F., & Fisk, F. Strength of adult ego following bereavement. *American Journal of Orthopsychiatry*, 1960, **30**, 788–798.

Hill, O. W., & Price, J. S. Childhood bereavement and adult depression. *British Journal of Psychiatry*, 1967, **113**, 743–751.

Hill, R. *Families under stress.* New York: Harper, 1949.

Hoffman, L. W. The father's role in the family and the child's peer-group adjustment. *Merrill Palmer Quarterly*, 1961, **7**, 91–105.

Hoffman, M. L. Father absence and conscience development. *Developmental Psychology*, 1971, **4**, 400–406 (a).

Hoffman, M. L. Identification and conscience development. *Child Development*, 1971, **42**, 1071–1082 (b).

Holstein, C. E. The relation of children's moral judgment level to that of their parents and to communication patterns in the family. In R. C. Smart & M. S. Smart (Eds.), *Readings in child development and relationships.* New York: Macmillan, 1972. Pp. 484–494.

Ingham, H. V. A statistical study of family relationships in psychoneurosis. *American Journal of Orthopsychiatry*, 1949, **106**, 91–98.

Jacobson, G., & Ryder, R. G. Parental loss and some characteristics of the early marriage relationship. *American Journal of Orthopsychiatry*, 1969, **39**, 779–787.

Jenkins, R. L. The varieties of children's behavioral problems and family dynamics. *American Journal of Psychiatry*, 1968, **124**, 1440–1445.

Johnson, M. M. Sex-role learning in the nuclear family. *Child Development,* 1963, **34,** 319–333.

Jones, E. *Raising your child in a fatherless home.* New York: MacMillan, 1963.

Kagan, J. Socialization of aggression and the perception of parents in fantasy. *Child Development,* 1958, **29,** 311–320.

Kaufman, I., Peck, A. I., & Tagiuri, C. K. The family constellation and overt incestuous relations between father and daughter. *American Journal of Orthopsychiatry,* 1954, **24,** 266–277.

Kaye, H. E. et al. Homosexuality in women. *Archives of General Psychiatry,* 1967, **17,** 626–634.

Kayton, R., & Biller, H. B. Sex-role development and psychopathology in adult males. *Journal of Consulting and Clinical Psychology,* 1971, **36,** 235–237.

Kayton, R., & Biller, H. B. Perception of parental sex-role behavior and psychopathology in adult males. *Journal of Consulting and Clinical Psychology,* 1971, **36,** 235–237.

Keeler, W. R. Children's reaction to the death of a parent. In P. H. Hoch & J. Zubin (Eds.), *Depression.* New York: Grune, 1954. Pp. 109–120.

Kelly, F. J., & Baer, D. J. Age of male delinquents when father left home and recidivism. *Psychological Reports,* 1969, **25,** 1010.

Klein, C. *The single parent experience.* New York: Avon, 1973.

Landis, J. T. A reexamination of the role of the father as an index of family integration. *Marriage and Family Living,* 1962, **24,** 122–128.

Landis, P. H. *Making the most of marriage.* New York: Appleton-Century-Crofts, 1965.

Landy, F., Rosenberg, B. G., & Sutton-Smith, B. The effect of limited father-absence on the cognitive and emotional development of children. Paper presented at the meeting of the Midwestern Psychological Association, Chicago, May 1967.

Lansky, L. M. Patterns of defense against conflict. Unpublished doctoral dissertation, University of Michigan, 1956.

Lawton, M. J., & Sechrest, L. Figure drawings by young boys from father-present and father-absent homes. *Journal of Clinical Psychology,* 1962, **18,** 304–305.

Lazowick, L. M. On the nature of identification. *Journal of Abnormal and Social Psychology,* 1955, **51,** 175–183.

Lederer, W. Dragons, delinquents, and destiny. *Psychological Issues,* 1964, **4** (Whole No. 3).

Lee, P. C., & Wolinsky, A. L. Male teachers of young children: A preliminary empirical study. *Young Children,* 1973, **28,** 342–352.

Lefkowitz, M. M. Some relationships between sex-role preference of children and other parent and child variables. *Psychological Reports,* 1962, **10,** 43–53.

Leichty, M. M. The effect of father-absence during early childhood upon the

Oedipal situation as reflected in young adults, *Merrill-Palmer Quarterly,* 1960, **6**, 212–217.

Leiderman, G. F. Effect of family experiences on boy's peer relationships. Unpublished doctoral dissertation, Harvard University, 1953.

Leiderman, G. F. Effect of parental relationships and child-training practices on boys' interactions with peers. *Acta Psychologica,* 1959, **15**, 469.

Leighton, L. A., Stollak, G. E., & Ferguson, L. R. Patterns of communication in normal and clinic families. *Journal of Consulting and Clinical Psychology,* 1971, **36**, 252–256.

Leonard, M. R. Fathers and daughters. *International Journal of Psychoanalysis,* 1966, **47**, 325–333.

Lerner, S. H. Effect of desertion on family life. *Social Casework,* 1954, **35**, 3–8.

Lessing, E. E., Zagorin, S. W., and Nelson, D. WISC subtest and IQ score correlates of father absence. *Journal of Genetic Psychology,* 1970, **67**, 181–195.

Levin, H., & Sears, R. R. Identification with parents as a determinant of doll play aggression. *Child Development,* 1956, **37**, 135–153.

Levin, R. B. An empirical test of the female castration complex. *Journal of Abnormal Psychology,* 1966, **71**, 181–188.

Lidz, T., Parker, N., & Cornelison, A. R. The role of the father in the family environment of the schizophrenic patient. *American Journal of Psychiatry,* 1956, **13**, 126–132.

Liverant, S. MMPI differences between parents of disturbed children and nondisturbed children. *Journal of Consulting Psychology,* 1959, **23**, 256–260.

Lockwood, D. H., & Guerney, B. Identification and empathy in relation to self-dissatisfaction and adjustment. *Journal of Abnormal and Social Psychology,* 1962, **65**, 343–347.

Luckey, E. B. Marital satisfaction and parental concept. *Journal of Consulting Psychology,* 1960, **24**, 195–204.

Lynn, D. B. *Parental and sex-role identification.* Berkeley: McCutchan, 1969.

Lynn, D. B. *The father: His role in child development.* Belmont, Calif.: Brooks/Cole, 1974.

Lynn, D. B., & Sawrey, W. L. The effects of father–absence on Norwegian boys and girls. *Journal of Abnormal and Social Psychology,* 1959, **59**, 258–262.

MacDonald, A. P., Jr. Internal–external locus of control: Parental antecedents. *Journal of Consulting and Clinical Psychology,* 1971, **37**, 141–147.

MacDonald, M. W. Criminal behavior in passive, effeminate boys. *American Journal of Orthopsychiatry,* 1938, **8**, 70–78.

Madow, L., & Hardy, S. E. Incidence and analysis of the broken family in the background of neurosis. *American Journal of Orthopsychiatry,* 1947, **17**, 521–528.

McClelland, D. C., & Watt, N. F. Sex-role alienation in schizophrenia. *Journal of Abnormal Psychology,* 1968, **73**, 226–239.

McCord, J., McCord, W., & Howard, A. Family interaction as an antecedent to the direction of male aggressiveness. *Journal of Abnormal and Social Psychology*, 1963, **66**, 239–224.

McCord, J., McCord, W., & Thurber, E. Some effects of paternal absence on male children. *Journal of Abnormal and Social Psychology*, 1962, **64**, 361–369.

McDermott, J. F. Parental divorce in early childhood. *American Journal of Psychiatry*, 1968, **124**, 1424–1432.

McPherson, S. Communication of intents among parents and their disturbed adolescent child. *Journal of Abnormal Psychology*, 1970, **76**, 98–105.

Medinnus, G. R. Adolescents' self-acceptance and perceptions of their parents. *Journal of Consulting Psychology*, 1965, **29**, 150–154 (a).

Medinnus, G. N. Delinquents' perception of their parents. *Journal of Consulting Psychology*, 1965, **29**, 5–19 (b).

Meerloo, J. A. M. The father cuts the cord: The role of the father as initial transference figure. *American Journal of Psychotherapy*, 1956, **10**, 471–480.

Miller, B. Effects of father-absence and mother's evaluation of father on the socialization of adolescent boys. Unpublished doctoral dissertation, Columbia University, 1961.

Miller, W. B. Lower-class culture as a generating milieu of gang delinquency. *Journal of Social Issues*, 1958, **14**, 5–19.

Mischel, W. Preference for delayed reinforcement: An experimental study of cultural observation. *Journal of Abnormal and Social Psychology*, 1958, **56**, 57–61.

Mischel, W. Preference for delayed reward and social responsibility. *Journal of Abnormal and Social Psychology*, 1961, **62**, 1–7 (a).

Mischel, W. Father-absence and delay of gratification. *Journal of Abnormal and Social Psychology*, 1961, **62**, 116–124 (b).

Mischel, W. Delay of gratification, need for achievement, and acquiescence in another culture. *Journal of Abnormal and Social Psychology*, 1961, **62**, 543–552 (c).

Mishler, E. G., & Waxler, N. E. *Interaction in families.* New York: Wiley, 1968.

Mitchell, D., & Wilson, W. Relationship of father-absence to masculinity and popularity of delinquent boys. *Psychological Reports*, 1967, **20**, 1173–1174.

Monahan, T. P. Family status and the delinquent child. *Social Forces*, 1957, **35**, 250–258.

Moulton, P. W., Burnstein, E., Liberty, D., & Altucher, N. The patterning of parental affection and dominance as a determinant of guilt and sex-typing. *Journal of Personality and Social Psychology*, 1966, **4**, 363–365.

References 151

Moynihan, D. P. *The Negro family: The case for national action.* Washington, D.C.: United States Department of Labor, 1965.

Mussen, P. H. Some antecedents and consequences of masculine sex-typing in adolescent boys. *Psychological Monographs,* 1961, **75,** No. 2 (Whole No. 506).

Mussen, P. H., & Distler, L. Masculinity, identification, and father–son relationships. *Journal of Abnormal and Social Psychology,* 1959, **59,** 350–356.

Mussen, P. H., & Distler, L. Child-rearing antecedents of masculine identification in kindergarten boys. *Child Development,* 1960, **31,** 89–100.

Mussen, P. H., & Parker, A. L. Mother nurturance and the girls' incidental imitative learning. *Journal of Personality and Social Psychology,* 1965, **2,** 94–97.

Mussen, P. H., & Rutherford, E. E. Parent–child relationships and parental personality in relation to young children's sex-role preferences. *Child Development,* 1963, **34,** 589–607.

Mussen, P. H., Young, H. B., Gaddini, R., & Morante, L. The influence of father–son relationships on adolescent personality and attitudes. *Journal of Child Psychology and Psychiatry,* 1963, **4,** 3–16.

Nash, J. The father in contemporary culture and current psychological literature. *Child Development,* 1965, **36,** 261–297.

Nash, J., & Hayes, T. The parental relationships of male homosexuals: Some theoretical issues and a pilot study. *Australian Journal of Psychology,* 1965, **17,** 35–43.

Nelsen, E. A., & Vangen, P. M. The impact of father absence upon heterosexual behaviors and social development of preadolescent girls in a ghetto environment. *Proceedings of the 79th Annual Convention of the American Psychological Association,* 1971, **6,** 165–166.

Neubauer, P. B. The one-parent child and his Oedipal development. *The Psychoanalytic Study of the Child,* 1960, **15,** 286–309.

Norton, A. Incidence of neurosis related to maternal age and birth order. *British Journal of Social Medicine,* 1952, **6,** 253–258.

Nowicki, S., Jr., & Segal, W. Perceived parental characteristics, locus of control orientation, and behavioral correlates of locus of control. *Developmental Psychology,* 1974, **10,** 33–37.

Nye, F. I. Child adjustment in broken and unhappy unbroken homes. *Marriage and Family Living,* 1957, **19,** 356–361.

O'Connor, P. J. Aetiological factors in homosexuality as seen in R.A.F. psychiatric practice. *British Journal of Psychiatry,* 1964, **110,** 381–391.

Oltman, J. E., & Friedman, S. Parental deprivation in psychiatric conditions: III. In personality disorders and other conditions. *Diseases of the Nervous System,* 1967, **28,** 298–303.

Oltman, J. E., McGarry, J. J., & Friedman, S. Parental deprivation and the broken home in dementia praecox and other mental disorders. *American Journal of Psychiatry*, 1952, **108**, 685–694.

Ostrovsky, E. S. *Father to the child: Case studies of the experiences of a male teacher.* New York: Putnam, 1959.

Papenek, M. L. Authority and sex roles in the family. *Journal of Marriage and the Family*, 1969, **31**, 88–96.

Payne, D. E., & Mussen, P. H. Parent–child relations and father-identification among adolescent boys. *Journal of Abnormal and Social Psychology*, 1956, **52**, 358–362.

Pedersen, F. A. Relationships between father-absence and emotional disturbance in male military dependents. *Merrill-Palmer Quarterly*, 1966, **12**, 321–331.

Peterson, D. R., Becker, W. C., Hellmer, L. A., Shoemaker, D. J., & Quay, H. C. Parental attitudes and child adjustment. *Child Development*, 1959, **30**, 119–130.

Pettigrew, T. F. *A profile of the Negro American.* Princeton, N.J.: Van Nostrand, 1964.

Phelan, H. M. The incidence and possible significance of the drawing of female figures by sixth-grade boys in response to the Draw-A-Person Test. *Psychiatric Quarterly*, 1964, **38**, 1–16.

Poffenberger, T. A. A research note on father–child relations and father viewed as a negative figure. *Child Development*, 1959, **30**, 489–492.

Pollak, G. K. Sexual dynamics of parents without partners. *Social Work*, 1970, **15**, 79–85.

Pope, B. Socioeconomic contrasts in children's peer culture prestige values, *Genetic Psychology Monographs*, 1953, **48**, 157–200.

Portnoy, S. M., Biller, H. B., & Davids, A. The influence of the child care worker in residential treatment. *American Journal of Orthopsychiatry*, 1972, **42**, 719–772.

Reuter, M. W., & Biller, H. B. Perceived paternal nurturance–availability and personality adjustment among college males. *Journal of Consulting and Clinical Psychology*, 1973, **40**, 339–342.

Rexford, E. N. Antisocial young children and their families. In M. R. Haworth (Ed.), *Child psychotherapy.* New York: Basic Books, 1964. Pp. 58–63.

Robey, A., Rosenwald, R. J., Snell, J. E., & Lee, R. E. The runaway girl: A reaction to family stress. *American Journal of Orthopsychiatry*, 1964, **34**, 762–767.

Robins, E., Schmidt, E. H., & O'Neal, P. Some interrelations of social factors and clinical diagnosis in attempted suicide. *American Journal of Psychiatry*, 1957, **114**, 221–231.

Rogers, W. B., & Long, J. M. Male models and sexual identification: A case from the Out Island Bahamas. *Human Organization*, 1968, **27**, 326–331.

Rohrer, H. H., & Edmonson, M. S. *The eighth generation.* New York: Harper, 1960.

Rosenberg, C. M. Determinants of psychiatric illness in young people. *British Journal of Psychiatry*, 1969, **115**, 907–915.

Rosenberg, M. *Society and the adolescent self-image*. Princeton, N.J.: Princeton University Press, 1965.

Rosenthal, M. S., Ni, E., Finkelstein, M., & Berkwits, G. K. Father–child relationships and children's problems. *Archives of General Psychiatry*, 1962, **7**, 360–373.

Rothbart, M. K., & Maccoby, E. E. Parents' differential reactions to sons and daughters. *Journal of Personality and Social Psychology*, 1966, **4**, 237–243.

Rubenstein, B. O., & Levitt, M. Some observations regarding the role of fathers in child psychotherapy. *Bulletin of the Menninger Clinic*, 1957, **21**, 16–27.

Rushing, W. A. Adolescent–parent relationships and mobility aspirations. *Social Forces*, 1964, **43**, 157–166.

Rutherford, E. E., & Mussen, P. H. Generosity in nursery school boys. *Child Development*, 1968, **39**, 755–765.

Rychlak, J., & Legerski, A. A sociocultural theory of appropriate sexual role identification and level of personality adjustment. *Journal of Personality*, 1967, **35**, 31–49.

Saghir, M. T., & Robbins, F. *Male and female homosexuality,* Baltimore: Williams and Wilkins, 1973.

Salzman, L. Psychology of the female: A new look. *Archives of General Psychiatry*, 1967, **17**, 195–203.

Santrock, J. W. Paternal absence, sex-typing, and identification. *Developmental Psychology*, 1970, **2**, 264–272 (a).

Santrock, J. W. Influence of onset and type of paternal absence on the first four Eriksonian developmental crises. *Developmental Psychology*, 1970, **3**, 273–274 (b).

Santrock, J. W. Relation of type and onset of father-absence to cognitive development. *Child Development*, 1972, **43**, 455–469.

Santrock, J. W. Father absence, perceived maternal behavior, and moral development in boys. *Child Development*, 1975, **46**, 753–757.

Santrock, J. W., & Wohlford, P. Effects of father absence: Influences of, reason for, and onset of absence. *Proceedings of the 78th Annual Convention of the American Psychological Association*, 1970, **5**, 265–266.

Schaefer, E. S. Children's reports of parental behavior: An inventory. *Child Development*, 1965, **36**, 413–424.

Schlesinger, B. The one-parent family: An overview. *Family Life Coordinator*, 1966, **15**, 133–137.

Schoeppe, A., Haggard, E. A., & Havighurst, R. J. Some factors affecting sixteen-years-olds' success in five developmental tasks. *Journal of Abnormal and Social Psychology*, 1970, **75**, 30–37.

Schuham, A. I. Power relations in emotionally disturbed and normal family triads. *Journal of Abnormal Psychology*, 1970, **75**, 30–37.

Sears, P. S. Doll-play aggression in normal young children: Influence of sex, age, sibling status, father's absence. *Psychological Monographs*, 1951, **65** (Whole No. 6).

Sears, P. S. Child-rearing factors related to playing of sex-typed roles. *American Psychologist*, 1953, **8**, 431. (Abstract)

Sears, R. R. Relation of early socialization experiences to self-concepts and gender role in middle childhood. *Child Development*, 1970, **41**, 267–289.

Sears, R. R., Pintler, M. H., & Sears, P. S. Effect of father-separation on preschool children's doll-play aggression. *Child Development*, 1946, **17**, 219–243.

Sears, R. R., Rau, L., & Alpert, R. *Identification and child rearing*. Stanford: Stanford University Press, 1965.

Seward, G. H. Cultural conflict and the feminine role: An experimental study. *Journal of Social Psychology*, 1945, **22**, 177–194.

Sexton, P. C. *The feminized male: Classrooms, white collars, and the decline of manliness*. New York: Random House, 1969.

Shortell, J. R., & Biller, H. B. Aggression in children as a function of sex of subject and sex of opponent. *Developmental Psychology*, 1970, **3**, 143–144.

Siegman, A. W. Father-absence during childhood and antisocial behavior. *Journal of Abnormal Psychology*, 1966, **71**, 71–74.

Slater, P. E. Parental behavior and the personality of the child. *Journal of Genetic Psychology*, 1962, **101**, 53–68.

Sopchak, A. L. Parental identification and tendency toward disorder as measured by the MMPI. *Journal of Abnormal and Social Psychology*, 1952, **47**, 159–165.

Spelke, E., Zelazo, P., Kagan, J., & Kotelchuck, M. Father interaction and separation protest. *Developmental Psychology*, 1973, **9**, 83–90.

Stanfield, R. E. The interaction of family variables and gang variables in the aetiology of delinquency. *Social Problems*, 1966, **13**, 411–417.

Steimel, R. J. Childhood experiences and masculinity–femininity scores. *Journal of Consulting Psychology*, 1960, **7**, 212–217.

Stendler, C. B. Possible causes of overdependency in young children. *Child Development*, 1954, **25**, 125–146.

Stephens, W. N. Judgments by social workers on boys and mothers in fatherless families. *Journal of Genetic Psychology*, 1961, **99**, 59–64.

Stephens, W. N. *The Oedipus complex: Cross-cultural evidence*. Glencoe, Illinois: Free Press, 1962.

Stolz, L. M. et al. *Father relations of war-born children*. Stanford: Stanford University Press, 1954.

Suedfield, P. Paternal absence and overseas success of Peace Corps volunteers. *Journal of Consulting Psychology*, 1967, **31**, 424–225.

Sutton-Smith, B., & Rosenberg, B. G. *The sibling.* New York: Holt, Rinehart & Winston, 1970.

Tasch, R. J. The role of the father in the family. *Journal of Experimental Education,* 1952, **20**, 319–361.

Tasch, R. J. Interpersonal perceptions of fathers and mothers. *Journal of Genetic Psychology,* 1955, **87**, 59–65.

Thompson, N. L., Schwartz, D. M., McCandless, B. R., & Edwards, D. A. Parent–child relationships and sexual identity in male and female homosexuals and heterosexuals. *Journal of Consulting and Clinical Psychology,* 1973, **41**, 120–127.

Thrasher, F. M. *The gang.* Chicago: University of Chicago Press, 1927.

Tiller, P. O. Father-absence and personality development of children in sailor families. *Nordisk Psyckologi's Monograph Series,* 1958, **9**, 1–48.

Tiller, P. O. *Father separation and adolescence.* Oslo, Norway: Institute for Social Research, 1961.

Toby, J. The differential impact of family disorganization. *American Sociological Review,* 1957, **22**, 505–512.

Tolor, A., Brannigan, G. G., & Murphy, V. M. Psychological distance, future time perspective, and internal–external expectancy. *Journal of Projective Techniques and Personality Assessment,* 1970, **34**, 283–294.

Torgoff, I., & Dreyer, A. S. Achievement inducing and independence granting synergistic parental role components: Relation to daughter's parental role orientation and level of aspiration. *American Psychologist,* 1961, **16**, 345. (Abstract)

Trapp, E. P., & Kausler, D. H. Dominance attitudes in parents and adult avoidance behavior in young children. *Child Development,* 1958, **29**, 507–513.

Travis, J. Precipitating factors in manic-depressive psychoses. *Psychiatric Quarterly,* 1933, **8**, 411–418.

Trenaman, J. *Out of step.* London: Methuen, 1952.

Trunnell, T. L. The absent father's children's emotional disturbances. *Archives of General Psychiatry,* 1968, **19**, 180–188.

Tuck, S. Working with black fathers. *American Journal of Orthopsychiatry,* 1971, **41**, 465–472.

Tuddenham, R. D. Studies in reputation: III. Correlates of popularity among elementary school children. *Journal of Educational Psychology,* 1951, **42**, 257–276.

Tuddenham, R. D. Studies in reputation: I. Sex and grade differences in school children's evaluations of their peers. II. The diagnosis of social adjustment. *Psychological Monographs,* 1952, **66** (Whole No. 333).

Wahl, C. W. Antecedent factors in family histories of 392 schizophrenics. *American Journal of Psychiatry,* 1954, **110**, 668–676.

Wahl, C. W. Some antecedent factors in the family histories of 568 male schizophrenics of the U.S. Navy. *American Journal of Psychiatry*, 1965, **113**, 201–210.

West, D. J. Parental relationships in male homosexuality. *International Journal of Social Psychiatry*, 1959, **5**, 85–97.

West, D. J. *Homosexuality*. Chicago: Aldine, 1967.

Westley, W. A., & Epstein, N. B. *Silent majority*. San Francisco: Jossey-Bass, 1970.

White, B. The relationship of self-concept and parental identification to women's vocational interests. *Journal of Consulting Psychology*, 1959, **6**, 202–206.

Whiting, J. W. M., Kluckhohn, R., & Anthony, A. The function of male initiation ceremonies at puberty. In E. E. Maccoby, T. M. Newcomb, & E. L. Hartley (Eds.), *Readings in social psychology*. New York: Holt, 1958. Pp. 359–370.

Winch, R. F. The relation between loss of a parent and progress in courtship. *Journal of Social Psychology*, 1949, **29**, 51–56.

Winch, R. F. Some data bearing on the Oedipus hypothesis. *Journal of Abnormal and Social Psychology*, 1950, **45**, 481–489.

Wohlford, P., & Liberman, D. Effects of father absence on personal time, field independence, and anxiety. *Proceedings of the 78th Annual Convention of the American Psychological Association*, 1970, **5**, 263–264.

Wohlford, P., Santrock, J. W., Berger, S. E., & Liberman, D. Older brothers' influence on sex-typed, aggressive, and dependent behavior in father-absent children. *Developmental Psychology*, 1971, **4**, 124–134.

Wood, H. P., & Duffy, E. L. Psychological factors in alcoholic women. *American Journal of Psychiatry*, 1966, **123**, 341–345.

Wright, B., & Tuska, S. The nature and origin of feeling feminine. *British Journal of Social Psychology*, 1966, **5**, 140–149.

Wylie, H. L., & Delgado, R. A. A pattern of mother–son relationship involving the absence of the father. *American Journal of Orthopsychiatry*, 1959, **29**, 644–649.

CHAPTER 4

# The Father's Role in the Child's Social Network

MICHAEL LEWIS

*Educational Testing Service*

MARSHA WEINRAUB

*Virginia Polytechnic Institute and State University*

When we talk only of the role and nature of fathers or mothers, we lose sight of the fact that, though these social objects are different, they are in many respects similar. Any discussion of the meaning of parents must be embedded in the larger context of the child's biological–social needs. When viewing it in this fashion, we are forced to broaden our definitions and considerations. In this essay we discuss the child's social world and social needs, focusing on the father's role as it fits within this social network.

A visitor from Mars might report that, as far as most psychologists on Earth are concerned, the only social object in the infant's life is its mother. The effect of the mother on the infant, the effect of the infant on the mother, and the types of interactions that characterize the mother–infant relation have been investigated in great detail. However, the infant's dealings with other members of its family and with the family's friends and acquaintances are treated as though they do not exist or at least as though

This paper was supported in part by a contract from NICHD to the first author (Contract Number NO1 HD 42803), and by a grant from the Small Projects Grant Program at Virginia Polytechnic Institute and State University (Project Number 1892500) to the second author.

they are relatively unimportant. Such overconcern with the importance of the mother to the exclusion of all others offers a very narrow view of the influences on early social and cognitive development. This general failure to consider the child's total social network is, in part, a historical function, whose outlines must first be presented before we consider the social network itself.

## HISTORICAL PERSPECTIVE

The general concern for motivation within psychological inquiry rests on the attempt to answer the simple question of why organisms behave. Inquiry into concepts such as needs, drives, and motives are all attempts to answer this question. Different theoretical approaches have different associated terms. We focus on drives, because much of American psychology was and is concerned with this formulation.

Drive theorists (and others) distinguished two major types of drives: basic biological or primary drives and secondary or derived drives. Primary drives were thought to be those activating and/or directing functions tied specifically to the biological functioning of the organism, such as feeding and drinking; secondary or derived drives were thought to be those functions created through the satisfaction of the primary drives. An example of such a derived drive might be dependency or love.

It was to such a conceptualization of the biology of man and theories of motivation that both Harlow's and Bowlby's initial work was directed. In Bowlby's earliest effort (1951) he concluded that the proper care, attention, and love of a caretaker were necessary for the young human organism to survive. Without such care the infant not only might fail to thrive but also might even die. In effect, by evoking the criteria of survival or failure to thrive, Bowlby was able to argue that the love and care of an adult for the young of the species was not a secondary but a primary drive. Like Harlow's work of the 1950s Bowlby's arguments thrust care and love from its derived and thus nonbiological position back into the arena of biology. Meanwhile American psychologists such as Sears (Sears, Maccoby, & Levin, 1957) were trying to reduce psychoanalytic concepts to learning theory. In so doing they made dependency into a secondary drive derived from the child's need for food.

Harlow and Bowlby, along with Spitz (1945), showed that the lack of love and attention of an adult were sufficient for the organism to fail to thrive and even die. If the need for food was primary because the organism could not thrive or live without it, so too was the need for love and care. Love could then be reintroduced into the study of human behavior (see, for example, "Learning to Love," Harlow & Harlow, 1966)—a result not too surprising for those psychologists who had adhered to the more dynamic theories of motivation proposed by Freud and others at the beginning of the 20th century.

In his theory of attachment Bowlby (1969) went one step further than the original demonstration of the primary importance of love for the development of the human infant. By wishing to make love a biological necessity and imperative of development and growth, Bowlby argued for the biological unity of mother and infant. For him the mother–infant dyad was a biological entity endowed with unique features. It was distinguished from all other relationships and was derived from biological and evolutionary pressures.

Following Bowlby's lead many researchers (e.g., Ainsworth, 1964; Schaffer & Emerson, 1964) became interested in investigating the special features of the mother–child relationship. The resulting literature, which became known as the attachment literature, served an important function by refocusing our concerns on the infant's early relationship to the caretaker, which has been seen as having a *central* or primary role in effecting and determining subsequent intellectual as well as social development. It is becoming more and more obvious, however, that the young child's social, affective, and intellectual development are not solely determined by the mother–infant relationship. Data from both the nonhuman primate and the human studies make it clear that the child's peer relationships occur concurrently with its maternal relationship within the first years of life (e.g., Chamove, 1966; Goodall, 1971; Harlow & Harlow, 1969; Lee, 1975; Lewis & Rosenblum, 1975). Consideration of the infant's relationships with significant others such as fathers, grandparents, and siblings also suggests that these begin early in life and do not necessarily lag behind, nor are they necessarily derived from the child's relationship with the mother (e.g., Lewis, Young, Brooks, & Michalson, 1975; Schaffer & Emerson, 1964). Unfortunately the attachment literature's emphasis on the mother–infant relationship has resulted in such an exclusive view of it that other social and nonsocial (object) relationships are ignored or played down. Moreover, the conceptualization of attachment and its operational definitions limit its applications to studies of other members of the child's social network. What is needed is a conceptual framework that not only allows for but also stimulates investigation of the numerous important social interactions that influence early development.

## THE SOCIAL NETWORK

We wish to offer a more general view of social behavior based on the simple premise that man is by nature a social animal and is a part of a large social network from the very beginning of life. Although no encompassing social network theory is currently available, certain propositions are necessary for such a theory. In the following discussion such a set of propositions is presented. These are broad statements made as simple as possible. Rheingold and Eckerman (1975) have also discussed general features of social behavior in propositional form.

Proposition 1.  *Man Is by Nature a Social Animal and from Birth Enters into a Social Network.*

This statement is meant to imply that the human need for social interaction is as basic an attribute as the need for air. Social contact is a biological imperative. Moreover, the child is preprogrammed to respond to social stimuli and to elicit responses from others.

Proposition 2.  *The Social Network Is Made Up of a Variety of Social Objects, Including at Least Females and Male Adult Caretakers, Siblings, Other Relatives, and Friends.*

This proposition is self-explanatory. It is included merely to emphasize the need to consider social objects other than the mother.

Proposition 3.  *The Social Network Is Made Up of Social Objects, Functions, and Situations.*

The definition of "social object" is difficult. It may not be the case that only persons are responded to as social objects. Certainly many adults (and cultures—for example, the English) consider animals as possessing attributes commonly considered human. Likewise, children do the same. Even nonanimals such as plants are given human attributes by some adults. What the infant considers "human" is an even more difficult question. Nevertheless we hold to the simple view that a social object refers to a human being, understanding that this is an incomplete definition, since what constitutes a social object may vary both ontogenetically and culturally–historically.

Functions and situations are still harder to define. Whereas some attempts have been made to create a taxonomy of objects—for example, living/nonliving, animal/vegetable—there has been little attempt at a taxonomy of functions and situations. Functions include feeding, bathing, changing, and playing. Situations can usually be defined by physical locations—the feeding table, the bathroom, the playground—although feeling states can also be considered, for example, an anxious situation. For a more nearly complete analysis of what constitutes a situation, see Pervin (1975).

Proposition 4.  *Social Objects, Functions, and Situations Are Only Partially Related.*

Social objects refer to people, and social functions are those activities that take place within the social network (see above). Situations refer to the context of a social network and as such have a relationship to function. For example, feeding behavior, a social function, takes place under specific situations, although Lewis and Freedle (1973) report that it takes the first year before parents join physical locations (room in the house) with specific functions. Whereas feeding and bathing functions and situations have relatively little variance, we could possibly find functions and situations that are markedly variable. Social objects and social functions are often related. For example, "mothering" (a function) and mother (an object) are in many cases highly related. We merely point out that the relation between social object, social function, and social situation may be variable.

Proposition 5.   *The Social Network Is Embedded in and Varies as a Function of a Larger Social Environment.*
     Any individual social network must be embedded in both a historical and cultural context and is not invariant with respect to these dimensions.

Proposition 6.   *The Child from Birth on Is an Active Participant in the Social Network.*
     The child from birth enters into interactive relationships within the social network. Within these relationships the child's behavior is both initiating and response. Moreover, the child's primary mode is active rather than passive in constructing and responding to the network.

Proposition 7.   *The Child's Social Behavior and the Composition of the Social Network Change as a Function of Development Status.*
     The effects of experience and maturation as well as ontogenetic status affect the social network, both to change its composition (objects) and to influence its functions and situations.

Proposition 8.   *The Child Has a Repertoire of Behaviors That Are Distributed Within the Social Network as Befits the Object, Function, and Situation of the Specific Interaction.*
     The set of behaviors a child has available can be distributed as a function of the specific interaction. Specific behaviors or subsets of behavior are not restricted to certain social objects but are distributed as a function of the interaction of social objects, functions, and situations.
     There are two corollaries to this proposition:

8a.   *Within an Individual Child's Social Network, Certain Objects Tend to Fill Certain Functions in Certain Situations.*

8b.   *When More Than One Object Fulfills the Same Function, Tension Is Introduced into the System.*

Proposition 9.   *The Child Acquires Knowledge Through Direct and Indirect Interaction with the Social Network.*

The child's knowledge is acquired from its social experiences, although the nature and the manner of acquisition of this knowledge are not currently understood. Direct interaction always involves the child as one of the participants in each interaction and occurs when all the participants are present. It is also possible for the child to be influenced by and to learn from interactions among members of the network when the members themselves are not present. The effects of such interactions might be said to be indirect. The notion of indirect effects has particular import in any discussion of the role of the father because, in our culture at least, the father is usually not the child's primary caretaker and is often absent during the day.

Proposition 10.   *The Structural Aspects of the Social Network Include Interactions and Relationships That Are Arranged in a Hierarchical Order. Interactions and Relationships May or May Not Directly Correspond.*

Interactions are specifiable behaviors or sets of behaviors that are observable and therefore measurable. Relationships are inferred from interactions but are difficult to specify and, hence, are not easily measurable. For example, the behavior between a mother and her child constitutes an interaction. Knowledge of the relationship may be helpful in predicting the particular interaction. Conversely observing the interaction between two individuals without knowing the relationship between them may be helpful in predicting it. After watching a woman interacting with a child—feeding it, for example—we might infer that she is the child's mother, but such an association between interaction and relationship is not always observable. What interaction between a man and a child might lead us to infer that the man is the father of the child?

We have now outlined some broad propositions that might launch a social network theory. Theory building, development of new methodologies, and data collection can all be guided by them. We use this broad framework to examine specifically the nature and role of fathers. This model can be used to explore any of the child's social interactions, whether with adults or peers. The propositions of particular import for the discussion of the father's role in the child's development are the following: (1) the social network is made up of a variety of social objects; (2) social objects, functions, and situations are not necessarily related; (3) the child has a repertoire of behaviors that are distributed within the social network as befits the object, function, and situation of the specific interaction; and (4) the child acquires knowledge through direct and indirect interaction within the social network.

# THE NATURE OF PATERNITY

Before going on to the role of the father, we must deal with the nature of paternity. This may appear to be a rather frivolous topic, and yet careful consideration shows that the biological definition of *father* tells us absolutely nothing about the father's behavioral relationship to the child, though this is not so for the mother. Whereas the father is undistinguished from other male adults, the mother of the child is biologically obvious. In fact, for most primates, the adult female is not monogamous, and paternity cannot, therefore, be determined. Thus neither child nor adult can be certain who the father is. Even within monogamous relationships knowledge of the association between sexual relations and childbirth is required to permit determination of paternity. Compare this situation to that of the mother. Her relationship to the child clearly distinguishes her from all other women. Her biological relationship to the child—first through pregnancy and childbirth and then nursing—makes known to her, to all other individuals, and to the child that she is "mother."

Not only can the mother be defined through her unique biological function, but also much of her behavior toward the child is likewise defined. Thus relationship and interaction for the mother are both biologically defined. The mammalian mother by definition must feed her child. With feeding, other interactions naturally follow; for example, the mother provides satisfaction for the child's warmth, tactile, and kinesthetic needs. These early patterns then build into somewhat predictable interactions in most environments. By 1 year of age, it is not surprising at all that children go to their mothers in times of hunger, fatigue, and fear. Thus for mothers, the biological relationship predicts the expected behavioral and cultural mother–child relationship. Fathers present, however, a different case. Knowing that a man is father of the child tells us nothing about that man's relationship to the child. The father serves no apparent survival function, except perhaps protection and help in the provision of food, warmth, shelter, and stimulation. This function is not, however, as immediately apparent as the mother's interaction is. Moreover, although this paternal role may have helped to perpetuate the species, children could have survived if fathers did not perform their role. They could not, however, have survived if someone did not perform the maternal role. Thus whereas the mother–child relationship is tied to biological dispositions, the father–child relationship is less attached to biology and more free to vary, the continuum of interaction intensity and quality being more heavily determined by other considerations.

Since there are no predictable, biological, predisposed interaction patterns for fathers, the father–infant relationship is more difficult to discern.

It is not surprising that we have no patterns or archetypes for the father as we have for the mother. Parenthetically, as women free themselves from their biological niche, by bottle feeding and substitute caregiving, their role vis à vis the child will become likewise more difficult to discern.

This analysis returns us to the last proposition, in which we specified that relationships (such as parent) and modes of interaction are only casually related. In fact the degree of conjoining between relationship and interaction best differentiates motherhood and fatherhood. For motherhood the relationship and interactions are biologically tied. Thus one can predict types of interactions (such as feeding) from the mother–child relationship. For fatherhood there is little tie between the relationship and interaction. This uniquely defines the potential difference between the male and female in childrearing.

## THE ROLE OF THE FATHER

Our analysis to this point was not meant to suggest that the father's role is not as central to the development of the child as the mother's. On the contrary: for human beings, at least, the father's role may be different from the mother's, but it is also important and needs to be understood. The existing theoretical approaches to early socialization are in general inadequate to the task of understanding the father's role in early child development. According to classical psychoanalytic theory, only the mother is important in the child's first 2 or 3 years of life. The father does not become important until the child reaches the oedipal stage. Stimulus–response theories have pretty much ignored the father's role, since fathers are reputed to have very little interaction with the infant and young child. These theorists seem to assume that, because the father has little stimulus control or reward value for the child, he can have very little effect on the child's development. Finally ethological attachment theory is widely known for its emphasis on the mother to the exclusion of all other social objects (Bowlby, 1951; Kotelchuck, 1972; Lamb, 1975b). The father's value in providing economical and emotional support for the mother is assumed; his effect on the child either directly or indirectly through the mother is thereafter generally ignored.

Guided by the assumptions of the social network approach that we have just outlined, we look at several possible ways in which the father does have an important effect on the young child. As specified in proposition 9, the child can acquire knowledge about its social world through direct and indirect experience. Direct experience results from the interaction of the child with the social object, in this case, the father. Indirect experience results from the child's interaction with others who interact with the social object (father). Our hypothesis is that the mother's effect is mostly direct while the father's is indirect. It is to this difference and its resulting knowledge that we turn our attention. Whereas our hypothesis is that this is one of the major differential features of mothers and fathers, it may also apply to other social objects.

## DIRECT EFFECTS OF FATHERS

Direct effects refer to interaction between the social object and the child. Fathers can directly affect their children through specific activities and patterns of interaction as well as through introducing tension into the system. This tension results from the overlap of the father's specific activities with those of other people.

### Specific Activities

Fathers directly affect their children by interacting with them. To investigate these direct effects, both the nature of specific activities the father (or any social object) engages in with the child and the kinds of behaviors the father reinforces in the child have been examined.[1]

The stereotype of the bumbling father, unable to cope with the fragile infant and unknowledgeable in the ways of babies is rapidly coming under fire. Though it has been commonly assumed that females are naturally more capable than males of being "motherly" or nurturant to infants and young children, studies of both primates and human beings do not support this assumption. According to Mason (1965) there are many primate species in which the males have been observed to assist in the care of the young. In some cases, for example, the marmoset, the male is reported to carry the infant at all times except when it is being nursed or cleaned by the mother. There have even been some isolated reports of relatively stable adult male–infant relationships in which the male adult has served as a mother-substitute. Itani (1959) reports that there are some groups of Japanese macaques in which males of high social rank adopt and care for infants during the birth season.

---

[1] Clearly the differential behaviors and functions of the father in today's society are culturally determined and not immutable. Though in some families the father's role may be equal to the mother's, we are referring here to traditional roles of the father. We do not advocate these roles; we are only trying to offer a framework in which to ascertain and describe them in today's North American society.

Increasingly obstetricians, psychologists, and nurses are becoming aware of the male human being's responsiveness to newborns and infants (Bradley, 1962; Greenberg & Morris, 1974; Parke & O'Leary, 1975). As early as the first few days of life, fathers feel a powerful bond to the newborn. The new father perceives his infant as extremely beautiful and has a desire to touch and hold the baby. Fathers think the baby is perfect, and they are terribly absorbed, preoccupied, and elated. Parke and O'Leary (1975) studied in the hospital both lower-class and middle-class families with their newborns. Fathers were actually observed to interact with the newborn as much as or more than the mother. Most striking of Parke and O'Leary's observations was that fathers and mothers differed only slightly in the amounts of interaction. In fact, when both mothers and fathers were present with their infants, middle-class fathers engaged in more rocking and holding, and lower-class fathers, in more holding, more contemplating, and more physical and auditory stimulation of their infants than their wives did.

It has been suggested that there may be in fathers as in mothers a "sensitive period" in the development of the fathers' attraction toward and interest in the child (Greenberg & Morris, 1974). Though several observers have suggested that fathers who have not had contact with their infants during the first few months have difficulty showing affection for the child later on (Greenberg & Morris, 1974; Nash, 1965; Stolz et al., 1954), more research is needed to clarify how long such a period may be, when it might occur, and what factors may influence it. However, as more fathers are allowed and even encouraged to be present and assist in the pregnancy, birth process, and early stages of infancy, the father's role in the child's development may expand.

Studies of 1- and 2-year-old children interacting with mothers and fathers in structured playroom situations have suggested that there may be very few differences in children's behaviors toward mothers and fathers. Though some preference for mother on touching, staying near, and looking have been observed at 1 year of age (Cohen & Campos, 1974; Lewis, Weinraub, & Ban, 1973), by 2 years of age, few sex-of-parent differences are apparent (Lewis et al., 1973). Kotelchuck (1972) reports that children show very little parent preference until 12 months of age. After that approximately 55% of the children prefer the mother, 25% prefer the father, and 20% prefer either parent over a stranger. In addition mothers and fathers elicit approximately equal amounts of separation protest when they leave the room in the "strange situation" paradigm (Cohen & Campos, 1974; Kotelchuck, 1972; Spelke, Zelago, Kagan, & Kotelchuck, 1973). Most remarkable about these laboratory studies is the similarity of young children's behaviors toward mothers and fathers. There are, however, two points that should be taken into consideration in interpreting the results of these studies. Though these studies suggest that children will demonstrate behaviors toward their fathers that we usually think of as reserved for children with their mothers, children's everyday expression of these behaviors toward fathers must be questioned. Perhaps it would be helpful here to draw a competence-performance distinction. Although these studies suggest that fathers may certainly be as competent as mothers in eliciting approach and affectionate behaviors from their infants and young children when opportunity permits, all have observed infants and their fathers interacting under fairly special and highly unusual circumstances—a laboratory situation or the hospital room after birth. On the other hand, as is evident in Chapter 9, a different picture may emerge when more careful attention is paid to characterizing father–infant interaction in natural situations. The little data available on the extent of father–infant interaction in real life suggest that fathers interact very infrequently with their infants (Ban & Lewis, 1974; Pedersen & Robson, 1969; Rebelsky & Hanks, 1971) and take very little responsibility for infant caretaking. Of the 144 fathers with children from 9 to 12 months old that Kotelchuck (1972) interviewed, only 25% reported they had any regular caretaking activity. Newson (1963, 1968, reported in Lamb, 1975b) found from interviews of mothers of 1- and 4-year-old children that although 99% of the fathers played with their children, many of the fathers were not highly involved in everyday caretaking functions. Although 52% of the fathers were considered to take a highly participant part in their child's daily life, many of the remaining fathers reported only a "moderate share" in the child's activities. This meant that they did not participate in child care unless asked or under very special circumstances. Thus nearly half of these fathers contributed very little to the daily care of their children. Despite the fact that fathers may be as competent as mothers in responding nurturantly, they are much less frequently available on a regular basis to the child than are mothers. It would not be surprising, then, if in everyday circumstances, paternal activities were very much different from maternal activities.

Second, it is also very important to note that in all of the laboratory studies cited, the parents were instructed to respond naturally but not to initiate interaction with the infant. Under such conditions, the similarity of infants' behaviors toward mothers and fathers may not be surprising. It may be that sex-of-parent differences emerge in parent as well as infant behaviors only when parents freely interact with their infant. Sex-of-parent differences in *parental* behaviors in the free play situation should be examined in order to acquire a more complete understanding of sex differences in parent-infant interaction patterns.

## Patterns of Interaction

There also seem to be important qualitative differences in father– and mother–infant interactions. Most of the mother's time may be involved in caretaking, and father's time may be spent more in play. According to Newson, approximately 99% of the fathers played with their children regularly. Lamb (1975a) observed that mothers were more likely to hold their infants during caretaking activities, but fathers held them most often during play.

In general, fathers are less often at home with their children than mothers. Fathers are also less likely to be perceived by children as being involved in the daily tasks of homemaking. In a recent pilot study author Weinraub asked mothers of 3- and 4-year-old children who was responsible for a variety of tasks in and around their homes. The mothers were middle-class, well-educated women from the Princeton, New Jersey, area, most of them under 30 years of age. On 15 of 16 tasks (indoor house painting was the one exception) mothers agreed there was clear division by sex. Mothers reported that they were primarily responsible for making the beds, sewing, vacuuming, washing and ironing clothes, washing dishes, feeding the children, and arranging flowers, and fathers were responsible for carpentry, house repairs, repairing bicycles and toys, adjusting the water heater, mowing the lawn, lifting boxes, and taking out the trash. These data suggest that, although fathers are responsible for certain home-making tasks, these are done less regularly and are less likely to be observed by the young child. When the children were asked who did each of these tasks in their home, 3-year-old children were most likely to answer that mother was responsible for most of these tasks; 4-year-old children, however, were well aware of the division of labor, and their reports were in high agreement with their parents. In general, children's and adolescents' concepts of parental roles in the home suggest that they see mothers as engaged in taking care of children and homemaking, and fathers are seen as engaged in activities outside the home involving physical strength and endurance (Bronfenbrenner, 1961; Finch, 1955; Hartley, 1960).

Parsons and Bales (1955) have argued that sex roles are divided along instrumental and expressive lines. This sex-role differentiation is considered responsible for differences in mothers' and fathers' behaviors toward children. According to them the father's role is one of competence and mastery. The father is provider, judge, and ultimate disciplinarian. He is the child's model for planning ahead, delaying gratification, and interacting with the world outside the family. The mother, on the other hand, is expressive. She smooths over interpersonal relations and keeps the family functioning as a unit. She is affectionate, solicitous, conciliatory, and emotionally supportive. Though we believe that separation of these two modes —the expressive and the instrumental—along sex-role lines is unrealistic,[2] there is some evidence to support the fact that, at least within the family, fathers play a more instrumental role, linking the child to the larger society outside the family, and mothers play a more expressive, nurturant role. Interviews with mothers and fathers conducted by Stolz (1966) revealed that fathers were more likely to be concerned with children's education, moral values, personal values, and physical safety, and mothers were more concerned with their children's emotional adjustment and freedom from anxiety. Fathers were also more likely to say that socialization agents other than the mother, such as schools and the media, were beneficial to the child.

Interviews and observations of children suggest that children from preschool through high school perceived their mothers as more affectionate and nurturant, and fathers were perceived as more punitive and restrictive (e.g., Armentrout & Burger, 1972; Bronfenbrenner, 1961; Kagan, Hosken, & Watson, 1961). Mothers were often seen as more supportive and encouraging of their children, and fathers were seen as more action oriented. A study by Osofsky and O'Connell (1972) is particularly interesting; they observed 4- to 6-year-old girls in structured and unstructured interactions. Fathers tended to be less involved than mothers with their daughters. Fathers appeared to be more action oriented, either jumping into or totally withdrawing from physically helping their child with the task, and mothers were more supportive and encouraging of their daughter's efforts. Even more interesting was the girls' differential behavior with mothers and fathers. While with their fathers, girls spent more time working on the task; with their mothers they spent more time talking and seeking help and attention. These findings are congruent with Thomes' (1968) observation that elementary school children perceived their fathers' role in the home as teacher, disciplinarian, and protector and with Stehbens and Carr's (1970) observation that ninth-grade children saw their fathers as less involved in their lives, less child centered and less accepting of them as individuals than mothers.

*Sex Typing.* Fathers have also been considered to play a very large role in the child's—girls' as well as boys'—acquisition of sex-role typing (see, for example, Johnson, 1963). Although the father's influence on the

---

[2] Mothers must be instrumental to run a household efficiently and economically, and many mothers hold jobs as well as run households. Many fathers must be expressive as well as instrumental to perform competently in their jobs (especially if fathers are teachers, counselors, psychologists, administrators, or salesmen).

child's sex-role typing is still relatively undefined, data from the 1950's and 1960's suggest that fathers are much more actively and personally concerned with proper sex-role acquisition than mothers are (Aberle & Naegele, 1952; Goodenough, 1957; Lansky, 1967; Tasch, 1952). Fathers are particularly opposed to feminine behavior in their 2- to 4-year-old sons; they are likely to worry when their sons appear unaggressive and unwilling to defend themselves (Goodenough, 1957), but they rarely express such concern about unaggressiveness in their daughters (Lansky, 1967; Tasch, 1952). According to Aberle and Naegele (1952), middle-class fathers are very concerned that their children receive proper sex-role training. Fathers expect their sons to be masculine and to go on to college and a good job; they expect their daughters to be pretty, sweet, and affectionate and to get married. Mothers, on the other hand, are less likely to differentiate between sons and daughters (e.g., Bee, Van Egeren, Streissguth, Nyman, & Leckie, 1969) and have not been shown to have very strong attitudes about sex-appropriate behavior (e.g., Sears et al., 1957). Whether these greater sex-role concerns of the father hold true today, however, is open to question.

*Individual Differences.* These differences in fathers' and mothers' direct interaction are moderated by many variables. Social class is one variable that has been studied. Others are the sex and parity of the child.

In general middle-class fathers tend to be more involved in childrearing than lower-class fathers (see Lynn, 1974, for a more nearly complete review). Whereas middle-class wives expect their husbands to be as supportive of the children as they are, working-class wives expect their husbands to restrain the children (Kohn & Carroll, 1960). Not surprisingly then, lower-class fathers are also more likely to demand conformity and obedience than middle-class fathers, and middle-class fathers are more likely to read to their children, take their children to the library and on other trips, set educational standards, and make college plans for their children (Freeberg & Payne, 1967). Despite these differential views of the father's role, the lower-class father seems to have much less influence over family life (Benson, 1968), and more middle-class than lower-class children see their father as the family boss and disciplinarian (Fitzgerald, 1966). Middle-class fathers are more likely to assume a teaching role (Hess & Torney, 1967), to encourage curiosity in their children, and to be concerned with their children's future education (Kohn & Carroll, 1960). This differential conceptualization of the father's role in the two social classes may help to explain Radin's (1973) finding that, for 4-year-old children, paternal nurturance was related to high scholastic aptitude in the middle-class but not in the lower-class boys.

Various studies suggest that parental sex differences in responses to children may be affected by the sex of the child. In their study of parent–newborn interaction Parke and O'Leary (1975) observed that fathers are more likely to stimulate (especially touch and vocalize to) firstborn sons than later born sons or daughters of any birth order. Rebelsky and Hanks (1971) reported that fathers are more likely to decrease their vocalizations to daughters but not to sons in the second and third months of life. Gewirtz and Gewirtz (1968) report that Israeli fathers tend to stay longer in the children's house with their 4-month-old sons than with daughters. On the other hand, Pedersen and Robson (1969), who interviewed mothers about paternal interaction with infants, found no sex-of-child differences in the amount of time fathers spend playing with and caring for their 8- to 9-month-old infants, and Lamb (see Chapter 9 and 1976) reports no sex differences in mother– or father– infant interaction in infants of 7 to 13 months of age. With somewhat older infants, similar sex-of-parent, sex-of-child interactions have been reported.

The following differences have been reflected in the child's behaviors toward mothers and fathers. Spelke et al. (1973) observed that 1-year-old children were more likely to vocalize to the same-sexed than to the opposite-sexed parent. Lewis et al. (1973) observed that 1-year-old boys look more at their fathers than at their mothers. Likewise 2-year-old girls are more likely to play in the presence of their mothers than of their fathers. Interestingly, when 2-year-old children are with their same-sexed parent, looking at the parent is highly correlated with amount of play. Lamb (1975a) reported that, at 8 months of age, all children prefer to play with their fathers rather than with their mothers. Further, Lynn and Cross (1974, in Lynn, 1974), examining preschool children's parent-play preferences, found that, as young as 2 years, both boys and girls prefer to play with their fathers.

Although sex-of-parent and sex-of-child differences in the nature of the direct interaction between parent and child are still not clear, the research that exists so far suggests that the sex of the interactors, as well as social class and possibly even birth order, may contribute to individual differences in the direct interaction between parent and child.

*Tension Introduction.* Another way fathers (or other social objects) might directly affect their children is simply by interacting with the child in ways similar to the mothers' but just slightly different. We refer to this particular process by which the father affects the child as *tension introduction.* Tension is introduced into a social network when more than one person fulfills a social function or interacts with the child in a particular context. Tension develops as the child learns to discriminate between the cues and the responses of the different persons. As in bilingualism, learning to differentiate the similar but different cues emitted by two (or more) people may prolong the period of learning to interact smoothly with each person. Moreover, having two social objects does not necessarily increase the amount of social interaction the child may experience, since it has been shown that the presence of the father tends to reduce the amount of mother–child interaction (Parke & O'Leary, 1975). Having to relate to two similar but slightly different persons may, however, force the child at an early age to learn to be sensitive to social cues, to discriminate subtle differences between individuals, and to tolerate the frustration generated during the process of learning differential expectations about fathers' and mothers' behaviors.

A purely conjectural theory is that the absence or reduction of intense interaction with different social objects (like father) may influence the appearance of stranger anxiety in the 8- to 9-month-old infant. One might hypothesize that learning to deal with at least two different social objects (mothers and fathers or mothers and grandmothers—it does not matter what combination of two) enables the child to "solve" the problem of difference and as such reduces the tension produced by the appearance of a complete stranger. This possibility is currently being investigated by using the amount and number of early differential social objects as the independent variable in stranger-anxiety studies.

At a later age the presence of two adult authority figures with similar but different opinions and expectations regarding the child's behavior forces the child to learn to deal with differences of opinion and to consider more than one side of an argument or issue. Thus the presence of two social objects should be expected to increase the child's analytic skills. Finally the fact that these two social objects may have different opinions of the child's worth makes it more likely that, if one person's opinion of the child is extreme and unjustified, the other parent's opinion may counteract the negative influences of the first parent's opinion. Thus self-concept may be affected by the presence of two parents as opposed to one parent.

Tension production and resolution is an interesting conception; unfortunately at present, there exists very little empirical support for such a position. In general the literature contains few studies bearing on this mode of influence. In the infancy literature there are none. Studies of father absence showing that it may affect the child's intellectual development (e.g., Santrock, 1972; Sutton-Smith, Rosenberg, & Landy, 1968) point to the possible role of the father in tension introduction, although this evidence is somewhat controversial (see Herzog & Sudia, 1973). Studies indicating that father absence influences the child's analytic reasoning skills offer somewhat stronger support (see, for example, Barclay & Cusumano, 1967; Carlsmith, 1964; Sciara, 1975). However, the severe confounding of most studies of father absence limits the extent of support they can offer.


## INDIRECT EFFECTS

Although the father affects the young child directly through interactions, these are limited in quantity. This may be the reason why the father's role has been so largely ignored. The father may, however, exert great influence on the young child indirectly—by affecting the child's social network.

In general, fathers spend little time with their young infants. From interviews with mothers, Pedersen and Robson (1969) concluded that fathers played with their 9-month-old infants approximately 8 hours a week—that is slightly more than an hour a day, including weekends. They also noted great variability in how much time fathers reportedly spent with their infants. The reports ranged from 45 minutes to 26 hours a week. Rebelsky and Hanks (1971) reported that fathers spent an average of only 37.5 seconds a day verbally interacting with their 3-month-old or younger infants. From interviews with middle-class fathers, Ban and Lewis (1974) found that they played with their 1-year-old children on the average of 15 minutes a day. They observed that the amount of time fathers spent with their children only weakly if at all predicted the child's observed behavior. Though Pedersen et al. (1973) observed that the amount of time the father interacted with his 5- to 6-month-old child predicted the child's alertness, responsiveness, and interest in the environment, it was also the case that father-present children had more toys than father-absent children. Other studies have not reported correlations between amount of time spent with father and the child's behavior. With another sample Pedersen and Robson (1969) found that estimates of the amount of time fathers either played with or were available to their children were not correlated with measures of the child's attachment to the father, as measured by the child's greeting behavior toward the father. Moreover, Kotelchuck (1972) reported that the amount of time fathers interacted with their children was not related to the child's behavior toward the father in the laboratory.

The data, though sparse, indicate, first, little direct interaction between fathers and 1-year-old children and, second, little relationship between amount of interaction and socioemotional or cognitive development. Indirect modes of influence (at least some of them) may be more prepotent at this time. The indirect modes are (1) the father's emotional support of other members of the social network—particularly the wife–mother, (2) the father's being referred to and discussed by others in his absence, and (3) the father's being related to and interacting with other social objects in the child's social network.

## Emotional Support

Individuals within the social network affect not only the child's behavior but also the behavior of other dyads, and triads, and so forth, within the network. Bronfenbrenner (1973), referring to this as a "second-order" effect, has stressed its importance. Yet it seems evident that the father's emotional as well as economic support for the mother (and vice versa, of course) can affect even the very young child in a variety of ways. For example, by allaying the mother's doubts, anxiety, and frustrations and by making her feel more self-confident and secure, the father can enable the mother to be more responsive to the child. Clearly an unhappy wife may be an unhappy mother. In addition growing up in a loving, relatively consistent, and stable family atmosphere, the young child may be more relaxed, self-confident, and more likely to perceive social interaction as a pleasant, enjoyable occupation.

It is becoming increasingly recognized (Lynn, 1974; Schaefer, 1974) that one of the ways fathers may contribute to children's development is through emotional support of the mother. Many of the effects of father absence may be explained by the differences in the mother's behavior toward her children and not necessarily the father's absence per se. In many cases mothers whose husbands are absent must provide economic support for the family. Whether or not they want to work, they must. They must also do all the household tasks by themselves with little help from people outside the family. Lynn reports several studies (e.g., Kriesberg, 1967; Parker & Kleiner, 1966; Tiller, 1958) in which mothers without husbands on a regular or temporary basis described some of the difficulties they experience. They felt much worse off psychologically and were not so goal oriented. They were more concerned about the children's educational achievements than other mothers, they made more inappropriate efforts to help their children, and they were more likely to be dissatisfied with the child's level of work and less likely to be involved with the schools or to aspire to a college education for their children. Finally mothers whose husbands were temporarily absent on a regular basis led less active social lives, worked less outside the home, were more overprotective of children, and were more likely to be concerned with their child's obedience and manners rather than with happiness and self-realization. Hoffman (1971) suggests that not having a husband might make a woman feel "busier and more harassed and hence impatient with the child and oriented toward immediate compliance rather than long-range character goals" (p. 405). As a result these mothers might be more likely to use power assertion as opposed to induction as a disciplinary technique. In Hoffman's studies, single mothers reported expressing less affection for their sons. Since there were no differences in expression of affection for daughters, it may be that mothers can compensate for the effects of father absence, but they may do so only with daughters.

Pedersen (1975) has contributed one of the few studies of the ways in which each person in the social network influences and is influenced by other members. He observed high interrelationships for the families of boys but not girls among the following factors: (1) infant's alertness, motor maturity, and irritability; (2) the mother's feeding competence; (3) the father–infant play, positive and negative affect; and, most relevant here, (4) the father's esteem for the mother as "mother" and the amount of tension and conflict in their marriage. Pedersen suggests that the father's warmth and affection may help to support the mother and make her more effective. Finally the study by Parke and O'Leary (1975) suggests that the father's interest in the infant is likely to enhance the mother's interest. When mothers were with their husbands, they were more likely to explore the infant and smile at the infant than when they were alone. Moreover, the father's attitudes toward the infant may be contagious. When mothers were with fathers, they tended to touch their male infants more than their female infants. There were no sex-of-child differences in touching, however, when the mother and child were alone.

### Representational Modes

Representational activities occur under at least two conditions: (1) whenever there are more than two individuals in a social network and (2) whenever one individual is separated from another and cannot be directly experienced. In the first condition the child's knowledge of the father and the child's relationship to the father are created by a third social object (most often the mother but not uncommonly grandparents, friends, and older siblings). For example, the mother might say, "That's daddy's briefcase" or "Daddy's going upstairs to wash up for dinner. Why don't you go with him." A grandparent might say "You look just like your father."

The second representational activity involves the re-presenting of an absent object. This ability, an attribute of human beings, is more likely to occur the more frequently the object is absent. This separation of the object from the child that allows for the development of representation has been called "distancing" by Sigel (1970). Distancing requires the child to construct, elaborate, and label the absent one and thus promotes abstraction. Distancing may play a larger role in the father–child than in the mother–child relationship. The absence of the father frequently requires the child to represent him or think about him in his absence. Children may spend less time thinking about mother in her absence only because she is less frequently absent.

Unfortunately there is very little research into the effects of different representational modes, especially in early childhood. One recently conducted study does, however, provide support for differential use of distancing with mothers and fathers. Brooks and Lewis (1975) studied the first labels used by infants aged 9 to 36 months. While nine different pictures were presented singly to each child (mother, father, adult male and female, self, male and female infant same age as subject, male and female children about 10 years old), only the data on the labeling of mother and father interest us here.

At 15 months, the age of first labeling, 25% of the infants labeled pictures of their fathers correctly; no infants labeled pictures of their mothers. By 18 months, all infants labeled pictures of their fathers correctly. Some used the label "daddy" incorrectly; that is, they overgeneralized the label. In contrast only some of the 18-month-old infants used the label "mommy" for their mother, and there was very little overgeneralization. Mothers of the 15-month-old infants confirmed this mother–father difference in labeling. They reported that "daddy" preceded "mommy" in their children's first speech. This finding has been noted by others (e.g., Jakobson, 1962).

This result is highly counterintuitive, but its explanation may be relevant to our discussion. Why should the "daddy" label be acquired before the "mommy" label? Two possible explanations within the representational mode are suggested. These are, in fact, the two modes described earlier. Infants may hear their mothers labeling their fathers more often than the reverse, and this experience—knowing about a second social object from a third social object—may account for the phenomenon. In a recent test of this possibility Dunn (personal communication) checked the verbal transcripts of 38 different mother–infant pairs seen in their homes for at least 2 hours of observation and recording. The children were 14 months old and the families were all British. Dunn counted 103 "mommy" and 43 "daddy" references in more than 5000 utterances. Thus the frequency of utterances fails to support the explanation of differential label use.

The second possibility is provided by the distancing hypothesis, which states that representation is acquired best when there is distance between social objects. The failure of sheer numbers of reference to account for differential labeling implies this hypothesis may have merit. Further support for it comes from two sources. First, the labeling of "mommy" most characteristically took place in Dunn's study around an ongoing activity the mother was performing. For example, a mother might comment, "Mommy is tying your shoe." This is not so for "Daddy" labels, which most often took place in discussions of activities not taking place at that time, as in "Daddy will come home early tonight." Thus the "daddy" label may be learned in the absence of the social object, but the "mommy" label may be learned in the presence of the social object. A second source of support for the distancing hypothesis comes from an observation by Rosenblum (personal communication), who reports that macaque monkeys reared only with their mothers—and never seeing another monkey—have difficulty in finding her (recognizing) when placed in a situation where their mother and other female monkeys are present. Again the result is counterintuitive if we believe that representation is best built up over repeated experience with the object; the more experience the greater the representation. Representation may be best constructed with the child's experiencing both presence (interaction) and absence of the other social object in some as yet unknown ratio.

Whereas this aspect of knowledge about the father—his label—is just one feature, this example does point out that indirect experience can affect the child's knowledge about social objects. This is not, of course, restricted to the father. In the Brooks and Lewis study (1975) of differential labeling, four mothers worked or left the house more frequently than the others. It was the children of these mothers who used the "mother" label earliest.

Three studies have suggested that children often do think about their fathers, even in their absence, and this may account for the lack of findings regarding effects of father absence in some studies. Bach (1946) observed urban elementary school children whose fathers had been away from 1 to 3 years in World War II. These children included their fathers in doll play and fantasy about as often (23%) as father-present children (25%) did. The attitudes toward the father strongly affected the child's fantasies. Baker, Fagan, Fischer, Janda, & Cove (1967) found a similar continued participation in the child's fantasies despite his absence. Crain and Stamm (1965), studying elementary school children whose fathers had been away for 3 months or less, found them very similar to the control children.

The effects of distancing are not, of course, limited to the fathers. If the mother is away from home for a good portion of the day but is referred to in her absence, this too may facilitate distancing. Kohen-Raz (1968, in a review by Etaugh, 1974) gave Bayley tests to infants from 1 to 27 months of age in kibbutzim, private homes, and institutions. Boys in private homes whose mothers were working away from the homes had higher developmental quotients than children whose mothers stayed home.

## Transitivity

A complex property of some relationships composing a social network is that they are "transitive." We suggest the term *transitive* to refer to the fact that, if the mother has a relationship to person "X," then the child also forms a relationship to person "X," regardless of whether or not the child has ever directly interacted with that person. In the case of the father, the child's relationship to its mother and the mother's to the child's father facilitate the child's to the father, regardless of the amount of direct interaction between child and father. Transitivity may be necessary in all extended social networks. According to this principle, relationships can be created or enhanced by indirect relationships. For example, if I love and am loved by my mother and she loves and is loved by my father, then it follows that I love and am loved by my father, even in the absence of my father's interaction toward me. Transitivity is a sophisticated mental process requiring and enhancing knowledge about self as well as the ability to recognize complex, indirect relationships. This same principle of transitivity can be applied to relationships between child and grandparent, which are mediated through the child's relationship with its parents and the parents' with their parents. Transitivity is very important in influencing a child's relationship with his grandparents, especially when the children have little direct interaction with their grandparents because of distance or other reasons. We have observed that many children express deep feeling for grandparents rarely seen, much more than for a friend of the family whom they see considerably more often. A transitivity explanation would take the following form: $a$ loves $b$ (I love my father), $b$ loves $c$ (my father loves his father), therefore $a$ loves $c$ (I love my grandfather). The example further points out that these transitivity relationships can also be determined by the intensity of the direct relationships. If $a$ loves $b$ is weak or if $b$ loves $c$ is weak, then $a$ loves $c$ should also be weak.

The literature contains some data on older children that have a bearing on this issue. Mary Romm (1969, in Lynn, 1974) has characterized the mother's role as very important in the father–daughter relationship. If the daughter believes that her mother truly cares about the father and loves and respects him, then she can also feel free to develop a close relationship with her father without guilt and resentment toward her mother. Once the girl has experienced a close and warm relationship with her father, she can transfer the same feelings toward her father toward a man her own age when the time comes. Others have also emphasized the importance of the father in the daughter's acquisition of femininity. According to Hetherington (1967) femininity in girls is related to the father's approval of the mother as a model as well as the father's own masculinity and his reinforcement of the daughter's participation in feminine activities. The mother's femininity is not, however, related to the daughter's femininity.

## CONCLUSION

We have suggested that the failure to conceptualize adequately the child's social network has done a disservice to the complex fabric of social relationships that the child is capable of establishing and learning. The lack of models of the social network has constrained research efforts regarding the child's relationship not only to the father but also to peers (see Lewis & Rosenblum, 1975), grandparents, uncles, aunts, friends, and others.

We have suggested some important propositions that may facilitate study of the social network. We have focused on the various ways one has of acquiring knowledge about others. Although most research has concentrated on the direct effects of social objects, we have argued for the consideration of additional and alternative modes of influence, which we have tried to specify. Members of the social network may affect the child directly or indirectly. Direct modes of influence include special activities and patterns of interaction and introduction of tension into the system. Indirect modes of influence include emotional support, representation, and transitivity. These modes of influence affect and are affected by cognitive as well as socioemotional development.

In our society fathers and mothers may differ mostly in terms of the modes through which the child interacts with them. Biologically the mother is tied to the direct mode of interaction and knowledge, and the father to the more indirect modes. This difference may be responsible not only for how we view mothers and fathers—mothers as nurturant, fathers as action oriented—but also for how we view men and women in general. The female—mother—is soft, nurturant, protective because her interactions consist of these types of direct activities; these interactions have their origins in biological function. The male—father—is aloof, distant, authoritarian, and action oriented as a result of his indirect relationship to the child. As technology gives us the opportunity to transcend our biology, however, these distinctions between mother and father, female and male should be open to change.

# REFERENCES

Aberle, D. F., & Naegele, K. D. Middle-class fathers' occupational role and attitude toward children. *American Journal of Orthopsychiatry*, 1952, **22**, 366–378.

Ainsworth, M. D. S. Patterns of attachment behavior shown by the infant in interaction with his mother. *Merrill-Palmer Quarterly*, 1964, **10**, 51–58.

Armentrout, J. A., & Burger, G. K. Children's reports of parental childrearing behavior at five grade levels. *Developmental Psychology*, 1972, **7**, 44–48.

Bach, G. Father fantasies and father typing in father-separated children. *Child Development*, 1946, **17**, 63–80.

Baker, S. L., Fagan, S. A., Fischer, E. G., Janda, E. J., & Cove, L. A. Impact of father absence on personality factors of boys. I. An evaluation of the military family's adjustment. Paper presented at American Orthopsychiatric Association meeting, Washington, D.C., March 1967.

Ban, P., & Lewis, M. Mothers and fathers, girls and boys: Attachment behavior in the one-year-old. *Merrill-Palmer Quarterly*, 1974, **20**, 195–204.

Barclay, A., & Cusumano, D. R. Father absence, cross-sex identity and field-dependent behavior in male adolescents. *Child Development*, 1967, **38**, 243–250.

Bee, H. L., Van Egeren, L. F., Streissguth, A. P., Nyman, B. A., & Leckie, M. S. Social class differences in maternal teaching strategies and speech patterns. *Developmental Psychology*, 1969, **1**, 726–734.

Benson, L. *Fatherhood: A sociological perspective*. New York: Random House, 1968.

Bowlby, J. *Maternal care and mental health*. Geneva: WHO, 1951.

Bowlby, J. *Attachment and Loss*, Vol. I. *Attachment*. New York: Basic Books, 1969.

Bradley, R. Father's presence in delivery rooms. *Psychosomatics*, 1963, **3**, 474–479.

Bronfenbrenner, U. Some familial antecedents of responsibility and leadership in adolescents. In L. Petrullo & B. M. Bass (Eds.), *Leadership and interpersonal behavior*. New York: Holt, Rinehart & Winston, 1961. Pp. 239–271.

Bronfenbrenner, U. Interactions among theory, research and application in child development. Paper presented at the meetings of the Society for Research in Child Development, Philadelphia, March 1973.

Brooks, J., & Lewis, M. Person perception and verbal labeling: The development of social labels. A version of this paper was presented at the meetings of the Society for Research in Child Development, Denver, April 1975, and the meetings of the Eastern Psychological Association, New York City, April 1975.

Carlsmith, L. Effects of early father absence on scholastic aptitude. *Harvard Educational Review*, 1964, **34**, 3–21.

Chamove, A. S. The effects of varying infant peer experience on social behavior in the rhesus monkey. Unpublished master's thesis, University of Wisconsin, 1966.

Cohen, L. J., & Campos, J. J. Father, mother, and stranger as elicitors of attachment behaviors in infancy. *Developmental Psychology*, 1974, **10**, 146–154.

Crain, A. J., & Stamm, C. S. Intermittent absence of fathers and children's perception of parents. *Journal of Marriage and the Family*, 1965, **27**, 344–347.

Dunn, J. Personal communication. October 1975.

Etaugh, C. Effects of maternal employment on children: A review of recent research. *Merrill-Palmer Quarterly*, 1974, **20**, 71–98.

Finch, H. M. Young children's concepts of parent roles. *Journal of Home Economics*, 1955, **47**, 99–103.

Fitzgerald, M. P. Sex differences in the perception of the parental role for middle and working class adolescents. *Journal of Clinical Psychology*, 1966, **22**, 15–16.

Freeberg, N. E., & Payne, D. T. Dimensions of parental practice concerned with cognitive development in the preschool child. *Journal of Genetic Psychology*, 1967, **111**, 245–261.

Gewirtz, H. B., & Gewirtz, J. L. Visiting and caretaking patterns for Kibbutz infants: Age and sex trends. *American Journal of Orthopsychiatry*, 1968, **38**, 427–443.

Goodall, J. L. Some aspects of mother–infant relationships in a group of wild chimpanzees. In H. R. Schaffer (Ed.), *The origins of human social relations*. New York: Academic Press, 1971. Pp. 115–128.

Goodenough, E. W. Interest in persons as an aspect of sex difference in the early years. *Genetic Psychology Monographs*, 1957, **55**, 287–323.

Greenberg, M., & Morris, N. Engrossment: The newborn's impact upon the father. *American Journal of Orthopsychiatry*, 1974, **44**, 520–531.

Harlow, H. F., & Harlow, M. K. Learning to love. *American Scientist*, 1966, **54**, 244–272.

Harlow, H. F., & Harlow, M. K. Effects of various mother–infant relationships on rhesus monkey behaviors. In B. M. Foss (Ed.), *Determinants of infant behavior, IV*. London: Methuen, 1969. Pp. 15–36.

Hartley, R. E. Children's concepts of male and female roles. *Merrill-Palmer Quarterly*, 1960, **6**, 83–91.

Herzog, E., & Sudia, C. Children in fatherless families. In B. M. Caldwell & H. N. Ricciuti (Eds.), *Review of child development research*, Vol. 3. Chicago: University Press, 1973.

Hess, R. D., & Torney, J. *The development of political attitudes in children*. Chicago: Aldine, 1967.

Hetherington, E. M. The effects of familial variables on sex typing, on parent–child similarity and on imitation in children. In J. P. Hill (Ed.), *Minnesota symposia on child psychology*, Vol. 1, Minneapolis: The University of Minnesota Press, 1967. Pp. 82–107.

Hoffman, M. L. Father absence and conscience development. *Developmental Psychology*, 1971, **4**, 400–406.

Itani, J. Paternal care in the wild Japanese monkey, *macaca fuscata fuscata*. *Primates*, 1959, **2**, 61–93.

Jakobson, R. Why "Mama" and "Papa"? In *Selected writings of Roman Jakobson*. The Hague: Mouton, 1962.

Johnson, M. M. Sex role learning in the nuclear family. *Child Development*, 1963, **34**, 319–333.

Kagan, J., Hosken, B., & Watson, S. Child's symbolic conceptualization of parents. *Child Development*, 1961, **32**, 625–636.

Kohn, M. L., & Carroll, E. E. Social class and the allocation of parental responsibilities. *Sociometry*, 1960, **23**, 372–392.

Kotelchuck, M. The nature of the child's tie to his father. Unpublished doctoral dissertation, Harvard University, 1972.

Lamb, M. E. Infants, fathers, and mothers: Interaction at 8 months of age in the home and in the laboratory. Paper presented at the meetings of the Eastern Psychological Association, New York, April 1975 (a).

Lamb, M. E. Fathers: Forgotten contributors to child development. *Human Development*, 1975, **18**, 245–266 (b).

Lamb, M. E. The one-year-old's interaction with its parents. Paper presented to the meetings of the Eastern Psychological Association, New York, April 1976.

Lansky, L. M. The family structure also affects the model: Sex-role attitudes in parents of preschool children. *Merrill-Palmer Quarterly*, 1967, **13**, 139–150.

Lee, L. C. Toward a cognitive explanation of peer interaction. In M. Lewis & L. Rosenblum (Eds.), *Friendship and peer relations: The origins of behavior*, Vol. IV. New York: Wiley, 1975. Pp. 207–221.

Lewis, M., & Freedle, R. Mother–infant dyad: The cradle of meaning. In P. Pliner, L. Krames, & T. Alloway (Eds.), *Communication and affect: Language and thought*. New York: Academic Press, 1973. Pp. 127–155.

Lewis, M., & Rosenblum, L. (Eds.), *Friendship and peer relations: The origins of behavior*, Vol. IV. New York: Wiley, 1975.

Lewis, M., Weinraub, M., & Ban, P. Mothers and fathers, girls and boys: Attachment behavior in the first two years of life. Paper presented at the meetings of the Society for Research in Child Development, Philadelphia, March 1973.

Lewis, M., Young, G., Brooks, J., & Michalson, L. The beginning of friendship. In M. Lewis & L. Rosenblum (Eds.), *Friendship and peer relations: The origins of behavior*, Vol. IV. New York: Wiley, 1975. Pp. 27–66.

Lynn, D. B. *The father: His role in child development*. Monterey, California: Brooks/Cole Publishing Company, 1974.

Mason, W. A. The social development of monkeys and apes. In I. DeVore (Ed.), *Primate behavior: Field studies of monkeys and apes*. New York: Holt, Rinehart & Winston, 1965.

Nash, J. The father in contemporary culture and current psychological literature. *Child Development*, 1965, **36**, 261–297.

Osofsky, J. D., & O'Connell, E. J. Parent–child interaction: Daughters' effects upon mothers' and fathers' behavior. *Developmental Psychology*, 1972, **7**, 157–168.

Parke, R. D., & O'Leary, S. Father–mother–infant interaction in the newborn period: Some findings, some observations, and some unresolved issues. In K. Riegel & J. Meacham (Eds.), *The developing individual in a changing world. Vol. 2. Social and environmental issues.* The Hague: Mouton, 1975, in press.

Parsons, T., & Bales, R. F. *Family, socialization and interaction process*. Glencoe, Illinois: Free Press, 1955.

Pedersen, F. A. Mother, father and infant as an interactive system. Paper presented in the symposium *Fathers and Infants* at the meetings of the American Psychological Association, Chicago, August 1975.

Pedersen, F. A., & Robson, K. S. Father participation in infancy. *American Journal of Orthopsychiatry*, 1969, **39**, 466–472.

Pedersen, F. A., Rubenstein, J. L., & Yarrow, L. J. Father absence in infancy. Paper presented at the meetings of the Society for Research in Child Development, Philadelphia, March 1973.

Pervin, L. Definitions, measurements, and classifications of stimuli, situations, and environments. Research Bulletin 75–23. Princeton, N.J.: Educational Testing Service, 1975.

Radin, N. Observed paternal behaviors as antecedents of intellectual functioning in young boys. *Developmental Psychology*, 1973, **8**, 367–376.

Rebelsky, F., & Hanks, C. Fathers' verbal interaction with infants in the first three months of life. *Child Development*, 1971, **42**, 63–68.

Rheingold, H. L., & Eckerman, C. O. Some proposals for unifying the study of social development. In M. Lewis & L. Rosenblum (Eds.), *Friendship and peer relations: The origins of behavior*, Vol. IV. New York: Wiley, 1975. Pp. 293–298.

Rosenblum, L. Personal communication. October 1975.

Santrock, J. W. The relation of type and onset of father absence to cognitive development. *Child Development*, 1972, **43**, 455–469.

Schaefer, E. S. The ecology of child development: Implications for research and the professions. Paper presented at the meetings of the American Psychological Association, New Orleans, August 1974.

Schaffer, H. R., & Emerson, P. E. The development of social attachments in infancy. *Monographs of the Society for Research in Child Development,* 1964, **29**(3, Serial No. 94).

Sciara, F. J. Effects of father absence on the educational achievement of urban black children. *Child Study Journal,* 1975, **5**, 45–55.

Sears, R. R., Maccoby, E. E., & Levin, H. *Patterns of child rearing.* New York: Row, Peterson, 1957.

Sigel, I. The distancing hypothesis: A causal hypothesis for the acquisition of representational thought. In M. R. Jones (Ed.), *Miami Symposium on the Prediction of Behavior, 1968: Effect of early experiences.* Coral Gables, Florida: University of Miami Press, 1970. Pp. 99–118.

Spelke, E., Zelazo, P., Kagan, J., & Kotelchuck, M. Father interaction and separation protest. *Developmental Psychology,* 1973, **9**, 83–90.

Spitz, R. A. Hospitalism: An inquiry into the genesis of psychiatric conditions in early childhood. In A. Freud et al. (Eds.), *The psychoanalytic study of the child.* New York: International Universities Press, 1945.

Stehbens, J. A., & Carr, D. L. Perceptions of parental attitudes by students varying in intellectual ability and educational efficiency. *Psychology in the Schools,* 1970, **7**, 67–73.

Stolz, L. M. Old and new directions in child development. *Merrill-Palmer Quarterly,* 1966, **12**, 221–232.

Stolz, L. M. et al. *Father relations of war-born children.* Stanford, California: Stanford University Press, 1954.

Sutton-Smith, B., Rosenberg, B. G., & Landy, F. Father-absence effects in families of different sibling compositions. *Child Development,* 1968, **38**, 1213–1221.

Tasch, R. J. The role of the father in the family. *Journal of Experimental Education,* 1952, **20**, 319–361.

Thomes, M. M. Children with absent fathers. *Journal of Marriage and the Family,* 1968, **30**, 89–96.

# CHAPTER 5

# The Role of the Father:
# An Anthropological Perspective

MARY MAXWELL WEST

*Harvard University*

and

MELVIN J. KONNER

*Harvard University*

In both popular and scientific literature on the family there has recently been an increased interest in the role and behavioral capabilities of fathers. Whereas past literature deals with the role of the father in sex-role and moral development and addresses the process of identification, the most recent literature shows slightly different emphases—more concern with the attachment and nurturant potential of fathers, with the biological bases of parental behaviors, and with the exact content of father–child interaction. This chapter examines parental behavior in cross-phylogenetic and cross-cultural perspective in an effort to describe and interpret the range of human paternal behavior and characterize it as a feature of the behavior of the species. Various forms of paternal behavior are discussed, but the primary focus is on caregiving and nurturant behavior.

We approach this effort in six steps: (1) description of a model of male parental investment arising from a new body of theory in evolutionary biology that is making a dramatic impact on ethology and anthropol-

We are grateful to John and Beatrice Whiting for inspiration and guidance and for developing many of the key ideas in the cross-cultural data; to Sarah Blaffer Hrdy, John Sodergren, and Martin Etter for helpful discussion and references; to Steven Stepak for preparation of the manuscript; and to Irven DeVore and Robert Trivers for the original synthesis and provocative presentation of the theory at the core of our discussion.

ogy; (2) review of the evidence on how this model applies to the natural variation in the behavior of animals; (3) ethnographic sketches of fathering and family relations in five exemplary cultures, showing the range of human male parental investment and its association with different subsistence adaptations; (4) presentation of quantitative data on male parent–offspring relations among the !Kung San (Bushmen), an African gathering and hunting culture representing the basic sociocultural form characterizing our own ancestors during almost all of human evolution; (5) presentation of quantitative data on 80 human cultures of all subsistence types, illustrating changes since the gathering and hunting era; and, (6) discussion of plasticity in male parental investment, especially in human beings, and a characterization of the role of fathers in our own culture.

## NATURAL SELECTION AND PARENTAL BEHAVIOR

### Male Parental Investment

To consider parental behavior in the framework of natural selection theory, we must first note that the predominant behavior patterns in a species are those that have maximized individual reproductive success during evolution. This is because the genes of those individuals who respond to any situation in a way that is reproductively advantageous to them are present in a higher frequency in subsequent generations. Thus differences in parental behavior between species (or any separately breeding populations) represent different strategies that maximize individual reproductive success in the separate species. Furthermore, where there is variation in parental care patterns *within* a species, we would expect that it is related to different environmental conditions and that the various strategies would function to maximize reproductive success in particular ecological settings. In these species a flexible program for parental behavior is available and is used adaptively.

In this section we discuss relations between adult males and infants cross-phylogenetically in terms of male "parental investment," a concept developed by Trivers (1972), which considers parental behaviors as they are operated on by natural selection. Trivers defines parental investment as "any investment that enhances the offspring's chance of surviving at the cost of the parent's ability to invest in another offspring" (1972; p. 139). He states that the relative parental investment of the sexes governs sexual selection (courtship and mating patterns), sexual dimorphism, patterns of competition, and adult sex ratio. He offers the following examples

of male parental investment, here applying mainly to birds: provision of
food for the female during the breeding period, finding and defending a
nesting place, building the nest, defending the female, brooding the eggs,
feeding and protecting the young, and, in group-living species, defending
the group. A continuum describing the interrelationships among variables
discussed by Trivers and others he cites is roughly sketched in Table 1.
While not all aspects of this model are testable, those features that are
quantifiable underlie a good deal of current research, and we use it to
guide the discussion in this chapter. Data supporting different sections of
the model have been collected for many species (Trivers, 1972; Wilson,
1975). Examples are given of species at different points on the continuum,
including man. The distances from left to right are merely ordinal and
do not represent an interval scale.

Man is located on this continuum between monogamy and polygyny
because monogamy with some incidence of polygyny is the most common
form of marriage in nonindustrial cultures. Even where monogamy is the
rule, pair bonding is less permanent than in many monogamous birds, and
men sometimes have secondary unofficial spouses, whereas women usually
do not. Polyandry is extremely rare in human societies. On a world sample
of nonindustrial cultures (Murdock & White, 1969), forms of marriage are
distributed as follows: 1% polyandry, 17% monogamy, 51% occasional
polygyny, and 31% common polygyny. Furthermore adult sex differences
in human beings are in keeping with the left side of the continuum: human
males are slightly larger and heavier than females and have a higher
metabolic rate and higher mortality.

**Table 1.   Continuum of Parental Investment and Related Variables**

|  | Elephant seal | Baboons, Macaques | Monogamous birds Man  Marmosets | Polyandrous birds |
|---|---|---|---|---|
| Parenting | Male parental investment lower than female parental investment | | Male and female parental investment about equal | Female parental investment lower than male parental investment |
| Mating system | Polygyny | | Monogamy | Polyandry |
| Courtship | Male–male competition for females, female choice | | Low intrasex competition | Female–female competition for males, male choice |
| Adult sex differences | Males larger, higher metabolic rate, perhaps more brightly colored, etc. | | Low sexual dimorphism | Females larger etc. |

Research in this area faces problems in measuring some of these variables and in demonstrating their relationship to reproductive success. In measuring parental investment, for example, how do we determine whether feeding the young represents more investment than defending the troop, especially if this is frequent and the male risks his life in defense activities? The concept of parental investment seems to work best in this model when continuous care of individual offspring, especially carrying or feeding them, is considered high parental investment. It is well to keep in mind that defense activities constitute parental investment. But this form of investment, directed as it is relatively indiscriminately toward all the offspring in a group, does not affect relations between specific males and specific young, which are the main concern of this book.

High male parental investment is rare among vertebrates, especially among mammals. Whereas there are 8000 species of monogamous birds and some polyandrous species, among mammals both long-term pair bonding and significant male care of young are rare. In mammals the female is uniquely adapted to care for the young, and the male is not necessarily joined to the mother–offspring unit. In most mammals the parents do not remain together after copulation, and the male contributes no parental investment except the sperm. The best mammalian examples of high male parental investment are certain species of wild canids and nonhuman primates. Among wild canids both sexes feed the young by regurgitation after the hunt, a pattern resembling that of pair-bonding birds. The female is provisioned if she is unable to hunt, as are other "baby-sitters" or individuals unable to hunt in the group-living canids (Fox, 1975; van Lawick & van Lawick-Goodall, 1971). In several species of New World monkeys the male is reported to carry the young (a pair of twins) the majority of the time and to provision the young in some cases (Epple, 1975; Mason, 1966; Mitchell & Brandt, 1972; Ruvolo, unpublished). The amount of direct "care" of offspring by human fathers is much less than in these species of canids or New World monkeys, but the human father does provide for and defend the female and offspring. Provision of resources and defense are the most important forms of male parental investment in human beings. We examine the variance in human paternal behavior in detail in the next section.

Why has the role of males become more prominent in these species? They have in common the need to care for slow-developing—"altricial"—young (Eisenberg, 1966; p. 68). But there are many altricial species in which the father does not have a large role. Blaffer Hrdy (personal communication) notes that the extensive carrying of young by male marmosets may simply be related to twinning; nursing two slow-developing primate young is such a burden for the female that other care devolves upon the male. Jolly (1972; p. 212) speculates that the selective advantages of the human pair-bonded family may be related to scarcity of resources on the savannah, the probable environment of most of human evolution; to a need to protect females and young; and to long infant dependency. Recent experimental research by Dudley (1974a, 1974b) on the California mouse, which usually lives in isolated pairs and exhibits high amounts of male parental care, shows that the male's presence significantly increases the pups' chances of survival and their weight gain, especially in conditions of noncontinuous presence of the mother or of early weaning. (Under natural conditions foraging requires the mother to be frequently absent— more so if there are scarce resources.) A field study of marmots in two different settings (Barash, 1975) shows that males interacted with their young more in the less populated setting. Here they lived in the same burrows with the mother and offspring, but in the more populated setting they made separate burrows and interacted less frequently with their offspring and more frequently in vigilant and defense encounters with other adult males. Barash cites field work by McKinnon on orangutans in two settings: where there were more predators and competitors, males joined the mother–offspring unit (presumably protecting and guarding their parental investment); where there were fewer predators and competitors, the males lived separately. These studies indicate that both scarcity of resources and requirements for defense are important determinants of the male's proximity to the mother–offspring unit and of the forms of male parental investment he gives. If defense or male–male competition are required, he may be distant or close; if caretaking is required, he is close. Although such studies of marmots and orangutans may seem remote from the study of human fathers, we propose to show that ecological factors influence human fathering as well.

### Male Parental Investment, Social Organization, and Ecology

Ecological factors have also been stressed by various workers who focus on differences in social organization across groups of related species (e.g., Crook, 1970; Eisenberg, 1966; Fox, 1975). It is probably impossible to draw conclusions that would apply cross-phylogenetically about specific ecological determinants of male parental investment. But relationships between male parental investment and social organization can be distinguished, and ecology is the final framework within which both of these must be considered. In this section we review male parental investment and social organization in canids and nonhuman primates with brief references to ecology.

Within both canids and nonhuman primates are found gradients of social organization—some species are asocial, some live in isolated pairs with offspring, and some live in larger groups. The longest pair bonds occur where the pair lives separately, as in coyote and golden jackal pairs, who remain together beyond the breeding and rearing season. In pack-living canids, the bond between a mated pair persists during the rearing period and may persist subsequently in the wolf, but this is not fully verified (Fox, 1975; p. 445). Although data on male parental investment in the three types of social organization are not complete, it appears to be highest in the isolated pairs. In observations of dingos, an asocial species, the adult male visited the den regularly and was greeted affectionately but was not seen to provide food (Corbett & Newson, 1975). Among coyotes, however, who form isolated pairs, the male provides food for his mate in late pregnancy when she does not hunt and to the pups when they begin to eat solid food (Gier, 1975). In the pack-living African wild dogs, all pack members share in the feeding and protection of the young (Estes & Goddard, 1967), suggesting that the contribution of the father to his own offspring alone may be less than in the coyote. Since packs are extended family units (Fox, 1975), the sharing of caretaking is probably an example of kin-directed altruism (Hamilton, 1964). Fox (1975) relates the three types of social organization to ecological factors—mode of hunting and size of prey, food availability and dispersion, and predation pressure.

Reviews of the literature on primates (Blaffer Hrdy, 1976; Jolly, 1972; Mitchell & Brandt, 1972; Redican, Chapter 11) present evidence that different *forms* of male parental investment—especially "care" versus "protection"—accompany different forms of social organization and ecological conditions. Male care of infants does not follow phylogenetic trends and may be more related to ecology (Jolly, 1972). The gibbons and various New World monkeys that exhibit the most caretaking are arboreal and omnivorous and live in isolated pairs or extended families. These include the marmosets, tamarins, calimico, night monkey, and titi. In marmosets, for example, the male may assist at birth, receiving and washing the infants, and he assumes the major responsibility for carrying and grooming the infants until they become physically independent. The extent of provisioning of food is less well known, but male and female parents share food and allow the young to take food from them. The female has priority access to food after parturition (Snyder, 1972).

The Old World monkeys, gorillas and chimps, do not give continuous care of infants but often protect, retrieve, and defend them (as well as the troop). Males respond rapidly to infants' distress cries. In some species play is found, and in most there are distal forms of association such as orienting to or traveling beside an infant. Baby-sitting and adoptions occasionally occur. These species are all group living and at least partly terrestrial and engage in brief consortships or promiscuous mating. Precise assessment of male parental investment is difficult because paternity is usually not known. In Old World monkeys, especially, adult male–infant relations are oriented around male–male competition and dominance in the group. The association found here of male–male competition, greater sexual dimorphism, diffusion of paternity, and low male parental investment is in keeping with the left side of the continuum in Table 1. There is much less carrying of infants than in New World monkeys, and when it occurs, it is often not caretaking but "agonistic buffering"—carrying an infant, sometimes roughly, to inhibit the aggression of another male in a tense encounter. This goes hand in hand with the protective reaction of males to infants: carrying an infant can inhibit another male's aggression because males have a protective response to them. Other interactions found with infants seem also to be more beneficial to the adult male's reproductive success than to the infant's and thus seem not to represent forms of actual male "parental investment" (see Blaffer Hrdy, 1976, for review of adult male–infant relations in terms of reproductive success). For example, Hamadryas baboon males attend to female infants who will later become sexual partners for them in their harems. Males may associate with infants to achieve a higher rank, which improves their reproductive success. Crook and Goss-Custard (1972) note that male "care" of young in Japanese macaques may permit a rise in social rank of the male if the infant receiving attention is kin to higher ranking animals. Ransom and Rowell (1972) report that mature male baboons sought contact and interaction with high-ranking females and their offspring but rarely with low-ranking mothers. How much these attentions benefit the infant's eventual reproductive success is not known. Where "care" is given, it is more frequently from leaders, who are more likely to be the fathers of the infants in the troop, since it has been shown that the dominant males have greater access to females at the time of ovulation (see Redican, Chapter 11). For example, leaders among Japanese macaques apparently take over the care of 1- and 2-year-old infants when their mothers are delivering new infants. Each of the two Barbary macaque males in one observed troop carried, retrieved, and protected an infant and ignored other infants. (This species shows more interaction between males and infants than most Old World species.) The greater attention of leaders to infants may be a function of their higher degree of paternity and thus represent actual parental investment, but even in these cases male parental investment is certainly lower than female. In Old World monkeys, protection and distal associations between males and infants are the primary forms of male parental investment, and these are related to the hierarchical nature of the group. Male parental investment has a different form and different origin from that in New World monkeys.

A comparison of the three mammalian cases in which long-term pair bonding occurs shows that there are important differences in several features (Table 2). In canids, the male's importance lies in providing food resources, which in this carnivorous species requires continuous hunting. In omnivorous humans, there is less extreme reliance on hunting, but the male is an important provider of various resources. The number of young and way of locating them also differ. The three cases represent three quite different phylogenetic adaptations, but they have in common long-term pair bonding and significant association between male and female parents and offspring.

## THE ROLE OF THE FATHER IN CROSS-CULTURAL PERSPECTIVE

The remainder of this chapter deals with relations between human fathers and their children, especially infants, in cross-cultural perspective. The following five ethnographic sketches give an idea of the range of styles of fathering and family relations in nonindustrial cultures. We have chosen five major modes of subsistence that represent different solutions to providing for basic human needs. Just as male parental investment was seen to vary with social organization and ecology in the last section, so it varies across human cultures with different subsistence adaptations. The examples are all drawn from the large sample used for analyses presented in a subsequent section.

Table 2. Comparison of Mammalian Species with Relatively Long Pair Bonds

| | Coyote, Golden Jackal | New World Monkeys | Man |
|---|---|---|---|
| Number of young | Several | Twins | Single |
| Location of young | Cached | Carried | Carried |
| Role of male in provisioning female and young | High | Low | High |
| Importance of meat in diet | High | Low | Medium |
| Female sexual receptivity | Noncontinuous | Noncontinuous | Continuous |
| Relationship of pair to other conspecifics | Isolated | Isolated | In group |

## The Father in Five Major Subsistence Adaptations

*!Kung San (Bushmen), in northwestern Botswana in 1970. Source: Konner (fieldwork).* The !Kung are typical warm-climate gatherers and hunters living in a semi-arid region of northwestern Botswana. Subsistence derives 60 to 80% from vegetable foods collected and prepared by women. Meat hunted by men supplies the remaining 20 to 40%. Each sex works about half the days in the week, allowing much leisure. The family is usually monogamous with a small (5 or less) percentage of polygynous marriages, in the context of a seminomadic band of about 30 people representing the extended families of either or both spouses.

Indulgence of infants and young children is as high as has ever been described for a human population, and older children are given much freedom and few responsibilities. Women carry infants more than half the waking hours, sleep with them, and nurse them several times an hour. Almost no restrictions are placed on premarital sex, but traditional marriage is early adolescence for girls and young adulthood for men.

Since fathers are not occupied in subsistence activities for half the days of the week and are often available for parts of the remaining days, their potential contact with infants and children is high. They often hold and fondle even the youngest infants, though they return them to the mother whenever they cry and for all forms of routine care. Young children frequently go to them, touch them, talk to them, and request food from them, and such approaches are almost never rebuffed. Boys are not expected to become involved in hunting activity until early adolescence at the soonest and then follow their fathers and uncles on hunts for years before being able to conduct hunts themselves. Information transfer on such hunts has an "observational learning" rather than a "teaching" character. The same may be said about the transfer of spiritual medicine, though this is rarely acquired from the young man's own father. Traditional male initiation rites involve making boys dance in the cold for a few days, frightening them in the dark and making small cuts on their foreheads to signify their accession to manhood. Homicidal violence occurs in this society, but wars were apparently very rare historically, and no wars had occurred for many decades at the time of study. Preparation for fighting did not occupy the men in any way, and learning to fight was not considered an important skill for boys.

*Rwala Bedouin, north Arabian desert, in 1913. Source: Musil (1928).* Distance between the father and young children, strong emphasis on male authority, and cultivation of fierceness in conjunction with frequent warfare are typical of many cultures whose primary mode of subsistence is animal husbandry—the "herders." Though the Masai and Dodoth raise cattle rather than camels and horses, family relations are similar to the Bedouin. The animals are the focus of their lives, providing transportation, food, and cash resources. Raiding and warfare are also important activities, to acquire booty and new territory and to seek revenge. The men alone manage and control the subsistence activities and engage in the fighting, and the women labor hard at domestic chores. In this polygynous, patrilineal, and patrilocal group, the men have strong authority; the father is a master over both women and children. The tent is divided into separate men's and women's compartments, and the men eat separately from the women and children. Until their 7th year, children remain with their mother in the women's compartment, "going to their father only for an occasional talk." Boys are circumcised by their father when they are between three and seven, in ceremonies that last several days:

A she-camel is sacrificed . . . the women carry the bread and meat to the father's tent, where on this occasion anybody may enter and eat his fill. After dinner the father (or nearest relative) takes on his lap the boy, dressed in black on that day. He pretends to show him something, and then cuts off his prepuce with a sharp knife. . . .

The older boys spend more time with their father and other men, attending to the horses, bringing fuel and water to the men's quarters, and learning to shoot and go on raids by midadolescence. Younger children are disciplined with a stick by mother or father, but older boys are punished for disobedience by their father with a saber or dagger.

By cutting or stabbing them the father not merely punishes the boys but hardens them for their future life. In the opinion of the Bedouin the son who disobeys is guilty of rebellion, for which the proper punishment is the saber.

*Lesu Village in New Ireland, Melanesia, in 1930. Source: Powdermaker (1933).* Lesu is typical of many cultures in the Pacific islands in which the primary mode of subsistence is small-scale gardening in combination with fishing. Fishing, done mainly by men, and taro gardening, done mainly by women, are equally important, each providing 40% of subsistence. The household is usually a monogamous, nuclear family, although a few men have two wives, each with separate houses. The sexes keep separate in public life, and men's houses exist where older boys, unmarried men, and men whose wives are pregnant or nursing sleep at night. But in family life the sexes are affectionate and intimate, and the family is described as a close-knit unit. The husband quite frequently takes care of the baby while his wife is busy in the garden or with her cooking.

He will sit in the compound in front of the house, or on the beach, with the infant, playing with him, fondling and petting him. . . . The father and mother are equally tender towards their child, as are also other male and female relatives. A man plays with his child for hours at a time, talking pure foolishness to the baby. . . . Whenever there is a group of natives together . . . or men idling on the sand, the child is tossed about from one to the other, fondled, patted, jumped up and down, and kissed. . . . Or they may croon one of the dance songs to the infant.

Children from 3 to 6 are rarely left alone; they are either with their parents in the village, or, if the latter are away in the gardens or fishing, they are with their older brothers or sisters.

When the parents are in the village, the little child follows them about. They are present at all the adult activities, dance rehearsals, rites, communal preparations of food, etc. . . . thus their education is begun in the observance of those activities in which they will later participate. . . . At all rites, and in social life, the boys are with the men and the little girls are with their mothers.

As children grow older, there is a gradual increase in their participation in the village life, but girls are kept busier than boys.

[The boys] watch the adult male activities but do not participate as actively as the girls do in the women's work. When the men are fishing the boys are present, eagerly watching it all, but they do not participate.

At age 9 to 11, elaborate initiation rites mark a boy entrance into adult society. They endure for many months and involve much feasting and dancing. At the height of the rites, the adult men and women engage in a spirited fight, hurling stones and coconut shells and exchanging jeering talk. The men enter a specially built enclosure, where the boys are circumcised, while the women dance in sympathy for them. The father holds his son steady while another man does the cutting. The boys are then secluded from women for several weeks while they are instructed by the older men. Finally they are ritually returned to society.

Although fighting between villages occurred in the past, it appears to have been on a small scale.

*Thonga of the Ronga subtribe, east coast of South Africa, in 1895. Source: Junod (1927).* The Thonga represent simple field agriculture— small-scale grain and vegetable agriculture done mainly by women— which is here found in combination with herding, done mainly by men. As in Lesu, the women's gardening is a substantial direct contribution to subsistence, but here polygyny is more common, and the men do herding instead of fishing. The family is the extended polygynous family, each wife having her own hut within the large family compound. The man's ideal is to acquire several wives who bear him many children, and large herds of cattle, with which he can acquire wives for his sons.

Relations between fathers and infants are dramatically different from those in Lesu. The men do not relate to infants and young children except in occasional ritual events. Taboos prevent the father from almost any contact with infants under 3 months. Babies are cared for by the mother and older siblings, and upon weaning, toddlers go to live with the grandparents for a few years. The distance between fathers and young children does not seem to be due to lack of free time, since the ethnographer specifically comments on this:

> . . . their life is far from being as active as that of the woman . . . their duties only require of them isolated effort from time to time . . . a great part of their time is devoted to paying visits . . . we can fairly estimate at three months the time required for the work which they have to do for the village and for the community. The remaining months are devoted to pastimes and pleasures.

When slightly older, the girls help their mothers and the boys tend goats.

> If they are negligent, the father will thrash the boys when they come back. . . . The [father] relationship implies respect and even fear. The father, though he does not take much trouble with his children, is nevertheless their instructor, the one who scolds and punishes. Absolute obedience is due him on the part of his sons and daughters.

Though no data are given on the frequency of feuding or warfare, there are an elaborate structure of war costumes and weapons and an army numbering about 2000.

*Koreans of Sondup'o village, Kanghwa Island, in 1950. Source: Osgood (1951).* This community represents advanced agriculturalists—plow agriculture with intensive rather than extensive land use. Advanced agriculture differs from the small-scale agriculture of Lesu and Thonga in that men are in charge of it, the use of the plow makes a larger scale possible, and it comes to dominate over any other subsistence activities of the culture. Analysis of a large sample (presented below) shows that in advanced agriculture there is greater variance in the father's closeness to the family than in other subsistence types. But on the average they are midway between the harshness of the Thonga and Rwala and the warmth of !Kung and Lesu fathers.

The family is monogamous and usually extended, with patrilocal residence and patrilineal inheritance. The oldest son inherits all the father's property. The father is described as "stern and somewhat distant" from his children.

The father is likely to be tolerantly affectionate to the little [daughter] but becomes more removed as she grows up. . . . The relationship between father and son has an ambivalent quality . . . it is not a union of familiarity and demonstrable affection. . . . The father becomes the symbol of the disciplinarian and is apt to be a strict one in practice. . . . The son must show utter respect regardless of how he really feels. . . . [The children] run to their mothers for relief and she is known as the "kind parent," he as the "stern" one.

Young children are cared for by the mother and older siblings; older children go to school. The mother works some in the fields, but most of her work is domestic. The father is separated from his children during the day because he works in the fields, and children only occasionally help with this. The state provides for police and defense.

## Dimensions of the Human Father's Role

These and other cases show that styles of fathering vary within a certain range and can be viewed in relation to family structure and the work activities of adult men and women. The elements that vary are:

1. the number of wives the father has and is responsible to, and the number of children he has and is responsible to;
2. the amount of authority he has over these;
3. the amount of time that he is in proximity or contact with his wive(s) and children at different ages, and the qualities of the interactions that occur;
4. the amount that he, as opposed to his wife or others, cares for his children;
5. the amount that he, as opposed to his wife or others, is responsible for direct or indirect teaching of skills and values;
6. the amount that he participates in ritual events connected with his children;
7. the amount that he, as opposed to his wife or others, works to provide the primary subsistence needs of the family or community;
8. the amount that he and others engage in fighting to defend or increase resources of the family or community.

Since some variation in paternal behavior exists and, as we later see, is related to basic environmental conditions (indicated by subsistence adaptation), human males can be said to possess a flexible program for paternal behavior.

Relations between some of these elements are suggested by the case studies and other cross-cultural data. (They are tested on a large sample in a later section.) In the two cases above in which the father has very little contact with young children (Rwala and Thonga), polygyny and warfare are common, and obedience to paternal authority is stressed. The role of the father is to procreate, defend, command, and punish. In two of the three cases above in which women are directly involved in subsistence activities (Lesu and !Kung), fathers are closer to infants and children. In the third (Thonga), fathers are distant, and polygyny and warfare are present. Whiting and Whiting (1975a) have proposed that distant fathering is associated with the necessity for rearing and training boys to be warriors, where accumulated resources have to be defended and no special defense forces are provided by the state.

From these and other ethnographies we find also that, in less modern cultures, children of 6 to 8 years begin to learn adult skills by observing or participating in adult activities: one role of the father is to teach subsistence skills. In modern states where specialized labor exists and caste systems are absent, schools have taken over this function and the father's (and mother's) role as teacher is diminished. Another role of fathers in many cultures has been noted by B. Whiting (personal communication): the father "plays" with his children, but the mother has the more serious and final responsibility for their care.

Lamb (1975) cites several studies of his own and others that confirm this distinction in American families and raises another possible aspect of the Western father's role: to introduce the child to the world outside the home. This would seem to apply where the mother does not work outside the home. But in many non-Western societies, the amount of time spent by father, mother, and children "around the house" varies, and so does the nature of their work; it is possible that a child may not associate mother with "home" and father with "outside of home" so strongly. In many non-Western cultures, the most likely source of introduction to the "outside world" is actually the juvenile play group, which also introduces the child to adult skills and values (Konner, 1975). American middle-class children and their mothers are unusually socially isolated compared to those in many other cultures. If a mother is not employed, she can stay at home all day quite self-sufficiently and go out only for shopping. Furthermore the wealthier the neighborhood, the more space and privacy exists between dwellings; children may not be able to form their own playgroups easily, especially young children. The American middle-class father may thus become the only one who can "introduce the child to the outside world," but his authority in this role is reduced (compared to other cultures) by his inability to educate his child directly in subsistence activities. Moreover, what the mother does at home is often comparatively frivolous—it is not pressing work that is essential to subsistence. As a result the mother may exhibit indecisiveness. B. Whiting (personal communication) has noted this quality in American mothers as compared with busier mothers in some non-Western cultures.

We now turn to quantitative data, first on fathers among the gathering and hunting !Kung San (Bushmen) and then on a world sample of 80 cultures, all nonindustrial subsistence types, covering all contexts for paternal behavior up to the present.

## Father–Child Proximity Among !Kung Hunter–Gatherers

In this section we present data describing the level and pattern of male parental behavior among the !Kung San (Bushmen) of Botswana, a typical warm-climate gathering and hunting group. These data serve two purposes for the argument in the chapter. First, warm-climate gathering and hunting is the mode of subsistence adaptation that characterized 98 to 99% of human and protohuman history (Lee & DeVore, 1968). Thus the forces of natural selection operating on human fathers and their relations with their children during the time when the basic nature of such relations was being formed are in evidence in this context. Second, the !Kung are classified as "high" on closeness of fathers to infants and young children in a sample of 80 independent nonindustrial societies (Barry & Paxson, 1971). They thus represent the upper end of the range of direct male care of offspring seen in the ethnographic record and, by inference, in the human past. General aspects of their culture and child care patterns, and of the behavior of fathers toward children, have already been described. Some quantitative data on behavior of fathers toward infants and toward 2- to 6-year-old children are described here.

The data on infants come from 15-minute observations divided into contiguous 5-second time blocks; 43 infants were observed six times at from one to four age points. Observations were distributed throughout the daylight hours and over all days of the year. An observation was not begun unless the infant was awake, not in the sling at the mother's side, not suckling, and within 15 feet of the mother. Onset of observation was in no way made contingent on availability of the father. Table 3 displays the data on the number and percentage of observations of boys and girls in two age groups in which fathers interacted with the infant in any way. Overall incidence of father participation for the sexes and ages combined is 13.7%. Fathers are significantly more likely to interact with boys than with girl infants at the older ($\chi^2 = 4.61$, $p < .05$) but not at the younger age level.

Precisely comparable measures for mothers are not available, because observation was contingent on mothers' presence. We estimate that randomly distributed 15-minute time samples would have a less than 1%

**Table 3.   Number of Infant Observations with Father Interaction**

|  | Boys | | | Girls | | |
|---|---|---|---|---|---|---|
| Age | Total Observations | Father Present | % | Total Observations | Father Present | % |
| 0–26 weeks | 112 | 13 | 11.6 | 59 | 2 | 3.4 |
| 27–99 weeks | 130 | 29 | 22.3 | 94 | 10 | 10.6 |

chance of showing no interaction between mother and infant, so that a figure to compare with the 13.7% figure would be something above 99%. This comparison somewhat inflates the participation of fathers, since the amount of interaction within the 15 minutes is greater for mothers than for fathers. But it provides some basis for comparison with mother– and father–infant interaction in samples with which the reader may be familiar.

The actual amount of interaction and its breakdown into four sub-categories of caretaker–infant proximity are shown in Table 4. Because of small *n*'s the sexes are combined for the comparison of mother and father proximity patterns. Figures shown represent the average number of 5-second time blocks in which fathers or mothers were the primary caretakers, divided according to whether they were face-to-face, in physical contact, within 2 feet, or more than 2 feet away from the infant at the time. Two averages are given for the father—one averaged over all observations and one averaged over only those in which he was present.

Father participation, indicated by total father scores divided by father score plus mother score, is 2.3% at the younger age and 6.3% at the

**Table 4.   Frequency of Type of Proximity Expressed in the Average Number of 5-Second Blocks per 15-Minute Observation That Each Parent Was Primary Caretaker**

|  | Father (all observations) | Father (when present) | Mother (always present) |
|---|---|---|---|
| Age: 0–26 weeks | | | |
| Physical contact | 3.80 | 43.27 | 123.46 |
| Face-to-face | 0.74 | 8.46 | 11.56 |
| Within 2 feet | 0.09 | 1.07 | 10.54 |
| 2 to 15 feet | 0.00 | 0.00 | 0.11 |
| Age: 27–99 weeks | | | |
| Physical contact | 3.85 | 32.13 | 58.41 |
| Face-to-face | 0.25 | 1.43 | 3.69 |
| Within 2 feet | 2.26 | 13.00 | 32.91 |
| 2 to 15 feet | 0.77 | 4.41 | 8.38 |

older age. Despite these extreme differences in father and mother participation, the distribution of caretaking time among the four proximity categories is remarkably similar for mothers and fathers, including a parallel decrease with age in the relative contribution of physical contact. This suggests that the pattern of proximity to infants is similar for fathers and mothers, despite large differences in absolute total time and despite the fact that only mothers are involved in nursing and toileting of infants.

As for older children, the father was present in 30% of observations on 2- to 6-year-old children, also made throughout daylight hours and all days of the week. This contrasts with 19% on similar observations made in London by Konner for a comparative study (Blurton Jones & Konner, 1973). On observations of 3- to 11-year-old children in six cultures, including the United States, father presence ranged from 3 to 14%, with 9% in the United States (Whiting & Whiting, 1975b). Although these figures are not really comparable, owing to the different age ranges, !Kung fathers appear to be closer than fathers in other subsistence types, including industrial societies.

## Changes Since the Gathering and Hunting Era

In this section we present analyses of a world sample of 80 cultures on the relationship between father–infant proximity, family organization, and subsistence activities. Since all modes of subsistence except industrialized societies are included, these analyses cover all contexts for paternal behavior up to the present. The aim of these analyses is to determine the sociocultural conditions that influence the distance between the human father and his young children. The father–infant proximity scale, recently developed by Barry and Paxson (1971), is described in Table 5; the sample and all other scales are described in the Appendix. Although father–infant proximity does not necessarily indicate actual child care, it gives the opportunity for child care, and we have used it to index the potential for this form of male parental investment. Other forms—defense and provision of resources—are included in the discussion.

*Proximity of Fathers versus Mothers to Their Children.* Comparison of the distributions of Barry and Paxson's scale on father–infant proximity with their scale called "Nonmaternal Relationships" gives an idea of the differential proximity of fathers and mothers to their children (Table 5). The scales were not designed to be comparable, but review of several cases suggests that the closest fathers probably compare with "half or less of time" on the mother scale. For example, the mothers of Alor are rated at the extreme of the scale (5), and yet they certainly are frequently in proximity to their infants (DuBois, 1944). The scales are aligned in the table to facilitate comparison.

If "regular close relationship" between father and child is equated with "half or less of time" spent together by mother and child, then 4% of fathers are close to infants, compared with 98% of mothers. In early childhood, 9% of fathers are close, compared with 66% of mothers. These distributions show an extreme discrepancy between maternal and paternal proximity in infancy that lessens slightly in early childhood.

Although the father scale does not tell how much the fathers are actually caring for or interacting with their children, there is evidence that some amount of nurturance and dependency takes place. Father–infant proximity is correlated with "Nonmaternal Relationships" ($r = .36$, $p < .01$) and with "Earliness of Child Autonomy," which is defined as independence from earlier caretakers ($r = -.48$, $p < .01$). On a small sample, father–child proximity is correlated with "Dependency Satisfaction Potential" ($r = .42$, n.s.). We therefore interpret father–infant proximity in human fathers to involve at least some interaction and development of dependency.

*Subsistence Adaptation and Family Organization.* What conditions predict father–child proximity in nonindustrial cultures? Findings on subsistence adaptation and family organization show that fathers are closest where gathering or horticulture (small-scale vegetable and fruit growing

**Table 5.   Percent of Cultures with Various Degrees of Proximity Between Parents and Children (scales from Barry and Paxson, 1971)**

INFANCY (age 0-2)

| Role of Father | | Role of Mother | |
|---|---|---|---|
| No close proximity | 5 | 0 | Practically all care is by others |
| Rare  proximity | 15 | 0 | Most care except nursing by others |
| Occasional proximity | 37 | 2 | Mother's role is significant but . . . |
| Frequent proximity | 39 | 8 | Mother provides half or less of care |
| Regular close relationship | 4 | 44 | Principally mother, others important |
| | | 43 | Principally mother, others minor |
| | | 3 | Almost exclusively the mother |

EARLY CHILDHOOD (age 2-5)

| Role of Father | | Role of Mother | |
|---|---|---|---|
| No close proximity | 1 | 2 | Practically all time away from mother |
| Rare proximity | 11 | 33 | Majority of time away from mother |
| Occasional proximity | 19 | 39 | Half or less time with mother |
| Frequent proximity | 60 | 27 | Principally mother, others important |
| Regular close relationship | 9 | 0 | Almost exclusively mother |

as in the Pacific Islands) is the primary mode of subsistence and where combinations of polygyny, patrilocal residence, the extended family, or patridominant division of labor are absent. These variables are inter-related but, at least in this sample, are not highly correlated with each other. It is combinations of these conditions or their opposites that predict father–child proximity. The findings also suggest that the need for males to engage in warfare and the degree to which women provide subsistence resources are important underlying factors.

The relation of father–infant proximity to primary mode of subsistence is shown in Table 6. Dichotomizing the father–infant scale, fathers are most likely to be "close" in two of seven nonindustrial subsistence adaptations—"gathering" (as in !Kung) and "horticulture" (as in Lesu). Cultures with *extreme* dependence on hunting, such as the three in this sample, are probably not typical of most of human evolution. These findings are basically consistent with Whiting and Whiting's (1975a) finding on a larger sample that husband–wife intimacy is greater among cultures without accumulated resources or capital investments that must be defended. "Horticulturalists" are an exception in both our sample and theirs, but the Whitings note that these cultures are mainly in the Pacific islands and that insularity may provide a degree of protection. The Whitings pose a two-level interpretation of their findings on subsistence: husbands and wives are distant (in terms of sleeping arrangements) where warriors are needed to protect property, and distance between husbands and wives has the psychological effect of producing hyperaggressive males.

Other cross-cultural research has shown an association between relative father absence and violent or hypermasculine behavior. In the Whiting six-culture study, more cases of assault and homicide occur in the two father-distant cultures. There is also a notably different preoccupation

Table 6.  Father–Infant Proximity and Primary Mode of Subsistence in 80 Nonindustrial Cultures

| Primary Mode of Subsistence | Father-Infant Proximity | |
|---|---|---|
| | Distant | Close |
| Gathering | 1 | 7 |
| Hunting | 3 | 0 |
| Fishing | 6 | 4 |
| Herding | 4 | 1 |
| Simple agriculture | 12 | 6 |
| Horticulture | 3 | 10 |
| Advanced agriculture | 16 | 6 |

with and attitude toward violence and strife (B. Whiting, 1965). Bacon, Child, and Barry (1963) show that the frequency of the theft and personal crime is higher in societies with mother–child households. J. Whiting (1972) reports that, in another large sample, pursuit of military glory is associated with exclusive mother–son sleeping arrangements ($\phi = .40$). These findings are interpreted according to the "protest masculinity" hypothesis: where the mother dominates the infant's and young child's world but men dominate the adult world, protest masculinity develops in boys as a defense mechanism against cross-sex identity conflict. In many of these cultures, boys undergo severe initiation rites at adolescence (Burton & Whiting, 1961; Whiting, Kluckhohn, & Anthony, 1958). Whereas the association between father absence and aggressive behavior may hold across cultures of different types, it may not apply within cultures.

Findings on family organization are shown in Table 7. None of the elements alone predicts father–infant proximity above the .05 level, but when two or more are combined, they do ($\chi^2 = 7.67$, $\phi = .31$, $p < .01$). Of the few cultures with strictly monogamous and nuclear families—the typical form in our own culture—all have close fathers ($n = 6$). In extended families, monogamy or very low polygyny predicts close fathering only if residence is not patrilocal.

Warfare is suggested as a factor, since both polygyny and patrilocal residence are associated with internal warfare and feuding (Otterbein, 1968; Otterbein & Otterbein, 1965; van Velson & van Weterling, 1960). In many patrilocal or polygynous cultures, warfare and raiding are means of acquiring resources, including women. Bride theft and raiding for wives are found in polygynous cultures (Ayres, 1974), and even where women are not kidnapped, the communities that are at war with each other are often the same ones that intermarry. Patrilocal residence is related to warfare in that it enables father and sons to remain together when the sons marry. When these families accumulate, patrilocal clans are formed that act as small military organizations to defend the interests of the group when necessary. Recent work by Paige and Paige (1973) discusses the conditions necessary for the development of these clans (or "fraternal interest groups") and proposes that they exist in large part to assert paternity rights. In these cultures the male's reproductive strategy is to produce many children by having multiple wives, and a good deal of time is spent in accumulating and defending the resources necessary to acquire and maintain these wives, if not in actually kidnapping women.

The association of aggressive and defensive activities with polygyny is consonant with the continuum in Table 1. On the left side of the continuum, male–male competition is often associated with greater size and strength and higher metabolic rate in males than females, all of which

**Table 7.  Father–Infant Proximity and Family Organization**[a]

|  | Percent of Cultures with Distant Fathers |
|---|---|
| Polygyny ($n=24$) | 75% |
| Patrilocal or avunculocal residence ($n=51$) | 65% |
| Extended family ($n=43$) | 65% |
| Distant fathers in entire sample | 57% |

| Father–Infant Proximity | Family Organization | |
|---|---|---|
|  | Two or More of the Above | One or None of the Above |
| Distant | 31 | 15 |
| Close | 11 | 21 |

$$\chi^2 = 7.67, \phi = .31, p < .01$$

[a] These results are based on the Murdock and Wilson (1972) codes, which use the same ethnographic date as the Barry and Paxson (1971) ratings. Stronger results are obtained if Murdock's (1967) codes are used, but in some cases these are based on an earlier ethnographic date (father proximity and form of marriage, $\phi = .25$; father proximity and patrilocal residence, $\phi = .28$). It may be that traditional family organization continues to influence father–child proximity when family structure has recently changed.

are found in human beings. These male attributes can be used for aggressive activities when necessary, but this does not mean that they evolved for that purpose, nor does it dictate aggression as a part of the future. As we saw in the preceding section, the greater part of human evolution was probably characterized by the "close" end of the range of human paternal behavior and a relatively low amount of aggression and violence. The polygynous or patrilocal cultures, which occur in connection with accumulation of resources without specialized defense forces, represent the "distant" end.

The division of labor—the degree to which women versus men provide subsistence resources—is suggested as a factor since, in both gathering and horticulture (the close fathers), women make a high contribution to subsistence. Where the mother is especially busy and provides essential resources, we would expect that the father could be called on to help with child care. This hypothesis is not supported when Murdock's (1967) Atlas scale on contribution of men and women to subsistence is used but is supported if all subsistence types where women typically make a high contribution—gathering, horticulture, shifting agriculture are lumped ($\chi^2 = 6.6, \phi = .31, p = .011$).

In simple field agriculture, women are busy and provide important resources, but polygyny is common and fathers are mostly distant. It is interesting that in these cultures babies are often cared for by siblings, and toddlers will often go to live with their grandparents for a while. This suggests a model for predicting nonmaternal caretakers. Where the male's strategy for reproductive success includes polygyny and/or military activities, he does not contribute to child care, regardless of women's contribution to subsistence. When these are absent, he contributes, if the mother is busy with subsistence activities, especially if the family is not extended. When the father is absent and the mother's workload is high, grandparents and siblings help with child care. At present there are no really adequate scales on women's contribution or on warfare, and so the model cannot be properly tested.

We did test a rough version of this model that supported it (Table 8). We examined father–infant proximity interacting with form of marriage, division of labor, and extendedness. The scale on division of labor is the one described—it simply lumps subsistence types in which the contribution of women to subsistence is typically high (gathering, horticulture, and simple agriculture). The interactions of the four variables were assessed by use of the ECTA program from multidimensional contingency tables written by D. Oliver (Harvard University) for the method originally described by Goodman (1970). The testing of various models of interaction showed that the four variables are not independent ($\chi^2 = 39.97$, $p = .003$) but that the entire table can be explained by three separate two-variable interactions: fathering and marriage, fathering and women's contribution, marriage and women's contribution. Extendedness of family was not critical in the four-dimensional table. The table shows that the high contribution of women increases male parental investment unless the male's role prevents it: Where the contribution of women is high, fathers are close except where there is polygyny. Fathering in cultures with low polygyny shifts according to the contribution of women: Where it is high they are close, where it is low they are distant. But this should be tested with a better scale for contribution to subsistence.

In conclusion, across all nonindustrial culture types, fathers play a

Table 8.   Father–Infant Proximity in Relation to Form of Marriage, Division of Labor, and Extendedness (Number of Cultures with Distant Fathers/Close Fathers)

| Form of Marriage: | | Monogamy | | Low Polygyny | | High Polygyny | |
|---|---|---|---|---|---|---|---|
| Family Type: | | Ext. | Nucl. | Ext. | Nucl. | Ext. | Nucl. |
| Women's contribution to subsistence: | High | 1/2 | 0/2 | 2/6 | 5/12 | 4/1 | 4/1 |
| | Low | 6/1 | 0/5 | 12/3 | 7/1 | 3/1 | 2/0 |

minor role in relating to young children compared to mothers. Still there is some variation across cultures in father–child proximity and in the apparent style of fathering—indulgent and affectionate versus harsh and aloof. Some subsistence adaptations that have developed with the decline of nomadic foraging and with increased accumulation of resources have apparently presented conditions in which aggressive competition (local warfare) and polygyny become the most advantageous reproductive strategy for males. The competition is for both material resources and access to women—these are inseparable, and it results in defense's becoming the dominant form of male parental investment. This condition develops especially where herding is a primary or secondary mode of subsistence. The ecological dynamics of this situation are yet to be understood, but population growth and land use are suggested; for example, Divale and Harris (in press) argue that the complex of "male supremacist practices," including local warfare, polygyny, bride price, and others, exists to regulate population growth. If conditions allow or require the woman to provide a substantial portion of resources, there is increased probability of the father's involvement with young children, but probably only if his own subsistence or military activties do not take priority. As technology and political organization increase—as in advanced agriculture—women's role in agriculture and, hence, her subsistence contribution is often reduced, owing to the advent of the plow, and men's role in defense is reduced, owing to curtailment of local warfare and development of specialized defense forces. Monogamy is found, and provision of resources becomes the dominant form of male parental investment. Father–child proximity varies somewhat; it averages at the middle of the range, and variation is probably related to more specific details of the agricultural work such as type of crop and distance of fields from the home. The six-culture study (B. Whiting, 1963; Whiting & Whiting, 1975b) provides many data and insights on the relationship of these factors to family relationships.

## PLASTICITY IN MALE PARENTAL INVESTMENT

Our discussion of natural selection and parental behavior emphasized differences among species in forms of male parental investment, but examination of variability within species shows considerable plasticity and points to the importance of environmental factors. The most dramatic demonstration of this is the results of experimental pairing of adult male rhesus monkeys with infants (Gomber and Mitchell, 1974; Redican & Mitchell, 1973). Rhesus males in the wild show indifference to infants.

When paired in the laboratory, adult males and infants developed many attachment behaviors and engaged in high levels of physical contact and interaction. The male in the first experiment responded strongly to distress cries of the infant on maternal separation and to the infant's assuming a depressed posture in the cage. The "nurturance" or "attachment" that developed may spring from the protective response found throughout baboons and macaques in the field.

Plasticity in more natural conditions can also be demonstrated. In an anubis baboon case observed in the field by Ransom and Ransom (1971) where the mother gave abnormally low amounts of care to an infant, an adult male gave more and more attention to the infant. Adult male langurs in the field pay no attention to infants, usually avoiding the mothers and young, but in the captive colony they are interested in the young and nuzzle and inspect them (Dohlinow, 1975). The study of marmots by Barash (1975) described earlier shows different amounts of male attention to the young in populated and isolated settings. All these studies point to plasticity in the behavioral capabilities of males that is subject to environmental influences. Quantitative data sometimes also show marked individual differences within settings—for example, the amount of carrying done by male tamarins in Epple's (1975) laboratory study. Experimental studies such as Dudley's (1975b) on the California mouse (discussed above) that manipulate environmental conditions and measure both parental behaviors and development in the offspring are extremely helpful to understanding relations between ecological factors and parental behavior. In the crosscultural data we examined some sociocultural correlates of different forms and levels of human male parental investment in the narrow range that exists.

There is, however, some evidence for limits to the plasticity of these behaviors in the neural and endocrine systems. It is well known that testosterone administered experimentally acts to reduce nurturant behavior of various mammalian females. Male mice are more likely than female mice to kill strange pups presented to them, and the tendency of females to kill pups is increased by administration of testosterone, as a function of dosage (Davis & Gandleman, 1972). Administration of testosterone during the last 12 days of gestation in the rabbit results in postnatal scattering of young, cannibalism of young, failure to nurse, and depressed nest-building activity (Fuller, Zarrow, Anderson, & Denenberg, 1970). In a semi-free-ranging troop of rhesus monkeys, the only male seen to exhibit substantial amounts of nurturance toward infants was one who had been castrated (Breuggeman, 1973).

Other evidence suggests that physiological differences between the sexes underlying the differences in parental behavior extend beyond hormone levels. Preadolescent male rhesus monkys who have been raised in total social isolation are more aggressive and less nurturant toward infants presented to them for the first time than preadolescent females raised under the same deprived conditions are (Chamove, Harlow, & Mitchell, 1967). This means there is a residue of gender differentiation in parental behavior in monkeys who have had no social experience that could influence gender-specific behavior. Furthermore, the test is performed before adolescence, when dramatic sex differences in hormone levels appear.

Experiments with other species on the "fetal androgenization" phenomenon may help to explain this difference. Many experiments have demonstrated that administration of male sex hormones to female mammals at or near the time of birth acts to change the adult behavior of the females in a "masculinizing" direction. For example, in a study that measured retrieval, licking, crouching over, and nursing of strange pups, adult female rats who had received injections of androgen at 4 days of age behaved less maternally (and more like normal males) than nonandrogenized females did (Quadagno & Rockwell, 1972). In the same study males castrated at birth but not males castrated at 25 days of age showed more nurturant behavior than intact males, suggesting a possible sensitive period for the effects of androgens on nervous system circuits governing nurturant behavior in these animals. In bird species in which males play a role in care of offspring similar to or exceeding that of females, it is clear that the males have elaborate neural and endocrine adaptations that suit them for these behaviors (Lehrman, 1955), and such adaptations do not appear to be present in males of species in which parental investment is overwhelmingly female. What, if any, special physiologic adaptations may characterize males of primate or canid species with high male parental investment, such as marmosets, is not known, but this would be a suitable avenue for investigation.

For human beings the data are obviously more difficult to interpret. In the best extant cross-cultural study of child behavior (Whiting & Whiting, 1975b) girls of six widely separated cultures were found to be more likely to be with infants and to show more nurturance (offer more help and support) generally than boys the same age, and this sex difference increases from age 3 to 11. Previous work (Barry, Bacon, & Child, 1957) has, however, shown that virtually all cultures studied had socialization practices that would tend to produce such sex differences, and so the uniform sex difference in child behavior cannot be taken as a biologically based lack of plasticity. Furthermore cultures vary in socializing sex differences, and this factor is related to accumulation of resources (Barry, Child, & Bacon, 1959), which reinforces our earlier discussion of the cross-cultural data.

There is also, however, evidence that fetal androgenization contributes to sex differences in the nurturant behavior of human beings. This evidence comes from the leading laboratory working on gender anomalies in human infants, members of which for some years defended the concept of "psychosexual neutrality" in human beings at birth. This latter position has been jeopardized by the study of 10-year-old girls who for one reason or another had high levels of circulating androgen during the latter part of fetal life, and in whom this condition was corrected at the time of birth (Money & Ehrhardt, 1972). Interviews with these girls and with their mothers showed that they played less with dolls, were more "tomboyish," and were less likely to be looking forward to marriage and motherhood than a comparable sample of nonandrogenized girls were. This finding may be taken as initial evidence that circulating androgens effect changes in the human male during fetal life that dispose him less to develop nurturant behaviors than human females.

Still the evidence from studies such as Mitchell's (cited above) is compelling. It demonstrates that the male and female nervous systems are not so different as might be inferred from studies of naturalistic behavior and that under certain conditions the male nervous system can produce behaviors usually produced almost exclusively by females, and at something approximating the same order of magnitude of level of incidence. Although the conditions of the experiment are very special—they are protected from competition, are not required to forage, are in social isolation, have no sexual opportunities, and are presented with infants whose behavior is made quite special by the fact that they have just been removed from their own mothers—still, the finding that there are conditions in which males can be induced to show fully "maternal" forms of nurturant behavior shows the importance of environment in molding parental behavior. It is consonant with our understanding of our own cross-cultural evidence, though the degree of plasticity shown by the latter is much smaller.

Under what conditions, then, can we expect the highest degree of human male parental investment? Where polygyny and local warfare are absent, there is increased opportunity for it, but the division of labor and nature of subsistence activities are also important. Modern industrial cultures fit the first two conditions, but the third is an obstacle. Most fathers are the primary providers of income, and their work usually takes them away from their children. The urgency for the father's contribution to child care is increased if the mother must be away from home herself to provide resources, and if there are no other persons available—either relatives or child care facilities. These conditions are present in some working-class families in our own culture where the mother's income is necessary, the family is typically nuclear rather than extended, and high geographic mobility has separated parents from their kin. Increased unemployment for men together with slightly increased opportunities for women to enter the labor force may have produced more of these families recently: the husband takes on many domestic responsibilities while the wife works. Families of this type should be the subjects for research on the nurturant father.

It is less likely that high-income fathers will contribute, because where men have the opportunity to accumulate large cash (or property) resources, this becomes the more efficient form of parental investment—the goods passed between father and child is money rather than nurturance. In this case, even if the wife provides a substantial portion of resources, the husband is unlikely to take on child care; it is more efficient to pay for outside services.

What are our future prospects? There is no evidence that fathers cannot be very nurturant and fully adequate caretakers, but whether they will do so depends on sociocultural conditions—conditions that in modern cultures are largely economic. Within the general population many individual solutions are probably possible. Schooling, day care and contraception have released women, especially, from considerable amounts of parental investment, but in a slightly open capitalist society competition for resources is very keen and falls (so far) mainly on men. Compared to the past, we may be moving slightly toward the center of the continuum. The mating system is essentially monogamous, and the state provides specialized defense forces, so that males are not reared especially to be warriors. But other forms of political and economic competition have replaced local warfare. The exact characteristics of the fully monogamous or even the polyandrous position for human beings as a species are unclear. The monogamous position in which male and female parental investment equalize would probably be characterized by less keen competition for resources (requiring deliberate efforts to distribute resources more evenly or at least to allow equal access to them), more nearly equal division of labor, a low and equal degree of promiscuity for each sex, and some degree of isolation of the pair—as in marmosets or coyotes. Parents in modern cultures are becoming more isolated economically and geographically from their kin. Nuclear families and neolocal residence are the rule. These conditions may favor increased participation in child care by fathers, but it is unclear whether the economic conditions that would elicit the maximum amount will develop. Short of this, there is still an opportunity for close relationships between father and child that is as great as or greater than that in any other type of previous subsistence adaptation and that can be increased, depending on the situation of individual families.

## SUMMARY

A model derived from natural selection theory relating parental behavior to mating systems and several other variables is presented, and species with different forms and levels of parental behavior are compared. Some species show more male parental behavior than human beings, some less. The model predicts an association among a series of variables, including male parental investment, mating pattern, competition, and sex differences. Cross-cultural data show that fathers in nonindustrial subsistence types play a very small role compared to mothers—at least they are much less often in proximity to their children. But the degree of variation that exists in father–infant proximity can be related to subsistence adaptation and family organization: fathers are relatively close among gatherers, who represent the sociocultural form that existed for 99% of human history, and also where women do gardening and polygyny is absent. Furthermore all cultures with monogamous nuclear families have comparatively close fathers. Other findings suggest that distant fathering occurs, especially where there are accumulated resources that have to be defended (or acquired) in local warfare and raiding. Father–child proximity may also be related to the division of labor, but better scales are needed to test this. Plasticity in the level and forms of paternal behavior is evident in other species as well as in man and is related to environmental conditions, but some hormonal correlates of nurturant behavior are absent in human males. There is no evidence that, in spite of these hormonal differences, males cannot be fully adequate caretakers, but it is unclear whether sociocultural or economic conditions that would elicit the maximum amount will develop. Without being principal caretakers, there is still opportunity for fathers to develop close relationships with their children, and current sociocultural conditions are favorable to this outcome.

## REFERENCES

Ayres, B. Bride theft and raiding for wives in cross-cultural perspective. *Anthropological Quarterly*, 1974, **47**, 238–252.

Bacon, M. K., Child, I. L., & Barry, H. A cross-cultural study of correlates of crime. *Journal of Abnormal and Social Psychology*, 1963, **66**, 241–300.

Barash, D. P. Ecology of parental behavior in the hoary marmat (*Marmota caligata*): An evolutionary interpretation. *Journal of Mammalogy*, 1975, **56**, 613–618.

Barry, H., Bacon, M. K., & Child, I. L. A cross-cultural survey of some sex differences in socialization. *Journal of Abnormal and Social Psychology*, 1957, **55**, 327–332.

Barry, H., Child, I. L., & Bacon, M. K. Relation of child training to subsistence economy. *American Anthropologist*, 1959, **61**, 51–63.

Barry, H., & Paxson, L. M. Infancy and early childhood: Cross-cultural codes. *Ethnology*, 1971, **10**, 467–508.

Blaffer Hrdy, S. The care and exploitation of nonhuman primate infants by conspecifics other than the mother. In J. Rosenblatt, R. Hinde, & C. Beer (Eds.), *Advances in the study of behavior,* Vol. 6. New York: Academic Press, 1976.

Blaffer Hrdy, S. Personal communication, October, 1975.

Blurton Jones, N. G., & Konner, M. J. Sex differences in behavior of two- to-five-year-olds in London and among the Kalahari Desert Bushmen. In R. P. Michael & J. H. Crook (Eds.), *Comparative ecology and behavior of primates.* London: Academic Press, 1973.

Breuggeman, L. A. Parental care in a group of free-ranging rhesus monkeys *(Macaca mulatta). Folia Primatologica,* 1973, **20**, 178–210.

Burton, R. V., & Whiting, J. W. M. The absent father and cross-sex identity. *Merrill-Palmer Quarterly*, 1961, **7**, 85–95.

Chamove, A., Harlow, H., & Mitchell, G. Sex differences in the infant-directed behavior of pre-adolescent rhesus monkeys. *Child Development*, 1967, **38**, 329–335.

Corbett, L., & Newson, A. Dingo society and its maintenance: A preliminary analysis. In M. W. Fox (Ed.), *The Wild Canids.* New York: Van Nostrand Reingold, 1975.

Crook, J. L. The socioecology of primates. In J. H. Crook (Ed.), *Social behavior in birds and mammals.* New York: Academic Press, 1970.

Crook, J. L., & Goss-Custard, J. D. Social ethology. *Annual Review of Psychology*, 1972, **23**, 277–312.

Davis, P. G., & Gandleman, P. Pup-killing produced by the administration of testoterone propionate to adult female mice. *Hormones and Behavior,* 1972, **3**, 169–173.

Divale, W. T., & Harris, M. Population, warfare and the male supremacist complex: Female infanticide and warfare are part of a population regulation system among many band and village societies. *American Anthropologist,* in press.

Dohlinow, P. J. Lecture delivered at Institute on Evolution and the Development of Behavior, Institute of Child Development, University of Minnesota, 1975.

DuBois, C. *The people of Alor.* New York: Harper, 1944.

Dudley, D. Contributions of paternal care to the growth and development of the young in *Peromyscus californicus. Behavioral Biology*, 1974, **11**, 155–166 (a).

Dudley, D. Paternal behavior in the California mouse, *Peromyscus californicus. Behavioral Biology*, 1974, **11**, 247–252 (b).

Eisenberg, J. F. The social organizations of mammals. *Handbuch der Zoologie,* 1966, **8,** 1–92.

Epple, G. Parental behavior in *Saguinus fuscicollis* spp. (*Callithricidae*). *Folia Primatologica,* 1975, **24,** 221–238.

Estes, R. D., & Goddard, J. Prey selection and hunting behavior of the African wild dog. *Journal of Wildlife Management,* 1967, **31,** 52–70.

Fox, M. W. Evolution of social behavior in canids. In M. W. Fox (Ed.), *The wild canids.* New York: Van Nostrand Reingold, 1975.

Fuller, G. B., Zarrow, M. X., Anderson, C. O., & Denenberg, V. H. Testosterone propionate during gestation in the rabbit: Effect on subsequent maternal behavior. *Journal of Reproduction and Fertility,* 1970, **23,** 285–290.

Gier, H. T. Ecology and social behavior of the coyote. In M. W. Fox (Ed.), *The wild canids.* New York: Van Nostrand Reingold, 1975.

Gomber, J., & Mitchell, G. Preliminary report on adult male isolation-reared rhesus monkeys caged with infants. *Developmental Psychology,* 1974, **10,** 298.

Goodman, L. A. The multivariate analysis of qualitative data: Interactions among multiple classifications. *Journal of the American Statistical Association,* 1970, **65,** 226–256.

Hall, K. R. L., & DeVore, I. Baboon social behavior. In I. DeVore (Ed.), *Primate behavior: Field studies of monkeys and apes.* New York: Holt, Rinehart & Winston, 1965.

Hamilton, W. D. The genetical theory of social behavior, I, II. *Journal of Theoretical Biology,* 1964, **7,** 1–52.

Jolly, A. *The evolution of primate behavior.* New York: Macmillan, 1972.

Junod, H. A. *The life of a South African tribe* (2nd ed., 2 vols.). London, Macmillan, 1927.

Konner, M. J. Relations among infants and juveniles in comparative perspective. In M. Lewis & L. Rosenblum (Eds.), *Friendship and peer relations.* New York: Wiley, 1975.

Lamb, M. E. Fathers: Forgotten contributors to child development. *Human Development,* 1975, **18,** 245–266.

Lee, R. B., & DeVore, I. (Eds.) *Man the hunter.* Chicago: Aldine, 1968.

Lehrman, D. S. The physiological basis of parental feeding behavior in the ring dove. *Behavior,* 1955, **7,** 241–286.

Mason, W. A. Social organization of the South American monkey, *Callicebus moloch:* A preliminary report. *Tulane Studies in Zoology,* 1966, **13,** 23–28.

Mitchell, G., & Brandt, E. M. Paternal behavior in primates. In F. E. Poirier (Ed.), *Primate socialization.* New York: Random House, 1972.

Money, J., & Ehrhardt, A. A. *Man and woman, boy and girl.* Baltimore: The Johns Hopkins University Press, 1972.

Murdock, G. P. Ethnographic atlas. *Ethnology*, 1967, **6**, 109–236.

Murdock, G. P., & White, D. R. Standard cross-cultural sample. *Ethnology*, 1969, **8**, 329–369.

Murdock, G. P., & Wilson, S. F. Settlement patterns and community organization. *Ethnology*, 1972, **11**, 254–269.

Musil, A. *The manner and customs of the Rwala Bedouin.* New York: The American Geographical Society, 1928.

Osgood, C. *The Koreans and their culture.* New York: Ronald, 1951.

Otterbein, K. F. Internal war: A cross-cultural study. *American Anthropologist*, 1968, **70**, 277–289.

Otterbein, K. F., & Otterbein, C. S. An eye for an eye, a tooth for a tooth: A cross-cultural study of feuding. *American Anthropologist*, 1965, **67**, 1470–1482.

Paige, K. E., & Paige, J. M. The politics of birth practices: A strategic analysis. *American Sociological Review*, 1973, **38**, 663–677.

Powdermaker, H. *Life in Lesu.* New York: Norton, 1933.

Quadagno, P. M., & Rockwell, J. The effect of gonadal hormones in infancy on maternal behavior in the adult rat. *Hormones and Behavior*, 1972, **3**, 55–62.

Ransom, T. W., & Ransom, B. S. Adult male–infant relations among baboons *(Papio anubis). Folia Primatologica,* 1971, **16**, 179–195.

Ransom, T. W., & Rowell, T. E. Early social development of feral baboons. In F. E. Poirier (Ed.), *Primate socialization.* New York: Random House, 1972.

Redican, W. K., & Mitchell, G. A longitudinal study of parental behavior in adult male rhesus monkeys: I. Observations on the first dyad. *Developmental Psychology*, 1973, **8**, 135–136.

Ruvolo, M. Parental investment and sexual selection in marmosets. Unpublished manuscript, Harvard University, 1973.

Snyder, P. A. Behavior of *Leontopithecus rosalia* (The Golden Lion Marmoset) and related species: A Review. In D. D. Bridgewater (Ed.), *Saving the lion marmoset.* Wheeling, W. Va.: The Wild Animal Propagation Trust, 1972.

Trivers, R. L. Parental investment and sexual selection. In B. Campbell (Ed.), *Sexual selection and the descent of man 1871–1971.* Chicago: Aldine, 1972.

van Lawick, H., & van Lawick-Goodall, J. *Innocent killers.* Boston: Houghton Mifflin, 1971.

van Velsen, H. H. E. T., & Van Weterling, W. Residence, power groups and intra-society aggression. *International Archives of Ethnology*, 1960, **49**, 169–200.

Whiting, B. B. Sex identity conflict and physical violence: A comparative study. *American Anthropologist*, 1965, **67** (pt. 2), 123–140.

Whiting, B. B. (Ed.), *Six cultures: Studies of child rearing.* New York: Wiley, 1963.

Whiting, B. B. Personal communication, June 1974.

Whiting, B. B., & Whiting, J. W. M. *Children of six cultures: A psychocultural analysis.* Cambridge, Mass.: Harvard University Press, 1975 (b).

Whiting, J. W. M. The place of aggression in social interaction. In J. F. Short, Jr., & M. E. Wolfgang (Eds.), *Collective violence.* Chicago: Aldine-Atherton, 1972.

Whiting, J. W. M., & Child, I. L. *Child training and personality.* New Haven: Yale University Press, 1953.

Whiting, J. W. M., Kluckhorn, R., & Anthony, S. A. The function of male initiation ceremonies at puberty. In E. E. Maccoby, T. Newcomb, & E. Hartley (Eds.), *Readings in social psychology.* New York: Holt, 1958.

Whiting, J. W. M., & Whiting, B. B. Aloofness and intimacy of husbands and wives: A cross-cultural study. *Ethos,* 1975, **3**, 183–207.

Wilson, E. O. *Sociobiology: The new synthesis.* Cambridge, Mass.: Harvard University Press, 1975.

# Appendix

## SAMPLE AND SCALES FOR ANALYSES ON FATHER–INFANT PROXIMITY

### Sample

The sample is a subsample of 80 from Murdock and White's (1969) Standard Cross-cultural Sample, a world sample of historically and linguistically independent cultures. Cultures were selected that were rated by Barry and Paxson (1971) on the father scale at their highest confidence level. The resultant sample includes all subsistence types except for industrialized societies and is geographically distributed as follows:

| | | | |
|---|---|---|---|
| Africa | 12 | Oceania | 19 |
| Europe and Circum-Mediterranean | 10 | North America | 17 |
| Asia | 10 | South America | 12 |

### Scales

| | |
|---|---|
| Father–Infant Proximity (Tables 5–8) | Barry and Paxson (1971) |
| Father–Child Proximity (Table 5) | Barry and Paxson (1971) |
| Nonmaternal Relationships (Table 5) | Barry and Paxson (1971) |
| Earliness of Autonomy | Barry and Paxson (1971) |
| Dependency Satisfaction Potential | Whiting and Child (1953) |
| Primary Mode of Subsistence (Table 6, 8) | Murdock and White (1969) |
| Polygyny (dichotomized) (Table 7) (P/MN) | Murdock and Wilson (1972) (p. 260, col. 8) |
| Polygyny (trichotomized) (Table 8) (QS/NPR/M) | Murdock (1967) (p. 155, col. 14) |
| Extended/Nuclear Family (Table 7) (EFS/MNPQ) | Murdock and Wilson (1972) (p. 260, col. 8) |
| Extended/Nuclear Family (Table 8) (EFS/MNOPQRS) | Murdock (1967) (p. 155, col. 14) |
| Patrilocal–Avunculocal Residence (Table 7) (PA/BMN) | Murdock and Wilson (1972) (p. 261, col. 9) |

# CHAPTER 6

# *Fathers, Children, and Moral Development*

ESTHER BLANK GREIF

*Boston University*

Moral development is concerned with a child's acquisition of the rules that guide moral actions. All cultures have general guidelines specifying acceptable social behavior, and it is necessary for children to learn these standards. Since moral behaviors constitute a subset of general social behaviors, the process of socialization requires acquisition of moral standards. The study of moral development has focused on several aspects of morality, including internalization of moral codes, ability to make moral judgments, formation of moral character, and exhibition of moral behaviors.

The purpose of this chapter is to review the role of the father in moral development. More specifically I try to determine if the father plays a distinctive and unique role in children's moral development. As in other areas of child development the father has been relatively ignored as a major influence on a child's acquisition of rules and values. Studies attempting to examine parental influences on moral development typically have focused on the mother alone. This may reflect the difficulty in recruiting fathers to participate in studies. In addition it may reflect the view that mothers are more influential in children's development than fathers are, at least during the early years of development. Whereas it is true that mothers usually spend more time with children, it is not clear that fathers have, therefore, little impact on children's development. In fact it seems reasonable to assume that fathers play an important role in their children's moral development.

This chapter is divided into two major sections. The first section reviews the major approaches to moral development and examines the role of the father in the major theories of moral development. The second section reviews the empirical research literature concerned with fathers and children's moral development. I conclude with an evaluation of the current state of the field.

## APPROACHES TO MORAL DEVELOPMENT

The area of moral development is complex enough to include several different orientations. Typically researchers in this field have emphasized three major perspectives. The first is concerned with overt moral behaviors, such as cheating, stealing, and lying. The focus clearly is on moral behavior that can be exhibited and measured. This approach allows one to assess both interindividual differences in moral behaviors and intraindividual consistencies in moral behavior. Hartshorne and May (1928), for example, looked at the consistency with which people cheated in a variety of situations (intraindividual consistency) and found that individuals who cheated in one situation did not necessarily cheat under different circumstances. Their data were later reanalyzed by Burton (1963), who found that some individuals could be classified as more honest than others (interindividual differences).

One problem with this approach is in determining the criterion for moral behavior. One needs to specify what types of actions are moral, and sometimes it is difficult to reach consensus about this. Certain types of activities (e.g., murder, theft) are, however, generally viewed as morally wrong, and other activities are considered morally good (e.g., helping someone in need). Later in the chapter I review a variety of studies that use moral behavior as an index of moral development.

The second major approach concerns internal, emotional aspects of moral development (Aronfreed, 1969). The conscience (as an internal censor) and guilt are both indices of moral development. Unlike behavioral measures, affective aspects of moral development are frequently not apparent. For example, one cannot determine the amount of guilt an individual feels simply by observing that person. There are, however, certain behaviors that give clues to the internal state of individuals, such as confession of guilt. Thus, although behavior is often used as an index of development, the main emphasis of this approach is on internal, affective aspects of moral development.

The third approach is concerned with an individual's cognitions about morality (Kohlberg, 1963; Piaget, 1948). The focus here is on an individual's thoughts about moral issues, rather than on actual moral behavior or moral emotions. This emphasis leads one to study moral judgments, moral reasoning, and moral values. Concern is with what people say about moral issues, rather than what they actually would do or feel in a moral situation. Since many types of moral dilemmas are rarely encountered in daily life (e.g., a chance to save someone's life), information about cognitions is the only way to answer certain questions about moral development.

These three approaches are not mutually exclusive; rather, they are all legitimate aspects of moral development and can be studied separately or in combination.

## THEORIES OF MORAL DEVELOPMENT

### Psychoanalytic View

Generally the psychoanalytic view of moral development, as established by Freud (e.g., 1927), is concerned with internal aspects of moral development. The superego is the structure most tied to morality. According to Freud the superego acts as an internal censor. To determine the developmental antecedents of morality, we need to know how moral values become internalized and how the superego is formed. According to Freud moral development occurs during the early years of life, with parents as the major influence. Initially boys and girls both develop attachments to their mothers and start to identify with her and take on her characteristics. The identification with the mother is called anaclitic identification (Bronfenbrenner, 1960). Thus for the first few years of life, development for boys and girls is similar. When the phallic stage begins, however (around age 3 or 4), development for boys and girls diverges. At this time, Freud explains, a little boy begins to have incestuous desires for his mother. He is jealous of his father and wishes he could be rid of him. (This is called the oedipal complex, which is discussed in greater detail by Mächtlinger in Chapter 8.) Further, the boy is afraid his father will retaliate for the incestuous desires by castrating him. Realizing that he cannot get rid of his father, the boy deals with this castration anxiety by identifying with his father. That is, the boy assumes his father's characteristics and internalizes the standards and values his father represents. The rationale is simple: the father would not harm someone like himself; therefore, if a boy is like his father, he will not be castrated. Thus the boy resolves his oedipal complex by becoming like his father. This results in the formation of the superego, which includes the conscience and the ego ideal. Resolution of the oedipal complex is a crucial part of development, for the boy has not only acquired the appropriate sex-role characteristics but also has internalized the moral rules and values his father represents.

According to this view the father is essential for normal moral development of boys. Without a male figure present a young boy would not have castration anxiety and would have no reason, therefore, to resolve his oedipal complex. Although some moral development would occur because of identification with the mother, it seems that boys without fathers would have weaker superegos and would therefore be less moral than boys with fathers.

For girls development proceeds in a parallel fashion. Around the same time that boys are coping with desires for their mothers, the little girl is experiencing incestuous desires for her father. But unlike her male peers who are suffering from castration anxiety, the girl must deal with penis envy. The little girl blames her mother for her lack of a penis, and as a result she switches her love from her mother to her father. At this point there is no pressing reason for the girl to give up hopes for her father; unlike her male counterpart she does not fear castration. Freud's explanation for girls' ultimate identification with their mothers is rather weak; he says that girls simply give up hopes for their fathers and then identify with their mothers and thereby form their superegos. With the formation of the superego girls acquire their sex roles and their moral values. But because their identification with their mothers was not due to castration anxiety, Freud concedes that girls have less well-developed superegos than boys. Consequently girls are less morally mature. According to Freud (1950), "for women what is ethically normal is different from what it is in men. Their superego is never so inexorable, so impersonal, so independent of its emotional origins as we require it to be in men . . ." (p. 196).

In sum, the Freudian view suggests that fathers are quite necessary for normal development of boys and girls, although less so for girls. Thus this theory does support an important and unique role for the father.

## Cognitive Theory

The second major theory of moral development is cognitive theory, concerned with the relationship between an individual's moral development and his cognitive development. Major emphasis is put on moral reasoning and moral judgment rather than on moral behavior or emotions. Piaget (1948) is the originator of the cognitive view. He conceptualized moral development in two major stages: heteronomous morality and autonomous morality. Initially, during the heteronomous stage, children are moral realists. They believe that rules are immutable, and they display complete respect for authority. According to Piaget, "Any act that shows obedience to a rule or even to an adult, regardless of what he may command, is good; any act that does not conform to rules is bad" (p. 111). In addition, children at this stage "evaluate acts not in accordance with the motive that has prompted them but in terms of their exact conformity with established rules" (p. 112).

Around age 12, children begin to realize that rules are in fact man-made and are subject to change; they also become concerned with notions of justice and can take intention into account when assessing moral situations. To make this shift to the maturer form of moral development (autonomous reasoning, also called moral relativism), Piaget stresses the importance of peers. Nowhere does he make explicit the role of the father per se; instead, he talks about the roles of parents and peers. He suggests that parents, because they are authority figures, serve to keep children in the first stage of moral development. To mature, children need to have experiences away from parents (and other adults). As Piaget (1948) explains, "adult authority, although perhaps it constitutes a necessary moment in the moral evolution of the child, is not in itself sufficient to create a sense of justice. This can develop only through the progress made by cooperation and mutual respect—cooperation between children to begin with . . ." (p. 319).

Kohlberg elaborated a cognitive theory of moral development based on Piaget's stage sequence. Instead of two stages, Kohlberg describes six stages of moral development. At the preconventional level are Stage 1, defined by punishment and obedience orientation, and Stage 2, marked by instrumental relativist orientation. At the conventional level are Stage 3, the interpersonal concordance or good-boy orientation, and Stage 4, the authority and social order orientation. Finally, at the principled level are Stage 5, social contract orientation, and Stage 6, the individual principles orientation. Like Piaget, Kohlberg does not view the family as particularly essential for moral development, and he does not deal separately with the father's role. As Kohlberg (1969) states, "From our point of view, however, (1) family participation is not unique or critically necessary for moral development, and (2) the dimensions on which it stimulates moral development are primarily general dimensions by which other primary groups stimulate moral development" (p. 399). It seems, then, that for cognitive theorists, the father plays no unique role in children's moral development. Cognitive theorists also assume no difference between the moral development of boys and girls.

## Social Learning Theory

A third major theory of moral development is social learning theory. Whereas both psychoanalytic and cognitive theorists view moral development as a distinct area of development, social learning theorists view it as simply one aspect of development subject to the same laws of learning as other areas. Because of their interest in the antecedents of learning, social learning theorists are concerned mainly with the behavioral aspects of morality. Thus they deal with overt behaviors such as lying, cheating, and stealing, rather than with emotions or moral judgments. Since moral behavior reflects an individual's previous experience and learning, moral development is explained by using the basic learning paradigm. Major emphasis is put on the notions of reinforcement (reward and punishment) and modeling. Children are thought to acquire and exhibit behaviors for which they are rewarded. Thus if a child tells the truth about breaking his father's favorite pipe, and he is reinforced for being honest (e.g., his father thanks him for telling the truth), then he will continue to be honest. Conversely a child will exclude from his repertoire behaviors for which he is punished.

The notion of modeling deals with learning for which there is no explicit reinforcement. Children seem to acquire behaviors simply by watching them performed by others. Since parents are salient in children's lives, one would expect parents to have a good deal of influence over their children by the modeling process. More specifically, to the extent that the father acts as a model for the child's moral actions, one would expect him to play an important role in the child's moral development. In social learning theory, however, the father is not essential to moral development the way he is in psychoanalytic theory; that is, an appropriate model does not necessarily have to be the father. In general, research on modeling has shown that children are most likely to imitate warm, nurturant models (e.g., Mussen & Distler, 1960). Thus the father's role in children's moral development varies as a function of his characteristics as a role model. Finally although social learning theory does not specify differences between the moral development of boys and girls, there is some evidence to suggest that boys and girls respond differently to male and female models (Bandura, Ross, & Ross, 1963).

## Personological Approach

A fourth approach to moral development emphasizes the character structure of individuals (Hogan, 1973, 1975; Peck & Havighurst, 1960). Character is defined by the pattern of attitudes and motives that structure an individual's behavior. This view attempts to determine interrelationships between an individual's moral character and his moral actions. A basic assumption is that differences in character structure will lead to differences in moral behavior. Proponents of this view consider childhood to be the most important time for formation of moral character. Because they are the primary agents for socializing children, parents are crucial to their children's moral development. As Peck and Havighurst (1960) stated in their study of character development, "the evidence indicates that character is strongly—probably predominantly—shaped by family experience" (p. 106). The father's role is not, however, separated from the mother's. Rather, emphasis is placed on the importance of parents in general. It seems, then, that although the father can be important in children's moral development, he does not seem to play a unique role. In addition this approach does not focus on differential effects of the father on sons and daughters.

## Summary

To review briefly the theories discussed, we see that psychoanalytic theorists view the father as crucial for normal moral development, although they see the father as more important for moral development of boys than of girls. For social learning theorists, the father can play an important role, but his influence is not crucial. Similarly, for personological theorists, the father is significant but not essential; an adequate family life should be sufficient. Finally cognitive theorists suggest that fathers (and mothers) can actually hinder a child's moral development by preventing a child from questioning an authority figure. Thus the major moral development theories differ significantly in their positions on the importance of the father for a child's moral development.

## EMPIRICAL RESEARCH

Because of the variety of approaches to moral development, there is no organized body of literature examining the relation of the father to a child's moral development. Nevertheless there is some moral development research that includes the father, and a review of these studies can help us evaluate the current evidence for the father's role. In this section I review research concerned with overt moral behaviors, including resistance to temptation and delinquency. Then I deal with studies of affective aspects of morality and studies of moral character. Finally I review studies dealing with cognitive aspects of moral development.

### Studies of Moral Behavior

Research concerned with the antecedents of moral actions have generally used behaviors such as cheating, stealing, and resisting temptation as criteria for moral development. In addition, delinquency has frequently been considered an indicator of (low) moral development.

Sears, Rau, and Alpert (1965) conducted an extensive study of the childrearing antecedents of several aspects of development, including sex roles, aggression, dependency, and honesty. Forty 4-year-old children and their parents participated. The researchers obtained interview data from fathers and mothers about their methods of discipline (e.g., What do you think are the best ways of disciplining children?), their attitudes about childrearing (e.g., Do you think a child of $X$'s age should be given any regular jobs to do around the house?), and their impressions about their children (e.g., Would you describe $X$ as an affectionate child?). A variety of data was obtained from the children (e.g., from observations, doll play). Most relevant for our review are the correlations between children's resistance to temptation and fathers' responses to the interviews. Resistance to temptation was assessed by putting children in situations in which they had an opportunity to steal (candy), cheat, or do something they were told not to do (play with a toy). Sears et al. found that fathers of boys who were high on resistance to temptation were ambivalent toward their sons; they were both affectionate and hostile. Further these men believed strongly in teaching their sons the difference between right and wrong. The pattern was different for girls: fathers of honest girls did not seem ambivalent toward their daughters. Instead they displayed dissatisfaction with their daughters and frequently ridiculed them. The authors suggest that resistance to temptation in the girls was a result of "the girls' efforts to meet the high standards of achievement prescribed by both parents and quite literally demanded by the fathers" (p. 232). Thus it seems that a father's interactions with his child influence the child's moral development. Moreover different interaction patterns between fathers and sons and fathers and daughters seem to result in the same behavior patterns for sons and daughters.

Rutherford and Mussen (1968) examined generosity in 4½-year-old boys. Each child was given 18 pieces of candy and was asked to share the candy with two other children. A generosity score was defined as the number of candies the boy gave to other children. From these scores two groups were formed: nongenerous boys (they kept all 18 candies) and generous boys (they gave away 15 or more candies). Each boy then participated in a semistructured doll play situation, designed to assess his attitudes toward his parents and his perceptions of them. No data were obtained from the fathers themselves. A comparison of boys high and low in generosity indicated that the generous boys perceived their fathers as warmer and more nurturant. The investigators suggest that paternal nurturance provides the child with a good model and motivates him to adopt his father's behavior. In addition the authors suggest that generosity is part of a general pattern of moral behaviors acquired from identification with the father.

To examine the father's influence in fostering deviant behavior in his son, McCord and McCord (1957) examined the effects of the parent as role model. A group of boys considered to be "problem children" were matched with a sample of nonproblem boys. Average age of the boys was seven. Data about parents included ratings of parental behavior and attitudes toward the child, and judges' reports of methods of discipline. No data were collected from the parents directly. Various interesting findings were reported in this study; several are particularly useful for assessing the role fathers seem to play in their sons' moral development. First, paternal rejection and a deviant paternal model (e.g., the father was a criminal) often led to problem behavior in the boys. There was, however, an interaction between parents. Thus even if a father was rejecting and a poor role model, a warm mother could offset this and reduce the likelihood of her son's becoming a problem child. We must keep in mind in our assessment of the research on the role of the father that fathers do not function in isolation; rather, they are frequently in interaction with another parent, namely, the mother. A second interesting finding concerned discipline and parental role model: it seems that consistent discipline administered effectively counteracted the role model of a criminal father. Further, consistency rather than actual type of discipline (e.g., physical, psychological) was more important for transmission of values. The father as a role model becomes important only in the absence of consistent discipline and warm parents. As McCord and McCord (1957) conclude, the effect of a criminal father depends on other family factors. It is certainly not the case that sons of criminals will themselves be criminals. Rather, "children imitate their father's criminality when other environmental conditions (rejection, maternal deviance, erratic discipline) tend to produce an unstable, aggressive personality" (p. 375). It seems, then, that the father's influence on his son's moral development is not simply a result of modeling.

Other studies have examined moral behaviors in adolescents. Bronfenbrenner (1961) compared teachers' ratings of responsibility and leadership for 10th-grade boys and girls with the students' evaluation of their parents' childrearing practices. He found that, for boys, rejection, neglect, and lack of discipline from the father were associated with irresponsible behavior. For girls, on the other hand, strong discipline from the fathers was associated with irresponsibility. Further girls reported receiving more affection from their fathers than boys did. Bronfenbrenner concludes that paternal authority facilitates responsibility in boys and impedes it in girls.

MacKinnon (1938) was concerned with dishonesty in male college students. In his study, students were given a test and were told where the answers could be found. They were then instructed not to look at certain answers. The students were observed to see if in fact they would violate the prohibition. Of 74 students involved, 34 cheated. MacKinnon subsequently asked the students about their parental preferences and their impressions of relationships with their parents. Several interesting results appeared. First, 74% of violators, as opposed to 36% of nonviolators, preferred their mothers to their fathers, with only one violator preferring father to mother (11 nonviolators preferred their fathers). Second, violators reported greater use of physical (rather than psychological) punishment by their fathers than nonviolators did (78% vs. 48% for physical punishment; 22% vs. 52% for psychological punishment). There was, however, little difference in reports of mothers' methods of discipline. Finally nonviolators reported that their fathers' discipline was more effective than their mothers' and was feared more. In general the men who did not violate the prohibition against cheating perceived their fathers more positively than men did who violated the prohibition.

A study by Bandura and Walters (1959) compared male adolescents who exhibited antisocial aggression with a control group of adolescents who had similar demographic characteristics, but with no history of antisocial aggression. Information on childrearing practices and attitudes was obtained from interviews with mothers and fathers. One aspect of the research concerned the relationship between boys' aggression and their fathers' attitudes toward aggresive behavior. Bandura and Walters found that fathers of aggressive males encouraged aggression in their sons, although they made it clear that aggression should be outside the home, and discouraged aggression against themselves. (It seems that mothers of aggressive males also encouraged aggression.) Further, using a projective measure to assess hostile thoughts and feelings of the boys, they found that aggressive boys displayed more hostility toward their fathers than nonaggressive boys did. They also found that the two groups did not differ greatly in their descriptions of their mothers' discipline methods but did differ in their descriptions of their fathers' methods. "The total evidence . . . suggested that the aggressive boys had experienced fathers who were harsh and punitive in their handling of their sons and mothers who placed fewer limits on their behavior and were somewhat inconsistent and vacillating" (Bandura & Walters, 1959, p. 246). While there were clear-cut differences between father–son relationships and behaviors patterns for aggressive and nonaggressive males, the two groups differed in mother–son relationships, too. We cannot, therefore, attribute differences between the two groups solely to the effects of the father. Rather, as Bandura and Walters suggest, interactions with both parents are important for development.

Glueck and Glueck (1950) were interested in differences between delinquents and nondelinquents. Again using an all-male sample, they found that delinquents received erratic discipline from their fathers, who were either lax or overstrict. In addition to inconsistency, there was a good deal of physical punishment, and little use of reasoning or praise. Thus this study supports the view that paternal discipline is related to the child's later behavior patterns.

In summary, most of the studies reviewed deal exclusively with males; only those by Sears et al. (1965) and Bronfenbrenner (1961) included girls. Interestingly both these studies found that fathers treated their sons and daughters differently and achieved the same behavioral outcome. Further there seems to be an implicit assumption that the father is more important to the development of boys than girls, particularly with delinquent populations. This may be due to the view that fathers are important for sex-role development of boys. In general the studies reviewed indicate that the father does play an important role in children's moral development, as evidenced by significant relationships between fathers' role-model behaviors, discipline, and affectional techniques and children's behavior.

## Moral Affect

Another group of researchers has focused on affective aspects of moral development, particularly strength of conscience and guilt. Martin Hoffman and his colleagues have been contributors to this research area. In one study (Hoffman, 1971b), father identification was correlated with several aspects of moral development, including guilt, confession, internal moral judgment, and rule conformity. Subjects were middle- and lower class male and female seventh graders. Although no information was obtained from fathers directly, an identification measure was used as an index of the child's liking of his parents. The measure was based on a child's admiration, his desire to emulate, and his perception of similarity to his parents. As Hoffman explains, his measure was designed to assess conscious, rather than unconscious, identification. He found that father identification was correlated with rule conformity (moral behavior) for middle-class boys and girls, with internal moral judgment for middle- and lower class boys, and with moral values for middle-class boys. Guilt, confession, and acceptance of blame were not, however, related to identification. From these results Hoffman concluded that (conscious) identification may affect moral principles, but it does not seem to relate to emotional aspects of moral development.

A second study by Hoffman (1971a) examined the relationship between conscience development and father absence. Again using seventh-grade males and females, Hoffman assessed guilt following transgression, acceptance of blame, rule conformity, and moral values. He found that boys whose fathers were absent received lower scores on these measures for internal moral judgment. Further these boys were rated by their teachers as more aggressive than boys whose fathers were present. Interestingly there were no differences for girls. Again we see suggestive evidence that the father's presence is more important for the moral development of boys than for girls. Hoffman points out that several factors may account for the differences in moral development for boys with and without fathers. First is the lack of a paternal model; the boys do not have a consistent male figure around for them to model. Second, the absence of the father may result in lack of identification. Finally, it is possible that the absence of a father leads to changes in the mother's childrearing practices so that mothers without spouses treat their children differently.

Hoffman and Saltzstein (1967) obtained data on children's conscience development and their identification with parents and then acquired parental reports and child reports of parental discipline. Although there were some significant relationships between discipline techniques and moral development for mothers (e.g., use of induction was positively correlated with guilt; use of power assertion was negatively correlated with guilt), there were few significant relationships between fathers' discipline techniques and children's moral development. This is particularly surprising in light of data indicating that parental discipline techniques are important for children's development (Becker, 1964). From the lack of strong evidence indicating that fathers' discipline techniques have a specific impact on moral development, Hoffman (1970) suggests that the role of the father may be to provide a background role model, whereas the mother is the primary influence in moral development. As he explains, "individual differences in children's moral orientations may be due mainly to the mother's discipline" (p. 294). When, however, the father does not provide an adequate role model (e.g., father is absent, is a criminal, etc.), the father's importance in moral development becomes apparent.

Finally the study by Bandura and Walters (1959) described in the previous section noted that aggressive boys showed less identification with their fathers and exhibited less guilt than nonaggressive boys did. Because fathers of aggressive boys spent little time with their sons, Bandura and Walters concluded that "the disruption of the father–son relationship undoubtedly made identification with the father difficult, and consequently internalization of parental values was not completely achieved" (p. 311).

In summary, studies of moral affect support the view that fathers' impact on the moral development of boys and girls differs, fathers having a larger impact on boys. Father absence affected moral development of males but not of females. Interestingly paternal discipline techniques did not have a significant impact on internal aspects of moral development, including guilt and confession.

## Studies of Moral Character

The major study of moral character attempting to assess developmental antecedents of character was conducted by Peck and Havighurst (1960). Using a sample of 34 boys and girls, they collected data on personality characteristics and moral values of the adolescents over a span of 7 years. Data were also collected from parents. Although they found significant correlations between the mothers' and children's moral values, they found few significant correlations between the fathers' and children's values. Because of this, they concluded that fathers play no unique role in children's moral development. They suggest instead that "moral values may be learned equally well—or equally badly—from either parent. The quality of the child's morality depends on the moral qualities of the parent whom he takes for his model" (p. 123). In families where mothers and fathers have similar moral values, either parent can serve as the primary model.

Peck and Havighurst, examining several different character types among the adolescents, found that different family interaction styles were related to the character types. They note, therefore, that "character . . . appears to be predominantly shaped by the intimate, emotionally powerful relationship between child and parents, within the family" (1960, p. 175). But the father's role apart from the mother is not made clear. Instead they state that "for the most part, there was little evidence in most cases that the father exerted as powerful an influence on emotional and moral development as did the mother" (p. 118). Thus, it again seems that the father is important as a background figure.

## Cognitive Studies

The fourth major category of research deals with cognitive aspects of moral development. Focus here is on moral judgments, moral reasoning, and stated moral attitudes and values. Whereas most of the studies dealing with these aspects of moral development have not been concerned with developmental antecedents, and particularly with the father's role, there are a few studies that help us understand the possible role of the father.

Haan, Smith, and Block (1968) studied students who were in college during a student protest movement. They were interested in determining the relationships among Kohlberg's stages of moral development, behavior of the adolescents during the student protests, and familial variables. All data were obtained from the students, rather than from their parents. They divided subjects into three levels of moral reasoning based on their responses to Kohlberg's scale. Correlations were computed among these variables and familial variables. Findings included a curvilinear relationship between conflict with father and level of moral development for males. It seems that a high level of reported conflict with father was associated with the lowest moral development level, and a moderate conflict level was associated with highest moral development level. For women highest level of conflict with father was associated with the highest level of moral development. Again we see that similar father–child relationships (e.g., conflict) have different effects on boys and girls. According to self-reports about the influence of fathers, males at middle-level morality reported that their fathers influenced them a good deal, whereas males at the highest level morality reported that friends had greater influence than fathers. This finding is in accord with Piaget's notion that peers are important for moral development.

Weisbroth (1970) was interested in the relationship between Kohlberg's moral reasoning stages and parental identification for male and female adults. He assessed identification by using the semantic differential. For males identification with both parents was related to high moral judgments, and for females identification with father was related to high moral judgment. Thus his results suggest that the father plays an important role in moral development.

In summary, although few studies attempt to determine the relationship between fathers and the development of moral judgment and moral values in their children, the research reviewed suggests that fathers have a significant impact on their children's moral development. Again the effects are greater for males. These findings are somewhat discrepant with cognitive theory, which suggests that fathers are not necessary for normal moral development.

## DISCUSSION

The studies reviewed in this chapter suggest that fathers play an important role in determining children's moral development. Fathers' attitudes and behaviors, along with children's perceptions of their fathers, seem to affect moral development. But the relatively small number of studies on fathers and the methodological problems associated with research on father–child relationships make it difficult to understand the father's role.

The studies highlight some of the methodological problems. One major problem is lack of comparability across studies. Because there are several aspects of moral development (behavioral, cognitive, affective), researchers have different emphases. When they do focus on the same aspect of moral development, they frequently use different criteria to assess moral development. For example, whereas both Rutherford and Mussen (1968) and Sears et al. (1965) were interested in behavior, Rutherford and Mussen studied generosity, and Sears et al. looked at resistance to temptation. When the same criteria are used, the ways in which they are assessed often differ (e.g., willingness to cheat can be measured by using teacher ratings, interviews, projective measures, or experimental situations). These variations in the research literature make it difficult to compare studies.

Another problem with studies of fathers and children is the absence of data from fathers directly. The majority of studies obtain information about fathers' behavior and attitudes from self-reports of children or ratings from other people (e.g., Hoffman, 1971a, 1971b; Rutherford & Mussen, 1968). The few studies that obtained information directly from fathers used interview techniques. Although this is useful, additional data on fathers could be obtained in other ways (e.g., by observing father–child interactions in the home).

Since it is difficult to manipulate father–child relationships, most research on fathers and children has been correlational. Some experimental research has examined factors that influence children's moral development. For example, Bandura and McDonald (1963) studied the effects of models on children's moral judgments. It is not clear, however, that experimental situations adequately represent the family situation. Although correlational research frequently deals with complex variables, it is difficult to determine causal relationships. Thus a good deal of the research on moral development and father–child relationships does not explain how fathers affect moral development in their children.

Several variables may affect the results of these studies. One is socioeconomic status. Studies of childrearing practices among different classes suggest that middle- and lower class parents treat their children differently. Hoffman (1971a, 1971b) compared moral development of children in two social classes and found some differences between them.

Another variable is age of children. One would expect differences in moral development and in father–child relationships for children at different ages. Few studies have attempted to trace developmental changes in children's moral development in relation to the father's role.

A third variable is paternal discipline, which may affect the quality of the father–child relationship and in turn the child's moral development. Although Hoffman and Saltzstein (1967) found that paternal discipline is not related to internal aspects of moral development, it may be related to other aspects of moral development (e.g., behavior; cf. Glueck & Glueck, 1950).

A fourth variable is sex of the child. Several studies suggest that fathers affect the moral development of boys and girls differently. It seems that different interaction patterns between fathers and sons and fathers and daughters may lead to the same behavioral outcome in boys and girls. For example, Sears et al. (1965) found that paternal rejection resulted in honesty in girls, but paternal ambivalence (warmth and hostility) resulted in honesty in boys. Similarly both Bronfenbrenner (1961) and Haan et al. (1968) found that differences in paternal interactions with sons and daughters resulted in the same behaviors in children. These studies suggest that (1) fathers interact differently with their sons and their daughters; (2) the same behavior in boys and girls may develop in different ways; and (3) fathers may have different standards and goals for their sons and daughters. The area of sex differences in moral development should not be overlooked.

Finally father presence versus absence is an important variable. Studies comparing the effects of father presence and absence on moral development revealed significant differences for boys (Hoffman, 1971a). Since father absence is a complex variable, it is not clear which aspects influence moral development. For example, length of father's absence, age of child when father leaves, reason for father's absence, and the ways in which the mother deals with the absence are all factors that may affect a child (cf. Herzog & Sudia, 1973). Bacon, Child, and Barry (1963) conducted a cross-cultural study to see if limited interactions between boys and their fathers were correlated with crime. From a survey of 48 non-literate societies, they found that cultures in which boys had few opportunities to interact with their fathers had greater frequencies of theft and personal crimes. The authors suggest that, when contact with fathers decreases, juvenile delinquency increases. According to Bacon et al., boys without fathers will at some point exhibit what they view as extreme masculine behavior (e.g., crime). Further study of the effects of father absence in relation to moral development is necessary before we can reach any clear-cut conclusions.

The need for additional research on the father's role in determining children's moral development is clear. Nevertheless it appears that fathers do play a significant role. They affect children by serving as models and as disciplinarians and by contributing to the general family climate. Although it seems that fathers are more important for moral development of boys than of girls, the dearth of research on girls makes it difficult to determine the father's effect on his daughter. We have seen that children's moral development is influenced by both parents. Father–child, mother–child, and mother–father interactions all seem to contribute to a child's development. Future research might focus on the father–child relationship in conjunction with other family relationships.

## REFERENCES

Aronfreed, J. The concept of internalization. In D. A. Goslin (Ed.), *Handbook of socialization theory and research*. Chicago: Rand McNally, 1969.

Bacon, M. K., Child, I. L., & Barry, H. A cross-cultural study of correlates of crime. *Journal of Abnormal and Social Psychology*, 1963, **66**, 291–300.

Bandura, A., & MacDonald, F. J. Influence of social reinforcement and the behavior of models in shaping children's moral judgments. *Journal of Abnormal and Social Psychology*, 1963, **67**, 274–281.

Bandura, A., Ross, D., & Ross, S. A. A comparative test of the status envy, social power, and secondary reinforcement theories of identificatory learning. *Journal of Abnormal and Social Psychology*, 1963, **67**, 527–534.

Bandura, A., & Walters, R. H. *Adolescent aggression*. New York: Ronald, 1959.

Becker, W. C. Consequences of different kinds of parental discipline. In M. L. Hoffman & L. W. Hoffman (Eds.), *Review of child development research*. Vol. 1. New York: Russell Sage Foundation, 1964.

Bronfenbrenner, U. Freudian theories of identification and their derivatives. *Child Development*, 1960, **31**, 15–40.

Bronfenbrenner, U. Some familial antecedents of responsibility and leadership in adolescents. In L. Petrullo & B. M. Bass (Eds.), *Leadership and interpersonal behavior*. New York: Holt, Rinehart, and Winston, 1961.

Burton, R. V. Generality of honesty reconsidered. *Psychological Review*, 1963, **70**, 481–499.

Freud, S. *The ego and the id*. London: Hogarth Press, 1927.

Freud, S. Some psychological consequences of the anatomical distinction between the sexes. In *Collected Papers*. Vol. 5. London: Hogarth Press, 1950.

Glueck, S., & Glueck, E. *Unraveling juvenile delinquency*. New York: Commonwealth Fund, 1950.

Haan, N., Smith, M. B., & Block, J. Moral reasoning of young adults: Political–social behavior, family background, and personality correlates. *Journal of Personality and Social Psychology*, 1968, **10**, 183–201.

Hartshorne, H., & May, M. A. *Studies in deceit*. New York: Macmillan, 1928.

Herzog, E., & Sudia, C. E. Children in fatherless families. In B. M. Caldwell & H. N. Ricciuti (Eds.), *Review of child development research*. Vol. 3. Chicago: University of Chicago Press, 1973.

Hetherington, E. M., & Deur, J. L. The effects of father absence on child development. In *The young child: Review of research*. Vol. 2. Washington, D.C.: National Association for the Education of Young Children, 1972.

Hoffman, M. L. Moral development. In P. H. Mussen (Ed.), *Carmichael's manual of child psychology*. Vol. 2. New York: Wiley, 1970.

Hoffman, M. L. Father absence and conscience development. *Developmental Psychology*, 1971, **4**, 400–406. (a)

Hoffman, M. L. Identification and conscience development. *Child Development*, 1971, **42**, 1071–1082. (b)

Hoffman, M. L., & Saltzstein, H. D. Parent discipline and the child's moral development. *Journal of Personality and Social Psychology*, 1967, **5**, 45–57.

Hogan, R. Moral conduct and moral character: A psychological perspective. *Psychological Bulletin*, 1973, **79**, 217–232.

Hogan, R. The structure of moral character and the explanation of moral action. *Journal of Youth and Adolescence*, 1975, **4**, 1–15.

Kohlberg, L. The development of children's orientation toward a moral order: I. Sequence in the development of moral thought. *Vita Humana*, 1963, **6**, 11–33.

Kohlberg, L. Stage and sequence: The cognitive–developmental approach to socialization. In D. A. Goslin (Ed.), *Handbook of socialization theory and research*. Chicago: Rand McNally, 1969.

Maccoby, E. E. The development of moral values and behavior in childhood. In J. A. Clausen (Ed.), *Socialization and society*. Boston: Little Brown & Co., 1968.

MacKinnon, D. W. Violation of prohibitions. In H. A. Murray (Ed.), *Explorations in personality*. New York: Oxford University Press, 1938.

McCord, J., & McCord, W. The effects of parental role model on criminality. *Journal of Social Issues*, 1957, **13**, 66–75.

Mussen, P. H., & Distler, L. Child-rearing antecedents of masculine identification in kindergarten boys. *Child Development*, 1960, **31**, 89–100.

Peck, R. F., & Havighurst, R. J. *The psychology of character development*. New York: Wiley, 1960.

Piaget, J. *The moral judgment of the child*. Glencoe, Ill.: The Free Press, 1948.

Rutherford, E., & Mussen, P. Generosity in nursery school boys. *Child Development*, 1968, **39**, 755–765.

Sears, R. R., Rau, L., & Alpert, R. *Identification and child rearing*. Stanford, Calif.: Stanford University Press, 1965.

Weisbroth, S. P. Moral judgment, sex, and parental identification in adults. *Developmental Psychology*, 1970, **2**, 396–402.

Wright, D. *The psychology of moral behaviour*. Baltimore: Penguin, 1971.

CHAPTER 7

# The Role of the Father in Cognitive, Academic, and Intellectual Development

NORMA RADIN

*University of Michigan*

In spite of the many deficiencies in the literature discussed here, it is important to summarize what is known about the father's role in the child's intellectual functioning so that some myths can be dispelled; for example, that father absence is highly damaging to the academic performance of black children. Further the mass of data about maternal influence on the child's cognitive development tends to mask the influence that fathers exert. The relative scarcity of discussions about fathers suggests his role is unimportant. As the ensuing summary suggests, this is indeed an invalid conclusion. Finally an examination of the knowledge that is available may facilitate the generation of new hypotheses and highlight fruitful directions for future research.

## LIMITATIONS TO THE LITERATURE

### Deficiencies Common to Research on Mothers and Fathers

The nature of cognitive functioning itself creates difficulties for anyone attempting to analyze the influence of any single variable or individual. Biller (1971) and Lynn (1974), in their books on fathers, both stated that biological and environmental factors interact in their contribution to the child's intellectual growth; both recommended caution in analyzing the influence that fathers might exert. Lynn pointed out that, even when there is a similarity in some particular aspect or style of thinking between father and child, it is difficult to determine how much can be attributed to genetic heritage and how much to social influence of the father.

Many other researchers in child development, such as Bayley (1968), Honzik (1963), Maccoby and Jacklin (1974), and Zigler and Child (1969), have also discussed genetic influences on cognitive development. For example, Maccoby and Jacklin stated that there is evidence of a recessive sex-linked gene that contributes an element of high spatial ability to cognitive competence, and this element is more commonly found in men than in women. Honzik, using the longitudinal data from the Berkeley Guidance study, discovered that girls' IQ correlated significantly with fathers' education at 3 years of age, but the correlation between boys' IQ and fathers' education did not become significant until 7 years of age. Honzik attributed this differential pattern to a sex difference in the rate of mental growth, girls maturing in cognitive functioning earlier than boys. She felt it was probable that the maturing of the central nervous system proceeds more slowly in the male than in the female as it does in other aspects of physical growth, such as height. Perhaps the most useful comment on the complex nature–nurture question was made by Zigler and Child (1969), who said, "One does not have to decide whether the individual's physical constitution and the behavior he emits are a common product of an underlying genetic structure, whether the behavior results from the constitution, or whether the behavior emerges from environmental response to the constitution, in order to appreciate the importance of constitutional factors" (p. 464).

The preponderance of research on middle-class families endemic to research on mothers contaminates the information available on fathers as well. Generalizations about the findings to other groups are, therefore, questionable. Particularly scarce are investigations of fathers in Chicano, Puerto Rican, and Oriental families. Such data would be of great importance to those interested in cognitive development, for the academic performance of these youngsters differs considerably (Coleman, Campbell, Hobson, McPartland, Mood, Weinfeld, & York, 1966). Another difficulty prevalent in the study of maternal behavior and pervading research on father behavior is the question of direction of influence in correlational investigations. All researchers in the field indicate that it is possible that the father is responding to the behavior evinced by the child rather than the reverse. Osofsky and O'Connell (1972) have shown experimentally that this phenomenon occurs; Bell (1968) showed in a *tour de force* that many classic studies can be reinterpreted if one assumes the child rather than the parent is the initiator of the interaction. Hoffman (1975) responded that in some instances it is reasonable to assume that parents initiate more interactions than children but agreed that in others it is not. The possibility also exists that the influence system is cyclical, as Clarke-Stewart (1973) demonstrated with maternal behavior, and that child behavior affects father behavior, which in turn affects child behavior, which in turn affects father behavior, and so on.

No attempt is made in this review to interpret all findings in terms of the child's impact on the father, as well as the father's impact on the child. It is assumed that both directions of influence exist; the discussion focuses, however, on the possible effect the father has on the child. There is no question, as Harrington, Block, and Block (1975) pointed out in interpreting their data, that the young boy's inability to solve a problem may well arouse hostility and rejection in the father. One can never be certain it is the father's hostility that is interfering with the boy's problem-solving capabilities. But since this chapter's goal is to analyze the possible influence fathers exert on their children's capabilities, and not possible causes of fathers' behavior, the direction of influence given emphasis is from adult to child.

## Deficiencies Unique to Studies of Fathers

Perhaps the most severe limitation to the available research literature is the absence of long-term investigations of paternal behavior comparable to the Berkeley Growth Study or the Fels Research Institute investigation wherein repeated observations of maternal behavior and child's cognitive performance were made. Thus correlational data on father's behavior and child's intellective ability through the years do not exist. A second limitation unique to father research is that many studies purporting to focus on fathers use data obtained entirely from mothers or from children, probably because housewives and students are more readily available. Mothers' views of fathers' behavior are, of course, important, as are the perceptions of the children. Such information cannot, however, replace direct observation of how fathers behave with their youngsters or of fathers' views directly expressed. Data obtained from different family members are not isomorphic and cannot be used interchangeably.

An additional constraint on father data is that many of the studies on paternal childrearing involve mothers' as well as fathers' interacting with their children. This method is rarely used in research on maternal behavior. It is difficult to know how the father would behave with his child if his wife were not present. No study thus far has involved a father's interacting with his child alone, and again when his wife is present, so that a comparison might be made. There are some suggestions in the data available, discussed later, that different correlational patterns may exist between father and child behavior when they interact alone and when they interact with the mother present. Although information about paternal behavior in the presence of other family members is essential, it is also necessary to have data about paternal behavior in the absence of his wife. The man who is fulfilling the husband and father role simultaneously may behave quite differently from the man who is only playing the father role. Further, fathers who "perform" in front of their wives may feel obligated to meet the women's role demands of the father in addition to, or instead of, meeting his own or his child's expectations. Thus there may be a tendency to play the stern disciplinarian when mother is watching, but not when she is absent; or roughhouse play may differ in view of mothers. We do not know at this point.

A complication that may be unique to a study of fathers is the importance of the economic context in which the behavior occurs. Parsons and Bales' (1955) description of the father as playing the instrumental role in the family is still largely valid, although conditions are changing. It is still primarily the father who is the family's link with the world of work and whose status in the family depends to a great extent on his ability to fulfill that role. As Strodtbeck (1958) succinctly phrased it, "The father's occupational success is something else again . . . if he fails in his function of 'bringing home the bacon'—of adapting successfully outside—his power is reduced at home, too" (p. 189). Since paternal power has been shown by a number of investigators, discussed later, to mediate the child's modeling of the father, paternal employment status may well affect his influence on his youngsters. There are suggestions that there may be racial, ethnic, and class differences in this area. Schulz (1969) pointed out that many black fathers play an expressive role in the family that is not dependent on his employment status. We know too little about paternal behavior at present to understand how the child's cognitive development might be affected by extensive unemployment or underemployment of the father, beyond the obvious financial deprivation of the family.

Another problem in attempting to understand the role of fathers in the child's cognitive development is the abundance of research data assessing his influence by his absence. Herzog and Sudia (1970) presented strong evidence that little is known about the effect of father absence per se, because so many other variables confound the findings, including reactions of other family members to his absence, his relationship to the mother and child before his departure, the economic condition of the family, the child's age when the father left, the reason for his leaving, and the support system available. Sutton-Smith, Rosenberg, and Landy (1968) have shown that even the birth order of the children of each sex can influence the impact of the father's absence. Thus it is important to examine the conditions present, rather than focus on an individual no longer there, and too few studies do this.

Finally much of the information about the father's influence on the cognitive competence of the child is contradictory, partially as a result of the different samples and methodologies employed. Bing (1963), Lytton (1973), and Sears (1965), among others, have underscored the fact that diverse results are obtained in the study of parent–child relations when different research strategies are used. A few trends do, however, emerge and appear to have substantial support. These are discussed first, and the more tenuous trends and findings follow.

## EMERGENT TRENDS

### Link Between Fathers and Sons

The most pronounced theme emerging about fathers and their children's intellectual growth is that the bond between fathers and sons is stronger than that between fathers and daughters. There are two probable reasons for this. One is the tendency for boys to identify with and model their fathers, particularly from about 4 to 9 years of age. The second is that fathers appear to identify with their sons, so that they react in a different way to sons than to daughters; they become more invested in the young boy's activities, abilities, and behavior patterns.

*Theoretical Support.* Insofar as boys' identification with fathers is concerned, learning theorists, such as Gewirtz and Stengle (1968), assert that the boy imitates his father because he is rewarded for doing so. Further, since an intermittent reinforcement schedule produces the most persistent behavior, a considerable amount of imitation can result from relatively little reinforcement. Because behaviors that are frequently rewarded acquire reinforcement value themselves, other learning theorists, such as Baer and Sherman (1964) pointed out that imitation itself can become rewarding. Bandura (1962), a social learning theorist who believes that modeling can take place even without external reward, described identification as virtually synonymous with imitation. Both involve matching the behavior, attitude, or emotional reactions exhibited by the models. Other child development theorists, such as Kagan (1958), Mussen and Rutherford (1963), and Sears (1953), discussed the relationship of reinforcement and imitation in other terms. They demonstrated that children imitate models who are nurturant or rewarding and that this modeling is particularly strong with a model who resembles themselves. According to Mowrer (1950), in developmental identification it is assumed that parental characteristics will be adopted to the extent that the parent is an important source of nurturance and reward. Thus boys are likely to imitate fathers who are loving and warm, even if the youngsters are not specifically rewarded for doing so.

Nelsen and Maccoby (1966) discussed another type of identification, that with the aggressor-or defensive identification in Mowrer's terminology. Mowrer hypothesized that defensive identification is a function of the threat qualities of the parent. Using other words but conveying the same idea, Nelsen and Maccoby suggested that boys identify with fathers they fear, to relieve their anxiety. Other have focused on father power rather than fear of the father. Mussen and Distler (1960) and Hetherington and Frankie (1967) found that paternal power or dominance fostered the boy's identification with his father. Kohlberg and Zigler (1967) proposed that boys must develop the concept of constancy of identity before they can identify with their fathers. Once the child learns that his sex is invariant, he seeks as a model someone of the same sex, begins to use his father as his primary model, and ultimately identifies with his male parent. Finally, according to Maccoby and Jacklin (1974), sex identification and same-sex modeling are initiated by the child, not the adult; these result from self-socialization by the youngster and show up in "rudimentary form" as early as 3 years of age.

There may be disagreement about the basis for identification among theorists and researchers, but there is little about the fact that young boys identify with, imitate, and/or model their fathers. It is suggested here that, as boys identify with their fathers, they emulate not only attitudes, values, roles, gestures, and emotional reactions but problem-solving strategies, thinking processes, and vocabulary as well. This matching of child's to adult's intellective behavior should foster the cognitive development of young boys.

As to counteridentification or parent identification with the same-sex child, Aberle and Naegele (1952), Gewirtz and Gewirtz (1968), Maccoby and Jacklin (1974), Rothbart (1971), and Sears (reported by Maccoby and Jacklin), found evidence of it. Counteridentification may also partially explain the phenomenon observed by Farber (1962) that fathers are particularly upset when their retarded child is a boy. Aberle and Naegele discussed parent identification with the same-sex child at some length, stating, ". . . whereas the father's present situation represents to him his son's probable future situation (broadly speaking), the son's present behavior may represent to the father his own past. . . . Perhaps difficulties now observed in the son were once successfully overcome by the father, sometimes after a struggle, and these may now be unconsciously reactivated. The identification may thus intensify the degree to which the father attempts to counteract the disturbing behaviors in his son, attempting at the same time to stifle the same tendencies in himself" (p. 374).

Such counteridentification may be related to the findings discussed by Goodenough (1957), Lynn (1974), and Maccoby and Jacklin (1974), among others, that greater emphasis is given by fathers than mothers to the appropriate sex-role behaviors of their children, particularly their sons.

Counteridentification is more likely to facilitate than hinder the boys' cognitive growth, although the opposite possibility exists. If the father's counteridentification results in his spending more time with the boy, encouraging his academic pursuits, it should facilitate cognitive growth. If, on the other hand, counteridentification leads to critical, domineering, paternal behavior, it could be damaging.

Thus it appears that young boys are particularly sensitive to their father's behavior and respond more strongly to fathers than to mothers; fathers in turn are particularly sensitive to, or empathic with, the behavior of their young sons and react in a more differentiated way to sons than to daughters. By the time the son approaches adolescence, the picture may change. Rosen and D'Andrade (1959) suggested that boys and their fathers may see each other as competitors. Maccoby and Jacklin (1974) supported this view, stating that fathers may begin to treat older children as they do adults of that sex, and ". . . there are simply discreet elements of flirtation with the opposite sex child and elements of rivalry with the same sex child" (p. 316). It is highly likely that such a rivalrous paternal stance will be detrimental to the boy's cognitive functioning, particularly if the hostility and power of the father are not restrained.

Investigations that found a relation between paternal behavior, or presence, and the young boy's cognitive development are summarized below. They can all be interpreted to a considerable extent, in terms of boys' identification with their fathers, and/or fathers' identification with sons, and/or rivalry between father and son. Although some of the studies report data for older children, the researchers, for example, Dyk and Witkin (1965) and Rosen and D'Andrade (1959), either implicitly or explicitly assume that the parental behavior assessed at one point in time had been taking place for some time earlier. Thus the findings reflect an ongoing process whose consequences were evidenced at the time the study was conducted.

*Quantity of Contact.* Pedersen, Rubenstein, and Yarrow (1973) found that, for black boys 5 to 6 months of age, the amount of interaction between father and child was positively correlated with measures of the son's cognitive functioning, for example, scores on the Mental and Psychomotor Developmental Indices from the Bayley Tests of Infant Development. The correlations with daughters' scores did not even approach significance. Father absence, a variable computed in a different way, was similarly negatively and significantly correlated with sons' cognitive competence but not with daughters'. Because no differences could be found in the behaviors of the mothers, Pedersen et al. concluded that the link between father and son was direct and not mediated by the women. No hypothesis was offered, however, about the nature of the link except the negative one that the children were obviously too young to have been modeling anyone. One could interpret the results as evidence of counter-identification by fathers that resulted in different behaviors by fathers of sons and fathers of daughters. The nature of the interaction between father and child was not investigated, merely the amount. Perhaps, just as qualitatively different paternal behavior with sons and daughters 4 years of age was found (Radin & Epstein, 1975a), paternal behavior with 6-month-old boys and girls may be different, at least in black families.

Blanchard and Biller (1971) studied third-grade boys who were of average intelligence and from working-class and lower middle-class backgrounds. They assessed the effect of different levels of father availability on academic performance. The findings showed that boys whose fathers interacted frequently with them (more than 2 hours per day) received higher grades than boys whose fathers infrequently (less than 6 hours per week) interacted with them, controls being provided for age of child, IQ, socioeconomic status, and sibling constellation. When four groups, (1) early father absent (beginning before age 5), (2) late father absent (beginning after age 5), (3) low father present (less than 6 hours per week), and (4) high father present (more than 2 hours per day) were compared, it was found that the rank order for school grades, the cited variables being controlled, was the following: first, high father-present boys, who were doing superior work; second, the late father-absent and low father-present boys, who were both functioning somewhat below grade level; and third, the early father-absent boys, who were generally under-achievers. In the study the reason for absence or the mothers' reaction to the absence was not assessed, but so many other variables were controlled that the research has major significance.

Supporting Blanchard and Biller's findings that early father absence has a greater impact than later absence on boys' intellectual performance were the data collected by Carlsmith (1964). Investigating the College Board Aptitude scores of middle-class high school boys, she found that those who were father absent early in their childhood were more likely than boys who were father present to have a feminine patterning of aptitude test scores ($Vm$), that is, a higher verbal than mathematics score. The incidence of feminine patterning was negatively related to the child's age at the onset of the father's absence and positively related to the length of his absence. Carlsmith attributed the findings to sex-role identification. She hypothesized that the greater incidence of higher $Vm$ scores in boys who were father absent early in life was due to the boys' identifying with their mothers rather than with their fathers, since the $Vm$ pattern of aptitude scores reflects an underlying "feminine conceptual approach." It was further assumed that the cognitive styles are maintained throughout childhood and adolescence, despite the return of the father to the family. There is much in common between Carlsmith's view and the view presented in this chapter. In both cases it is suggested that a cognitive style can be modeled as any other behavioral style can.

Other studies pertaining to quantity of paternal contact are discussed in the section on Father Absence. The Carlsmith investigation was reviewed at this point because of its relevance to father identification.

*Quality of Contact.* Nelsen and Maccoby (1966) replicated Carlsmith's work to test an alternate explanation of the feminine patterning of scores of father-absent males. They posed a tension-interference hypothesis: that stress and tension interfere more with cognitive functioning basic to mathematical ability than with that involved in verbal ability. Thus stress caused by a number of factors could produce a $Vm$ pattern in males. To test this theory, they examined the Scholastic Aptitude Test scores of college freshmen and related the patterning of verbal and mathematics scores to various experiences the students had reported as having with their parents. One of the major findings was that there was support for the sex-role identification theory of Carlsmith, but only for males, not females. Supporting this theory were the findings that males who were father absent had higher verbal than mathematics scores, and males whose fathers were frequently absent from home for extended periods more often showed the $Vm$ pattern than males whose fathers were not frequently absent. In addition, in keeping with the theory, males who reported having talked over their personal problems with their fathers, and not having feared their fathers, tended to obtain high mathematics than verbal scores. Support for defensive identification was also found, according to the investigators. Boys who reported being punished only by their fathers had higher mathematics scores in relation to their verbal scores than males who were not punished only by their fathers.

A recent extensive review of the relevant literature by Maccoby and Jacklin (1974) revealed that, of the four well-established sex differences the authors could find, one was that girls have greater verbal ability than boys and another was that boys excel in mathematical ability, beginning at about age 12. These differences did not appear to be due to biological factors, as was true of the remaining two well-established sex differences.

Thus the findings concerning father influence in this area gain in significance.

Mutimer, Laughlin, and Powell (1966) found that boys 8 to 12 who read well preferred to be with their fathers; girls who read well preferred to be with their mothers. Shaw and White (1965), in an investigation of high school students with above-average intelligence, obtained results indicating that the boys who had a B average or better perceived themselves as more similar to their fathers than boys with a below-B average. Further, father and son self-ratings were correlated in the high-achieving group but not in the low-achieving group. Girls with high grades saw themselves as more like their mothers than their fathers. Similar results were obtained by Teahan (1963), who compared low- and high-achieving college freshman. High-achieving males completed an attitude questionnaire as their fathers did; low-achieving males did not. In contrast high-achieving females' questionnaires resembled their mothers'; low-achieving girls' questionnaires did not. The author speculated that the disparity seen between attitudes of low-achieving girls and their mothers, and between low-achieving males and their fathers, might be due to a possible lack of identification with these parental figures. Also supportive of the relationship between developmental identification and cognitive competence of young boys were the findings of Andersland and Kimball. In the Andersland (1968) investigation paternal rejection was related to underachievement in high school boys but not in high school girls. In the Kimball (1952) study very intelligent adolescent boys who had poor relations with their fathers had lower grades than the group whose relationship with their father was considered average.

In my own observational research (Radin, 1972, 1973; Radin & Epstein, 1975a) with preschool children, described in detail at a later point, paternal nurturance was found to be significantly related to cognitive competence in white boys, particularly middle-class youngsters. In contrast Baumrind's (1971) observational study of middle-class preschool children found no significant correlation between these two variables. The difference in methodology employed in the two studies may help explain the divergent results. In the Baumrind investigation both mother and father were present; in our research, only the father and child were present with the interviewer. Perhaps fathers behave differently when their wives are present; perhaps children perceive the behavior differently. Further research on the question is needed.

There is considerable evidence that paternal authoritarianism and hostility have detrimental effects on young men attending college, and on boys likely to become college students. Teahan (1963) found that fathers of low-achieving, male and female freshmen were more punitive in their attitudes than fathers of high achievers. Cross and Allen (1969) discovered that high-achieving college men had fathers they viewed as accepting and child centered; Heilbrun's (1973) data showed that late adolescent males who experienced aversive paternal control, that is, much control in a context of low nurturance, had thinking deficits. Baumrind's (1971) study revealed that authoritarian attitudes expressed on a questionnaire by middle-class fathers were negatively associated with the cognitive competence of young boys, although observed authoritarian behaviors were not. Data from our study (Radin & Epstein, 1975a) demonstrated that observed paternal restrictiveness was negatively correlated with measures of cognitive ability in preschool, middle-class boys and in lower class boys as well.

Harrington, Block, and Block (1975), in an observational study of 3-year-old, middle-class children, noted that father hostility, rejection, and impatience were associated with the intolerance of ambiguity in boys but not in girls. The girls' performance was affected by their mothers' behavior. Although intolerance of ambiguity is not usually considered a component of cognitive ability, as Harrington et al. described the attribute, it may well hinder the ability to solve complex problems; jumping to a solution before examining all aspects of a problem should surely reduce the child's problem-solving competence.

Overall the literature shows that paternal punitiveness and hostility are associated with limited cognitive ability in middle-class males. There is little evidence that fear of father facilitates their cognitive growth. The Nelsen and Maccoby (1966) study suggesting that defensive identification enhances mathematics skill contradicts this trend, but males who scored high in mathematics in this study did not fear their fathers. Thus some other factor, such as paternal dominance, may be involved rather than punitiveness. Perhaps a middle-class boy who fears his father is also fearful about exploring the environment, and the child's cognitive growth is thereby hindered, regardless of his identification with his father. Both modeling of an adult and freedom to explore may be needed for optimum intellectual development. Developmental identification may supply both of these essential factors by fostering imitation and also suggesting to the child that interaction with the environment (of which has father is a part) is likely to be reinforcing. Defensive identification may provide only the first element.

*Paternal Power.* Several studies underscored the importance of paternal power in boys' cognitive performance, possibly because of the role that power plays in enhancing identification with the child's father. Bowerman and Elder (1964) observed that 13- to 18-year-old, middle-class and lower class boys who were high achievers had fathers who were the most powerful individual in the family and were democratic in their relationship with the children. Majoribanks (1972), from an extensive study of 11-year-boys in England, concluded that father dominance correlated significantly, although at a low level, with boys' verbal ability on a standard achievement test. There is also evidence that low father power fosters cognitive competence in boys. Strodtbeck (1958) found that low father power vis-à-vis his son and wife was associated with high independence and mastery values by boys 14 to 17 years of age; according to Strodtbeck these values are generally associated with high achievement. The one point of agreement between the work of Strodtbeck and that of Bowerman and Elder is that power assertion by the father over the son does not facilitate achievement or achievement striving. Rosen and D'Andrade's (1959) study of paternal influence on achievement in young boys supports this view. These researchers, studying achievement motivation in lower class and middle-class white boys in grades four through six, concluded that, for high motivation to achieve to develop, the boy needs more autonomy from his father than from his mother. The father who gives the boy a relatively high degree of autonomy "provides him with the opportunity to compete on his own ground, to test his skill, and to gain a sense of confidence in his own competence" (p. 216). Although intellectual achievement and motivation to achieve are not the same, they are highly correlated when need achievement is assessed by projective techniques (Strodtbeck, 1958), and this was the procedure followed in the Rosen and D'Andrade study.

The different results regarding paternal power obtained by Bowerman and Elder, and Marjoribanks on one hand, and by Strodtbeck, and Rosen and D'Andrade on the other, may be reconciled when the methods used by the two groups are examined. The former investigators relied on questionnaire data about general paternal behavior; the latter group conducted observational studies in which fathers were watched as they interacted with their sons, completing tasks. There is evidence, discussed in greater detail later, that paternal interference, or even involvement, in the boy's mastery efforts may be detrimental to the youngster's cognitive growth. Paternal behavior in nonmastery situations may have different consequences for his offspring. Thus the divergent results may be explained by the use of different methodologies. Perhaps a father who is perceived as competent and strong, but who permits his son to master tasks and solve problems independently, provides the most fertile background for the youngster's intellectual growth.

*Paternal Self-Confidence.* Grunebaum, Hurwitz, Prentice, and Sperry (1962) studied elementary-school-aged boys of average IQ who were 2 years below grade level. They discovered that the boys had fathers who felt inadequate and considered themselves failures. Supporting their findings were those of Busse (1969), who found that flexibility in thinking (defined as considering alternative solutions to problems) of 11-year-old, lower class, black boys was related to the fathers' feelings of power toward his spouse, the world, and his offspring. Possibly a model who is ineffectual fosters ineffective problem solving in those who emulate him. An alternative possibility is that the powerless father is not as readily modeled as one perceived as powerful. Related to the Grunebaum and Busse findings were those of Honzik (1967). Describing some data obtained in the longitudinal Berkeley Study, Honzik reported that the father's satisfaction with his own occupation was significantly correlated with his son's IQ from ages 5 to 15 but not with his daughter's. The father who is pleased with his own job may present a more nearly adequate and self-confident model for his son to emulate.

*Cognitive Style.* The literature on cognitive style tends to support the view that boys' approach to problem solving is influenced by their relationship with their fathers. Various terms have been used to describe an approach that involves disembedding details of a problem from its context or ignoring irrelevant cues in the environment in solving certain types of problems. The cognitive style is sometimes called analytic, as opposed to global, or field independent, as opposed to field dependent. Dyk and Witkin (1965), in their research on young boys, reported a significant correlation between an analytic approach and some components of intellectual competence, such as space ability, and between an analytic approach and several nonverbal items on the Wechsler Intelligence Scale for Children, such as block design and object assembly. Corah (1965), in keeping with the findings of Dyk and Witkin, obtained significant associations between scores on tests of field independence and the verbal IQ of adult males, adult females, and young girls, but not of young boys. Thus there appears to be an overlap between field independence and intellectual competence, and the findings pertaining to the latter are relevant to the former.

Several investigations have found that a positive father–son relationship is related to field independence. Dyk and Witkin (1965), using 10-year-old, middle-class, white boys as subjects, learned that field-independent boys were more likely to indicate warm father–son relationships on the Thematic Apperception Test than field-dependent boys. Seder's (1957) study of suburban families, as reported by Dyk and Witkin, revealed that fathers of field-dependent boys, but not of girls, spent relatively little time with their sons, and the time was spent in relatively passive activities such as watching television. Seder also learned that fathers of "global" boys used more physical punishment and verbal aggression than fathers of "analytic" boys, whose punishment tended to be more restrained. This relationship did not hold for girls. Analytic boys were punished more often, however, by their fathers than by their mothers, a finding resembling Nelsen and Maccoby's (1966) observation that college males with higher mathematics than verbal scores were punished by their fathers rather than by their mothers. The similarity is not surprising in view of the relationship often found between an analytic approach, mathematical ability, and spatial ability (Bing, 1963; Carlsmith, 1964; Maccoby & Jacklin, 1974). Barclay and Cusumano (1967) reported that father-absent adolescent boys were more field dependent than those whose fathers were present, a finding again resembling those of Nelsen and Maccoby and Carlsmith concerning the more limited mathematical ability of father-absent males in high school and college.

Lynn (1969) hypothesized that there was a curvilinear relationship between father availability and field independence. According to Lynn, when there is a moderate amount of father availability, the boy has an idea of masculine role but has to interact actively with his environment to develop his masculine role fully. Thus if the boy's father is constantly available, the boy does not develop an analytic, independent stance in interaction with his environment. Support for this hypothesis came from research on Eskimo boys who spend a good deal of time with their fathers. Berry (1966) and MacArthur (1967) found that Eskimo boys imitate their fathers more closely but are not more field independent than girls. Sherman and Smith's (1967) study also gave support to the Lynn hypothesis, for they found that orphans receiving full-time care from male counselors were less field independent than males from normal families. Some additional indirect support for the Lynn proposition appeared in the data obtained by Corah (1965), who correlated scores of field dependence of middle-class fathers and their children. Little evidence was found of a relationship between fathers' and sons' scores, but there was a significant association between the scores of fathers and daughters. Thus it appears that the process by which fathers influence their sons' cognitive style may not be modeling. This leaves the possibility open that the development of independence while interacting with the environment may be one of the antecedents of field independence.

*Sex Differences.* Our own work strongly supported the hypothesis that developmental identification with fathers fosters, or is associated with, cognitive competence in 4-year-old boys but not girls (Radin, 1972, 1973; Radin & Epstein, 1975a, 1975b). The data have consistently shown paternal nurturance to be linked with intellectual ability in the young boys and paternal restrictiveness to be linked with lack of such competence. There was no evidence of defensive identification or of an association between paternal punitiveness and intellectual ability. Rather the conclusion was reached that paternal restrictiveness tended to hinder the boy's identification with his father and, hence, with the youngster's cognitive development. The link between fathers' behavior and girls' cognitive competence was negligible.

Two studies with white families were conducted. The first, a pilot study for the second, involved only boys, with one-half of the sample middle-class and the other half lower class families. The second study contained both boys and girls and three social classes, middle, working, and lower. The methodology used in both studies was the same. Fathers were interviewed at home in the presence of only their 4-year-old child. The child was asked to be in the room so that he/she could perform some tasks at the end of the interview. It was assumed that the child would make some demands on the father during the interview that he would have to handle or anticipate in some way. These paternal behaviors provided the raw data that were recorded on audio tape and subsequently coded, with 25 predetermined categories. The interviewer's notations about nonverbal paternal behavior were also coded. The categories were as behaviorally specific as possible, for example, praised the child, asked the child a question. The child was administered intelligence tests within a few weeks, and the father's behaviors were correlated with the child's test scores. In the pilot study the Stanford–Binet Intelligence Scale and the Peabody Picture Vocabulary Test were used; in the larger study the Stanford–Binet and some standardized Piagetian tasks were employed.

In both studies paternal nurturance was positively and significantly associated with cognitive measures of the boys. Paternal restrictiveness was negatively associated. In the pilot study paternal behaviors were placed in these categories on an a priori basis. In the second study separate factor analyses were performed on fathers' behaviors with boys and fathers' behaviors with girls. For boys four factors emerged, two clearly nurturant and two essentially restrictive. Although there were class differences (for example, the restrictive variable was more important than the nurturant variable in the lower class), in general, nurturance was positively associated and restrictiveness negatively associated with cognitive competence.

For girls the picture was sharply different. Six different factors emerged from the factor analysis and only one of the six factors was associated with a child's cognitive score, and this in only one social class subgroup. In view of the large number of correlations performed, this may well have been due to chance factors. Evidence also emerged of differential paternal behavior with sons and daughters. Although there had been a significant sex difference in the mean frequency of only 2 of the 25 behavior categories, the factor structure underlying fathers' behavior with boys was completely different from that underlying fathers' behavior with girls. For sons, as indicated above, there were two nurturant and two restrictive factors. For girls, however, six factors emerged, three of which were ambivalent; for example, they contained contradictory behaviors such as meeting explicit needs and ignoring explicit needs or requesting and ordering aversively. This mixed-message phenomenon did not occur in any of the boys' factors. The interpretation given to the finding was that the ambivalent message coming from the father to the daughter tended to alienate her and reduce the likelihood of the girl's using him as a model for problem solving, intellectual striving, or vocabulary development. Thus his behaviors were unrelated to her cognitive scores. Even the three unambivalent factors that were either restrictive or nurturant were unrelated to measures of the girls' intellective competence. It was suggested that 4-year-old girls were using their mothers as their primary model, as a previous study (Radin, 1974) using the same methodology has shown. The findings of Lynn and Cross (1974) concerning the preference of 4-year-old girls for their mothers over their fathers tended to support this hypothesis.

It is difficult to explain the reason for the mixed messages directed toward the young girls, but one possibility is that there is some element of flirtation in the father's relationship with his preschool daughter. Maccoby and Jacklin (1974), discussing this phenomenon, stated that it usually, but not always, occurred when the children were older. Our data give evidence that it may well take place at a much earlier age, as Johnson (1963) suggested it did in her analysis of paternal behavior with boys and girls. If this quasi-flirting is taking place, it may well involve an effort on the father's side to put distance between himself and his young daughter— hence the loading on one factor of contradictory behaviors.

*Sex-Stereotyped Behavior with Daughters.* These findings suggest that fathers, to some extent, may respond to their daughters in the stereotypic ways that males behave with females. Aberle and Naegele's (1952) study of middle-class men found fathers expressing just such views. The men interviewed gave evidence that they were oriented toward their sons as future occupants of middle-class occupational roles for which certain behaviors were of great importance. Their orientation toward their daughters was, however, as future occupants of different middle-class roles, wife and mother, for which their own standards were less exacting. In keeping with these orientations the men voiced serious concerns about their sons', but not their daughters', success in school and attendance of a good college. Among the concerns voiced about girls, but not boys, was that they marry and not be too bossy.

Lynn (1974) also supported the hypothesis that fathers tend to respond to their daughters in a sex-stereotyped manner. He expanded on this concept by indicating that such stereotypic behavior may interfere with the cognitive development of daughters, for fathers may perceive intellectual growth and achievement as masculine and, hence, not as feminine qualities to be enhanced in daughters. A father who treats his daughter in a fashion that elicits a traditionally feminine reaction may thus retard her intellectual and academic development. If, however, he sets up a relationship in which she can model his intellectual efforts and achievement motivation and be reinforced for doing so, he can heighten these attributes in his daughter.

The juxtaposition of both alternatives summarizes much of the data about fathers' role in their daughters' cognitive growth. Possibly because both types of fathers' behavior toward young girls exist, contradictory evidence about their influence pervades the literature.

## Father–Daughter Trends

*Moderate Distance and Autonomy.* One salient difference in the research on boys and girls is that paternal warmth is virtually never negatively associated with cognitive functioning in boys, but there is evidence that too much warmth may be detrimental to the development of intellective capacity in young girls. Honzik (1967), using the longitudinal data of the Berkeley Guidance Study, found that friendliness of the father toward his daughter, but not a close bond or expressions of affection, was significantly and positively related with the girls' IQ at 7 to 9 years of age. A close bond between father and son was, however, positively related with the IQ of boys. Similarly suggestive that distance from the father may benefit the girls' cognitive growth was the finding that, ages 2 and 3, "Father Energy Level" was negatively associated with the IQ of girls but not of boys. Conceivably an energetic father in this largely middle-class sample would be more physically involved with his children, or more intensely involved, and this behavior did not facilitate the intellective growth of his daughter.

The data of Crandall, Dewey, Katkovsky, and Preston (1964) did not fit the pattern exactly, but there is some evidence in their study that a moderate distance between father and daughter enhances the girl's intellectual competence. Crandall and her colleagues found that the academic achievement of girls, but not of boys, in grades two through four was positively correlated with positive paternal reactions to their intellective efforts and negatively correlated with negative reactions. But fathers who encouraged and instigated intellectual pursuits in girls had less proficient daughters. They interpreted the latter finding as resulting from paternal reactions to daughters of low ability. Other interpretations can, however, be made, particularly in view of the absence of a significant correlation between paternal instigative behavior and boys' intellective ability. It is possible that some distance and autonomy from fathers fosters girls' cognitive functioning. High paternal praise for daughters' intellectual efforts may also denote a father who does not hold stereotypic views of girls as nonintellectual individuals. Thus these fathers may provide an enhancement of cognitive functioning, provided they do not become too involved in the girls' work.

Supporting the hypothesis that some degree of paternal distance and cognitive competence in girls are positively associated were the findings of Teahan (1963), who compared parental attitudes of high- and low-achieving college freshmen. It was found that the fathers of high-achieving girls expressed less dominating attitudes and less approval of ignoring the girls than the fathers of low-achieving girls. Thus an orientation that involves neither dominance nor ignoring appears to be associated with academic achievement in college women. The same pattern was not found for high-achieving college men. Similar results were obtained by Heilbrun, Harrell, and Gellard (1967), who also studied college women. They observed that the subjects did best on tasks requiring an analytic style of thinking when they viewed their fathers as exerting little control over them and expressing little nurturance. More relevant to autonomy than to moderate distance were the findings of another study by Heilbrun (1973) that female undergraduates did poorly on cognitive tasks under stress when they perceived their fathers as exerting aversive control over them.

Investigating preschool children, Baumrind (1971) obtained results similar to those of Heilbrun, who studied 18-year-old women. Baumrind discovered that observed paternal authoritarianism with preschool-aged girls was negatively associated with the youngsters' cognitive performance. Our study with a similar age group noted no significant correlations between these variables (Radin & Epstein, 1975a). The difference in results may be attributable to the different observational methodologies in regard to the mother's presence, discussed previously. Some support for this suggestion was seen in the study by Harrington et al. (1975), which used a procedure similar to ours; fathers and preschool-aged girls were observed interacting without mothers present. Harrington's results, like ours, demonstrated that there was not a significant correlation between fathers' negative behavior and girls' cognitive competence. Perhaps fathers are a bit more restrained when alone with their daughters. Further research is needed to clarify the issue.

Bing's (1963) study presented data derived from maternal reports of paternal behavior and offered limited support to the paternal-distance hypothesis. The results showed that closeness between father and daughter, within a context of strictness, was beneficial to the girls' intellectual growth. The amount of time fathers spent reading to their daughters was seen to be positively associated with verbal achievement of fifth-grade girls but not of sons. Paternal strictness was also positively related to verbal achievement in girls but not in boys. Bing explained her results by reasoning that fathers who were strict with their daughters would have more feminine girls, and this would be associated with verbal achievement. Thus, contrary to Lynn's (1974) views, Bing postulated that fostering of femininity by fathers can enhance at least one type of intellectual competence in young girls. No data on the relationship between numerical ability and reading time, or numerical ability and strictness, were presented in the paper.

One study appears to contradict the hypothesis that some distance and autonomy from fathers fosters the cognitive growth of young girls. Cain (1971), using data supplied by the youngsters, found that high arithmetic achievement in Mexican–American children 7 to 13 years of age, was associated with father's love; low reading achievement was related to his casual attitude. Possibly father–child relationships within a Chicano culture are qualitatively different from those in Anglo families. There is a dearth of data about paternal behavior in Mexican–American families. Perhaps love and control are not expressed the same way in these families; possibly values Chicano families hold about the extended family interact with fathers' behavior to produce effects unique to that setting. We simply do not know.

*Paternal Pressure.* There are indications from both Baumrind's (1971) and our (Jordan, Radin, & Epstein, 1975) studies of preschool children that young girls, but not young boys, are hindered by paternal pressure to advance or grow. Baumrind found in her largely middle-class sample that early maturity demands and discouragement of infantile behavior by the child's father, as assessed by questionnaire data, were negatively correlated with the girl's IQ but not the boy's. Our investigation yielded similar results; early paternal demands for mastery and late independence granting, also assessed by questionnaire, were negatively associated with intellective scores of lower class, 4-year-old girls. In contrast, for middle-class boys, late independence granting was positively associated with the boys' IQ and scores on Piagetian tasks.

*Influence on Mathematics Skills.* Several researchers have observed that the relationship between a father and his daughter affects the girl's mathematical skills. The assumption is often made that relatively close contact with the father tends to foster her adoption of the father's masculine approach to thinking. Landy, Rosenberg, and Sutton-Smith (1969), studying the American College Entrance Examination scores of college sophomores, found that the $Q$ (quantitative) scores of women whose fathers were not present were significantly lower than $Q$ scores of women whose fathers started working on the night shift after the girls were 10 years of age. There were no significant differences in the language scores of the two groups. Since there were no differences in the $Q$ scores of the total absent group and of the group whose fathers started working on the night shift when the girls were 0 to 4 years of age, or 5 to 9, the authors concluded that the ages of 1 through 9 composed a critical period for the development of quantitative skills in girls and that fathers who are available to girls influence this development.

Another study by the same investigators (Sutton-Smith et al., 1968) supported this conclusion. The ACE scores of college freshmen, with and without fathers, were compared in students coming from families of different size and sibling composition. The details of the interaction with these variables are discussed in the section on Father Absence, but relevant to $Q$ scores was the finding that there was a significant difference between father-present and father-absent groups in $Q$ score only for females, except in one small subgroup, but in $Q$ and $L$ (language) scores for males. In addition it was found that women whose fathers' absence started when they were less than 9 years of age obtained lower $Q$ scores than women whose fathers' absence commenced after the age of 10. The age of onset of absence was not a significant variables for men.

It is not clear why quantitative skills should be linked to fathers' presence, especially for girls. A possible clue was offered by Rosenberg and Sutton-Smith (1966) who postulated that independence as a personality trait mediates an interest in stimuli emanating from a variety of sources, particularly the world of objects. The authors added, "It is this interest in the object world that has often been said to underlie the superiority of boys in quantification and problem solving" (p. 27). When conditions foster the girls' emulation of brothers, described by Sutton-Smith et al. (1968) as being already oriented toward independence by sex-typed reinforcement, the sisters' quantification scores are enhanced. Bing (1963) also linked independence and mathematical ability, and Lynn (1969) saw a connection between independence in the environment and field independence. One can extrapolate from the statement about brothers that any factor that fosters emulation by females of males—brothers or fathers—may have a beneficial effect on quantitative skills, and this may explain the possible link between father absence and low $Q$ scores for women in college. The correlation obtained by Corah (1965) between field-independence scores of fathers and daughters would tend to support the view that women's analytic or mathematical ability may be based to some extent on modeling their fathers' thinking processes in this area.

## Trends Common to Boys and Girls

*Participation in Problem Solving.* There are indications, although the data are not in complete agreement, that extensive participation of the father in the child's intellective efforts does not facilitate the youngster's cognitive development. Boerger (1971) studied variables associated with pressure to achieve in fathers of boys in grades five and six. His data showed that paternal participation was negatively and linearly related to achievement; that is, the fathers claiming the least participation in responding to a mailed questionnaire had the highest achieving sons, and as participation increased, achievement decreased. A post hoc analysis of the data showed that the negative correlation was centered in arithmetic rather than in language arts or science. The results were interpreted as suggesting that, although the fathers of high-achieving boys hold high aspirations for them, these fathers tend to be only indirectly involved in their sons' academic activities, for example, providing opportunities and materials for achievement, without actually directing specific tasks. Fathers of low-achieving boys, on the other hand, appear to involve themselves directly in completion of school tasks.

Crandall et al. (1964) found that fathers' participation in boys' intellective activities were negatively associated with the boys' arithmetic achievement. The Crandall data also revealed that fathers who encouraged and instigated the intellectual pursuits by daughters had girls who were less proficient in school. Solomon, Houlihan, Busse, and Parelius (1971) conducted an observational study of black fifth-grade children and their parents in a problem-solving situation. The investigators found that a moderate amount of paternal involvement facilitated the girls' intellectual functioning, as assessed by school tests and grades. For girls a moderate amount of paternal encouragement to engage in independent efforts, free of hostility and efforts to dominate the girl, was associated with high academic achievement. For boys this curvilinear relationship did not exist. Rather, no behavior of the father (in isolation from behavior of the mother) during the puzzle-solving session was significantly associated with the boys' academic competence. In addition the researchers found a negative relationship between paternal participation in the child's efforts to solve problems and the child's tendency to use efficient and constructive problem-solving techniques. Solomon and his colleagues reported studying the data carefully to determine if there was evidence, as Crandall

had suggested, that parents were responding to poor academic performance in the child. They found only a slight tendency for fathers to participate more if they felt their child had low ability. The explanation
offered by the Solomon group for the negative relationship between the
father's participation and achievement behavior by the child was that the
child may become more distracted when his/her father becomes involved
in the problem-solving effort.

Busse's (1969) study of black, lower class parents teaching tasks to
their fifth-grade sons concluded that moderately active paternal participation while the boys were working on the tasks was associated with flexible
thinking in the youngsters. Further, fathers who expressed preference for
a moderately active role with their children in a questionnaire had sons
higher in flexible thinking than fathers did who preferred either a very
active role or an ignoring role.

Our own research suggested that lack of involvement when 4-year-old
children were solving puzzles was related to cognitive competence in the
youngsters (Radin & Epstein, 1975b). At the conclusion of the interview
with the fathers, the children were given tasks to work on, such as jigsaw
puzzles, and fathers were told they could help if they wished. Whereas
nurturant paternal behaviors during the interview were associated with
intellective competence of the boys, paternal nurturance during the
problem-solving segment was negatively correlated with IQ and other
cognitive measures. For girls the correlation was not significant, but there
was a trend in this direction. When the total sample was grouped together,
there was a negative and significant correlation between a group of behaviors labeled nurturant and intellective measures of the children. A
cluster of paternal behaviors labeled restrictive was not related to the
cognitive measures. Regrouping the father behaviors into other categories
produced similar results. The behaviors were divided into Father Responses to Requests for Help from the Child and Father-Initiated Behaviors. Each of these categories was negatively correlated with cognitive
measures for the total sample and for boys. The total number of father
interactions during the task-solving segment was also negatively associated with cognitive measures for the total sample and for boys. The only
positive significant correlations with intellective scores were found with
one father's initiating behavior, "spontaneously announcing to the child
that he won't help with the puzzles or showing no interest in the child's
progress." This variable correlated positively with Piagetian measures
again for the total sample and for boys.

It was possible to gain some clues about the direction of influence because the children were tested 1 year later on the same intellective measures. For girls the cluster of nurturant paternal behaviors observed the

previous year was now negatively related to measures of the girls' cognitive competence. Thus there was evidence that paternal efforts to be helpful were detrimental to the girls' cognitive growth; it was not a case of fathers helping inept daughters. Similarly for boys and for the total sample, paternal restrictiveness, not correlated with concurrent measures of the youngsters' cognitive competence, was negatively correlated with the scores 1 year later. Thus again the direction of influence appeared to be from father to child; order giving and threats during the child's efforts to solve tasks hindered intellective development.

The contrast in correlations between paternal nurturance during the interview and boys' IQ, and between paternal nurturance during problem solving and boys' IQ, was surprising. It appears that very similar behavior by fathers can have very different meaning in different contexts. As with paternal power, paternal nurturance and help-giving may have generally beneficial effects, but not when the youngster is engaged in mastery efforts.

*Mother as Mediator.* Thus far all the investigations reviewed and trends delineated have referred to a direct link between father and child. But another channel of influence may exist, an indirect link whereby fathers influence children through the impact the men have on mothers. There is evidence that maternal behavior may sometimes mediate the relationship between the father's behavior and the child's cognitive functioning. Honzik's (1967) report on the Berkeley Guidance Study showed that paternal friendliness toward the mother fostered the girls' intellective growth. According to Honzik this variable yielded the largest number of significant correlations with the daughters' test scores between 21 months and 15 years. Honzik attributed this to the likelihood that the father's attitude toward the mother produced a compatible milieu conducive to the daughter's intellectual development. It is difficult to understand why this compatible milieu did not foster the boys' cognitive development as well. There was virtually no association between sons' IQ and fathers' friendliness to mother. An alternate explanation is that fathers' warm behavior toward their wives may enhance the women's warmth toward their children, and this may foster the girls' identification with mothers. As a consequence the daughters' intellectual growth may be stimulated through their emulation of their mothers' problem-solving strategies and thinking processes. One of Honzik's results tended to support this view. A close, friendly mother–daughter relationship was significantly correlated with the girls' test scores in the preschool years. Another study (Radin, 1974) similarly found an association between maternal warmth and the intellectual competence of preschool girls.

Additional support for the mother-as-mediator concept was seen in the

Dyk and Witkin (1965) study of middle-class mothers of 10-year-old boys. Wives who felt their husbands did not participate in childrearing fostered a global approach in their sons. Lynn (1974) speculated that this indicates that the father's role in the family influences the mother's attitudes and her behavior toward her child. Dyk and Witkin suggested it was related to father–son relations but emphasized that a father's behavior toward his wife may significantly affect her mothering. For example, he may add to her security by accepting her; he may add to her uncertainty by criticizing her. In addition his personal needs may cause her to modify her behavior with their children.

In our study paternal expectations regarding daughters appeared to affect mothers' behavior with the girls (Radin & Epstein, 1975a). Fathers' long-term and short-term academic expectations, as assessed by a questionnaire, were positively and significantly correlated with measures of the girls' cognitive functioning; his observable behaviors were not. It was hypothesized that his future expectations may have been communicated to his wife, who may then have altered her own expectations and behavior with the young girl. Some support for this view was found in relation to another factor on the questionnaire labeled "mother stimulates child," for example, mother assists child with learning. The "mother stimulates" factor was significantly related to the intellective competence of girls but not of boys.

## STATUS CHARACTERISTICS

In addition to what the father does, or feels, or thinks, the socioeconomic rank the father holds appears to relate to his children's cognitive competence. Many significant correlations have been reported, but the reason for the relationship remains obscure. The material resources, such as books, that an affluent parent can provide may be important. The trips to museums, motivated peers, successful models in the neighborhood, and so forth, may all be relevant, as Coleman et al. (1966) have shown. Genetics may also play a part. One is left with the question raised earlier about the role of constitutional and environmental factors in any significant correlation between father's and child's characteristics.

Jencks, Smith, Acland, Bane, Cohen, Gintis, Heyns, and Michelson (1972) reported the following correlations between nonfarm males' cognitive ability at 11 years of age and data about the father: with father's education, $r = .300$; with father's occupation, $r = .300$. The correlations for the adult nonfarm males' cognitive ability and their fathers' characteristics were as follows: with father's education, $r = .305$; with father's occupation, $r = .314$. To obtain a numerical value for the father's occupation in this calculation, the occupation was rated, by the Duncan scale where possible. The male's score at 11 was usually the sixth-grade aptitude test score. The adult male's cognitive score was one of the military classification test scores.

Honzik's (1963) data were similar. Using a sample of individuals described as representative of the children born in Berkeley between January 1, 1928, and June 30, 1929, Honzik obtained the correlations shown in Table 1 between father's education and the child's IQ at different ages.

The results did not differ much when Honzik employed an index of the father's social class, the Warner Index of Status Characteristics, which was based on father's occupation, the source of his income, house type, and dwelling area. The correlation between this measure and the girls' IQ reached significance at age 3, when it was .27; the correlation reached significance at age 5 for boys, when it was .37. Majoribanks' (1972) study of 11-year-old English boys from the middle and lower class yielded similar results. The correlation between total score on the SRA Primary Test of Mental Ability was .31 ($p < .01$) with father's education and .43 ($p < .01$) with father's occupation. Thus the studies by Honzik, Jencks et al., and Marjoribanks all reported correlations between father's education and boy's IQ at age 11 between .30 and .35; the figures are remarkably consistent.

The studies of Baumrind (1971) and Kohn and Rosman (1973) and our investigation (Radin & Epstein, 1975b) presented correlational data between father's education and intelligence scores of children of 4 to 6

Table 1.    Correlations Between Father's Education and Child's IQ[a]

| Age of Child in Years | Correlations for Boys | Correlations for Girls |
|---|---|---|
| 1¾ | .01 | .17 |
| 3 | −.08 | .32* |
| 4 | .10 | .36* |
| 5 | .23 | .34** |
| 6 | .17 | .43** |
| 7 | .34** | .44** |
| 8 | .27** | .41** |
| 9 | .29** | .41** |
| 10 | .27** | .40** |
| 12–13 | .35** | .42** |
| 14–15 | .41** | .33** |

[a] The data are from Honzik (1963).
* $p < .05$.
** $p < .01$.

years of age. Baumrind obtained a correlation of .25 for girls 4 years of age and .09 for boys. Neither figure was significant. Similar figures were obtained when a measure of the father's occupation was used in the correlation instead of his education. Kohn and Rosman combined father's education and occupation into one index, the Hollingshead Two-Factor Index of Social Position. A correlation of .24, which was significant, was obtained between the IQ of kindergarten boys and the Hollingshead Index. According to the authors the correlation obtained in their study was lower than many reported in the literature (typically .40 between parent's occupation and child's intelligence) because their sample consisted of 5-year-old males, and the work of Honzik and others indicated that social class variables do not usually become predictive of boys' IQ until 5 or 6 years of age.

Our study also employed the Hollingshead Two-Factor Index of Social Position and found the correlations with IQ at the end of the kindergarten year to be .12 for boys (not significant) and .34 ($p<.01$) for girls. The correlations between father's education and IQ were similar, .08 for boys and .31 for girls. Thus there is some consistency in correlational pattern across studies, although not as much as there was for 11-year-old children. This is not surprising, since the IQ has stabilized by that time, and at the ages of 4 through 6, it is just beginning to stabilize (Honzik, 1963). The data from the Baumrind, Honzik, Kohn and Rosman, and Radin studies show that the range of correlations for boys aged 4 through 6 was .09 to .24 and for girls from .25 to .36. The correlations were clearly higher for girls; there was not even an overlap. Further, in the studies that included both boys and girls, the correlations were consistently higher for girls.

None of these studies reported correlations over .50 between father's characteristics and child's cognitive competence. Thus one can say that, at most, less than 25% of the variation in the child's cognitive score is attributable to the social class status of the child's father. Both the Baumrind and Radin studies obtained higher correlations between observed paternal behavior and the child's IQ than between father's education and the youngster's IQ.

## FATHER ABSENCE

The most contradictory evidence concerning the father's role in the child's intellective functioning centers about the impact of his absence. There are data indicating that father absence is detrimental, that it affects the youngster's cognitive style, that it has no effect, and that it may even stimulate the child's cognitive performance.

## Cumulative Damage

Among those who reported a negative impact are Deutsch (1960) and Deutsch and Brown (1964), who studied the school performance of black children, primarily lower class, in New York City. Deutsch found that 10- to 13-year-old children without fathers scored lower on academic tests than their classmates with fathers. Deutsch and Brown found no significant difference in achievement of father-present and father-absent youngsters in the first grade, but by fifth grade a significant difference appeared. The researchers attributed these results to a cumulative damaging effect of father absence. On the other hand Santrock and Wohlford (1970) compared lower class white boys in fifth grade who were father present and father absent and discovered that the lowest grades were obtained by boys whose fathers' absence began recently, when the youngsters were 6 to 9 years of age. This suggested that recency of the departure was more critical than the total number of years of absence. Additional data reported by Santrock and Wohlford supported the cumulative-damage hypothesis. They found that the next worst grades, after those whose fathers had recently died or left home, were obtained by boys whose fathers' absence commenced when the youngsters were less than 2 years of age; the next lowest grades appeared among boys who became father absent when they were 3 to 5 years old.

## Sex Differences

Shelton's (1969) findings resembled those of Deutsch and Brown (1964). He compared junior high school students from Iowa who were father absent and father present and found the former group was significantly lower in academic grade point average, when IQ was controlled. In addition there was evidence that the family dissolution had a greater impact on boys than on girls. The boys who were father absent obtained significantly lower grades than the father-absent girls, although there were no differences in the grades of father-present boys and girls. Further, although father-absent boys scored significantly below father-present boys, there was no difference in the grades of father-present and father-absent girls.

The data obtained by Lessing, Zagorin, and Nelson (1970) gave additional support to the hypothesis that there are sex differences in the impact of father absence. These investigators found that the father-absent youngsters, all of whom were between 9 and 15 years of age and had been father absent for at least 2 years, obtained lower Performance IQ scores on the Wechsler Intelligence Scale than their father-present counterparts, regardless of sex or social class. However, boys, but not girls, who were father absent obtained lower scores than their father-present peers on the arithmetic subtest. There were no differencs in Full Scale IQ, Verbal IQ, or Performance IQ between father-absent boys and girls. All of the children had been referred for diagnosis to a research institute and were considered a clinic sample by the authors. This factor may account for the difference in findings regarding father-absent girls between the Shelton study and that of Lessing et al.; the impact appeared to be much greater in the latter investigation.

In an extensive study Santrock (1972) explored the differential impact, on lower class, white children, of father absence due to death versus father absence due to divorce, desertion, or separation. The interaction of the child's sex and age with onset of the absence was also investigated by examining the children's third- and sixth-grade scores on standard achievement tests. The major conclusions were that sex of child, age of onset of absence, and reason for absence were all significant variables mediating the impact of father absence on the child's academic and intellective performance. In general, boys were found to be more damaged by father absence than girls. For example, the test scores at sixth grade were lower for father-absent boys than for girls, regardless of the reason for the father absence. However, both boys and girls who were father absent for any reason scored lower on third-grade achievement tests than their father-present peers. For both boys and girls greater impairment was found when the father's absence was due to divorce, desertion, or separation that when it was due to death. This finding tends to contradict the myth that husband–wife relations were likely to be poor before a divorce or separation and, hence, that the children are relatively little damaged by the marriage's dissolution.

Father absence due to divorce, desertion, or separation occurring before the age of 5 was more damaging than when the absence for the same reason occurred between ages 6 and 11 for children of either sex. The ages of 0 through 2 were particularly vulnerable ones for both boys and girls when the father left home because of divorce, desertion, or separation. In contrast, when the father's absence was due to death, the most vulnerable age for boys was 6 through 9. The author speculated that they might still be suffering from the trauma of the loss. There was no evidence of cognitive impairment in the boys whose fathers died before the age of 2; there was even a trend for such boys to be superior in IQ to their father-present peers. An additional difference between boys and girls was their reaction to the presence of a stepfather in the home. If one entered a family in which the father's absence was due to divorce, desertion, or separation before the child was 5, the academic scores of boys improved; those of girls did not. Thus the study tended to support the proposition that modeling of the same-sex parent influences the cognitive functioning of young boys.

## Age of Onset of Absence

In addition to the Santrock investigation several other studies focused on the child's age at onset of the father's absence. Maxwell's (1961) investigation of British children, 8 to 13 years of age and under treatment in a psychological clinic, revealed that those who were father-absent starting when they were more than 5 years of age were below average on the Wechsler Intelligence Scale. Those whose fathers' absence commenced when the children were less than 5 were not below average. Although both boys and girls were included in the study, no breakdown was given by sex of child. In mathematics Sutton-Smith and his colleagues (1968) found the ages of 1 through 9 to be the vulnerable period for girls. The total number of years the father was absent was not important. Shelton (1968) found, however, that age at the time of family dissolution was unrelated to achievement among three subgroups of junior high school children. Santrock found both the sex of the child and reason for the father's absence influenced the most vulnerable age of onset of absence. Thus there appears to be little consensus about a single critical age when the death or departure of the father is most damaging.

## Impact on Young Children

Kohn and Rosman (1973) reported no significant differences in Stanford–Binet IQ of father-present and father-absent kindergarten boys from three social classes. Both white and black youngsters were included in their sample. Many other cognitive measures were used as well, but for "very few" were significant correlations obtained with father absence. The authors stated that these results supported their previous findings that family intactness was not very relevant for cognitive functioning at kindergarten age. This conclusion would be in accordance with the findings of Deutsch and Brown (1964) in their study of black first-grade children. Coleman et al. (1966) similarly found no difference in ability test scores of father-present and father-absence kindergarten children in a sample that included black and white youngsters.

## Race and Ethnicity

The importance of ethnicity in father absence was demonstrated in Coleman's study when the 6th-, 9th-, and 12th-grade achievement test scores were examined. There were no differences in school achievement between black or white students from structurally intact homes and their peers from non-intact homes. There were, however, significant differences for other minority groups, particularly Oriental Americans, Mexican Americans, and to a lesser extent, Puerto Ricans. Although Coleman and his colleagues did not comment on the fact, it appeared that cultures in which fathers tend to be very powerful are most adversely affected by their absence. The authors noted, however, that "Contrary to much that has been written, the structural integrity of the home (principally the father's presence or absence) shows very little relation to achievement for Negroes. It does, however, show a strong relation to achievement for other minority groups" (p. 302).

Other researchers similarly failed to find differences in cognitive performance between father-present and father-absent black youngsters. Wasserman (1969) found father-absent, lower class, black boys, 10 to 16 years of age, no worse than their father-present peers in academic work, although approximately 60% of both groups repeated a grade. Cortes and Fleming (1968) found no difference in achievement between lower class, black boys, 9 to 11 years of age, who were with father or without fathers or father substitutes. Both groups were below norms on standard achievement tests, particularly in arithmetic. Hess, Shipman, Brophy, and Bear (1968) studied 4-year-old, urban, black children and found no difference on a number of cognitive measures such as the Stanford–Binet Intelligence Scale and the Columbia Mental Maturity Scale between father-present and father-absent youngsters. Perhaps the lower class, black child is already so overwhelmed by adversity that the additional handicap of fatherlessness does not have a critical impact.

**Affluence and Giftedness**

Hilgard, Neuman, and Fisk (1960) investigated a representative sample of 19- to 49-year old men from a University town who had lost their fathers in childhood. The findings indicated that the men were highly successful academically and occupationally. Albert (1969), as reported by Biller (1971), analyzed the family background of geniuses and discovered a high rate of father loss during childhood. He attributed this phenomenon to the possibility that father-absent, gifted children were freer to explore their environment and develop a more creative type of behavior. Biller (1971) offered an alternative explanation. He posed the possibility that an intense relationship with an intellectually oriented mother may have facilitated the development of the gifted, father-absent children. In support of this view, Biller cited the findings of Levy (1943) that middle-class, maternally overprotected boys did superior work in school, especially in subjects requiring verbal skill; their mathematics performance was not at the same high level. This finding is consistent with the Carlsmith (1964) conclusion that fathers play an important role in the development of mathematical ability in boys. Lessing et al. (1970) found that working-class children with no father earned a significantly lower Verbal IQ and Full Scale IQ on the Wechsler Intelligence Scale than their father-present peers, but middle-class, father-absent children showed a significantly higher mean Verbal IQ than father-absent children from the same background. According to the authors, "The pervasive cognitive deficit found among working-class, father-absent children is most plausibly interpreted as a massive stress reaction to the loss of many resources provided by the father, in the absence of any compensatory gains" (p. 192). This suggests that middle-class families are able to continue providing material resources to their youngsters, even after the departure or death of the father, and the children are thereby able to withstand the loss more effectively. Lessing et al. did not, however, indicate what the compensatory gain experienced by middle-class, father-absent children could be. Perhaps it is closeness to an intellectually oriented mother that Biller discussed.

## Family Structure and Composition

The importance of the family structure and composition on impact of father absence was made salient by the research of Sutton-Smith, Rosenberg, and Landy (1968). They compared the American College Entrance Examination scores of father-present and father-absent, middle-class, college sophomores from one-child, two-child, and three-child families. Also examined were the effects of birth order and sex of siblings. The findings showed that, for the majority of the sample, quantitative, language, and total scores were lower for father-absent than father-present students, regardless of the student's age at onset of the father absence or length of time the father was away. The father-absence effects were, however, more pervasive for males than for females and were strongest in the three-child families, moderate in the two-child families, and minimal in one-child families. Whereas both sexes were affected in three-child families, males were more often affected in two-child families, and females in one-child families. Surprisingly the greatest differences between father-present and father-absent students were produced when the child had an opposite-sex sibling. Thus a sibling of the same sex appeared to attenuate the damaging impact of father absence; for example firstborn males with a younger sister showed a significant difference between father-present and father-absent peers, but firstborn males with a younger brother did not. The authors made several attempts to explain this finding but concluded that the nature of the interaction was unclear and further research was needed.

The work of several investigators relevant to father absence that was discussed in earlier sections is summarized very briefly. Five-month-old black boys, but not girls, who were father absent or who experienced low father interaction, scored lower on cognitive measures than their father-present counterparts in the Pedersen et al. (1973) study. Blanchard and Biller (1971) found that third-grade boys who were father absent starting when they were more than 5 performed better than peers whose father absence commenced when they were less than 5. The grades of boys with little father interaction resembled those of the boys father absent after age 5. High school boys who were father absent in their early childhood were shown by Carlsmith (1964) to have higher verbal than mathematics scores. The incidence of this feminine pattern was correlated with length of father absence and age of onset of absence. Male college freshmen in the Nelsen and Maccoby (1966) investigation who were father absent were significantly higher in verbal scores than in mathematics scores than their father-present peers. Landy, Rosenberg, and Sutton-Smith (1969) found that college women who were father absent as a result of their fathers' working the night shift obtained lower quantitative scores, but not lower language scores, when the absence occurred before they were 9. Finally Barclay and Cusumano (1967) reported that father-absent boys were less field independent than their father-present counterparts.

## Trends Regarding Father Absence

Several trends emerge from the array of contradictory and nonoverlapping evidence concerning father absence. It appears that father present/father absent is not a dichotomous variable and should not be treated in that fashion. More relevant is the amount of father involvement with the child. Mathematics scores appear to be more sensitive to paternal involvement than verbal scores, particularly for college students and college-bound high school students, where separate quantitative and verbal scores are readily attainable. Other skills related to mathematics also appear to be responsive to father involvement. Although the evidence is not uniform, most data suggest that father absence is most damaging when the child is less than 5 years of age. The effect of the damage on cognitive performance does not, however, become evident until the youngster is at least 8 years old. The reason the father is absent affects the impact of his absence on the child's intellective growth, and a recent death appears to be more debilitating than a recent divorce or separation. There is some evidence that, in ethnic groups which tend to be patriarchal, father absence has the most debilitating effect.

It is clear that the effect of diminished paternal involvement with children must be examined in the context of the entire family. When the circumstances are relatively positive, for example, university-based families, or middle-class families with one child, father absence appears to have little detrimental effect on the intellectual functioning of the child and may even stimulate the child's cognitive growth in some instances, particularly in verbal ability. When the circumstances are extremely impoverished, for example, lower class, black families, the additional damage wrought by father absence may be minimal. Father absence may have the greatest impact when conditions are intermediate, as is the case with working-class families. The subtlety of the findings regarding family structure and composition opens a Pandora's box of questions concerning the possible interaction effects of father absence with social class, ethnicity, and cause of absence in families of given structure and composition. The number of permutations and combinations to be studied is overwhelming. It is hoped that some operating principles will eventually be discovered to create order out of the mass of data that will be collected.

## SUMMARY

In spite of the problematic data available on the father's role in the child's cognitive development, several trends, varying in strength, can be detected. Paternal nurturance appears to be closely associated with the cognitive competence of boys, but not girls. A close relationship between father and son seems to foster an analytic cognitive style in the child. There are indications that powerful fathers foster their sons' cognitive development, provided the power is not used to intimidate the boys while they are engaged in mastery efforts. As to girls, some degree of autonomy and distance from fathers appears to be associated with cognitive proficiency, although specific father interest in his daughter's academic progress appears to stimulate her intellective growth. For both males and females authoritarian paternal behavior tends to be associated with reduced academic competence, as does intense paternal involvement in problem-solving activities of the child. There is some indication that fathers can influence their children through the impact the men have on their wives; this is particularly evident for daughters.

Many variables appear to mediate the effect of father absence on the child's intellectual performance, including reason for his absence, child's age at onset of absence, sex of child, family composition, family structure, ethnicity, and socioeconomic status of the family. Father absence before the age of 5 appears to be the most damaging to the intellective functioning of young boys, except in the case of death, where recency is the more important variable. Father absence in the early years appears to result in a cognitive profile in college men more typical of females than of males, that is, a higher verbal than mathematics score. Father absence before the age of 9 tends to hinder the development of the girls' mathematical skills.

Less than 25% of the variance in the child's IQ is accounted for by fathers' education, leaving 75% to be accounted for by other variables. The relationship between the child's IQ and father's education becomes manifest at an earlier age for girls, about 3, than for boys, about 6. Whether the link between father's education and child's intellective competence is due to genetic heritage or environment, or both in varying degrees, is unknown at this time.

Obviously much additional research is needed to clarify the father's role in the child's cognitive growth. Among the most pressing needs are longitudinal studies with repeated observations of father's behavior and child's intellective performance, and investigations of paternal childrearing practices and their correlates in Oriental and Spanish-speaking families. Studies of father behavior in the presence and absence of his wife are also needed to determine the impact of maternal presence on father-child interactions.

One is left with the overall conclusion that, in spite of the limitations in the state of our knowledge, a father influences his children's mental development through many and diverse channels: through his genetic background, his manifest behavior with his offspring, the attitudes he holds about himself and his children, the behavior he models, his position in the family system, the material resources he is able to supply for his children, the influence he exerts on his wife's behavior, his ethnic heritage, and the vision he holds for his children. Finally, when he dies or separates from the family, the memories he leaves with his wife and children continue to exert an influence, perhaps equal to the impressions he made on the youngsters when he was physically present.

## REFERENCES

Aberle, D. F., & Naegele, K. D. Middle-class fathers' occupational role and attitudes toward children. *American Journal of Orthopsychiatry*, 1952, **22**, 366–378.

Albert, R. S. Early cognitive development among the gifted. Paper presented at the meeting of the Western Psychological Association, Vancouver, British Columbia, Canada, June 1969.

Andersland, P. B. Parental rejection and adolescent academic achievement. *Dissertation Abstracts*, 1968, **28** (11-B), 4751.

Baer, D. M., & Sherman, J. A. Reinforcement control of generalized imitation in young children. *Journal of Experimental Child Psychology*, 1964, **1**, 37–49.

Bandura, A. Social learning through imitation. In M. R. Jones (Ed.), *Nebraska symposium on motivation*. Lincoln: University of Nebraska Press, 1962. Pp. 211–269.

Barclay, A. G., & Cusumano, D. Father absence, cross-sex identity, and field-dependent behavior in male adolescents. *Child Development*, 1967, **38**, 243–250.

Baumrind, D. Current patterns of parental authority. *Development Psychology Monographs*, 1971, **4**, 1–103.

Bayley, N. Behavior correlates of mental growth: Birth to thirty-six years. *American Psychologist*, 1968, **23**, 1–17.

Bell, R. Q. A reinterpretation of the direction of effects in studies of socialization. *Psychological Review*, 1968, **75**, 81–95.

Berry, J. W. Temne and Eskimo perceptual skills. *International Journal of Psychology*, 1966, **1**, 207–229.

Biller, H. B. *Father, child, and sex role*. Lexington, Mass.: D. C. Heath and Company, 1971.

Bing, E. The effect of childrearing practices on development of differential cognitive abilities. *Child Development*, 1963, **34**, 631–648.

Blanchard, R. W., & Biller, H. B. Father availability and academic performance among third-grade boys. *Developmental Psychology*, 1971, **4**, 301–305.

Boerger, P. H. The relationship of boys' intellectual achievement behavior to parental involvement, aspirations, and accuracy of IQ estimate. *Dissertation Abstracts International*, 1971, **31**, 5191.

Bowerman, C. E., & Elder, G. H., Jr. Variations in adolescent perception of family power structure. *American Sociological Review*, 1964, **29**, 551–567.

Busse, T. V. Child-rearing antecedents of flexible thinking. *Developmental Psychology*, 1969, **1**, 585–591.

Cain, M. A. A study of relationship between selected factors and the school achievement of Mexican migrant children. *Dissertation Abstracts International*, 1971, **31** (8-A), 3947.

Carlsmith, L. Effect of early father absence on scholastic aptitude. *Harvard Educational Review*, 1964, **34**, 3–21.

Clarke-Stewart, K. A. Interaction between mothers and their young children: Characteristics and consequences. *Monographs of the Society for Research in Child Development*, 1973, **38** (6–7, Serial No. 153).

Coleman, J. S., Campbell, E. Q., Hobson, C. J., McPartland, J., Mood, A. M., Weinfeld, F. D., & York, R. L. *Equality of educational opportunity.* Washington, D.C.: Department of Health, Education, and Welfare, Office of Education, 1966.

Corah, N. L. Differentiation in children and their parents. *Journal of Personality*, 1965, **33**, 300–308.

Cortes, C. F., & Fleming, E. The effects of father absence on the adjustment of culturally disadvantaged boys. *Journal of Special Education*, 1968, **2**, 413–420.

Crandall, V., Dewey, R., Katkovsky, W., & Preston, A. Parents' attitudes and behaviors and grade-school children's academic achievements. *Journal of Genetic Psychology*, 1964, **104**, 53–66.

Cross, H. J., & Allen, J. Relationship between memories of parental behavior and academic achievement motivation. *Proceedings of the 77th Annual Convention, American Psychological Association*, 1969, 285–286.

Deutsch, M. Minority group and class status as related to social and personality factors in scholastic achievement. *Monographs of Sociology and Applied Anthropology*, 1960, **2**, 1–32.

Deutsch, M., & Brown, B. Social influences in Negro–white intelligence differences. *Journal of Social Issues*, 1964, **20**, 24–35.

Dyk, R. B., & Witkin, H. A. Family experiences related to the development of differentiation in children. *Child Development*, 1965, **36**, 21–55.

Farber, B. Effects of a severely mentally retarded child on the family. In E. P. Trapp & P. Himelstein (Eds.), *Readings on the exceptional child.* New York: Appleton-Century-Crofts, 1962. Pp. 227–246.

Gewirtz, H. B., & Gewirtz, J. L. Visiting and caretaking patterns for kibbutz infants: Age and sex trends. *American Journal of Orthopsychiatry*, 1968, **38**, 427–443.

Gewirtz, J. L., & Stengle, K. G. Learning of generalized imitation as the basis for identification. *Psychological Review*, 1968, **75**, 374–397.

Goodenough, E. W. Interest in persons as an aspect of sex difference in the early years. *Genetic Psychology Monographs*, 1957, **55**, 287–323.

Grunebaum, M. G., Hurwitz, I., Prentice, N. M., & Sperry, B. M. Fathers of sons with primary neurotic learning inhibition. *American Journal of Orthopsychiatry*, 1962, **32**, 462–473.

Harrington, D. M., Block, J. H., & Block, J. Behavioral manifestations and parental correlates of intolerance of ambiguity in young children. Paper presented at meeting of the Society for Research in Child Development, Denver, Colorado, April 1975.

Heilbrun, A. B., Jr. *Aversive maternal control.* New York: John Wiley and Son, 1973.

Heilbrun, A. B., Jr., Harrell, S. N. & Gillard, B. J. Perceived childrearing attitudes of fathers and cognitive control in daughters. *Journal of Genetic Psychology*, 1967, **111**, 29–40.

Herzog, E., & Sudia, C. *Boys in fatherless families*. Washington, D.C.: U.S. Department of Health, Education, and Welfare, 1970.

Hess, R. D., Shipman, V. C., Brophy, J. E., & Bear, R. M. *The cognitive environment of urban preschool children*. Chicago: The University of Chicago Press, 1968.

Hetherington, E. M., & Frankie, G. Effects of parental dominance, warmth, and conflict on imitation in children. *Journal of Personality and Social Psychology*, 1967, **6**, 119–125.

Hilgard, J. R., Neuman, M. F., & Fisk, F. Strength of adult ego following bereavement. *American Journal of Orthopsychiatry*, 1960, **30**, 788–798.

Hoffman, M. Moral internalization, parental power, and the nature of parent–child interaction. *Developmental Psychology*, 1975, **11**, 228–239.

Honzik, M. P. A sex difference in the age of onset of the parent–child resemblance in intelligence. *Journal of Educational Psychology*, 1963, **54**, 231–237.

Honzik, M. P. Environmental correlates of mental growth: Prediction from the family setting at 21 months. *Child Development*, 1967, **38**, 337–364.

Jencks, C., Smith, M., Acland, H., Bane, M. J., Cohen, D., Gintis, H., Heyns, B., & Michelson, S. *Inequality*. New York: Basic Books, 1972.

Johnson, M. M. Sex role learning in the nuclear family. *Child Development*, 1963, **34**, 319–333.

Jordan, B., Radin, N., & Epstein, A. S. Paternal behavior and intellectual functioning in preschool boys and girls. *Developmental Psychology*, 1975, **11**, 407–408.

Kagan, J. The concept of identification. *Psychological Review*, 1958, **65**, 296–305.

Kimball, B. The sentence completion technique in a study of scholastic underachievement. *Journal of Consulting Psychology*, 1952, **16**, 353–358.

Kohlberg, L., & Zigler, E. The impact of cognitive maturity on the development of sex-role attitudes in the years 4 to 8. *Genetic Psychology Monographs*, 1967, **75**, 89–165.

Kohn, M., & Rosman, B. L. Cognitive functioning in five-year-old boys as related to social–emotional and background– demographic variables. *Developmental Psychology*, 1973, **8**, 277–294.

Landy, F., Rosenberg, B. G., & Sutton-Smith, B. The effect of limited father absence on cognitive development. *Child Development*, 1969, **40**, 941–944.

Lessing, E. E., Zagorin, S. W., & Nelson, D. WISC subtest IQ score correlates of father absence. *Journal of Genetic Psychology*, 1970, **117**, 181–195.

Levy, D. M. *Maternal Overprotection*. New York: Columbia University Press, 1943.

Lynn, D. B. *Parental and sex-role identification.* Berkeley: McCutchan, 1969.

Lynn, D. B. *The Father: His role in child development.* Monterey, Calif.: Brooks/Cole, 1974.

Lynn, D. B., & Cross, A. D. Parent preference of preschool children. *Journal of Marriage and the Family,* 1974, **36**, 555–559.

Lytton, H. Three approaches to the study of parent–child interaction: Ethological, interview, and experimental. *Journal of Child Psychology and Psychiatry,* 1973, **14**, 1–17.

MacArthur, R. Sex differences in field dependence for the Eskimo: Replication of Berry's findings. *International Journal of Psychology,* 1967, **2**, 139–140.

Maccoby, E. E., & Jacklin, C. N. *The psychology of sex differences.* Stanford, Calif.: Stanford University Press, 1974.

Marjoribanks, K. Environment, social class, and mental abilities. *Journal of Educational Psychology,* 1972, **63**, 103–107.

Maxwell, A. E. Discrepancies between the pattern of abilities for normal and neurotic children. *Journal of Mental Science,* 1961, **107**, 300–307.

Mowrer, O. H. *Learning theory and personality dynamics.* New York: Ronald Press, 1950.

Mussen, P., & Distler, L. Childrearing antecedents of masculine identification in kindergarten boys. *Child Development,* 1960, **31**, 89–100.

Mussen, P., & Rutherford, E. Parent–child relations and parental personality in relation to young children's sex-role preferences. *Child Development,* 1963, **34**, 589–607.

Mutimer, D., Loughlin, L., & Powell, M. Some differences in the family relationships of achieving and underachieving readers. *Journal of Genetic Psychology,* 1966, **109**, 67–74.

Nelsen, E. A., & Maccoby, E. E. The relationship between social development and differential abilities on the scholastic aptitude test. *Merrill-Palmer Quarterly,* 1966, **12**, 269–289.

Osofsky, J. D., & O'Connell, E. J. Parent–child interaction: Daughters' effects upon mothers' and fathers' behaviors. *Developmental Psychology,* 1972, **7**, 157–168.

Parsons, T., & Bales, R. F. *Family, socialization, and interaction process.* New York: Free Press, 1955.

Pedersen, F. A., Rubenstein, J., & Yarrow, L. J. Father absence in infancy. Paper presented at the meeting of the Society for Research in Child Development, Philadelphia, Pa., March 1973.

Radin, N. Father–child interaction and the intellectual functioning of four-year-old boys. *Developmental Psychology,* 1972, **6**, 353–361.

Radin, N. Observed paternal behaviors as antecedents of intellectual functioning in young boys. *Developmental Psychology,* 1973, **8**, 369–376.

Radin, N. Observed maternal behavior with four-year-old boys and girls in lower-class families. *Child Development,* 1974, **45**, 1126–1131.

Radin, N., & Epstein, A. S. Observed paternal behavior and the intellectual functioning of preschool boys and girls. Paper presented at the meeting of the Society for Research in Child Development, Denver, Colorado, April 1975 (a).

Radin, N., & Epstein, A. S. *Observed paternal behavior with preschool children: Final report.* Ann Arbor, Mich.: The University of Michigan, School of Social Work, 1975 (b).

Rosen, B., & D'Andrade, R. D. The psychosocial origins of achievement motivation. *Sociometry*, 1959, **22**, 185–218.

Rosenberg, B. G., & Sutton-Smith, B. Sibling association, family size, and cognitive abilities. *Journal of Genetic Psychology*, 1966, **107**, 271–279.

Rothbart, M. D. Birth order and mother–child interaction in an achievement situation. *Journal of Personality and Social Psychology*, 1971, **17**, 113–120.

Santrock, J. W. The relation of type and onset of father absence to cognitive development. *Child Development*, 1972, **43**, 455–469.

Santrock, J. W., & Wohlford, P. Effects of father absence: Influence of the reason for the onset of the absence. *Proceedings of the 78th Annual Convention of the American Psychological Association*, 1970, **5**, 265–266.

Schulz, D. *Coming up black.* Englewood Cliffs, N.J.: Prentice-Hall, 1969.

Sears, P. S. Childrearing factors related to the playing of sex-typed roles. *American Psychologist*, 1953, **8**, 431. (Abstract)

Sears, R. R. Comparison of interviews with questionnaires for measuring mothers' attitudes toward sex and aggression. *Journal of Personality and Social Psychology*, 1965, **2**, 37–44.

Seder, J. A. The origin of differences in extent of indepedence in children: Developmental factors in perceptual field dependence. Unpublished bachelor's thesis, Radcliff College, 1957.

Shaw, M. C., & White, D. L. The relationship between child–parent identification and academic underachievement. *Journal of Clinical Psychology*, 1965, **21**, 10–13.

Shelton, L. A. A comparative study of educational achievement in one-parent families and in two-parent families. *Dissertation Abstracts*, 1969, **29** (8-A), 2535–2536.

Sherman, R. C., & Smith, F. Sex differences in cue-dependency as a function of socialization environment. *Perceptual and Motor Skills*, 1967, **24**, 599–602.

Solomon, F., Houlihan, D. A., Busse, T. C., & Parelius, R. J. Parent behavior and child academic achievement, achievement striving, and related personality characteristics. *Genetic Psychology Monographs*, 1971, **83**, 173–273.

Strodtbeck, F. L. Family interaction, values, and achievement. In D. C. McClelland, A. L. Baldwin, U. Bronfenbrenner, & F. L. Strodtbeck (Eds.), *Talent and society*. Princeton, N.Y.: Von Nostrand, 1958. Pp. 135–194.

Sutton-Smith, B., Rosenberg, B. G., & Landy, F. Father-absence effects in families of different sibling compositions. *Child Development*, 1968, **39**, 1213–1221.

Teahan, J. E. Parental attitudes and college success. *Journal of Educational Psychology*, 1963, **54**, 104–109.

Wasserman, H. L. Father-absent and father-present lower-class Negro families: A comparative study of family functioning. *Dissertation Abstracts*, 1969, **29** (12-A), 4569–4570.

Zigler, E., & Child, I. L. Socialization. In G. Lindzey and E. Aronson (Eds.), *The handbook of social psychology, III* (2nd Ed.). Reading, Mass.: Addison-Wesley, 1969. Pp. 450–589.

# CHAPTER 8

# Psychoanalytic Theory: Pre-oedipal and Oedipal Phases, with Special Reference to the Father.

VERONICA J. MÄCHTLINGER

*Berlin*

As Anna Freud (1965, 1972) points out, the interest in childhood events shown by psychoanalysts 50 years ago derived primarily from the psychoanalytic treatment and study of adult neurotics. From their patients they had learned that every adult neurosis was preceded by a childhood neurosis and that the emotionally stormy conflicts of the phallic–oedipal period, that is, the Oedipus complex and the problems attached to its resolution, formed the core of both infantile and adult neurotic disturbances. Looked at from the viewpoint of the adult neurotic patient, therefore, the phallic–oedipal phase tended to be seen as forming the lower end of a process of investigation that ended with adult neurotic symptoms.

From the point of view of contemporary investigations, however, the phallic–oedipal phase is regarded as lying at the upper end of a complex, interactional, developmental process, and the appearance of the Oedipus complex with its conflicts is itself taken as evidence that the personality of the child has attained a given degree of organization, structuralization, and integration. In this view, the specific form taken by these conflicts is seen as "set against the background of personal qualities and characteristics which have been established from infancy onwards, and shaped by the fixation points which have been left behind during development" (A. Freud, 1972).

The author would like to thank Miss Anna Freud for reading an earlier version of this manuscript and for her encouragement and helpful comments.

This change of emphasis occurred gradually. At first some psychoanalysts shifted their attention from adults to children themselves—in the beginning with the help of the development of child analytic techniques (A. Freud, 1946; Klein, 1932), and later through direct observations of infants and young children (Burlingham & Freud, 1944; Hartmann, 1950; E. Kris, 1950, 1951; M. Kris, 1957; Provence & Ritvo, 1961; Provence & Lipton, 1962; Spitz, 1945, 1950).

Particularly in the work of Anna Freud at the Hampstead Clinic, London, and that of Ernst Kris at Yale, the emphasis was increasingly placed, not on pathology alone, but on "an enumeration, description and explanation of *any* interference with optimal mental growth and development" (A. Freud, 1972—my italics). In this way both normal and pathological developmental processes from the beginning of life came under increasing scrutiny. As a result of this change in emphasis there has been a less exclusive preoccupation with neurotic phenomena and childhood neurosis as such, and instead a growing interest in and knowledge of normal developmental processes, together with the factors that contribute to the so-called developmental failures, which manifest themselves in the form of much more severe pathology—the psychotic and borderline psychotic disturbances. As Anna Freud points out (1972), earlier analysts were aware that these other types of pathology existed in children, but their interest in childhood neurosis, as opposed to these other forms, was based on their attempts to understand adult neurotic phenomena in terms of their childhood forerunners.

In other words the shift to earlier developmental phases has led to the focusing of a different kind of attention on pre-oedipal processes than was formerly the case: not only for their part in laying the foundations for later oedipal conflicts, but also for their importance in the development and organization of the growing personality structure.

It would be false, however, to leave readers with the impression that the first generation of analysts placed little emphasis on the importance of pre-oedipal—that is, oral and anal—developmental phases for later neurotic development. Their clinical formulations make this clear. An examination of Freud's summing-up of the case of the Wolf Man (S. Freud, 1918) for example, demonstrates clearly that the complex interrelating events of the pre-oedipal phases (especially the anal contributions) with the identifications and fixation points based on them, in interaction with chance environmental factors, were all considered to have played an essential role in shaping the final neurotic conflict structure.

It would be quite incorrect, therefore, to say that more emphasis is today placed on pre-oedipal phases than in the past; rather, one might say that, as a result of the kind of analytic investigations now being conducted, we know far more about the internal precipitates acquired during the pre-oedipal phases that have helped shape the child's characteristic ways of responding and thus influence the nature, course, and resolution of the oedipal conflicts themselves.

In this chapter I propose to outline the historical development of Freud's own views on the phallic–oedipal phase of development. Here I describe how Freud, faced with the problems raised by female sexuality as well as with the phenomenon of bisexuality in infancy, came to recognize the importance of events in the pre-oedipal phases for the nature of the conflicts later met with in the oedipal phase itself. A brief statement of Freud's views on the development of the superego—in boys and girls—then follows.

I also examine some of the more recent contributions to the oedipal and pre-oedipal developmental phases, with emphasis on the role of the father. This section deals with some attempts being made to formulate the father's role theoretically; with clinical and observational analytic investigations in which the father's importance is clearly recognized; with material gained from the simultaneous analysis of parents and children, in which the complexities of interaction between all family members are made clear; and with a consideration of the absent father in psychoanalysis. Finally a brief indication of the type of theoretical formulations being made about the influence of the pre-oedipal phases on superego development is given.

The approach represented in this review is that of contemporary developmental psychoanalysis.[1]

## THE DEVELOPMENT OF FREUD'S IDEAS CONCERNING THE PHALLIC-OEDIPAL PHASE AND ITS CONFLICTS

### Introduction

In this section the changes in Freud's views of what came to be called the "Oedipus complex" are described historically. I show how these changes were made in response to clinical observations that caused Freud to reconsider his previous theoretical formulations. Some of the most important of these changes were necessitated by the growing awareness that the processes

---

[1] In this review only those analytical views associated with the work and the principles developed by Anna Freud are considered. The theories developed by Melanie Klein, representing as they do a fundamental divergence from the approach that lays stress on the relevance and importance of infant observation as a psychoanalytic tool (see also Ritvo et al., 1963), are not reviewed, since Klein never considered the role played by fathers in the formation of infant personality.

in the development and dissolution of the oedipal conflicts were different in the two sexes. Although this may not now seem surprising, in view of the very nature of the Oedipus complex, we shall see how the assumption that the development of boys and girls followed parallel paths was at first accepted. An equally important clinical "discovery" that initiated essential alterations in Freud's original theory, was of the bisexual nature of infantile sexuality (i.e., the existence of both feminine and masculine strivings in both girls and boys), with its roots in earlier developmental phases.

## Early Ideas Concerning the Oedipus Complex

Freud's first use of the term *Oedipus complex* was in a paper on the psychology of love published in 1910 (Freud, 1910b). The concept itself had, however, taken fôrm very much earlier than this. What is probably the first mention of the subject is to be found in a letter to Fliess in May 1897. Here Freud wrote: "Another presentiment too tells me . . . that I shall very soon discover the source of morality." In a draft included in this same letter, he adds: "It seems as though this death wish is directed in sons against their father and in daughters against their mother." By October 1897 he commented in a letter that he now regarded love of the mother and jealousy of the father as a "universal event of early childhood" (Freud, 1897). It seems clear that Freud had, at this stage, already made the connection between the resolution of oedipal conflicts and the formation of the superego, or morality, that he would later develop.

In his formal published writings the subject does not appear until 1900 in *The Interpretation of Dreams*. Here it is mentioned in connection with the notion, also to be more fully developed later, that the resolution of this complex set of fantasies, wishes, and feelings was an important determinant of later neurotic difficulties.

It is the fate of all of us perhaps, to direct our first sexual impulse towards our mother and our first hatred and our first murderous wishes towards our father. Our dreams convince us that this is so. King Oedipus who slew his father Laius and married his mother Jocasta, merely shows us the fulfilment of our own childhood wishes. But more fortunate than he, we have meanwhile succeedeed, in so far as we have not become psychoneurotics, in detaching our sexual impulses from our mothers and in forgetting our jealousy of our fathers (Freud, 1900).

In 1923 Freud described the Oedipus complex as follows:

In the very earliest years of childhood (approximately between the ages of two and five) a convergence of the sexual impulse occurs of which, in the case of boys, the object is the mother. This choice of an object, in conjunction with a corresponding attitude of rivalry and hostility towards the father provides the content of what is known as the *Oedipus Complex* which in every human being is of the greatest importance in determining the final shape of his erotic life. It has been found to be characteristic of a normal individual that he learns to master his Oedipus complex, whereas the neurotic subject remains involved in it (Freud, 1923a).

It was also in 1923 that Freud described the complex as being a "cornerstone" of psychoanalytic theory (Freud, 1923a).

In his *Five Lectures on Psychoanalysis* Freud (1910a) details the conflicts inherent in the complex, shifting and divided feelings aroused by the oedipal situation:

The child takes both of its parents, and more particularly one of them, as the object of its erotic wishes. . . . The feelings which are aroused in these relations between parents and children and the resulting ones between brothers and sisters are not only of a positive and affectionate kind but also of a negative and hostile one. The complex which is thus formed . . . is doomed to early repression but it continues to exercise a great and lasting influence from the unconscious. It is to be expected that together with its extensions, it constitutes the "nuclear complex" of every neurosis . . . (Freud, 1910a).

Later in this same publication the reason for the far-reaching consequences of these conflicting feelings is brought out more clearly:

It is inevitable and perfectly normal that a child should take his parents as the first objects of his love. But his libido should not remain fixated on these first objects, later on it should merely take them as a model, and should make a gradual transition from them on to extraneous people when the time for the final choice of object arrives. The detachment of the child from his parents is thus a task that cannot be evaded if the young individual's social fitness is not to be endangered.

Here Freud states clearly that it is the failure to "resolve" oedipal attachments and detach the feelings from the original objects that is one of the sources of later neurotic problems.

## Problems Introduced by Female Sexuality

Underlying the explicit references to the small boy's development lay the implicit assumption that the little girl's development ran a parallel path to that of the boy, with the necessary changes in parental role occasioned by the child's sex. James Strachey, in his editorial note to Freud's important paper "Some Psychical Consequences of the Anatomical Distinction Between the Sexes" (1925), shows how this original assumption came to be discarded in the face of increasingly negative evidence. In 1916 Freud had written: "As you see I have only described the relationship of a boy to his father and mother. Things happen in just the same way with little girls, with the necessary changes: an affectionate attachment to her father, a need to get rid of her mother as superfluous . . ." (Freud, 1916). Even as late as 1923, in *The Ego and the Id*, in discussing the fateful and complicated processes attached to the dissolution of the oedipal conflicts, the assumption of an analogous developmental process is maintained. Later in the same year, however, in describing the phallic phase during which the Oedipus complex reaches its peak, Freud says: "Unfortunately we can describe this state of things only as it affects the male child; the corresponding processes in the little girl are not known to us" (Freud, 1923c).

As indicated in my introduction to this section, it was clinical material derived from female patients that made Freud increasingly dissatisfied with the "precise analogy" theory. A case of female paranoia and one of female homosexuality (Freud, 1915, 1920) as well as a study of beating fantasies, which was largely concerned with female sexuality (Freud, 1919), led Freud to state clearly that he had been "mistaken" in "the expectation of there being a complete parallel" between the sexes (Freud, 1919).

The clinical material that forced Freud to a revision of his earlier position led him to focus on the length and intensity of the pre-oedipal attachment to the mother. From this point onward much more stress was placed on the child's relationships to its parents before the oedipal phase of development. In a footnote added in 1935 to his *An Autobiographical Study* (Freud, 1925b), he writes: "The information about infantile sexuality was obtained from the study of men and the theory deduced from it was concerned with male children. It was natural enough to expect to find a complete parallel between the sexes; but this turned out not to hold." It is perhaps pertinent to state here that Freud rejected Jung's term *Electra complex* precisely because it stresses such a parallel between the sexes that he had come to think was mistaken: "I do not see any . . . gain . . . in the introduction of the term 'Electra Complex' and do not advocate its use" (Freud, 1920). From 1919 onward the differences between the sexual development of boys and girls have been extensively clarified.

In the 1925 paper on anatomical distinctions and their consequences Freud completely reassessed his views on the psychological development of women. Strachey also points out that this paper contains the germs of all his later work on the topic. A major difference noted between the Oedipus complex in boys and girls was that in girls the negative form of the complex (the early intense attachment to the mother, with its attendant perception of the father as a rival) precedes the positive form (in which the father is taken as the primary love object and the mother is seen as a rival for the father's affections.) The castration complex (see section on dissolution of the Oedipus Complex), which in girls takes the form of penis envy, results in the girl's turning away from her mother in disappointment and anger and leads to her entering the positive oedipal phase. Bisexuality (see below) also plays a role, in that feminine as opposed to masculine trends should ideally accompany this change of object. That this does not always occur is clinically well known.

With the turning away from the mother clitoroidal masturbation frequently ceases as well; and often enough when the small girl represses her previous masculinity a considerable portion of her sexual trends in general is permanently injured too. The transition to the father object is accomplished with the help of the passive trends in so far as they have escaped the catastrophe (Freud, 1931).

Freud himself never appeared to be entirely satisfied with his work on the sexuality of women. He had earlier (Freud, 1905) complained that the sexual life of women was "veiled in an impenetrable obscurity," and in 1926 he wrote: "We know less about the sexual life of little girls than of boys. But we need not feel ashamed of this distinction; after all the sexual life of adult women is a 'dark continent' for psychology" (Freud, 1926).

## The concept of Bisexuality

As pointed out in my introduction, a second factor played a part, together with female sexuality, in causing Freud to revise his theoretical formulations. This was the concept of bisexuality that had been introduced in 1923 in *The Ego and the Id*. In discussing the concept of identification and showing that its process is based on the child's earliest object relationships, he talks mainly about identifications with the father that replace the Oedipus complex. In a footnote he adds, however: "Perhaps it would be safer to say 'with the parents,'" that is, not just with the father. Here Freud introduces the idea that both sexes identify with both parents, and not just with the parent of the same sex. The boy, for example, has not merely an ambivalent attitude to his father and an affectionate one to his mother; at the same time he displays an affectionate "feminine" attitude to his father together with a corresponding jealousy of and hostility to his mother. "It is this complicating element introduced by bisexuality that makes it so difficult to obtain a clear view of the facts in connection with the earliest object-choices and identifications, and still more to describe them intelligibly" (Freud, 1923b).

What Freud has here described is the "positive" and the "negative" Oedipus complex in the boy (later to be described for both sexes). "Because there is a positive and a negative relationship for both the boy and the girl to each parent the oedipal relationship may be seen as a quadruple one" (Nagera, 1969). Freud explains how at the dissolution of the Oedipus complex . . .

. . . the four trends of which it is composed will group themselves in such a way as to produce a father-identification and a mother-identification. The father-identification will preserve the object-relation to the mother which belonged to the positive complex, and will at the same time replace the object relation to the father which belonged to the inverted complex: and the same will be true *mutatis mutandis* of the mother-identification.

The relative strength and intensity of the two identifications reflect, in any given child, the preponderance of one or the other sexual predisposition. Freud placed very great importance on this concept of bisexuality in determining the outcome of the oedipal situation—that is, whether the child ultimately identifies, in the resolution of the oedipal conflicts, with the father or with the mother. It is in this way that bisexuality plays a role in the "subsequent vicissitudes" of the Oedipus complex.

Bisexuality thus influences not only the form of the Oedipus complex (in its positive and negative aspects) but also its resolution. In this connection it is worth noting:

. . . one gets the impression that the simple Oedipus complex is by no means the commonest form, *but rather represents a simplification or schematization* which, to be sure, is often enough justified for practical purposes. Close study usually discloses the *more complete Oedipus complex which is twofold, positive and negative* and is due to the bisexuality present in children (Freud, 1923b— my italics).

For the purposes of this review, intended for nonanalytical readers, it is perhaps necessary to emphasize this statement, because of the descriptions usually encountered in psychological texts of the "simple, positive" Oedipus complex. The reality of these complex interrelationships, as Freud himself recognized, is more complicated and difficult to describe.

**The Dissolution of the Oedipus Complex**

The concept of bisexuality, with the positive and negative oedipal constellations based on it, is also relevant to the processes involved in the repression of the oedipal conflicts. In his 1924 paper on "The Dissolution of the Oedipus Complex," in which Freud first worked systematically on the sex differences already described, he discussed why the Oedipus complex should be repressed at all and what brought about this repression. After discarding several alternative hypotheses, he relied on clinical evidence, in concluding that the Oedipus complex in the boy is destroyed by the castration complex. Essentially the argument runs as follows: For the boy, both the positive and negative (roughly: masculine and feminine) oedipal configurations entail the threat of castration, and both must, therefore, be given up. In other words whether he takes the feminine oedipal position with regard to his father (mother identification) or whether he adopts the active, masculine position toward his mother (father identification), his penis is threatened—"the masculine one as a resulting punishment and the feminine one as a precondition" (Freud, 1924). In this conflict between his narcissistic investment of his penis and his libidinal investment of his parents, the narcissistic position in the boy "triumphs: the child's ego turns away from the Oedipus complex" (Freud, 1924). Freud then discussed how the "fact" of the female genitals made castration "imagineable," and drew attention to the fact that previous remarks and threats implying castration now have a deferred effect because of the nature of the conflicts in which the child finds himself. In his treatment of castration conflicts, as with the oedipal situation, Freud placed great emphasis on the role of individual, historical factors that shape the clinical picture.[2]

The dissolution of the girl's oedipus complex proceeds differently. In his paper on "Female Sexuality" (1931) Freud made use of "fresh clinical material" (Strachey—editorial note in *The Standard Edition*) and dealt with the importance to the girl of the pre-oedipal attachment to the mother, which, as remarked before, he regarded as particularly intense and long-lasting. For the girl to reach the positive oedipal constellation, she has to move away from her pre-oedipal attachment to her mother and "find her way to" her father. This is the second major change that the girl must make—the first (mentioned as early as 1905 in *Three Essays on the Theory of Sexuality*), being the task of giving up her "leading genital zone—the clitoris—in favour of a new zone—the vagina." This is a task with which boys are not confronted. The change of object—that is, substituting the father for the primary object, the mother—"is no less characteristic and important" for the girl's development than the first task. Freud stressed the "rich and many-sided" relationship of the pre-oedipal phases and discussed the well-known clinical phenomenon of women who "remain arrested in their original attachment to their mother and never achieve a true change-over towards men." He also paid tribute to the female analysts, for example, Ruth Mack-Brunswick, J. Lampl-de Groot, (1962), and Helene Deutsch, who, through the transferences of their female patients, were able to "perceive these facts more easily and clearly."

[2] It is perhaps pertinent to mention here the work of later analysts dealing with children reared under unusual circumstances, where both developmental observations and analytical treatment reveal marked deviations from the "typical" picture. (See Freud & Dann, 1951; Gyomroi-Ludowyk, 1963.)

To explain why and how the girl changes her object, Freud emphasized the differential meaning of castration for the two sexes. For the female child, castration is not a threat but an accomplished fact, in the sense that she has no penis and must come to terms with this fact. She may do this, but Freud indicated that there are several paths of development then open to her:

She may experience a general revulsion from sexuality, or she may cling self-assertively to her "threatened masculinity" (which path may lead to a manifest homosexual object-choice), or development may follow a third, very circuitous path, through which she reaches the normal female attitude, in which she takes her father as her object and so finds her way to the feminine form of the oedipus complex.

Thus we see how in the girl the positive Oedipus complex follows the prior pre-oedipal attachment to the mother, during which time the father may be seen as a rival for the mother's affections, and thus constitute the negative oedipal position. "Thus in women the Oedipus complex is the end result of a fairly lengthy development. It is not destroyed, but created, by the influence of castration." It is evident from this what Freud meant when he said that the castration complex in women ushers in the Oedipus complex, whereas in boys it leads to the destruction of oedipal feelings. Freud argued that the hostility many women show toward their mothers is based not only on the rivalry inherent in the positive oedipal position but also on the preceding pre-oedipal history of their relationship—and clinical experience would tend to support this contention.

In considering the factors that lead the girl to turn away from her mother and take her father as her primary love object, Freud mentioned "not a single factor but a whole number of them operating together towards the same end." Jealousy of siblings and others, which also complicate the boy's relationship with his mother, exert their effects on the girl too. The inherent ambivalence of all pre-oedipal attachments applies equally to boys and girls. However, the main reason why girls abandon their mothers is that they blame them for their lack of a penis. Once again, in discussing these events, Freud stressed the inconstant and chance factors—in terms of timing, masturbation history, and current state—that exert their effect on the individual course of events.

One of the consequences of pre-oedipal ambivalence in girls is that they turn away from their mothers with great hostility. Boys, Freud argued, are able to deal with this ambivalence by the mechanism of splitting, in which the hostility is directed against the father, although he added that one ought not to give such an answer until "we have made a close study of the pre-oedipal phase in boys."

In 1931, therefore, insight into the development of the girl preceded that of the boy. Understanding of the role played by the boy's pre-oedipal attachment to his mother succeeded recognition of the importance of the phase in girls (Lampl-de Groot, 1946). One reason for the importance of this phase in boys is that it may result in an identification with the mother in the form of a feminine attitude to the father—an identification that will have obvious consequences on subsequent attempts to resolve the oedipal conflicts, as well as on the structure of the complex itself. But for this review we are not concerned with the many and complex variations in adult male sexuality that can be traced back to the boy's long pre-oedipal attachment to his mother.

## Summary

We see, thus, that Freud's views underwent considerable change. The importance for both girls and boys of the pre-oedipal relationship to the mother (with its basic ambivalence), and the fundamental factor of bisexuality, led to far-reaching revisions of his view of the oedipal situation for the two sexes. Both of these factors exert their effects on subsequent developments as well, playing a role in the course of events as they occur at the dissolution of the oedipal complex. Since the superego is considered the "heir" to the Oedipus complex, it is to this aspect of the personality that we now turn our attention.

## Freud's Views on the Development of Superego Functions

As noted earlier, Freud considered that there was a close relationship between the resolution of oedipal conflicts and the development of the superego. In Chapter 3 of *The Ego and the Id* (Freud, 1923b), we find an account of the genesis of the superego functions, which are seen as derivatives of a transformation of the child's earliest object-cathexes into identifications, which take the place of the Oedipus complex.

In earlier writings—the paper on "Narcissism" (1914), *Group Psychology and the Analysis of the Ego* (1921), and *Mourning and Melancholia* (1917)—Freud had described his idea of the ego-ideal ("Man has set up an ideal in himself by which he measures his actual ego" [Freud, 1914]). "It would not surprise us if we were to find that a special psychical agency which performs the task of seeing that the narcissistic satisfaction from the ego-ideal is ensured, and which, with this end in view, constantly watches the actual ego and measures it by that ideal" (Freud, 1914).

The subsequent concept of the superego was an amalgamation of this "agency" and the ego-ideal. In *Mourning and Melancholia* Freud's ideas about this "critical agency" were further developed, in a discussion of identification, a topic to be discussed more fully in *Group Psychology and the Analysis of the Ego* in 1921, where Freud described how early identifications with the father initially co-exist with the pre-oedipal attachment to the mother without conflict. With the development of the oedipal feelings, however, they come together, and the boy's "identification with his father takes on a hostile coloring." The identification becomes ambivalent. Bisexuality now also plays a role since both the basic father—and mother—identification form a *"precipitate in the ego, consisting of these two identifications in some way united with each other. This modification of the ego retains its special position; it confronts the other contents of the ego as an ego-ideal or superego"* (Freud's italics).

Freud explained that the superego is not merely a conglomeration of early object choices; it also represents an "energetic reaction-formation" against them.

Its relation to the ego is not exhausted by the precept: "You *ought to be like this* (like your father)." It also comprises the prohibition: "You *may not be like this* (like your father)—that is, you may not do all that he does; some things are his prerogative." This double aspect of the ego-ideal derives from the fact that the ego-ideal had the task of repressing the Oedipus complex; indeed it is to that revolutionary event that it owes its existence (Freud, 1923b—Freud's italics).

That the repression of the Oedipus complex is a difficult task is made clear by Freud, who suggested that because the father is seen (by the boy) as the obstacle to the fulfilment of his oedipal wishes, the child uses his identification with his father to help him in this task. (The notion of "borrowed strength" is used here.) Because the father is, in this context, seen as an inhibiting authority, the superego acquires the flavor and character of the father, and the stronger the oedipal wishes and feelings are, and the more rapidly they are repressed "under the influence of authority, religious teaching, schooling and reading," the stricter will be the watchfulness of the superego over the ego in later periods of development "in the form of conscience or perhaps of an unconscious sense of guilt." Later Freud wrote: "We see, then, that the differentiation of the superego from the ego is no matter of chance; it represents the most important characteristics of the development both of the individual and of the species; indeed, by giving permanent expression to the influence of the parents it perpetuates the existence of the factors to which it owes its origin" (Freud, 1923b).

Thus Freud believed that when the boy abandons his erotic oedipal attachment to his mother, he replaces it with identifications with his father. At the same time, a qualitative change takes place in the nature of the sexual impulses involved ("a desexualisation—a kind of sublimation, therefore" occurs [Freud, 1923b]), and this "instinctual defusion" is important for the characteristics and strengths of the superego.

Again the processes involved in the development of superego functions in the girl differ from those in boys. The fear of castration does not and cannot play the same role in the dissolution of the Oedipus complex in girls that it does in boys—superego formation therefore also takes a different course. "The fear of castration being thus excluded in the little girl, a powerful motive also drops out for the setting up of a superego and for the breaking off of the infantile genital organization" (Freud, 1924). Freud thought that fear of loss of love and disappointment of oedipal wishes provide the motives for superego formation in girls. But because such motives do not have the strength of castration fear, the overcoming of the oedipus complex is, according to Freud (1933), much more problematical and incomplete in many women. "In these circumstances the formation of the superego must suffer; it cannot attain the strength and independence which give it its cultural significance, and feminists are not pleased when we point out to them the effects of this factor upon the average feminine character" (Freud, 1933). For Freud, therefore, the woman's superego "is never so inexorable, so impersonal, so independent of its emotional origins" as in men (Freud, 1925).[3]

## Summary

I have outlined the development of Freud's views on the Oedipus complex and its importance for personality development, noting the changes in the original theoretical concepts occasioned by the growing awareness of the importance of the pre-oedipal phases, with their attachments and identifications, and the concept of bisexuality. An important product of these developments was recognition of the divergent developmental paths taken by girls and boys—divergence that has implications for superego development.

[3] It would not be relevant, in this review, to discuss contemporary psychoanalytic considerations of the superego concept. The area is controversial. That psychoanalysts are still trying to understand the nature of the processes involved in the development of superego functions must be obvious. (See, for example, Beres, 1958; Hartmann, Kris, & Loewenstein, 1946; Hartmann & Loewenstein, 1962; Ritvo & Solnit, 1958; Sandler, 1960; Sandler, Holder, & Meers, 1963; Sandler, Kawenoka, Neurath, Rosenblatt, Schnurmann, & Sigal, 1962.)

It should be apparent that, during the development of psychoanalytic theories, psychoanalysts began to look more closely at the nature of the pre-oedipal relationships and to concentrate less exclusively on the oedipal phase itself. In the process, the importance of the pre-oedipal father relationship has been increasingly stressed. As we shall see in the next section, this relationship, always of importance clinically, has been accorded theoretical consideration as well—though such considerations are still in their infancy.

## PRE-OEDIPAL AND OEDIPAL DEVELOPMENTAL PHASES

In this section I attempt to show that, although psychoanalytic theory has tended to neglect the role of the father in the pre-oedipal phases of development, this is not true of developmental–analytical–observational studies, or of clinical psychoanalysis—which recognize the fundamental importance to the child of the early father relationship. The comparative neglect of the father in theory has not been matched with a similar clinical neglect of his role. Present or absent, the father is seen by clinicians to play a fundamental role in the psychological development of both sons and daughters.

### The Father's Role in Development

As early as 1944, Anna Freud and Dorothy Burlingham pointed out the importance of the father for normal development. In discussing the attempts made during the war to provide evacuated children with mother substitutes, they commented on the complete absence of similar endeavors to provide substitutes for the father's vital functions and wondered why this "conspicuous fact" had not received more attention or "created more concern regarding the normality of the child's upbringing" (Burlingham & Freud, 1944). They considered the "superficial" factors that might have led to the mother's being regarded as more important in the child's life than the father and stated their position clearly: "The infant's emotional relationship to its father . . . is an integral part of its emotional life and a necessary ingredient in the complex forces which work towards the formation of its character and personality" (Burlingham & Freud, 1944). Other writers, too, such as Winnicott (1960), Greenacre (1960), and Neubauer (1960) have similarly stressed the importance of the early father–infant relationship.

But in spite of this recognition of the father's importance, no systematic attempts were made at that time to consider his role and functions in theoretical formulations about the infant's early relationships with the world.

In 1966 Greenacre again called attention to this neglect of the father in psychoanalytical theories on the first 2 years of life, and in the same year, Leonard (1966) noted that although pathological father–daughter relationships had been described, no comprehensive account of normal and abnormal father–daughter interactions had been put forward.

The growing dissatisfaction with the lack of adequate theoretical formulations that would do justice to the wealth of clinical and observational material testifying to the early appearance and emotional significance of the father–infant tie was strongly expressed by Burlingham in her paper on the pre-oedipal father–infant relationship (1973). Burlingham also expressed the opinion that the relative neglect of the father had possibly contributed to a distortion of our thinking about the mother–infant relationship as well. She believes that the father assists the process of individuation in the small child.

Abelin (1971, 1975) has proposed a similar role for the father. Within the framework of Mahler's developmental theory concerning the successive stages of the infant's differentiation and separation–individuation from its mother (Mahler, 1972), Abelin postulated that the early tie to the father plays an essential role in the growth and autonomy of ego functions. As Abelin (1971) points out, a similar ego-developing and ego-strengthening function had been suggested for the father by Loewald (1951) and by Mahler and Gosliner (1955). But Abelin based his conclusion on a study of mother–infant pairs in which he had been surprised by the intensity and early appearance of the father–infant relationships, and on a later intensive, longitudinal, observational study of a mother, father, and infant (Abelin, 1975) and made more specific theoretical propositions about the timing and nature of the father's role in the development of ego functions.

Mahler distinguishes between the infant's biological birth and its psychological birth. The latter is seen as a "slowly unfolding intrapsychic process" (Mahler, 1972), to which she gives the name "the Separation–Individuation phase." This phase is preceded by the "symbiotic phase." Separation–individuation processes are themselves divided into four subphases: differentiation, practicing, rapprochement, and processes leading to libidinal constancy. Abelin stresses the practicing subphase of the separation–individuation process. This is the subphase that occurs between 7 through 10 and 15 through 16 months of age. It is further subdivided into an early practicing phase, characterized by the infant's first physical movements away from the mother (crawling, climbing, etc., though still "holding on" to her), and the practicing phase proper, in which the infant is capable of free, upright locomotion and widens his experience of the "other than mother" world. Freedom and the opportunity for exploration at some physical distance from the mother characterize this phase. Abelin (1975) proposes that it is in the practicing subphase that the infant's specific attachment to its father, involving the encouragement of exploratory behavior and offering opportunities for identifications based on strong positive attachments, plays a decisive role in aiding the processes of differentiation and individuation.

It should be clear, therefore, that psychoanalysts are aware of the importance of the father in early development but that this awareness has not been reflected in or translated into theoretical formulations except in a rather sporadic way. When we turn to observational and clinical material, however, we see that greater justice has been done to the father–infant relationship than the foregoing considerations alone would have led us to believe.

## Contemporary Clinical and Observational Studies

In this section, data from observational and analytical–clinical studies are presented to exemplify the rich and many-sided interactions between fathers and their children. As is often the case, examination of pathological forms and patterns of interaction throws some light on normal developmental processes. Obviously only a small selection of such clinical material can be discussed here. Contributions have been selected where they imply specific formulations regarding the role of the father.

Burlingham (1973), basing her views on both infant observations and clinical data, stressed that "much has gone on between fathers and their infants" long before the oedipal phase is reached. She proceeded to follow the development of this relationship using observational notes from the Hampstead Wellbaby Clinic, as well as analytical material derived from men patients who, in the course of their analyses, became fathers. Her descriptions of the early modes of interaction between fathers and infants are consistent with Lamb's (see Chapter 9) more systematic descriptions. Her observations suggested that some infants seem to "prefer" their fathers to their mothers, even where there is no question about the mother's capacity to care for the infant. (It is a well-known clinical phenomenon that infants turn to others [mainly fathers when they are available] when their mothers are either too anxious or depressed to respond to their needs.) Burlingham also suggested that, in families where the special care of the children weighs heavily on a mother and interferes with her more lighthearted responses, the less burdened husband may be ready and available to enter into a purely pleasurable father–infant relationship.[4]

It is the analytical material Burlingham discussed that is especially interesting, representing, as it does, the point of view of the father. Burlingham showed that one important determinant of the father's handling of his infant is the way in which he was treated by his own father (cf. Weissman, 1963). She wrote: "We have found that whatever handling the father has experienced from his own father, whether it has been loving, unfeeling, secure, lenient, understanding or inconsistent, this affects his own attitude and behavior towards the child." Fathers sometimes say that they know they are imitating their fathers and that they sometimes try consciously to behave differently but nevertheless continue to act as their fathers did, against their better judgement. A very early identification with the father is indicated.

Burlingham also pointed out that there are sex differences both in infant's reactions to fathers, and in father's reactions to their infants. Stressing the importance of such qualitative differences between the mother– and father–infant relationship, she concludes:

I cannot help feeling that in spite of and beyond the complexities of parental characters, and also in spite of the alleged modern equality of the sexes, many of the either female or male characteristics of the parents will continue to exist and, in response to them, the infants' *differentiated* emotional reactions and *differentiated* experiences of pleasure (Burlingham, 1973—my italics).

Weissman (1963), like Burlingham, paid special attention to the effects of fathers' personalities on their children—in this case, their sons. Using analytical material from adult male patients, he described specific forms of play between fathers and their sons, which in each case became one of the principal determinants of outstanding character traits in the sons. Each of the fathers had clearly carried over his own pathology into his interaction with his child in such a way that the whole structure of the child's personality was affected. In each of the patients described, play with their fathers had been unusually continuous and intense from the very earliest developmental phases onward. In one of the patients who had a child it was his awareness that he wished to repeat the game his father had played

---

[4] Personal observations among Zulu families in South Africa would tend to support this observation of Burlingham's. Zulu mothers traditionally perform all the domestic chores and have, therefore, little time or energy to play with their children. In those families where the father was present, usually for a relatively brief visit from the city, the purely pleasurable and playful interactions they had with their infants were especially striking.

with him that led to the examination of the effects it had had on his own development.

Another example of the pathological interaction between a father and son is given by Kolansky and Moore (1966) in an account of the simultaneous analysis of both. As is usual in this type of analytical research, it was possible to gain some insights into their mutual psychopathology and its effects on the child. In this adolescent boy the compliant personality he had developed in response to his father's needs could be analyzed only after the father had partially worked through the reasons for his need to ensure his son's passive allegiance (through beatings). This sequence was repeated often in the simultaneous analysis—the son's problems yielding to analytic intervention only after aspects of the father's neurosis had been analyzed. This process, in a manner of speaking, "freed" the son from the pathological interaction and enabled him to take a developmental step away from the pathological interaction with the help of his own analysis. The crux of the father's problem lay in his identification with his aggressively experienced father.

Sprince (1972) reported a similar case of pseudo-dementia in a 13-year-old boy. For our purposes the contribution of this study derives from the enormously important impact the boy's pre-oedipal contact with his father had on his development. Sprince pointed out that all the characteristics described by Hellman (1954) as being important in mothers who produce intellectual inhibitions in their children were in this case attributes of the father and characteristic of his relationship with his son. The boy's pre-oedipal relationship with his father was one in which close physical contact played an important part—perhaps because the mother had had a long illness and many hospitalizations that finally led to her death when the boy was 9 years old. The main source of the boy's pathology was a massive identification with his father and difficulty in regarding himself as someone separate from his father. Sprince suggested that the strength and nature of this identification resulted from particularly intense pre-oedipal physical contact between them.

Father–daughter as well as father–son relationships have been identified as pathogenic. Another case report (Moore, 1974) described the deleterious effects on a girl of a father who openly did not care for her. Moore showed how this 13-year-old girl, in analysis because of her promiscuous behavior, had found it impossible to give up her pre-oedipal attachment to her mother because her father found her unattractive and unintelligent. The father's attitudes and feelings, in making it difficult or impossible for the girl to enter the oedipal phase, had obvious effects on her development. In this case, therefore, it was also the absence of the necessary warmth, interest, and affection that was damaging to the developmental processes.

This particular theme is also dealt with by Leonard (1966) in a paper on fathers and daughters in which she discussed the significance of fathering for the psychosexual development of girls. She concentrated on the role fathers play in enabling girls to progress successfully to and through the oedipal phase of development. She emphasized, in addition, that the father can also have a profound effect on the mother's relationship with her children. From her analytical studies of adolescent girls Leonard concluded that a father who is present and participating in the girl's upbringing from pre-oedipal stages onward is essential to normal psychosexual development.

Another type of observational–clinical study, characteristic of developmental psychoanalysis, is exemplified by a study by Ritvo (1974). This paper presented data on a little girl, Evelyne, whose development was studied as part of the Yale longitudinal analytical research initiated by Ernst Kris. These studies combine detailed and intricate sets of observations with reconstructions from the analysis of the adults and children concerned. Evelyne had been studied from birth as part of such a longitudinal study and was later, at $3\frac{1}{2}$ years of age, taken into individual analysis, as was her father, whose attitudes to the child had played a decisive role in her development. The father had disliked the child from birth—and the material from both analyses illustrated how much the father's attitudes and pathology had contributed to her difficulties. In the total family situation the birth of two younger sisters had deprived Evelyne of her earlier exclusive relationship with her mother—a fact that had the effect of strengthening the impact of her father's dislike, since she was unable to turn to him. The father had wished for a son and did not conceal his disappointment at Evelyne's birth. The subsequent birth of two more daughters did nothing to gratify his original wish, but he was able to identify the physical skills of the two younger girls with boyish qualities and was thus able to form relationships with them. Evelyne, on the contrary, had from the very beginning been physically awkward, a fact that annoyed both parents but that acted as a complete barrier to the development of a relationship with her father. She tried doggedly for a long time to develop skills to please her father but was unable to do so. A severe obstruction of Evelyne's attempts to win her father's love emerged in his own analysis. He had identified this child with a hated elder sister, who, he felt, had interfered with his relationship with his own father and had been the cause of disappointments and frustrations, both personal and professional. This virtual absence of love from the father was coupled with an attitude of growing disappointment on the part of the mother—all of which led to the clinical picture of an intellectually inhibited and physically awkward child, whose feminine development could not proceed.

This case has been presented in such detail because it exemplifies contemporary psychoanalytical research, as conducted by Kris at Yale (see Ritvo, McCollum, Omwake, Provence, & Solnit, 1963) and Anna Freud in London. This approach demonstrates how artificial and misleading it is to isolate the effect of one parent on the development of the child. In this case as in others, the combined effects of the total family situation and the interactions between the mother, father, and siblings, and the particular mental and physical characteristics of the child herself, contributed to the final clinical picture.

Other simultaneous analytic studies support such a view. Examples drawn from the Hampstead series of simultaneous analyses of parents and children have been reported by Levy (1960) and Sprince (1962). They give an account of a severe disturbance in a girl whose mother was also taken into analysis. Here again one observes how the interactions of the mother, father, and daughter contributed to the final severe clinical disturbance. Concern for digestive and bodily processes obsessed both parents (in the form of excessive bodily care by both that continued far into childhood) and constituted an essential bond between the girl and her parents, forming the basis of her pathology.

Hellman, Friedmann, and Shepheard (1960) describe a simultaneous analysis of a mother and son, where, although the dominant parental pathology was certainly that of the mother, her attitude to the father (and the consequent distortion of the boy's perception of the father) grossly interfered with the relationship between the two of them and thus contributed to the boy's problems. The pathology of one parent can, in this way, interfere with the possibility of a relationship's being formed with the other.

From such clinical reports and analytic investigations it is clear that a father who is physically present, whether he interacts or fails to interact with his child, exerts a profound influence on the course of that child's development. But the importance of the absent father has long been familiar to psychoanalysts, and it is to this topic that we now turn.

### The Absent Father in Psychoanalysis

Peter Neubauer, in his paper on "The one-parent child and his oedipal development" (1960), reviews the literature on the effect of the absence of one parent on events in the oedipal phase. In practically all the cases he discusses, the absent parent is the father, and again in almost all cases the existence of fantasies about the missing parent, which play a part in the developmental process, is made clear. These fantasies have either an idealized or a punitive content, or both—the nature of the specific fantasy depending not simply on the sex of the child in relation to the parent's sex but also on the developmental phase of the child at the time of the loss of the parent. Neubauer described the case of a girl whose absent father exerted an (pathological) effect more powerful than the influence of the mother. Although the child showed no great pathology, the author postulated that, because of her father's absence, she suffered a "developmental deficiency" since she did not experience and work through the oedipal conflicts. She remained in a pre-oedipal relationship to her mother, and also to her absent father in fantasy, as "When a parent is absent, there is an absence of oedipal reality" (Neubauer, 1960).

Maetze (1969 and personal communication), in a paper on the psycho analytic treatment of students in Berlin, pointed out that the disturbances found in this clinical population may be partly due to the fact that, born at the beginning of, or during the early years of, the war, most of them had grown up in families where the father was absent. They had been exposed as infants and young children, therefore, not only to a distorted family structure and to a childhood without a father, but also to a mother who was herself reacting (often depressively) to the absence of her husband.

A particularly interesting account of observations made of small children's reactions to an absent or dead father is provided by Burlingham and Freud (1944). These observations support the above-mentioned statements by Neubauer concerning the importance of the child's fantasies about the missing parent, although their observations are not limited to children in the oedipal phase of development and therefore give examples of fantasies drawn from different developmental phases. Burlingham and Freud discussed children who, because of the war, were either temporarily or permanently without their fathers, and for whom no substitute "father" had been provided. They observed that, although many children appeared to have been able to accept separation from their fathers relatively easily, compared with separations from the mother, they were utterly unable to accept the fact of death when it occurred. All the orphaned children talked of their dead fathers as though they were alive, and even when they could grasp the fact of death, denied it in a fantasy form. (Ideas of rebirth, or a return from heaven were common.) In some of the children these fantasies appeared to be the spontaneous production of the children themselves—that is, they did not occur only in children whose mothers attempted to hide the truth from them. Infants Without Families remains a storehouse of detailed observations on the behavior and comments of children living under these abnormal and disrupted conditions. To give but one example of a child's comments about the father who he knew had been killed in an air raid: Peter (aged 4) said "My Daddy is taking me to the Zoo today. He told me last night; he comes every night and sits on my bed and talks to me." On another occasion he said: "My Daddy is killed, yes, my sister said so. He cannot come. I want him to come."

The authors noted that dead fathers seemed to be mentioned, if anything, more often than living ones and that the children presented a continual flow of fantasies about their activities and the presents they would be bringing when they visited. One girl maintained a similarly intense relationship to a living, but absent, father during a 2-year-long separation when she was between $3\frac{1}{2}$ and $5\frac{1}{2}$ years of age. She constantly expressed her homesickness for her father, using "almost abnormal" terms of endearment when referring to him. This idealization of the father in fantasy contrasted particularly strongly with the reality father—who was "elderly, morose," and "rather strict and uncompromising with his large family." In this girl's case the purely positive and loving elements in the father relationship were especially outstanding. Other examples were also given of children who formed the most passionate and loving fantasy relationships with fathers who were, in reality, often disappointing.

One of the most interesting observations is, however, that of Bob, who produced a fantasy father where no father existed in reality. The child was illegitimate and had never known his father. He had a good and close relationship to his mother and to her substitute in the nursery. Bob's fantasy father was better than everyone else ("his feet were bigger than anyone else's"; "he owned a big car with lots of wheels on it"; he had "golden hair and lovely pink eyes," etc.), and he grew very sensitive when anyone appeared not to accept his stories about his "father." What is interesting about this child's fantasy father was that the change in the fantasies over time reflected the child's own developmental needs and thus mirrored the changes in the role of the father in the course of development. From 2 years 8 months (when the "father" was first mentioned) to 4 years 6 months, the following changes occurred in the fantasy. At 3 years the father figure reflected someone that Bob could love and admire and be proud of (examples of such statements have been given above); around 3 years 5 months, during a phase when he was aggressive and disobedient, the fantasy father was used to express his own instinctual wishes and to condone his bad behavior ("I did it. But my Daddy told me to do it."); by 4 years the father figure had become the embodiment of everything that was wonderful in the world; and by 4 years 6 months he had taken over the function of correcting everything that was wrong with the world ("My Daddy has lots of bombs which don't break houses"—when he saw a bombed house, and "My Daddy has lots of dicky-birds which never die," when the nursery's bird died) and appeared to have taken over the role of the child's conscience in that he never again did anything that could be considered to be bad or wrong.

In sum, these observations show that fatherless children experience the most intense and persistent attachments to fantasy fathers, which they construct out of even the most minimal relationship or contact with any man at all.

Erna Furman (1974) has discussed reaction to the disappearance of a parent through death in her book *A Child's Parent Dies*. Because the children she discussed had been analyzed, the detailed information about the meaning for the child of the death of a parent, gives the book its special value. It would require more space than is available to do justice to this study, but it is perhaps possible to summarize the main arguments without too much distortion. Furman emphasized that, in determining the reaction to parental death, it is important to consider not only the age of the child and the developmental stage in which it finds itself at the time, but also a great variety of other factors: the actual details of the event and what the child makes out of these; the prior relationship to the lost parent and his/ her previous role in maintaining the child's physical and emotional well-being; whether or not external support is available to the child in the form of explanation, comfort, and acceptance of the feelings of loss and subsequent mourning; or whether the remaining adults, having difficulties with their own feelings about the death, are unable to help the child cope with its feelings and with the inevitable fantasies about the death. Once again, therefore, we see stress laid on the total personality picture of the child and the complex environmental situation in which it finds itself before, during, and after the death of a parent.

Let us now consider this question: What has been the effect on psychoanalysis of the insights gained from the developmental investigations of the pre-oedipal periods of a child's life? In very general terms one can say that the recognition of the manner in which these early experiences influence events in the phallic–oedipal phase itself has been reflected in the emphasis placed on such things as the tendency to develop conflicts, the foundations of specific and characteristic defense mechanisms, the ego's capacity to tolerate and deal with conflict, as well as on early fixation points and identifications. In other words the manner and form in which the child's personality is organized, and indeed its capacity to enter into the conflicts of the phallic–oedipal phase at all, are influenced by what has gone on before (see Ritvo, 1974; Tolpin, 1970). Such considerations are causing analysts to reconsider their definition of "Infantile neurosis"— a topic with which we are not directly concerned. But what is of present concern are attempts at a reassessment of the so-called forerunners of the superego, which have also taken their origin in this shift of emphasis from oedipal to pre-oedipal developmental processes. It is with these views that we are concerned in the section that follows.

## Precursors of Superego Functions

A full examination of this topic is not possible—nor indeed would it be appropriate, for we would then enter a field of current controversy in psychoanalysis. I have chosen, therefore, to indicate briefly the type of thinking about these early processes that is characteristic of the developmentally oriented approach to demonstrate how the conflicts faced during the phallic–oedipal phase are seen as developmental tasks for which the personality is prepared during pre-oedipal development.

Anna Freud (1965) points out that imitation of parents begins in early infancy and increases as awareness of the object world expands and motor skills improve. She considers that, where the early imitations have been experienced as pleasurable, processes of identification develop from them during the pre-oedipal developmental phases. These pre-oedipal identifications are based on the wish to change the self in the image of the parents. In the shape of the child's ideal self, they therefore form an important forerunner of the superego. Parental authority is added by introjections during and after the oedipal period. In this way, she suggests, the early identifications develop from merely desirable ideals into actual internal legislators. From this point on drive control is internally regulated, by feelings of well-being and self-esteem, or by feelings of guilt, replacing the previous dependence on, and fear of, the parents that previously controlled behavior. She does point out, however, that, in spite of this internalization, the child needs continued support and backing from the external world for some considerable time. Ritvo and Solnit (1958), in a paper relating early ego identifications to later superego formation, concentrated their attention on the internalization (early ego identifications) of parental restrictions and limitations of behavior. Using examples of children observed in the course of a longitudinal study, they showed how these internalization processes lead to identifications (of prohibitions), which in turn prepare the child for the internalization of the later prohibitions that belong to the oedipal phase. By taking as their examples children in whom this process of internalization seemed to have been interfered with, they suggested that the later capacity of the personality to form a superego is partially dependent on the fact that these early internalizations and identifications, as processes, have taken place. They suggested, therefore, that to say, as Freud did, that the superego is the heir to the oedipus complex is also to say that these processes of internalization have taken place sufficiently *to permit the formation of a superego at this time* that can function independently of ego processes. In other words, through essential processes occurring in the pre-oedipal phases, the personality attains a sufficient degree of organization for the oedipal conflicts to be solved through the formation of an internally functioning "legislator."

## SUMMARY

An examination of Freud's statements about the role of the father in child development shows that he placed his major theoretical emphasis on the events of the phallic–oedipal period and on the primary identifications that had occurred before this stage in the pre-oedipal period. He perceived the role of the father to differ, depending on the age of the child, the developmental phase under consideration, and the nature and quality of the relationship between the father and the child. The father was seen as an object of love and admiration (and thus important for identifications), as someone powerful and omnipotent and therefore either as a protector or as a punishing, inhibiting, and castrating figure. The adoption of these changes in the role proposed for the father resulted partially from the recognition of the importance of the pre-oedipal relationships and the concept of bisexuality, which drew attention to the early positive relationship to the mother as well as the father.

In contemporary psychoanalytic discussions of the father's importance (which is generally recognized), we have noted the contrast between the richness and diversity of the father–infant interactions as described in clinical and observational studies and the relative neglect of the father in systematic theoretical statements. This gap is slowly being bridged, however, and attempts are being made to incorporate the clinical recognition of the father's importance into theoretical formulations. Data from simultaneous analyses of parents and their children serve as continuous reminders of the dangers of simplification inherent in attempts to isolate artificially the role and functions of one parent from the full pattern of interaction between all members of a family.

## REFERENCES

Abelin, E. L. The role of the father in the separation–individuation process. In J. B. McDevitt & C. F. Settlage (Eds.), *Separation–individuation*. New York: International Universities Press, 1971.

Abelin, E. L. Some further observations and comments on the earliest role of the father. *International Journal of Psychoanalysis*, 1975, **56**, 293–302.

Beres, D. Vicissitudes of superego functions and superego precursors in childhood. *Psychoanalytic Study of the Child*, 1958, **13**, 324–351.

Burlingham, D. The pre-oedipal infant–father relationship. *Psychoanalytic Study of the Child*, 1973, **28**, 23–47.

Burlingham, D., & Freud, A. *Infants without families.* London: George Allen and Unwin, 1944.

Freud, A. *The psychoanalytical treatment of children.* London: Imago, 1946.

Freud, A. *Normality and pathology in childhood.* New York: International Universities Press, 1965.

Freud, A. The Infantile neurosis: Genetic and dynamic considerations. In *Problems of psychoanalytic technique and therapy, 1966–1970.* London: Hogarth, 1972.

Freud, A., & Dann, S. An experiment in group upbringing. *Psychoanalytic Study of the Child*, 1951, **6**, 127–168.

Freud, S. [Extracts from the Fliess papers]. *The standard edition* (Vol. 1). London: Hogarth, 1966. (Originally published, 1897.)

Freud, S. [*The interpretation of Dreams.*] *The standard edition* (Vol. 4). London: Hogarth, 1953. (Originally published, 1900.)

Freud, E. [*Three essays on the theory of sexuality.*] *The standard edition* (Vol. 7). London: Hogarth, 1953. (Originally published, 1905.)

Freud, S. [*Five lectures on psychoanalysis.*] *The standard edition* (Vol. 11). London: Hogarth, 1957. (Originally published 1910.) (a)

Freud, S. [A special type of choice of object made by men. *Contributions to the psychology of love*, 1.] *The standard edition* (Vol. 11). London: Hogarth, 1957. (Originally published 1910.) (b)

Freud, S. [On narcissism: An introduction.] *The standard edition* (Vol. 14). London: Hogarth, 1957. (Originally published, 1914.)

Freud, S. [A case of paranoia running counter to the psychoanalytic theory of the disease.] *The standard edition* (Vol. 14). London: Hogarth, 1957. (Originally published, 1915.)

Freud, S. [*Introductory lectures on psychoanalysis.*] *The standard edition* (Vol. 16). London: Hogarth, 1963. (Originally published, 1916–1917.)

Freud, S. [*Mourning and melancholia.*] *The standard edition* (Vol. 14). London: Hogarth, 1957. (Originally published, 1917.)

Freud, S. [From the history of an infantile neurosis.] *The standard edition* (Vol. 17). London: Hogarth, 1955. (Originally published, 1918.)

Freud, S. [A child is being beaten: A contribution to the study of the origins of sexual perversions.] *The standard edition* (Vol. 17). London: Hogarth, 1955. (Originally published, 1919.)

Freud, S. [The psychogenesis of a case of homosexuality in a woman.] *The standard edition* (Vol. 18). London: Hogarth, 1955. (Originally published, 1920.)

Freud, S. [*Group psychology and the analysis of the ego.*] *The standard edition* (Vol. 18). London: Hogarth, 1955. (Originally published, 1921.)

Freud, S. [Two encyclopedia articles.] *The standard edition* (Vol. 18). London: Hogarth, 1955. (Originally published, 1923.) (a)

Freud, S. [*The Ego and the Id.*] *The standard edition* (Vol. 19). London: Hogarth, 1961. (Originally published, 1923.) (b)

Freud, S. [The infantile genital organization: An interpolation into the theory of sexuality.] *The standard edition* (Vol. 19). London: Hogarth, 1961. (Originally published, 1923.) (c)

Freud, S. [The dissolution of the Oedipus complex.] *The standard edition* (Vol. 19). London: Hogarth, 1961. (Originally published, 1924).

Freud, S. [Some psychical consequences of the anatomical distinction between the sexes.] *The standard edition* (Vol. 19). London: Hogarth, 1961. (Originally published, 1925.) (a)

Freud, S. [An autobiographical study.] *The standard edition* (Vol. 20). London: Hogarth, 1959. (Originally published, 1925.) (b)

Freud, S. [The question of lay analysis.] *The standard edition* (Vol. 20). London: Hogarth, 1959. (Originally published, 1926.)

Freud, S. [Female sexuality.] *The standard edition* (Vol. 21). London: Hogarth, 1961. (Originally published, 1931.)

Freud, S. [*New introductory lectures on psychoanalysis.*] *The standard edition* (Vol. 22). London: Hogarth, 1964. (Originally published, 1933.)

Furman, E. *A child's parent dies. Studies in childhood bereavement.* New Haven and London: Yale University Press, 1974.

Greenacre, P. Considerations regarding the parent–infant relationship. *International Journal of Psychoanalysis*, 1960, **41**, 571–584.

Greenacre, P. Problems of overidealization of the analyst and of analysis. *Psychoanalytic Study of the Child*, 1966, **21**, 193–212.

Gyomroi-Ludowyk, E. The analysis of a young concentration camp victim. *Psychoanalytic Study of the Child*, 1963, **18**, 484–510.

Hartmann, H. Psychoanalysis and developmental psychology. *Psychoanalytic Study of the Child*, 1950, **5**, 5–17.

Hartmann, H., Kris, E., & Loewenstein, R. Comments on the formation of psychic structure. *Psychoanalytic Study of the Child*, 1946, **2**, 11–38.

Hartmann, H., & Loewenstein, R. Notes on the superego. *Psychoanalytic Study of the Child*, 1962, **17**, 42–81.

Hellmann, I. Some observations on mothers of children with intellectual inhibitions. *Psychoanalytic Study of the Child*, 1954, **9**, 259–273.

Hellmann, I., Friedmann, O., & Shepheard, E. Simultaneous analysis of mother and child. *Psychoanalytic Study of the Child*, 1960, **15**, 359–377.

Kolansky, H., & Moore, W. T. Some comments on the simultaneous analysis of a father and his adolescent son. *Psychoanalytic Study of the Child,* 1966, **21**, 237–268.

Klein, M. *The psychoanalysis of children.* London: International Psychoanalytical Library, 1932.

Kris, E. Notes on the development and on some current problems in psychoanalytic child psychology. *Psychoanalytic Study of the Child,* 1950, **5**, 24–46.

Kris, E. Opening remarks on psychoanalytic child psychology. *Psychoanalytical Study of the Child,* 1951, **6**, 9–17.

Kris, M. The use of prediction in a longitudinal study. *Psychoanalytic Study of the Child,* 1957, **12**, 175–189.

Lampl-de Groot, J. The pre-oedipal phase of development of the male child. *Psychoanalytic Study of the Child,* 1946, **2**, 75–83.

Lampl-de Groot, J. Ego ideal and superego. *Psychoanalytic Study of the Child,* 1962, **17**, 94–106.

Leonard, M. Fathers and daughters. *International Journal of Psychoanalysis,* 1966, **47**, 325–334.

Levy, K. Simultaneous analysis of a mother and her adolescent daughter. *Psychoanalytic Study of the Child,* 1960, **15**, 378–391.

Loewald, H. Ego and reality. *International Journal of Psychoanalysis,* 1951, **32**, 10–17.

Maetze, G. *Psychische storungen bei stundenten. Symposion von 22–24 März 1968 in Berlin.* Stuttgart: Sonderdruck Georg Thieme Verlag, 1969.

Mahler, M. On the first three subphases of the separation–individuation process. *International Journal of Psychoanalysis,* 1972, **53**, 333–338.

Mahler, M. Symbiosis and Individuation: The psychological birth of the human infant. *Psychoanalytic Study of the Child,* 1974, **29**, 89–106.

Mahler, M., & Gosliner, R. On symbiotic child psychosis: Genetic dynamic and restitutive aspects. *Psychoanalytic Study of the Child,* 1955, **10**, 195–212.

Moore, W. T. Promiscuity in a 13-year-old girl. *Psychoanalytic Study of the Child,* 1974, **29**, 301–318.

Nagera, H. (Ed.). *Basic psychoanalytic concepts on the libido theory.* London: George Allen and Unwin, 1969.

Neubauer, P. B. The one-parent child and his oedipal development. *Psychoanalytic Study of the Child,* 1960, **15**, 286–309.

Provence, S., & Lipton, R. S. *Infants in institutions.* New York: International Universities Press, 1962.

Provence, S., & Ritvo, S. Effects of deprivation on institutionalized infants: Disturbances in development of relationship to inanimate objects. *Psychoanalytic Study of the Child,* 1961, **16**, 189–206.

Ritvo, S. Current status of the concept of infantile neurosis: Implications for diagnosis and technique. *Psychoanalytic Study of the Child*, 1974, **29**, 159–181.

Ritvo, S., McCollum, A. T., Omwake, E., Provence, S., & Solnit, A. J. Some relations of constitution, environment and personality as observed in a longitudinal study of child development. In A. J. Solnit & S. Provence (Eds.), *Modern perspectives in child development*. New York: International Universities Press, 1963.

Ritvo, S., & Solnit, A. J. Influences of early mother-child interaction on identification processes. *Psychoanalytic Study of the Child*, 1958, **13**, 64–91.

Sandler, J. On the concept of the superego. *Psychoanalytic Study of the Child*, 1960, **15**, 128–162.

Sandler, J., Holder, A., & Meers, D. The ego ideal and the ideal self. *Psychoanalytic Study of the Child*, 1963, **18**, 139–158.

Sandler, J., Kawenoka, M., Neurath, L., Rosenblatt, B., Schnurmann, A., & J. Sigal. The classification of superego material in the Hampstead index. *Psychoanalytic Study of the Child*, 1962, **17**, 107–127.

Spitz, R. Hospitalism: An enquiry into the genesis of psychiatric conditions in early childhood. *Psychoanalytic Study of the Child*, 1945, **1**, 53–74.

Spitz, R. Relevancy of direct infant observation. *Psychoanalytic Study of the Child*, 1950, **5**, 66–73.

Sprince, M. The development of a pre-oedipal partnership between an adolescent girl and her mother. *Psychoanalytic Study of the Child*, 1962, **17**, 418–424.

Sprince, M. Die psychoanalytische Behandlung eines pseudodebilen hochintelligenten Jungen mit abnormen Verhaltensweisen. In E. Geleerd (Ed.), *Kinderanalytiker bei der Arbeit*. Stuttgart: Ernst Klett Verlag, 1972.

Tolpin, M. The infantile neurosis: a metapsychological concept and a paradigmatic case history. *Psychoanalytic Study of the Child*, 1970, **25**, 273–305.

Weissman, P. The effects of pre-oedipal attitudes on development and character. *International Journal of Psychoanalysis*, 1963, **44**, 121–131

Winnicott, D. W. The theory of the parent–infant relationship. *International Journal of Psychoanalysis*, 1960, **41**, 585–595.

# CHAPTER 9

# Interactions Between Eight-Month-Old Children and Their Fathers and Mothers

MICHAEL E. LAMB

*University of Wisconsin-Madison*

In recent years, students of infancy have begun to pay increasing attention to social development. With few exceptions, the focus has been on the infant–mother relationship, reflecting the assumption that, since mothers have traditionally been responsible for caretaking, they must be the most important persons in the infants' lives. Ainsworth (1969, 1973, and personal communication), Bowlby (1952, 1958, 1969), and Yarrow and Pederson (1972) have all explicitly stated their belief that the mother–infant relationship is the most important in the infant's life and that it is the prototype for subsequent relationships (Freud, 1940).

Whatever the importance of the mother–infant relationship, though, researchers and theorists realize that most infants grow up in the context of the family, in which there are other persons—fathers and siblings—to whom infants become attached and who conceivably play important roles

This study is one of a series of researches carried out in the Ecology of Human Development Program under a grant from the Foundation for Child Development. This study was undertaken as a dissertation project in partial fulfillment of the requirements for the degree of Doctor of Philosophy in the Graduate School at Yale University. The author expresses his gratitude to William Kessen, Katherine Nelson, Phoebe Ellsworth, Urie Bronfenbrenner and the reviewers of the Ecology of Human Development Program, Thomas M. Achenbach, Mary D. Ainsworth, and Greta G. Fein for their contributions to the conduct of the study and for critical reviews of the manuscript. Lee Wilkinson provided expert statistical advice. Thanks are also due to William K. Redican and Sheila Huddleston for their comments on preliminary drafts of the manuscript. Judith McBride, Kinthi Sturtevant, Sheila Huddleston, and, particularly, Jamie E. Lamb made invaluable contributions to the collection and reduction of the data. Finally thanks are due to the families who agreed to participate in the longitudinal project.

in socialization (Lamb, 1975; Sutton-Smith & Rosenberg 1970). Both Ainsworth (1967, 1973, and personal communication) and Yarrow (1974) have urged recently that research be focused on the father–infant relationship.

The first attempt to investigate the father–infant relationship was made by Schaffer and Emerson (1964), who questioned mothers about the likelihood of protest on the part of their infants when separated from their mothers or fathers in everyday situations. The data showed that the infants protested separation from their mothers more than their fathers around 9 months of age, though by 18 months most infants protested separation from the two parents equally.

Subsequently Lewis, Weinraub, and Ban (1972) reported that the infant's attachment to its mother was greater than that to its father at 1 year of age (when looking, vocalizing, touching, and being near were the measures used) but that the two attachments were of equal strength at 2 years of age. Cohen and Campos (1974) reported corroborative evidence: They found that 10-, 13-, and 16-month-old infants preferred their mothers to their fathers when "using the parent as a secure base," being near, and separation protest were the measures used. However, Kotelchuck (1972), Ross, Kagan, Zelazo, and Kotelchuck (1975), and Spelke, Zelazo, Kagan, and Kotelchuck (1973) failed to find any preference for mother over father in American infants ranging in age from 12 to 21 months when separation protest, vocalizing, and smiling were the measures used. They did find though that, in Guatemalan infants, such preferences were evident (Lester, Kotelchuck, Spelke, Sellers, & Klein, 1974).

With the exception of the studies by Schaffer and Emerson (1964) and Ross et al. (1975) this research has all been conducted in the laboratory. In the present study I observed infants interacting with both parents in their homes in the hope that in this way we would gain further insight into infant attachment to their fathers, even if it meant sacrificing some of the rigorous control that can be exercised in the laboratory.

In addition I wished to observe these children at the ages at which Bowlby (1969) believes they should be forming their first social attachments, and then to observe the development of the patterns of interaction with the two parents in the course of a longitudinal study. This chapter deals with the first series of observations, made when the infants were 7 and 8 months old.

One major problem faced by researchers in this area concerns the choice of appropriate measures. Bowlby and Ainsworth both emphasize that the most reliable test of whether an infant is attached to a person is to determine whether it reacts with grief to long-term separation, and this test cannot, of course, be used in research. Noting this problem, Ainsworth (1964) presented a list of behaviors (that she labeled attachment behaviors) and suggested that these were directed more frequently to attachment figures than to other persons. She stressed, as I (Lamb, 1974) have more recently stressed, that one should not equate the attachment behaviors with the attachment bond, of which they are but crude indices. In the absence of superior measures I relied partially on these attachment behaviors in the present study but sought to minimize the possibility of error by using a larger number of them than have been used in previous studies. Preference in the display of attachment behaviors, however, should not be equated with affective preference for the person, although most previous research on father–infant (and mother–infant) attachment has tended to treat the two as equivalent.

In planning the study I found it useful to draw on Bretherton's (1974) and Bretherton and Ainsworth's (1974) suggestion that we distinguish attachment and affiliative behavioral systems. Both theoretical and empirical considerations suggest that there are certain behaviors—such as wanting to be held by an adult or wanting to be comforted by one when distressed—that infants direct almost exclusively to attachment figures (or substitutes thereof in their absence), whereas there are other behaviors that are directed not only to attachment figures but also to other friendly adults. These are referred to, respectively, as the attachment and affiliative behaviors in this paper, though it is important to remember that both are subsets of the list of attachment behaviors proposed by Ainsworth (1964) and Bowlby (1969). Several behaviors representative of each system were recorded and analyzed in this study.

In addition to tabulating the frequency of these behaviors, I attempted to explore the nature of the relationships by focusing on two classes of interaction (play and physical contact) that permit an evaluation of the parents' contribution to the interaction. Physical contact (holding) is an important aspect of attachment relationships, for as both Ainsworth, Bell, Blehar, and Main (1971) and Bowlby (1969) emphasize, when attachment is viewed ethologically, the achievement of physical contact (particularly that implicit in being held by the protective adult) is a goal of the attachment behavioral system. Moreover, Ainsworth et al. (1971) and Ainsworth, Bell, and Stayton (1972) believe that the analysis of the infant's response to being held is one of the more reliable indices of whether it is attached to the person.

Much of the interaction between infants and their parents takes place in the context of social play, and thus I attempted to determine not only the response of the infants to play initiated by their parents but also the character of mother– and father–infant play. I was interested in determining how closely mother–infant and father–infant interaction resembled one another, since an implicit or explicit assumption of those who stress the need for research on father–infant interaction is that the impact of fathers may be different from the impact of mothers because of differences in the character of the interaction (Lamb, 1975; Nash, 1965; Yarrow, 1974). Previous research has not addressed this issue.

In sum this study was an attempt to investigate the mother–infant and father–infant attachments and to address again the question raised in previous research—namely, is it possible to show that mothers are preferred to fathers in the display of social behaviors? The study differed from previous studies in its reliance on a larger number of measures and in its focus on the interaction between the infants and their parents in their homes at younger ages than have typically been studied.

## METHOD

### Subjects

The subjects were 10 boys, 10 girls, and their parents, recruited as part of an ongoing longitudinal project on infant social development. Subjects were recruited from the birth records of the Yale–New Haven Hospital by means of an introductory letter, followed by a telephone call. Of the families contacted, 46% agreed to participate and were offered payment for their cooperation. The social status of the families was assessed by means of Hollingshead's (1957) Two Factor Index of Social Position; the mean rating on this scale was 29.3 (boys' families, 28.5; girls' families, 30.1, n.s.). There were six families in Social Class I, four in II, four in III, and six in IV. There were no families in Class V. All the subjects were white.

All but one of the parents were native-born Americans: 18 of the fathers and 16 of the mothers had been raised in the Northeast. Six families were Jewish, 10 Catholic. Four of the mothers worked part time or studied—and three of them scheduled these activities so that the fathers could attend to the infants. In all but one of the families the mother was the primary caretaker. Only four of the fathers regularly took primary responsibility for the child for any length of time. Only one family made regular use of extrafamilial substitute caretakers. Three of the boys and five of the girls were firstborns. Nine of the girls, but only 5 of the boys were capable of independent locomotion when observed.

### Procedure

The infants were observed in their homes when both parents were present. Each family was observed once when the infant was 7 and again when it was 8 months old. Each visit lasted between 1 and 2 hours. On the average each infant was observed for a total of 153.3 minutes. The visits were scheduled at the parents' convenience, the only stipulation being that both parents be home. Consequently most visits were made in the evenings, over weekends, or on days when the parents were not working. The parents were encouraged to continue with their routines, even if this involved leaving the room to perform chores, though they were asked to remain in the same room as the infant most of the time. In a questionnaire completed by the parents after this series of visits 90% stated that the investigators were observing the normal interaction between the infant and its parents. Two sets of parents stated that they felt inhibited by the presence of the investigators and were not as affectionate with the infants as they would normally have been. The infants' routines were not disturbed.

Each visit was made by the same two persons. One of them, referred to as the Visitor ($V$), attempted to interact with the parents and the child in the same manner as any visitor to the home would. Her purpose was to alleviate the parents' anxieties about being observed and to offer the infant the choice between interaction with the parents or with a responsive and participative stranger. She did not attempt to focus attention on the child. The second person, the Observer ($O$), dictated into a tape recorder a detailed narrative account of the infant's behavior and the contingent behaviors of the other persons present. The observer used a microphone sensitive enough to record his dictation at a level that was barely audible and thus minimally obtrusive. He detailed the infant's response to attempts by the adults to initiate interaction and took special care to record each instance of any of the following behaviors' being directed to one of the persons present: smiling at, vocalizing to, laughing or giggling in interaction with, touching, requesting to be picked up by, fussing to, or reaching to. $O$ continually reported the distance between the child and the four persons (Mother [$M$], Father [$F$], $V$, $O$) and noted when the infant was being held by one of them. When the infants were being held, $O$ noted whether there was any positive (reflected in the display of one of the social behaviors, listed above, or by jiggling or bouncing happily) or negative (reflected by fussing or stiffening) response. While $O$ was dictating, a timer was automatically marking on the tape the passage of each 15-second time period. The detailed accounts were subsequently transcribed by a typist, and the transcripts were thoroughly checked against the tapes for their accuracy before being analyzed.

The data reported in the first section of this paper were derived from those portions of the visits when $V$, $O$, $M$, and $F$ were all present in the same room as the child. With this restriction applied, there were on average 122.25 minutes of observation for each child. A trained coder tabulated each instance of the attachment behaviors, noting to whom the behavior was directed, and whether the infant was in proximity (within 3 feet [0.9m]) of the person concerned. In addition, in each 15-second unit, it was noted whether the child was within proximity of any of the persons. "Being within proximity" was also considered an attachment behavior. Each time the infant was reported to have moved from a distance of more than 3 feet of a person to within proximity, an *approach* was scored.

The definitions of smiling, vocalizing (all nondistress utterances other than giggling or laughing) and laughing require little explanation, but several of the coding and observational conventions should be noted. First, since I was interested in the voluntary social behavior of the infants, *touching* was not scored during holding, unless the infant made attempts to extend contact, for example, by pulling the person's hair. Second, since touching often accompanied *reaching*, reaching was not coded unless the infant failed to touch the person. This convention makes the two mutually exclusive and thus independent measures. In a similar attempt to ensure independence of measures, *looking* was coded differently, depending on whether the infant merely looked or also smiled or vocalized to the person (i.e., in all cases of smiling or vocalization, looking also occurred). *Looking* in this report refers to instances where the infant merely looked at the person concerned.

*A request* by the infant *to be picked up* was usually manifested by fussing, reaching to, vocalizing, or clinging to the person concerned, and thus the measure is not independent of these others, although it did not correlate with any of them. Judgments about the infant's desire to be picked up were often aided by the parents' interpretations and responses.

*Fussing* to a person was coded only when the infant clearly directed its distress calls to that person. If an episode of fussing or crying occurred, it was coded only once, regardless of duration.

For the analysis reported in the second section, a trained coder searched the transcripts for each occurrence of physical contact or play with mother ($M$), father ($F$), or visitor ($V$). *Physical contact* was defined as the contact implicit in the infant's being held—the infant had to be raised off the ground and supported by the adult. *Play* interactions were difficult to define concisely. They were the occasions when the adult engaged in interaction with the infant or attempted to stimulate the infant, other than by simply vocalizing, smiling, or engaging in caretaking activities. Since episodes of both play and physical contact often extended across brief separations from the other parent, or began when one parent was not present, it was decided that the analysis should be based on the entire transcripts rather than solely on those periods when both parents were present throughout the interaction.

Having defined the instances of *physical contact,* the coder then noted
(1) by whom the infant was held; (2) the duration of the hold, measured
by the number of 15-second units over which the hold continued; (3) the
nature of the infant's response; and (4) the purpose of the hold.

The nature of the infant's response was rated on a 7-point scale, with
each point behaviorally defined. The points were as follows: 1 point—
very negative (cry, fuss, or squirm to be put down); 2—negative (stiffen);
3—neutral (no observable positive or negative response); 4—content (sink
in, cuddle); 5—mildly positive (smile, vocalize, or stop fussing); 6—
positive (scramble, squeal with delight); 7—very positive (laugh, jiggle,
bounce). If the response was mixed (both positive and negative), the two
extreme scores were averaged.[1]

The purpose of the hold was classified as being either for *caretaking*
(transport to or from changing, feeding, or bathing; being held for feeding;
etc.); *discipline/control* (carrying the infant away from forbidden activities); *play* (picking the infant up to engage it in play); *affection* (picking
the infant up simply to cuddle, kiss, or hug, etc.); *soothing* (picking up the
infant when it is distressed for the purpose of comforting it); and *other*
(all holds that could not be categorized in any of the previous five
categories).

Having defined each instance of *play,* the coder then noted (1) with
whom the interaction took place; (2) the duration of the play episode;
(3) the nature of the infant's response; and (4) the type of play activity.
An initial attempt to distinguish play initiated by the infant from that
initiated by the adult proved fruitless; almost all play interactions were
initiated by the adult.

The nature of the infant's response was rated on a 7-point scale, with
each point behaviorally defined. The scale was as follows: 1—very negative (fuss, cry); 2—negative (fuss-face); 3—neutral (no positive or negative response); 4—content (happy face, participation in the play); 5—
mildly positive (smile, vocalize); 6—positive (squeal, protest termina-
tion); 7—highly positive (laugh, jiggle, bounce). If the response was
mixed (both positive and negative) the two extreme scores were averaged.[2]

The play activity was classified as one of the following types: *conventional* (peek-a-boo; pat-a-cake, so-big); *physical* (rough-and-tumble type,
usually involving holding the infant off the ground); *minor physical* (e.g.,

---

[1] In fact mixed responses of this nature were rare, and so this procedure was seldom
necessary. Only 7.5% of the 397 instances of physical contact were so classified:
8.1% of the mothers' holds, 6.2% of the fathers', and 8.8% of the visitors'.

[2] Again such mixed responses were rarely observed. A mere 2.1% of the 708 instances
of play were so classified: 2.6% of the play bouts with mother, 2.4% of those with
father, and 1.5% of those with the visitor.

tickling, pretending to nibble the infant); *toy mediated* (using a toy or other physical object to mediate the interaction); and *idiosyncratic* (all those activities that could not be classified in the previous categories).

## Reliability

It was difficult to assess the reliability of the observations made by *O,* since the use of two observers in the home was deemed likely to disrupt the natural flow of interaction in most families.

Consequently the reliability was computed by recruiting an additional group of infants who were observed solely for the purpose of establishing the reliability of the observer's dictation, as well as by arranging for additional visits to the homes of several of the infants in the study.[3] On these visits the Observer and an assistant dictated parallel but independent accounts of the child's behavior and its interaction with the parents and another female assistant who accompanied the observers. The observers tried to position themselves as inconspicuously as possible and attempted to be far enough removed from one another so as not to overhear the other's dictation. This meant that their perspectives were usually different, increasing the probability of disagreement. The infants observed ranged in age from 7 to 24 months, but since the reliability of the observations was the same for all ages, they are combined for clarity of presentation. When the transcripts were coded in the manner described above, there was a high degree of agreement between the two observers, ranging from .75 (smiling and looking) to .93 (proximity). On average 80% of the time that a behavior was reported by one observer, it was also reported by the other.

In addition arrangements were made to observe seven of the mother–father–infant triads in a laboratory playroom, in the course of computing reliability estimates for other ongoing projects. Two observers, one of whom had never before seen the infants, were thus able to simultaneously observe and dictate independent accounts of the interactions from behind one-way mirrors. Physical contact did not occur frequently enough to permit the quantification of observer reliability, but in other respects, the descriptions by the two observers of the baby's play activity and attachment behavior were nearly identical. Agreement on the frequency of all behaviors except smiling was above .90 in each category (that is, 90% of the time that one observer reported an attachment behavior, it was also reported by the other observer). *O* consistently reported more smiling to

[3] These visits are still being made as the longitudinal projects proceed. At the time of writing a total of seven such visits had been made.

both parents than observer 2 did, because the window from which he observed each time afforded a better view of the children's faces when they were facing their parents. Agreement with respect to smiling was thus only .75.

All the transcripts were coded by one of the three persons working on the data analysis for the longitudinal projects. All coders trained on these and similar transcripts until agreement averaging 90% across all categories was achieved. During the coding, transcripts were periodically recoded by another coder, in situations such that neither coder knew that reliability was being assessed. Reliability in the tabulation of the social behaviors remained above 90%—that is, on 90% of the occasions that a behavior was coded by one person, it was also noted by the other. With respect to the play and physical contact interaction, the inter-coder agreement was above .85 in all coding categories.

In all cases the reliability of the coding and of the observations was equivalent for the mother-, father-, and visitor–infant interaction.

## RESULTS

### Attachment and Affiliative Behaviors

For all analyses reported in this section the scores for each infant were converted to rates per minute. This equalized the contribution of each infant to the group data and normalized the distribution of scores, so that transformations were not necessary.

A comparison of the data obtained at the two ages (7 and 8 months) showed no significant changes over time, either in the preferences or in the rate of display of the attachment behaviors to any of the adults. Consequently the data from the two visits were combined for the analyses reported in this chapter. The mean frequencies for the combined visits are displayed on Table 1.

A repeated-measures multivariate analysis of variance (MANOVA)[4]

[4] Multivariate Analysis of Variance (MANOVA) procedures attempt to achieve a maximum differentiation of groups in a multidimensional space. MANOVA proceeds by finding the successive orthogonal axes along which the groups' centroids are maximally distant. In maximizing the distance between the group centroids, the individual dependent variables are "weighted" in such a way that measures on which the groups are well differentiated account for a greater proportion of multidimensional variance than those measures on which the groups are poorly differentiated. The statistical algorithms have three implications for psychologists applying them.

First, because MANOVA actively seeks significant differentiation, it is a powerful

Table 1.    Mean Rates per Minute of Display of Attachment and
Affiliative Behaviors

| Behavior | Mother | Father | Visitor |
|---|---|---|---|
| Smiles | 0.140 | 0.276 | 0.220 |
| Vocalizes | 0.052 | 0.108 | 0.064 |
| Looks | 0.868 | 1.240 | 1.196 |
| Laughs | 0.040 | 0.092 | 0.056 |
| Approaches | 0.036 | 0.036 | 0.040 |
| Proximity[a] | 1.912 | 1.640 | 1.884 |
| Reaches to | 0.020 | 0.040 | 0.020 |
| Touches | 0.116 | 0.156 | 0.064 |
| Seeks to be held | 0.016 | 0.008 | 0.000 |
| Fusses to | 0.036 | 0.032 | 0.004 |

[a] Excluding time when the infants were being held.

using the rates of smiling, vocalizing, looking, laughing, touching, fussing, reaching, seeking to be held, approaching, and proximity (adjusted for the time that the infants were being held) as variables was computed to assess whether there was a consistent preference for any person. The results showed a significant preference for the fathers over the other two persons ($p<.001$, $p<.014$ for the two roots). Further MANOVAs comparing mothers with fathers, mothers with the visitor, and fathers with the visitor showed that the fathers were preferred to the mothers ($p<.05$) and to the visitor ($p<.05$), and the mothers were preferred to the visitor ($p<.01$). The MANOVAs were also significant when seeking to be held was not included as a measure, because of its nonindependence.

---

statistical procedure. By searching for axes on which the groups are most distant from one another, the procedures capitalize on the intergroup variance that exists.

Second, the weights are "derived" for their statistical properties, rather than for their psychological significance. Since multiple measures of psychological phenomena are seldom equally veridical or adequate, the researcher may have his/her own conception of the importance that would be attached to individual measures in determining psychological significance. This subjective "weighting" may not correspond to the statistically derived weights, though the degree of disparity may vary. It is the researcher's responsibility to consider this factor in the evaluation of results.

Third, if three groups are compared in pairs for statistical differentiation, centroids A and B and centroids B and C may be a significant distance apart from one another in the multidimensional space (A>B, B>C), without this implying that centroids A and C are significantly differentiated (A>C) because the weights computed and applied in each paired comparison will differ. Consequently apparent intransitivities and nonlinearities can, and do, occur.

Most of the multivariate and univariate analyses were computed by using the MANOVA program developed by the University of North Carolina Psychometric Laboratory (Cramer, 1967). The theoretical foundation of multivariate statistics is explained by Bock (1975), Harris (1975), and Morrison (1967).

All comparisons were then repeated using separate MANOVAs for the affiliative and attachment behavioral systems and these results are presented on Table 2. The results of the mother–visitor and father–visitor comparisons were unequivocal. Affiliative behaviors (smiling, looking, vocalizing, and laughing) were not directed significantly more often to either parent than to the visitor. Univariate analyses of variance (ANOVAs) showed only that infants vocalized more often to their fathers than to the visitor ($p<.05$), but both looked ($p<.01$) and smiled ($p<.10$) at the visitor more often than at their mothers. In all, though, these affiliative measures do not reveal clear-cut preferences for the parents over a relative stranger.

However, the attachment behaviors considered together in MANOVAs provided evidence of strong parental preferences. The preference for the fathers was significant by MANOVA ($p<.01$), as were several of the univariate tests as well—specifically, touching ($p<.01$), fussing to (p< .01), and reaching ($p<.10$). Likewise the multivariate preference for the mothers over the visitor was also unambiguous ($p<.001$). Infants fussed to ($p<.001$), sought to be held by ($p<.01$), and touched ($p<.10$) their mothers more often.

Whereas these data lend support to the hypothesis that preference for significant adults would most likely be expressed in the differential display of the attachment rather than the affiliative behaviors, major interest was in the mother–father comparison. The affiliative behaviors were directed toward fathers far more often than to mothers ($p<.005$). Univariate tests showed that smiling ($p<.012$), vocalizing ($p<.001$), looking ($p<.005$), and laughing ($p<.055$) all occurred more often in interaction with fathers.

A MANOVA of the attachment behaviors produced results that were far more ambiguous, however. Though significant differentiation of the centroids ($p<.05$) was achieved, and an overall preference for the fathers was indicated, only one of the variables even approached significance in individual tests (reaching, $p<.10$).[5] For this reason, and because there was such variability among the measures (some showing nonsignificant preferences for mothers, others for fathers), it seems misleading to conclude that fathers are superior attachment figures on the basis of these results. The measures cannot be considered equally adequate indices of a desire for proximity or contact. Reaching, the measure weighted most

[5] The standardized discriminant function coefficients in this analysis were such as to weight more heavily reaching—a variable showing preference for the fathers—while weighting negatively requests to be picked up and proximity—two measures showing nonsignificant preferences for the mothers.

heavily in the MANOVA, is a more equivocal index of proximity seeking than wishing to be picked up, fussing, or touching—none of which showed preferences for either parent. Thus I think it most parsimonious to conclude, not that infants are "more attached" to their fathers than to their mothers, but rather than they are attached to both parents. There is certainly no evidence to support the hypothesis that infants of this age show significant preferences for their mothers.

On Tables 2 and 3 are displayed the patterns of infant preferences for the three adults. As noted above, it is clear that discrimination of the visitor is most marked on the attachment measures—those related to close physical contact and the desire for it. The indices of the affiliative system showed fewer and less consistent preferences for the parents. Between the parents the attachment system indices show no preference for either parent, although distal or affiliative interaction is much more common with fathers.

Table 2. Patterns of Preferences in the Display of Attachment and Affiliative Behaviors

| Behavior | $M$ vs. $F$ | $F$ vs. $V$ | $M$ vs. $V$ |
|---|---|---|---|
| Vocalizes | $F>M$*** | $F>V$* | – |
| Smiles | $F>M$* | – | $V>M$+ |
| Looks | $F>M$** | – | $V>M$** |
| Laughs | $F>M$+ | – | – |
| Approaches | – | – | – |
| Proximity[a] | – | – | – |
| Reaches | $F>M$+ | $F>V$+ | – |
| Touches | – | $F>V$** | $M>V$+ |
| Seeks to be held | – | – | $M>V$** |
| Fusses to | – | $F>V$** | $M>V$*** |

[a] Excluding time when the infants were held.
+ $p<.10$
* $p<.05$
** $p<.01$
*** $p<.001$

Table 3. Patterns of Preferences Within the Two Behavior Systems

| System | $M$ vs. $F$ | $F$ vs. $V$ | $V$ vs. $M$ |
|---|---|---|---|
| Affiliative | $F>M$*** | – | – |
| Attachment | $F>M$* | $F>V$** | $M>V$**** |
| All Measures | $F>M$* | $F>V$* | $M>V$** |

* $p<.05$
** $p<.01$
*** $p<.005$
**** $p<.001$

## Sex and Social Class Differences

There were fewer significant and near-significant sex and social class differences than one would expect by chance.

## Play Interactions

Overall there was neither a great number of play episodes nor a greater amount of time spent in play with fathers than with mothers, but the average response to play with fathers was significantly more positive than to play with mothers ($\bar{X}_F = 4.9$; $\bar{X}_M = 4.4$; $p < .05$).[6] Similarly, although fathers did not play for a significantly greater amount of time nor engage in more frequent play sequences than the visitor, the average duration of each ($\bar{X}_F = 3.0$; $\bar{X}_V = 2.3$; $p < .05$) and the average response ($\bar{X}_V = 4.1$; $p < .01$) were greater in the father–infant interactions. However, although the visitor initiated play more often than the mothers ($p < .05$), she did not spend more time in play than they did, and the average response to each play bid by her was somewhat less positive than by the mothers ($p < .10$).

More importantly there were differences in the types of play initiated by the two parents. Fathers tended to initiate a greater number of *physical* ($p < .10$) and *idiosyncratic* ($p < .05$) games. Figure 1 displays more clearly the differences and similarities between the character of mother–infant and father-infant play.

On the other hand the visitor differed from both parents, particularly in her greater reliance on *toy-mediated* play than either the mothers ($p < .001$ for number; $p < .05$ for duration), or the fathers ($p < .001$ for number; $p < .05$ for duration), and her tendency to initiate more *conventional* play than either parent ($p < .10$). Both mothers ($p < .05$ for number; $p < .01$ for duration) and fathers ($p < .01$ for number; $p < .05$ for duration) engaged in more *idiosyncratic* play than the visitor, and the fathers engaged in more *physical* play than she did ($p < .05$ for number; $p < .01$ for duration).

## Sex Differences

Mothers showed a tendency ($p < .10$) to initiate more play with daughters than with sons ($\bar{X}_g = 12.3$; $\bar{X}_b = 6.8$), and fathers and the visitor did not initiate more play with children of either sex. There were no sex differences in the responses to play bids by the adults.

---

[6] All comparisons in this section and the next were computed by using matched (dependent) t-tests.

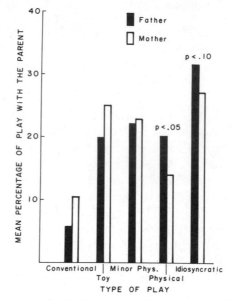

**Figure 1.** The percentage, for both parents, of the total number of play episodes, classified by type of play.

Within individual categories the only significant finding was that mothers initiated more ($p<.05$) and spent more time in ($p<.05$) *conventional* play with girls than with boys, though the girls were not more positively responsive to this play with their mothers. They responded more positively than boys, however, to *conventional* play with the visitor ($p<.05$) and *toy-mediated* play with their fathers ($p<.01$).

## Social Class Differences

There were fewer significant social class differences (the 10 families in Classes I and II compared with the 10 in Classes III and IV) than one would expect by chance. This suggests that, at least with very young infants, parents of different socioeconomic status play with their children in essentially the same manner and to the same extent.

## Physical Contact

Although infants did not seek to be picked up more frequently by their mothers than by their fathers, mothers held the infants far more often ($p<.01$) and for far longer ($p<.05$) than fathers did. However, the average response to physical contact was significantly more positive with fathers than with mothers ($\overline{X}_F = 3.9$; $\overline{X}_M = 3.4$; $p < .05$). The reason for this may lie in the fact that *caretaking* ($p < .01$ for number; $p < .05$ for duration) and *discipline/control* ($p < .05$ for number; $p < .05$ for duration) holds were much more common with the mothers, whereas a much greater portion of the time during which the infants were held by their fathers was for the purpose of play ($p < .001$). Presumably then, the more positive response to being held by fathers reflected the fact that fathers often picked up infants to play whereas mothers typically picked up infants to perform caretaking functions. When *play* holds are excluded, there is no difference between the responses to mothers and fathers ($p > .50$). Figure 2 presents the frequency of the different types of physical contact with mothers and fathers.

Since the visitor attempted not to interfere with caretaking routines, it is not surprising, and of relatively little importance, that the infants were held significantly more often and significantly longer by the mothers, overall ($p < .001$) and for all purposes ($.001 < p$'s $< .057$) except *play*. Fathers also held the infants more often and for longer than the visitor overall ($p < .001$) and for *discipline/control, caretaking, soothing,* and

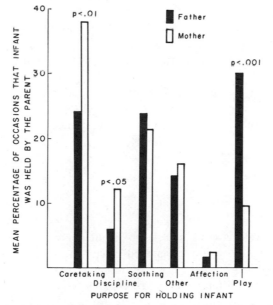

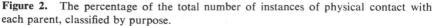

**Figure 2.** The percentage of the total number of instances of physical contact with each parent, classified by purpose.

*play* $(.001 < p\text{'s} < .045)$. The average response to being held by the visitor did not, however, differ significantly from the average response to either the mothers or the fathers, either over all categories combined or within individual categories.

## Sex Differences

Boys were held longer than girls by their fathers $(\overline{X}_b = 60.6; \overline{X}_g = 32.7; p < .05)$ and mothers $(\overline{X}_b = 83.4; \overline{X}_g = 48.2; p < .10)$, though the duration of each hold tended to be longer with both mothers $(p < .05)$ and fathers $(p < .05)$. A large proportion of this physical contact was for *soothing*, which tended to account for more of the time boys were held by their mothers or fathers than girls $(p < .10)$. Although these *soothing* holds did not occur more frequently with boys, each such hold by the mothers lasted longer on average $(p < .05)$ than with girls, who tended to respond more positively to these holds $(p < .10)$. Boys tended $(p < .10)$ to respond more positively to *other* holds by mothers than girls did, but overall there was no sex differences in the responsiveness to physical contact.

## Social Class Differences

There were few class differences. The 10 infants from families ranked as either Class I or II were held more often by their fathers for *caretaking* purposes than were children from Class III and IV families $(\overline{X}_u = 2.3; \overline{X}_l = 0.9; p < .01)$. There was also a tendency $(p < .10)$ for "upper class" infants to be held for *other* purposes for a greater amount of time by the visitor.

Thus the data suggest that fathers from "upper class" families may participate more extensively in caretaking activities but otherwise indicate that the amount of physical contact and the response to it is uniform across social class.

## DISCUSSION

The results presented in this chapter provide clear support for the belief that fathers as well as mothers are important persons in the lives of their infants. Both parents were "preferred" over the visitor, and what was most interesting in this regard was that the measures that were most important in this discrimination were those—seeking to be picked up, fussing to, reaching to, and touching—that clearly relate to close physical contact and the desire for it. This is in agreement with the findings of Tracy, Lamb, and Ainsworth (1974, 1976), who also reported that the clearest indication of discrimination between mothers and an unfamiliar visitor/observer was to be found in measures similar to these.

These measures showed a discrimination of the visitor from both parents in the present study and yet did not discriminate between the two parents. Although fathers were preferred to mothers over all measures, our analysis showed that the preference was accounted for largely by vastly more affiliative interaction with fathers, whereas on the measures related to close physical contact and distress no preference was demonstrated. If one distinguishes between the attachment and affiliative systems, as proposed by Bretherton (1974) and Bretherton and Ainsworth (1974), the results indicate that, on those measures that are most clearly related to the attachment behavioral system, the parents are not differentiated, but on those measures that may be better indices of the affiliative system, the fathers are preferred to the mothers. Thus, at least in the context in which these families were observed, there is an indication that infants relate to mothers and fathers in different ways. Infants appear to relate to their mothers mainly as attachment figures (sources of security), whereas the fathers are not only attachment figures quite as satisfactory as the mothers but also are the focus of more frequent distal affiliative behaviors as well. At least in part, this may relate to differences in the types of interaction that the parents initiate.

Further evidence that mothers and fathers assume different roles in relation to their infants is apparent in the analysis of the play and physical contact. Whereas the fathers did not play more often with the infants than the mothers did, the type of play in which they engaged differed. The fathers were more likely to engage in idiosyncratic and rough-and-tumble types of play, and it may be because of the greater variety and unpredictability of the play with the fathers that the response to play with them was more positive than with the mothers. Similar reasons may account for the fact that the response to play with both parents was more positive than with the visitor, whose play was clearly more stereotyped.

The analysis of physical-contact interaction yields additional information regarding the manner in which the mothers and fathers may be differentiated in the eyes of their infants. The mothers held the infants far more than the fathers did, but this was usually for caretaking or controlling the infant's activities. They seldom picked up or held the infants for play, whereas infants were held by their fathers most often for this purpose. It was this that accounted for the fact that the response to physical contact with the fathers was more positive than with the mothers.

In sum these results certainly suggest that to regard fathers as occasional mother substitutes is to disregard the fact that there are substantial and, I believe, important differences in the character of mother–infant and father–infant interaction (Lamb, 1975). The results suggest that, when both parents are present, fathers are more salient persons than mothers: They are more likely to engage in unusual and more enjoyable types of play and, hence, appear to maintain the infants' attention more than the mothers do. Nevertheless the role of father as playmate does not appear to prevent his being seen as an attachment figure as well; indeed he is apparently seen in this role as often as mother (at least at the times when the observations were made; it is conceivable that, at other times of the day, this would not be true). Unfortunately the present study does not permit us to determine to what extent the father–infant interaction observed was supported by the presence of the mother; in her absence, would the father–infant interaction have been the same? We intend to focus further attention on this question.

Kotelchuck (1972) and Spelke et al. (1973) did not find preference for the mothers in infants of 12 months of age and above, but they were unsuccessful in their attempts to investigate preferences in children younger than this. In general our results do not support the conclusion of most previous research that mothers were preferred to fathers by infants of 10 to 16 months of age (Cohen & Campos, 1974; Lewis et al., 1972). Besides the fact that our subjects were younger than theirs, there are several other differences in research strategy. These researchers observed their subjects in laboratory settings, and there is evidence that infants behave differently in such situations (Lamb, 1976). Lewis et al. (1972) observed the infants with each parent separately and recorded only four behaviors. Cohen and Campos (1974) used a design that required interruptions of the infant's activity every minute. Further both studies requested parents not to initiate interaction, whereas the parents in our study were encouraged to behave as they would normally. Given this number of differences, it is not possible to account for the different conclusions reached without further research. I believe, however, that the results of my study reinforce the belief that fathers are indeed salient persons in the lives of their infants and that there is a great deal of interaction between fathers and infants. Furthermore there is evidence that the characters of mother–infant and father–infant interaction differ substantially. Future research must focus on the specification of these differences, attempt a determination of whether they are evident in other ecological settings than that observed in this study, and, perhaps most importantly, determine whether the differences bear any consistent relationship to the roles of mother and father insofar as these are relevant to the socialization of the child.

There is another issue that is of increasing social relevance but that I was unable to address directly in this study—namely, the adoption of parental roles. In all but one of the families observed, the primary care-taker was the mother. Certain of the analyses—for example, that of physical contact—reflect the identification of the mother with caretaking functions, and it is impossible to avoid wondering whether the patterns of interaction might not have been different if the fathers had played a substantial, or perhaps primary, role in caretaking. As the cultural presumption that the female parent should automatically assume the primary nurturant role comes under scrutiny (even if deviations are rare), it becomes necessary to ask whether there would be any adverse or advantageous effects of being cared for primarily by the male parent. We cannot yet give an answer to this question. Within the traditional nuclear family, though, it seems that both parents are affectively salient, that the relationships with them differ in their character, and that the interaction differs with respect to both context and content. If we are to understand sociopersonality development, then, we can no longer afford to examine only the mother–child relationship but must appreciate the complexity and multidimensionality of the infant's social world.

# REFERENCES

Ainsworth, M. D. Patterns of attachment behavior shown by the infant in interaction with his mother. *Merrill-Palmer Quarterly*, 1964, **10**, 51–58.

Ainsworth, M. D. *Infancy in Uganda*. Baltimore: The Johns Hopkins University Press, 1967.

Ainsworth, M. D. Object relations, dependency and attachment: A theoretical review of the infant–mother relationship. *Child Development*, 1969, **40**, 969–1025.

Ainsworth, M. D. The development of infant–mother attachment. In B. M. Caldwell & H. N. Ricciuti (Eds.), *Review of child development research III*. Chicago: University of Chicago Press, 1973.

Ainsworth, M. D., Bell, S. M., Blehar, M. C., & Main, M. B. Physical contact: A study of infant responsiveness and its relation to maternal handling. Paper presented to the biennial meeting of the Society for Research in Child Development, Minneapolis, April 1971.

Ainsworth, M. D., Bell, S. M., & Stayton, D. J. Individual differences in the development of some attachment behaviors. *Merrill-Palmer Quarterly*, 1972, **18**, 123–143.

Bock, D. *Multivariate statistical methods in behavioral research*. New York: McGraw-Hill, 1975.

Bowlby, J. *Maternal care and mental health*. Geneva: WHO, 1952.

Bowlby, J. The nature of the child's tie to his mother. *International Journal of Psychoanalysis*, 1958, **39**, 350–373.

Bowlby, J. *Attachment and loss* (Vol. 1). *Attachment.* New York: Basic Books, 1969.

Bretherton, I. Making friends with one-year-olds: An experimental study of infant–stranger interaction. Unpublished doctoral dissertation, The Johns Hopkins University, 1974.

Bretherton, I., & Ainsworth, M. D. Responses of one-year-olds to a stranger in a strange situation. In M. Lewis & L. A. Rosenblum (Eds.), *The origins of fear.* New York: Wiley, 1974.

Cohen, L. J., & Campos, J. J. Father, mother, and stranger as elicitors of attachment behaviors in infancy. *Developmental Psychology*, 1974, **10**, 146–154.

Cramer, E. M. *Revised MANOVA program.* Chapel Hill, N.C.: Psychometric Laboratory, University of North Carolina at Chapel Hill, 1967.

Freud, S. [*An outline of psychoanalysis.*] New York: Norton, 1949. (Originally published, 1940.)

Harris, R. J. *A primer of multivariate statistics.* New York: Academic, 1975.

Hollingshead, A. B. The two-factor index of social position. Unpublished manuscript, 1957 (Available from A. B. Hollingshead, Department of Sociology, Yale University, New Haven, Connecticut 06520).

Kotelchuck, M. The nature of the child's tie to his father. Unpublished doctoral dissertation, Harvard University, 1972.

Lamb, M. E. A defense of the concept of attachment. *Human Development,* 1974, **17**, 376–385.

Lamb, M. E. Fathers: Forgotten contributors to child development. *Human Development,* 1975, **18**, 245–266.

Lamb, M. E. Proximity-seeking attachment behaviors: A critical review of the literature. *Genetic Psychology Monographs*, 1976, **93**, 63–89.

Lester, B. M., Kotelchuck, M., Spelke, E., Sellers, J. J., & Klein, R. E. Separation protest in Guatemalan infants: Cross-cultural and cognitive findings. *Developmental Psychology*, 1974, **10**, 79–85.

Lewis, M., Weinraub, M., & Ban, P. Mothers and fathers, girls and boys: Attachment behavior in the first two years of life. Educational Testing Service Research Bulletin (Princeton, N.J.), 1972.

Morrison, D. F. *Multivariate statistical methods.* New York: McGraw-Hill, 1967.

Nash, J. The father in contemporary culture and current psychological literature. *Child Development*, 1965, **36**, 261–297.

Ross, G., Kagan, J., Zelazo, P., & Kotelchuck, M. Separation protest in infants in home and laboratory. *Developmental Psychology*, 1975, **11**, 256–257.

Schaffer, H. R., & Emerson, P. E. The development of social attachments in infancy. *Monographs of the Society for Research in Child Development,* 1964, **29** (Serial No. 94).

Spelke, E., Zelazo, P., Kagan, J., & Kotelchuck, M. Father interaction and separation protest. *Developmental Psychology*, 1973, **9**, 83–90.

Sutton-Smith, B., & Rosenberg, B. *The sibling*. New York: Holt, Rinehart & Winston, 1970.

Tracy, R. L., Lamb, M. E., & Ainsworth, M. D. Locomotor proximity seeking in the first year of life as related to attachment. Paper presented to the Southeastern Society for Research in Child Development, Chapel Hill, N.C., March 1974.

Tracy, R. L., Lamb, M. E., & Ainsworth, M. D. Infant approach behavior as related to attachment. *Child Development*, 1976, **47**, in press.

Yarrow, L. J. (Chmn.) Parents and infants: An interactive network. Symposium presented at the Annual Convention of the American Psychological Association, New Orleans, August 1974.

Yarrow, L. J., & Pederson, F. Attachment: Its origins and course. *Young Children*, 1972, 302–312.

# CHAPTER 10

# The Infant's Relationship to the Father: Experimental Evidence

MILTON KOTELCHUCK

*University of Massachusetts—Boston*

The influence of the father on the infant's early social development has been virtually ignored by developmental psychologists. There have been almost no studies directly observing fathers and their young children interacting. This lack of research with fathers has not, however, stopped theorists from commenting about him. The popular prejudice (e.g., Gorer, 1948) is that, because fathers are not at home during the day and childrearing falls primarily on the mother, they are unimportant during the child's early years.

Indeed psychologists have tried to reify the concept of the mother– infant bond by developing a scientific rationalization for what is really the status quo in childrearing practices today. It is argued that children "innately" and "uniquely" relate only to their mothers and that they have no natural ties to their fathers. Bowlby (1969), for example, declares infants to be monotropically matricentric in orientation, meaning simply that the child has a propensity for going toward one person (monotropic) and that the person that the child has a propensity to relate to is the mother (matricentric). To Bowlby and other psychologists this bond is biologically rooted; it is instinctual and inbuilt. By implication the father–infant relationship must be of lesser importance, if it exists at all. These beliefs are, however, lodged in speculation.

What hard evidence is there to support the notion that children relate uniquely to their mothers? Here psychologists have a definitive answer: There is no evidence whatsoever. It has always been merely assumed that children have a natural preference for their mothers.

Until recently fathers had been studied only in their absence (e.g.,

Biller, 1970), a situation analogous to studying the effects of gravity by observing objects after they have fallen. The typical design makes the dubious assumption that father-present families minus father-absent families equal the role of the father. The father-absence literature has severe methodological problems, principally that the entire family structure changes when the father leaves, and, hence, any developmental differences cannot be attributed solely to the absence of the father (e.g., Lynn & Sawrey, 1959).

Why study the importance of the father–infant relationship by looking at the father's absence? It makes more sense to assess directly the influence of the father's presence on the child's early social development. The assumption of limited paternal importance could be directly tested by comparing the infant's response to its mother with the infant's response to its father. Starting in 1972 this author (1972) and subsequently a series of other researchers (e.g., Cohen & Campos, 1974; Lamb, 1975 and Chapter 9; and Lewis, Weinraub, & Ban, 1972) began directly studying father–infant interaction. This chapter is an effort to summarize the findings of one group of these studies.

A direct assessment of the infant–father relationship is not a difficult experimental task. It merely requires that one ignore the cultural assumption of the father's unimportance and bring him into an experimental situation and watch his interaction. To this end a semistructured attachment paradigm was developed. The aim was to examine the child's behavior in an unfamiliar playroom as a function of the presence or absence of its mother, father, or an unfamiliar female. This design emphasizes the infant's spontaneous reactions to the three adults, and not adult-initiated interaction with the infant. It is structured to allow for a direct comparison of the infant's responses to the mother, the father, and the stranger.

One important difference from other previous attachment studies was the inclusion of the father in the design. Most other experimentalists have looked only at the mother and the stranger (e.g., Ainsworth & Bell, 1970; Fleener & Cairns, 1970; Rheingold, 1969). Indeed, these studies generally show that children relate extensively and exclusively to the mother; children cried when the mother left, stayed close to her, and interacted with her, while ignoring the unfamiliar stranger. These results very logically, but incorrectly, led to the conclusion that little children have a "special" relationship to their mothers. Only by introducing a second familiar person into such a design, as in the present design, can one address the question of exclusive preference.

The experiment begins with the infant located in the center of a large playroom (24 ft. × 21 ft.) surrounded by toys and facing the parents, who were seated at one end of the room. The parents have been instructed not to initiate interaction with the child but to sit quietly and read. They are to respond naturally, but briefly, if the child approaches them or if the child is upset. It is emphasized to the parents that the child's spontaneous reactions to the situation were of primary interest. The strangers have similar instructions. Every three minutes one of the adults is signaled either to enter or depart from the room, according to one of the following schedules.

Each schedule is composed of 13 episodes. Each episode lasts 3 minutes or 39 minutes in total. Half the children follow the first schedule, in which the father departs first, and half the second, in which the mother departs first. For either schedule, a parallel set of events occurs for each of the three adults (e.g., the mother leaves the room twice, once with the father remaining and once with the stranger remaining; the father leaves twice, once with the mother remaining and once with the stranger remaining; the stranger leaves twice, once with mother remaining and once with father remaining; the mother enters twice, once with the father present and once with the stranger present, and so forth). These balanced schedules allow for an unconfounded comparison of the child's response to each of the three adults. The duration of the child's playing, crying, proximity to a person, touching a person, proximity to the door, vocalizations, smiles, fixations, and interactions are coded minute by minute throughout the 39-minute session. Data from similar conditions are pooled to determine the extent to which the infants behaved differentially toward the mother, father, and stranger.

There were four studies in this series using this design (Kotelchuck, 1972; Lester, Kotelchuck, Spelke, Sellers & Klein, 1974; Ross, Kagan, Zelazo, & Kotelchuck, 1975; Spelke, Zelazo, Kagan, & Kotelchuck, 1973).

**Table 1.   Order of Presence in the Experimental Room**

| Episode | Order 1 | Order 2 |
|---|---|---|
| 1 | Mother and father | Mother and father |
| 2 | Mother | Father |
| 3 | Mother and stranger | Father and stranger |
| 4 | Stranger | Stranger |
| 5 | Stranger and father | Stranger and mother |
| 6 | Father | Mother |
| 7 | Father and mother | Mother and father |
| 8 | Father | Mother |
| 9 | Father and stranger | Mother and stranger |
| 10 | Stranger | Stranger |
| 11 | Stranger and mother | Stranger and father |
| 12 | Mother | Father |
| 13 | Mother and father | Father and mother |

In total about 300 children were used, ranging in age from 6 to 24 months. Most of the studies used middle-class, firstborn children in the Boston area. For this chapter, only the first but largest of the studies is examined in detail ($N = 144$, with 12 boys and 12 girls at each of 6, 9, 12, 15, 18, and 21 months of age). The other results are mentioned only to supplement and expand on the findings from the first investigation.

The results from all four studies clearly indicate that infants and toddlers relate to their fathers. Contrary to the beliefs of Bowlby and others, there appears to be no unique mother–child bond; children are not monotropically matricentric.

An examination of Figures 1 to 4 from Kotelchuck (1972) indicates that children protest the departures of both parents, but not the stranger's. It can be seen in Figure 1 that boys and girls decrease play when both the mother and father leave the room but increase play when the stranger departs ($F[2,240] = 74.09$, $p < .001$). The change score was determined by subtracting the amount of play for the 3 minutes before departure from the 3 minutes following departure. These graphs combine both sexes and both experimental orders, and hence each age represents 24 children. The difference between the child's response to the departures of the mother and of the stranger or to the departures of the father and of the stranger were highly significant. This is a qualitative, as well as quantitative difference. The differences between the mother and father were significant only at 12 and 18 months.

As can be seen, separation protest follows a curvilinear pattern; 6- and 9-month-old children did not protest the departure of any person. The first significant reaction to separation occurred at 12 months. Children's play diminished following the departure of the mother at 12 months compared to either 6 or 9 months, and there was less play following the mother's departure than following the stranger's departure at 12 months. The departure of the father produced a marked reduction in play for the first time at 15 months ($15 > 9$ months), and there was less play following the fathers' departures than following the strangers' departures. From 15 months onward, there were highly significant differences in the child's play behavior following the departures of both the mother and father compared to the stranger's. As Figure 1 indicates, disruption of play following departures of either parent was greatest at 18 months ($18 > 6$, 9, 12, 15 months, $p < .01$) and then lessened at 21 months ($21 < 18$, $p < .01$), reflecting an abatement of separation distress. There were no sex or experimental order differences in separation protest.

Other measures show similar patterns. Figure 2 indicates that the infants increase crying following departures of both parents ($F[2,240] = 32.12$, $p < .001$) and decrease crying after the stranger departures. How-

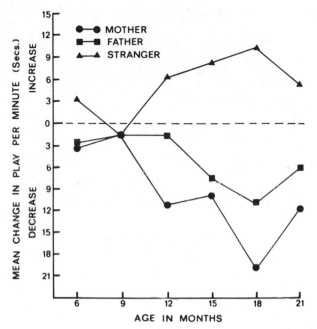

**Figure 1.** Mean change in duration of play following departure of each adult as a function of age of infant.

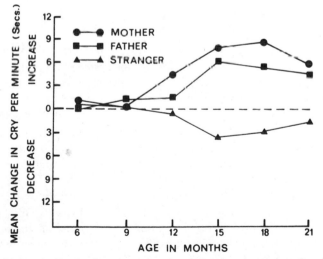

**Figure 2.** Mean change in duration of crying following departure of each adult as a function of age of infant.

333

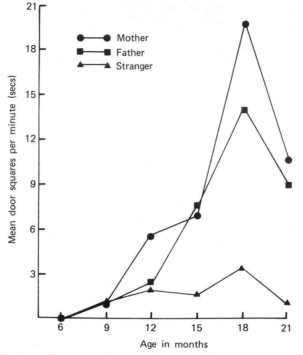

**Figure 3.**   Mean duration in proximity to the door following departure of each adult as a function of age of infant.

ever, this effect first reached statistical significance at 15 months for both parents. There were no mother–father differences. Similarly Figure 3 shows that children more often followed their parents to the door and were more likely to remain there following their departures than they were following the strangers' departures $(F[2,240] = 35.17, \ p < .001)$. Approaching the door commenced at 12 months, increased rapidly to a maximum at 18 months, and then declined somewhat at 21 months $(18 > 15, 21, \ p. < .01)$ for both parents. Again there is clear similarity of response to the mother and father.

The arrival of the parents was often a stressful period; children did not immediately return to playing but often continued crying and would frequently cling to their parents for extensive periods of time. Figure 4 shows that, upon reunion, children would cling to both their mothers and fathers and avoid the stranger $(F[2,240] = 52.71, \ p < .001)$. From 12 months of age, clinging was extensive though it declined with age as the children needed less and less comfort before play resumed.

Duration of touching was typical of all interactive measures; strangers

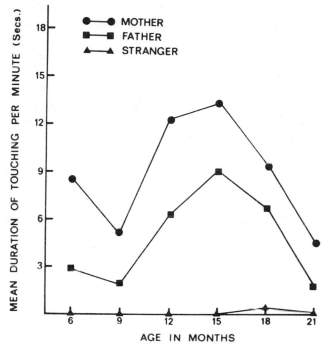

**Figure 4.** Mean duration of touching each adult upon arrival into the playroom as a function of age of infant.

were almost totally avoided, and both the mother and the father served extensively as bases of security and interaction for the child. Children, starting at 12 months, remained proximal, initiated interaction, smiled, and vocalized extensively to both the mother and the father and markedly avoided the stranger. These positive measures of parent–child relationships remained stable across ages and episodes and did not show the decline characteristic of the separation measures.

The previous figures reveal a high degree of similarity in the child's response to the mother and the father, in sharp contrast to the response to the stranger in the laboratory situation. The departures of both mothers and fathers are upsetting to the children; the departures of the strangers were greeted positively. Children extensively interacted with both their mothers and fathers and almost totally avoided the strangers.

The extent to which the children were content with either parent and the similarity of response to their departures and arrivals threaten the argument that the mother–child relationship is distinctively different from the father–child relationship. This is not to say that there were no differences, but the child's response to the father more closely resembled the child's response to its mother than the response to the stranger. The few mother–father differences that occurred in the analyses did not fit a discernible pattern. There is little evidence for the suggestion that there are important differences between the child's relationship to its mother and father.

These findings have not only occurred in laboratory situations but have also been replicated in the home situations (Ross et al., 1975) and cross-culturally in Guatemala (Lester et al., 1974). Children relate in basically the same way to mothers and fathers; early infant social behaviors are directed similarly toward both parents. In sum what these four studies show is that, when a second familiar person is introduced into the structured laboratory situation, the supposed uniqueness of the infant–mother bond seems to disappear. The infants do not spontaneously show a unique behavioral response to the mother but respond similarly to fathers and mothers.

Although no single measure can define a relationship, practically any

Table 2.  Number of Children in Parental Proximity on Arrival Greater than 15 Seconds

| Age in Months | None | Mother Only | Father Only | Both Mother and Father |
|---|---|---|---|---|
| 6 | 13 | 3 | 2 | 6 |
| 9 | 6 | 6 | 5 | 7 |
| 12 | 1 | 7 | 1 | 15 |
| 15 | 1 | 5 | 1 | 17 |
| 18 | 0 | 4 | 1 | 19 |
| 21 | 2 | 3 | 2 | 17 |

Table 3.  Mother–Father Difference in Duration Proximity When Both Parents Present

| Age in Months | Mother Greater than Father | Mother Equals Father | Father Greater than Mother |
|---|---|---|---|
| 6 | 9 | 14 | 1 |
| 9 | 9 | 9 | 6 |
| 12 | 14 | 6 | 4 |
| 15 | 13 | 3 | 8 |
| 18 | 12 | 5 | 7 |
| 21 | 11 | 5 | 8 |

measure examined reveals more mother–father similarities than differences. If, for example, one examines the number of children who spent at least 15 seconds near a person on arrival (Table 2), it is clear that, from 12 months onward, the majority of children, of their own initiative, stayed close to both their mothers and their father. Children who showed solitary relationships were in the minority. Whereas most of these children related only to their mothers, a few infants at every age responded only to their fathers. Pooling the number of children who are responsive to either of their parents on this and five other measures, one can approximate (albeit tentatively) the number of relationships the child has: 61% of the children, 12 to 21 months of age, showed relationships with both their mothers and fathers; 23% had only maternal relationships; 9% had only paternal relationships; and 7% showed no relationships. More than 70% of the children in this study were responsive to their father's presence. The modest mother–father differences seen in the previous graphs may be a reflection of the lesser number of children showing paternal than maternal relationships.

Although most children related to both parents, it remains reasonable to ask which is the principal or preferred relationship. Preference can be determined by examining whether the child's response to his mother or to his father is greater. For example, if one examines the duration of proximity to the mother and father in episodes where both parents are present, that is, the episodes where both parents are in the playroom and the child has a choice of whom to go to (Table 3), no clear-cut pattern of preference emerged before 12 months. From 12 months onward, the majority of children showed a maternal preference, but a surprisingly high percentage of children demonstrated equal or paternal preference. Other measures show a similar pattern.

Although the exact number of children who prefer mothers or fathers varies, depending on the measure chosen, approximately 55% of the 12- to 21-month-old children showed maternal preferences, 20% joint preferences, and 25% paternal preferences. Thus present data strongly imply that a monotropic, matricentric model of early infant interpersonal preference is simplistic.

The percentage of children relating to mothers and fathers and the percentage of children showing maternal or paternal preferences in the present experimental design agree remarkably well with the findings of Schaffer and Emerson's (1964) maternal interview study. They interviewed 60 Scottish mothers every 2 weeks from birth to 12 months and again at 18 months. Schaffer and Emerson independently estimated that 80% of 18-month-old infants are attached to their fathers (compared with 70% from the Kotelchuck, 1972, study) and that 51% of the 18-

month-old infants showed maternal preferences, 19% paternal preferences, and 16% joint preferences (compared to 55%, 25%, and 20%, respectively, from the Kotelchuck, 1972, study).

## HOME CARETAKING AND INTERACTION CORRELATES OF FATHER–INFANT BEHAVIOR

Since infants can clearly relate to their fathers, one can ask what parameters influence the development and depth of their relationships. In this section, I will explore tentatively the influences of the amount of paternal caretaking and interactions with his child at home on the child's laboratory behavior.

In all four experiments, maternal and paternal home caretaking and interaction data were obtained from a joint interview with the mother and the father following the completion of the experimental session. The interview sought to determine who took care of the child, who changed the child's diapers, who fed the child, how long each parent played with the child, and so forth. (It is recognized that parental reports have limitations and are somewhat unreliable; consequently these data should be thought of as hypothesis-generating rather than as definitive.)

I had expected that the supposedly changing role of the father in our society would be reflected in their child-care practices; this was not the case. The traditional observation that mothers take care of their children and fathers take minimal responsibility for childrearing were confirmed in these studies. In the Kotelchuck (1972) study in a middle-class Boston sample, mothers had principal childrearing responsibilities. Mothers were present for more time with the children than the fathers were, 9.0 versus 3.2 hours ($p<.001$), and were available essentially for the child's whole waking day. Mothers spent more time feeding than the fathers, 1.45 hours versus 0.25 hour ($p<.001$), and spent more time than fathers cleaning the child, .92 hour versus .15 hour ($p<.001$).

The distribution of the caretaking responsibility dramatizes the extensiveness of maternal caretaking in a middle-class sample. Of the mothers, 64% were totally and solely responsible for the child care; 9.1% shared caretaking responsibility jointly with another person. Only 7.6% of the fathers shared infant-caretaking responsibilities equally with their wives, and only 25% had any regular daily caretaking responsibilities. In other words 75% of middle-class fathers in Boston did not physically care for their children on a regular day-to-day basis. Even more remarkably, 43% of all the fathers reported they never changed diapers at all!

Mothers spent more absolute time in play with their children than the fathers did, 2.3 to 1.2 hours ($p<.01$), a difference that is statistically significant but that showed the least mother–father difference of any home variable. These data reveal that fathers were involved only in a minimal amount of the child's care, especially those tasks of childrearing that are often viewed as routine and somewhat boring. Fathers spent, however, a greater percentage of time (37.5%) in enjoyable play activities with the child than mothers did (25.8%). The exact consequence of the differences in proportion of play to total time spent with the child is unclear, but it appears reasonable to suggest that the amount of play contributes to the father's attractiveness to his child despite his restricted availability.

Given the consistently minimal participation of fathers in caretaking at home and the fact that most children related to their fathers in the laboratory situation, it should not be surprising that there is little direct relationship between these two sets of data. Crude amount of caretaking or playing is not the critical variable in determining with whom the child is comfortable or to whom the child relates. In all the studies infants and toddlers relate similarly to their mothers and fathers, irrespective of the vast differences in mother–infant and father–infant caretaking and interaction. There is no simple 1:1 relationship between home caretaking and laboratory behavior.

Yet there is evidence that paternal caretaking practices make a difference. Four additional findings have emerged from the various studies. First, there is a minimum level of paternal caretaking necessary for a relationship to exist. In the original study (Kotelchuck, 1972), those few children who did not relate to their fathers (operationally defined as infants who did not spend at least 15 seconds in his proximity on his arrival) came overwhelmingly from families with the lowest caretaking fathers ($\chi^2 = 7.9$, $p<.01$).

In the replication in Guatemala (Lester et al, 1974), where Guatemalan men have almost nothing to do with their young infants and, hence, father interaction with young infants is virtually nonexistent, children responded differently to their fathers than they did in the United States.

As can be seen in Figures 5 and 6, compared to Figures 1 and 2, Guatemalan children related to fathers less than with the mothers but more than with the strangers. In Guatemala, where paternal caretaking is extremely low, it does make a difference in the children's behavior. These findings are similar to Biller's (1974) findings that children in families with the father absent or very inaccessible seemed behaviorally similar. Perhaps some minimal level of interaction is necessary for a child to be basically comfortable with a person.

Second, the children's preferences and the extensiveness of their interaction with fathers in the laboratory are partially related to paternal care-

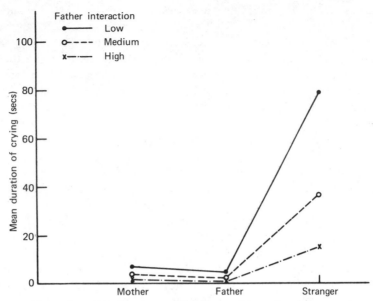

**Figure 5.** Mean duration of crying while alone with each adult as a function of level of interaction with father. Copyright (1973) by the American Psychological Association. Reprinted by permission.

taking at home. Significant positive correlations are found between overall proximity to the father and extent of his caretaking, in the Kotelchuck (1972) study ($r=.35$, $p<.01$) and in the Ross et. al. (1975) study ($r=.43$, $p<.01$). The highest home caretaking-laboratory behavior intercorrelation was found in the Ross et. al. (1975) study; ($r=.51$, $p<.01$) between paternal proximity in the joint mother–father-present episodes (1, 7, 13) (i.e., episodes in which the child has a choice of which parent to go to) and the number of diapers changed by the father per week!

Third, the age span of intense separation protest is shortened for the infant in families with multiple caretakers. More simply, infants with two parents who actively take care of them tend to show separation protest later and terminate it earlier than children with only a single maternal caretaker do. This incidental finding from the original study was clearly demonstrated in the study of Spelke et al. (1973), in which we systematically stratified and selected our sample ($N=36$) into three groups of high-, medium-, or low-interacting fathers on the basis of an extensive interview before the standard experimental situation.

As Figure 7 shows, the group of children responded to the separation episodes differently for the play ($F[4, 60]=2.68$) and the cry ($F[4, 60]=3.32$) measures. It can be seen clearly from the results that children who

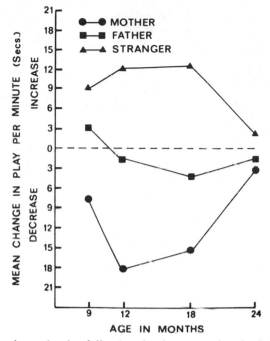

**Figure 6.**   Mean change in play following the departure of each adult (Guatemala).
Copyright (1974) by the American Psychological Association. Reprinted by permission.

are not cared for by their fathers (those cared for by their mothers only)
show extensive distress and protest in the laboratory situation when left
alone. Children whose fathers are active caretakers (those children with two
active caretaking parents) tend to find the experiment an enjoyable play session and are not distressed when left alone with strangers. Babies whose
fathers were in the intermediate group responded with an intermediate level
of distress and enjoyment. Since protest usually commences by 12 months,
it can be argued that high paternal caretaking slows the onset of protest in
their children. Consistent with this hypothesis is the observation gleaned
from the original study that, at 21 months of age, when protest normally sub-
sides, many infants in the high paternal caretaking families are distressed,
but those in the low paternal, exclusive maternal, caretaking families display protest. Thus the age span of protest when left alone appears shorter
for infants with extensive paternal caretaking.

Fourth, there were virtually no sex differences in any of the studies.
Boys and girls responded similarly to the experimental manipulations;
they did not respond differentially to their parents.

An interesting sex difference did emerge in reports of the fathers' interaction with the infants. In the Boston area fathers of firstborn children

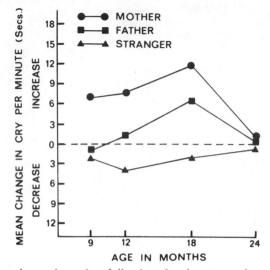

**Figure 7.** Mean change in crying following the departure of each adult (Guatemala). Copyright (1974) by the American Psychological Association. Reprinted by permission.

report that they play about half an hour a day longer with their firstborn sons than with their firstborn daughters $(p<.01)$. What the long-term effect of this will be is not clear. At 21 months of age, however, the oldest age looked at in the original study, boys played more and interacted more with their fathers than with their mothers. Early specific sex by parent interactions did not appear significant in the statistical analyses, although it is possible that the effects begin to be manifested only at older ages, such as 21 months of age.

Overall the findings that have emerged from an examination of the home–laboratory correlates from the four studies demonstrate that the level of paternal caregiving has a direct effect on how children interact with their fathers in a laboratory situation. The long-term effects of having fathers care for their infants have yet to be explored. It is hoped that, in the near future, there will be many studies delineating his effect on the child's later sex-role development, aggression, cognitive style, and a host of other behaviors.

## CONCLUSION

This chapter started by asking this question: Is it true that infants relate uniquely to their mothers? It is hoped that the experimental evidence presented in this chapter has convinced the reader that children can and do form active and close relationships with their fathers during the first 2 years of life. Children do not innately and instinctively relate only to their mothers. The presumed uniqueness of the mother–child relationship is ephemeral. The child's response to either parent in experimental situations is clearly more a function of the nature of the parent–child interaction than of a predisposed biological disposition.

# REFERENCES

Ainsworth, M., & Bell, S. Attachment, exploration, and separation: Illustrated by the behavior of one-year-olds in a strange situation. *Child Development*, 1970, **41**, 49–67.

Biller, H. Father absence and the personality development of the male child. *Developmental Psychology*, 1970, **2**, 181–201.

Biller, H. The mother–child relationship and the father–absent boys' personality development. *Merrill Palmer Quarterly*, 1971, **17**, 227–241.

Biller, H. B. *Paternal deprivation: Family, school, sexuality, and society.* Lexington: Heath, 1974.

Bowlby, J. *Attachment and loss* (Vol. 1). *Attachment.* New York: Basic Books, 1969.

Cohen, L. J., & Campos, J. J. Father, mother, and stranger as elicitors of attachment behaviors in infancy. *Developmental Psychology*, 1974, **10**, 146–154.

Fleener, D., & Cairns, R. Attachment behaviors in human infants: Discriminative vocalizations on maternal separation. *Developmental Psychology*, 1970, **2**, 215–223.

Gorer, G. *The American People: A Study of National Character.* New York: Norton, 1948.

Kotelchuck, M. The nature of the child's tie to his father. Unpublished doctoral dissertation, Harvard University, 1972.

Lamb, M. E. Fathers: Forgotten contributors to child development. *Human Development*, 1975, **18**, 245–266.

Lester, B. M., Kotelchuck, M., Spelke, E., Sellers, J. J., & Klein, R. E. Separation protest in Guatemalan infants: Cross-cultural and cognitive findings. *Developmental Psychology*, 1974, **10**, 79–85.

Lewis, M., Weinraub, M., & Ban, P. Mothers and fathers, girls and boys: Attachment behavior in the first two years of life. *Educational Testing Service Research Bulletin* (Princeton, N.J.), 1972.

Lynn, D., & Sawrey, W. The effects of father absence on Norwegian boys and girls. *Journal of Abnormal and Social Psychology*, 1959, **59**, 258–262.

Rheingold, H. The effects of a strange environment on the behavior of infants. In B. M. Foss (Ed.), *Determinants of Infant Behavior, IV*. New York: Barnes and Noble, 1969.

Ross, G., Kagan, J., Zelazo, P., & Kotelchuck, M. Separation protest in infants in home and laboratory. *Developmental Psychology*, 1975, **11**, 256–257.

Schaffer, H. R., & Emerson, P. E. The development of social attachments in infancy. *Monographs of the Society for Research in Child Development*, 1964, **29** (Serial No. 94.)

Spelke, E., Zelazo, P., Kagan, J., & Kotelchuck, M. Father interaction and separation protest. *Developmental Psychology*, 1973, **9**, 83–90.

# CHAPTER 11

# Adult Male-Infant Interactions in Nonhuman Primates

WILLIAM K. REDICAN

*Department of Psychobiology and Physiology*
*Stanford Research Institute*

So salient is the role of the mother in caring for dependent young among human and many nonhuman animals that an entire class of animals (Mammalia) is named after one of her life-giving functions. Indeed, *mama* is a word for "breast" used by groups as distant as Egyptians and Australian aborigines (Potter & Sargent, 1973).

The mother has been traditionally a focus of attention for ethologists and animal behaviorists. Explanations for this development are not difficult to devise. Among nonhuman primates, for example, the roles of the mother in sustaining the life of dependent neonates are directly evident through activities such as nursing, transport, restraint, retrieval, and protection. By contrast the relationships of immature animals to adult males are often indirect or at least difficult to observe or quantify. Generally speaking, close nurturant relationships between adult males and infants are relatively rare among nonhuman primates, but as we shall see, this generalization encounters prominent exceptions in certain groups.

Another factor that may have contributed to the relative neglect of male–infant interaction in nonhuman primates is largely a matter of historical circumstance. Groups that are most accessible and that have been studied most intensely—such as rhesus monkeys, baboons, and chimpanzees—also happen to show relatively infrequent male care of immature

The writing of this article was supported by NIH grant number HD04905, awarded by the National Institute of Child Health and Human Development, PHS/DHEW. I thank Dan Cubicciotti, Joel Kaplan, and Ron Schusterman for critically reading the manuscript.

**345**

animals. One would do well, then, in considering the pattern of this or of any other behavioral trait throughout groups of animals, to bear in mind that some groups have been much more extensively studied than others. Thus, if male caretaking activity has only rarely been reported for a particular species, it does not necessarily follow that there is a relatively lesser degree of this activity in that species than in others unless all species involved have been observed for approximately equal durations. *Caveat lector.*

The objectives for this paper are to present a reasonably comprehensive but far from exhaustive overview of behavioral interactions between adult male and immature nonhuman primates. An attempt is made to convey the basic dimensions of these relationships in a variety of species and to integrate some principles of sociobiology that may help account for observed patterns. Brief excursions dealing with birds and mammals other than primates are made to provide some perspective where appropriate.

The general organization of the paper is based on patterns of group organization, because fairly consistent relationships between parental caretaking activity and group organization are to be found. An alternative strategy is to arrange the material along taxonomic lines, proceeding species by species through the primate order. That approach offers clarity and expediency but does not readily demonstrate principles that transcend taxonomic lines. For reviews of various extents using this sort of organization, the reader is referred to papers by Hinde (1971), Mitchell (1969), Redican (1975), and Spencer-Booth (1970). A second alternative is to organize along degrees or types of male–infant interaction. (See, for example, papers by Mitchell & Brandt, 1972; and Raphael, 1969.) This approach was not employed in the present undertaking, because I have repeatedly been taught the lesson that it is wiser to let nature demonstrate Her or His own organization than to devise one by human conceptual criteria. An important review has also been presented recently by Blaffer Hrdy (1976).

Before proceeding any further, definitions of several terms are in order. An important one is *paternal.* The *Oxford English Dictionary* includes the following definitions of the term:

1. Of or belonging to a father or to fathers; characteristic of a father: fatherly;
2. Inherited or derived from a father; related through a father or on the father's side.

Since *father* is clearly central to the above, and indeed is cognate with (i.e., derived from the same root as) paternal, its definitions are included here:

1. One by whom a child is or has been begotten, a male parent, the nearest male ancestor. Rarely applied to animals.
2. = STEPFATHER. Now commonly regarded as a misuse.

In promiscuous, multimale social groups it is generally not possible to establish father–infant geneological relationships. Thus, both *paternal* and *father* are unacceptable terms for the behaviors in question unless kinship is clearly established.

The term *paternalistic* might be proposed as an acceptable alternative. It refers to paternalism, which has two meanings:

1. The principle and practice of paternal administration; government as by a father; the claim or attempt to supply the needs or to regulate the life of a nation or community in the same way as a father does those of his children.
2. The principle of acting in a way like that of a father towards his children.

Although one might accept the use of *paternalistic* on the basis of the second definition, the inclusion of the specific father–infant relationship in the definition makes the use of the term problematic in referring to promiscuous groups.

Deag and Crook (1971) used a terminology that both eliminates the problems associated with the terms considered thus far and provides a basis for uniformity. They described two types of interactions involving adult males and younger animals: (1) "male care," which includes activities such as holding, grooming, carrying, and protecting a neonate or infant by an adult male; and (2) "agonistic buffering," which is a more specialized term referring to the use of a neonate by an adult in regulating relationships with other individuals (usually other adult males).

The terms *male care* or *male parental care* are adopted in most cases in this chapter since they are free of geneological connotations, they have wide applicability, they are likely to be acceptable to researchers in various disciplines, and a set of corresponding terms (e.g., *female care* or *female parental care*) is available. These terms are here considered to be subsets of the class of behaviors referred to as "parental investment," defined by Trivers (1972), for example, as "any investment by the parent in an individual offspring that increases the offspring's chance of surviving (and hence reproductive success) at the cost of the parent's ability to invest in other offspring" (p. 139). As such, parental investment includes the metabolic investment in producing sex cells and any behavioral investment that benefits the young. It excludes efforts to find a mate or to compete with others for access to a mate.

For those readers with limited acquaintance with primate taxonomy and group organization, a brief survey of principal features may be helpful. There are two major divisions (suborders) of the primate order: prosimians ("before apes") and anthropoids ("like human beings"). Prosimians are small, nocturnal, and predominantly arboreal forms found in Asia and Africa. They have retained the sensory characteristics of "primitive" mammals, such as prominent sense of smell, scent glands, and claws and paws (instead of nails and hands) in some cases. Since information on prosimian behavior is still fragmentary, and they are distantly related to *Homo sapiens*, they will not be included in the present survey.

The remaining suborder, Anthropoidea, consists of three superfamilies: (1) New World monkeys, (2) Old World monkeys, and (3) apes and humans. New World monkeys are found only in South and Central America, where they have evolved from New World prosimians independently of other monkeys since the Eocene. New World monkeys are thus not ancestral to Old World monkeys, and any similarities between the two groups came about through parallel evolution. New World monkeys are all strictly arboreal and only one genus is nocturnal. Old World monkeys are found in Asia, Africa, and Europe (where a captive colony of Barbary macaques was established by the British on Gibraltar). They are a large and diverse group, occupying an extreme diversity of habitats (ranging from the foothills of the Himalayas to Ethiopian semideserts). Most are semiterrestrial. There are four principal groups of apes: gibbons and closely related siamangs, orang utans, gorillas, and chimpanzees. All are tailless, relatively large forms found in Asia and Africa. Their considerable cognitive capacities are well known. Forms of social organization of apes encompass a predominantly solitary one (orang utans), monogamous family units (gibbons and siamangs), and mixed groups (gorillas and chimpanzees). For more detailed information, the reader is referred to works by Chance and C. J. Jolly (1970), Eisenberg, Muckenhirn, and Rudran (1972), A. Jolly (1972), and Napier and Napier (1967).

## MONOGAMOUS GROUPS

A relatively small number of nonhuman primates live in monogamous family units. These units are composed of an adult male and female mated primarily for life, together with infants, young juveniles, and only occasionally one or two other adults. This form of social organization is seen in several New World monkeys, and gibbon and siamang apes.

Male care of infants is seen in marmosets and tamarins (New World monkeys) to perhaps the greatest extent among nonhuman primates (see Fig. 1). These groups are organized into the family units described above

**Figure 1.** A father pygmy marmoset (*Cebuella pygmaea*) carrying twin offspring. Pygmy marmosets are the smallest New World monkey and usually give birth to twins, unlike most primates (Napier & Napier, 1967). Twins are carried by the father until at least 6 weeks, transferring to the mother only for nursing (Ochs, 1964). (Photograph by Ron Garrison of the San Diego Zoo.)

(Snyder, 1974). Male marmosets (*Callithrix*) have been seen to assist during the births of infants, and they may premasticate food for infants during the first week. Males carry infants throughout the day, with the exception of nursing episodes every 2 to 3 hours, for the first 2 or 3 months of life. Males continue to carry young after weaning (Fitzgerald, 1935; Langford, 1963; Lucas, Hume, & Henderson Smith, 1927, 1937; Mallinson, 1971a; Stellar, 1960). Similar relationships have been seen in tamarins (*Saguinus* and *Leontideus*) (Hampton, 1964; Hampton, Hampton, & Landwehr, 1966; Mallinson, 1971b). Frequent father–infant contact is also seen in two other genera of New World monkeys: night monkeys (*Aotus*) and titi monkeys (*Callicebus*) (Mason, 1966; Moynihan, 1964).

It has been suggested that marmoset parents aggressively peripheralize offspring nearing maturity, so two adults of the same sex are not usually found within the same social group (Fitzgerald, 1935; Hampton et al., 1966; Epple, 1967). However, Rothe (1975) reported contrary findings, and recent field studies demonstrate that the peripheralization process may not be as widespread among marmosets and tamarins as had been believed. For example, both Neyman (in press and personal communication) and Dawson (in press), in the first major field studies of tamarins, observed several groups that included more than two mature adults. However, only one female and probably only one male were reproductively active in such groups (see also Epple, 1970, in press; Rothe, 1975).

The mature nonbreeding animals in free-ranging marmoset or tamarin groups may in fact be offspring of the resident bonded pair who remain into adulthood. Offspring have recently been seen to actively participate in caretaking of younger siblings, and this may form the basis of long-lasting associations. Hearn and Lunn (1975), for example, reported that the second set of offspring among their marmosets was carried largely by older siblings, who by then were approximately 6 months old. Similarly, Box (1975) found that adult male marmosets became progressively less involved in caretaking with successive sets of offspring.

Evidently the experience of interacting with or caring for younger siblings is necessary, at least among marmosets and tamarins, if juveniles are to develop into adults who display adequate parental caretaking. Adults lacking such experience do mate with each other and produce offspring, but they fail to adequately care for their progeny (Epple, 1975; Hearn and Lunn, 1975; Hoage, in press; Ingram, 1975). Thus, caretaking activities by siblings benefit not only the parents (by diminishing their caretaking burden) but the siblings as well (by preparing them for subsequent parental caretaking).

In general there is a striking association between monogamous social organization, an extensive investment of parental care by the male, and territoriality. In every genus of New World monkey in which there is pronounced male care (*Callithrix, Saguinus, Aotus, Cebuella,* and *Callicebus*), the social group consists of a monogamous pair (or pairs) and offspring of 1 or more years.[1] In every other genus of New World monkey

[1] There is insufficient evidence to conclude that *Leontideus* is or is not monogamous. It is said, however, to live in small groups (Forbes, 1897). Sufficient data are also unavailable for Goeldi's marmoset (*Callimico goeldii*). The situation is unclear for sakis, but there is some indication that adult males show interest in infants (Hanif, 1967).

the social group is polygamous. In at least four of the above genera that show pronounced male care, territoriality has also been documented. The converse does not necessarily apply, however, since some polygamous New World groups are also territorial (e.g., howler monkeys, *Alouatta*).

Before making sense of these patterns let us take a brief look at two of the smaller, arboreal apes: gibbons (*Hylobates*) and siamangs (*Symphalangus*). Both genera have a monogamous group organization and maintain virtually nonoverlapping territories (Carpenter, 1940; Chivers, 1971, 1972; Ellefson, 1968; McCann, 1933; McClure, 1964; Tenaza & Hamilton, 1971). Adult male gibbons in the wild have been observed to inspect and to groom neonates, and a male in a captive group of gibbons was seen to carry a small juvenile for the greater part of the day (Carpenter, 1940). As infant gibbons mature, they become more independent of their mothers and interact more frequently with their fathers (Berkson, 1966). As offspring near sexual maturity, however, they are threatened and aggressed by one or both parents until they eventually become peripheral to the natal group, and thus eventually establish additional monogamous units (Carpenter, 1940; Ellefson, 1968).

There is also extensive male–infant contact among siamangs. Chivers (1971, 1972) reported that infant siamangs are dependent on the mother for the first 12 to 16 months of life, but from that point onward they are carried by the father until independence is attained during the 3rd year of life. Siamang fathers groom and also sleep with juveniles, whereas mothers groom and sleep with infants. Maturing siamang offspring are also peripheralized from the natal group, but the process appears to be less severe than in the case of the gibbon (Chivers, 1971, 1972; Fox, 1972, 1974).

There are thus striking parallels between the three groups of monogamous primates examined in this review (marmosets and some other New World monkeys, gibbons, and siamangs). In addition to being monogamous, all three are also territorial, exhibit relatively frequent male parental care, and at least some engage in peripheralization of offspring nearing sexual maturity.

A useful concept in approaching the relationship between mating systems (e.g., monogamy) and parental investment (e.g., male care) is kinship selection. Mating systems in general can be categorized as follows. Monogamy ("one mate") is a situation in which one male and one female form a pair bond for varying intervals of time (a mating season to a lifetime). Polygamy ("many mates") is a generic term implying more than one mate in a single breeding season. Subcategories of polygamy are: (1) polygyny ("many women"), in which a given male mates with more than one female in a single breeding season; (2) polyandry ("many men"), in which a given female mates with more than one male in a single breeding season; and (3) promiscuity ("thoroughly mixed") or polybrachygamy ("many brief matings": Selander, 1972, p. 194), in which an individual mates with more than one other during a breeding period (i.e., both males and females have more than one mate). There are variations on these themes, to be sure. For example, Peter Scott (cited in Evans, 1974) reported that a male goose can form a lifetime monogamous bond with another male, but one of them may occasionally mate with a female. This ménage is apparently more successful in rearing offspring than male– female pairs, since the two males both protect the offspring. In the case of human beings, there is evidence of both monogamous and polygamous mating systems. Monogamous pair bonds (marriages) are clearly evident in many societies, and in a few they are regulated by mortal legal sanctions. Monogamous males and females are more nearly equal in size than polygamous animals, since they have relatively comparable social roles, and in the case of human beings, size dimorphism is no greater than that of many monogamous creatures. Neither are human males particularly more brightly colored than females, as is typically the case for polygynous and promiscuous species (see the discussion of polygamy, below). On the other hand many societies have institutionalized polygynous mating systems (e.g., harems [from Arabic *harama*, "he prohibited"]). Moreover, human males are ubiquitously reported to be more aggressive than females (Maccoby & Jacklin, 1974), a characteristic often seen in polygynous males competing with each other. In our society, at least, the advertisement of resources (e.g., hot rod/motorcycle/penthouse apartment) by males competing with each other for females can be likened to nonhuman mating systems in which male courtship displays precede polygynous copulation. Furthermore, although undecorated human males are not more conspicuously colored than females, as in the case of polygynous and promiscuous species, the presence of facial hair may function in intra-sexual aggressive displays much like bright coloration (see Hamilton, 1973).

Because it involves a far greater expenditure of energy to produce an ovum than a sperm cell, female gametes are the more limiting resource, and females are more likely to mate than males. It is to a male's evolutionary advantage to try to inseminate as many females as possible, since the expenditure of sperm involves such a relatively slight investment. A consequence of these contingencies is that animals are fundamentally polygamous (more specifically, polygynous), and hence monogamy is a derived state (Wilson, 1975, p. 327).

The concept of kin selection was first proposed by Darwin in *On the Origin of Species* (1859). As understood today, chiefly interpreted by Hamilton's (1964) important contributions, the concept suggests that the extent to which one animal is related to another is an important variable affecting the degree to which one will act to enhance the likelihood of survival of the other. In the long run individuals will take greater risks that increase the fitness of another if the latter is a close rather than distant relative. By behaving in such a way (e.g., protection) that the chances for survival of an offspring, for example, are increased, the individual is probably lowering its own fitness. This agent has, however, a genetic investment in the offspring, and if the shared genetic fitness of the agent plus offspring is increased in the next generation because of actions of the benefactor, such behavior will be selected for and flourish. In other words genes are selected that perpetuate themselves, and organisms are thus selected that aid closely related individuals. (For a helpful discussion of these and other concepts, the reader is referred to E. O. Wilson's *Sociobiology: The New Synthesis*, 1975, and Crook and Goss-Custard's review of social ethology, 1972.)

As applied to monogamous primates it is evident that young animals that a male protects and cares for are likely to be his own kin. Investments by the male in caretaking activity would tend to increase the probability that his genes would be propagated to subsequent generations. The involvement of both parents in caretaking activities probably makes twinning feasible in monogamous groups. In promiscuous groups adult males and immature animals vary in the extent of kinship relationships, and an investment in parental care may be of no evolutionary value to the adult male. One would thus expect to find less male parental investment in groups with promiscuous or polygynous mating systems. This is indeed the pattern that has been observed, but we are getting ahead of ourselves.

We have accounted, in a very brief way, for the relationship between relatively enhanced caretaking by males and monogamous mating systems. A question that remains is why territoriality is so often associated with these patterns. For an answer we first look to the birds, which as a group have been studied far more extensively than nonhuman primates. Male birds' involvement in the care of young is generally more extensive than male mammals' (Crook & Goss-Custard, 1972). As succinctly put by Orians (1969), "The physiology of mammalian reproduction dictates a minor role of the male in the care of the offspring, whereas among birds the only activity for which males are not equally adept as females is egg laying" (p. 596). Male birds collect food and nest material, find and defend a place for the female to lay eggs and to raise young, defend females, brood eggs, protect young, and provide learning opportunities for offspring (Trivers, 1972).

More than 90% of bird species are monogamous (most for a breeding season—some for life), and most monogamous species eat animal matter (e.g., insects) that is difficult for young to obtain themselves (Lack, 1968).

The evolution of monogamy is favored in those circumstances in which there is a relatively stable supply of food during mating seasons and where territories are defended. Territories ensure a food supply that is undisturbed and not chronically competed over, for both defendants and offspring. Where food is relatively low in nutrients (e.g., seeds, pulpy fruit, and nectar) and only present in seasonal abundance, mothers and offspring fend for themselves, males have little involvement in caretaking, and territories are not defended (Crook, 1964, 1965; Crook & Goss-Custard, 1972; Orians, 1969). As Horn (1968) demonstrated in his study of Brewer's blackbirds, when food is uniformly distributed in space and continually renewed in time, it is to a bird's advantage to defend whatever area that can be efficiently managed. In contrast, if food is unevenly distributed and sporadically renewed, the best strategy is to nest as a colony and forage in groups. Colonial grouping also provides enhanced protection against predators.

It would be shortsighted to suggest that the origins of mating systems and spatial behavior can be reduced simply to patterns of available resources. Other factors, such as predation, are of major importance. A male bird is unlikely to deliver food to mothers and/or offspring if predation pressure is great (Orians, 1969). He could conceivably attract predators to the nest, let alone risk his own life. As Wilson (1975) has suggested, "the territorial strategy evolved is the one that maximizes the increment of fitness due to extraction of energy from the defended area as compared with the loss of fitness due to the effort and perils of defense" (p. 269).

Parallels are evident in other groups of animals. Among mammals monogamy is most prevalent in terrestrial carnivores, for whom capturing high-energy food is a difficult task (Orians, 1969). Since many of them are thus at the top of the food chain, the need for wide dispersal is great, and one way of accomplishing this is through territoriality (Eisenberg, 1966, p. 52). In terms of parental caretaking, very complex forms of behavior have been observed in carnivores such as coyotes, wolves, jackals, hunting dogs, and foxes. They have been seen to bring food to pregnant females, to regurgitate food for young, to protect young and distract predators away from them, and to play with and transport young, and the fox has even been seen to "teach" the litter to hunt (Eisenberg, 1966).

To conclude this consideration of territoriality, let us return to nonhuman primates. Available data are not as complete, but there is evidence that the patterns observed in birds and carnivores may also apply to primates. In particular Gartlan and Brain (1968) reported that vervet monkeys in an area with abundant food resources had smaller, more clearly defined, and more strongly defended territories relative to conspecific groups in poor habitats.

# MULTIMALE, MULTIFEMALE GROUPS

A far more common form of social organization in nonhuman primates is one in which more than one mature male and more than one mature female, together with immature offspring, comprise the group. Most monkeys are organized in this pattern, and most are promiscuous.

Just as an understanding of kinship selection was important in the discussion of monogamy, some acquaintance with the concept of sexual selection is helpful in approaching polygamy. In 1871 Darwin described traits that offered no apparent survival benefits to individuals (e.g., colorful plumage, postures, and many displays). They did, however, confer advantages in terms of success in acquiring mates. Sexual selection is defined as a subset of natural selection and is described in terms of two components: (1) competition within one sex (usually the male) for access to mates of the opposite sex and (2) choice by members of one sex (usually female) of mates of the opposite sex. Sexual selection pressures brought about the evolution of secondary sexual characteristics such as horns, antlers, relatively large size, and aggressiveness that come into play during competition with members of one's own sex. In addition plumage characteristics and elaborate displays evolved to serve as means of attracting mates of the opposite sex.

As a consequence of sexual selection, therefore, many promiscuous monkeys in multimale, multifemale groups show pronounced sexual dimorphism in size, generally high levels of aggressiveness by males, and highly developed weaponry (e.g., canine teeth) in males. In general, relative to monogamous groups, there is a more pronounced differentiation of roles between males and females. Males are more energetic in activities such as vigilance, leadership, and protection of the group; females are more active in direct caretaking of offspring. In nonhuman primates, at least, the monogamous groups are without exception found in aboreal habitats, and polygamous ones in either arboreal, semiterrestrial, or terrestrial habitats.

Let us now consider several groups of Old World monkeys and apes. An emphasis is placed on macaques and baboons, about which most information is available.

## Rhesus Macaques

There is not a great deal of positive social interaction among adult males and infants in free-ranging groups of rhesus monkeys (*Macaca mulatta*). Adult rhesus males in North India, for example, have been described as "neutral or indifferent" toward infants and juveniles (Southwick, Beg, &

Siddiqi, 1965). Adult males frequently attack but only rarely associate peacefully with infants (Lindburg, 1971; Southwick et al., 1965). A male may pick up, bite, and throw an infant to the ground, especially while feeding. In the field study by Southwick et al. involving 762 hours of observation, on only three occasions were infants seen to play and associate peacefully with adult males for substantial lengths of time. Lindburg (1971) only twice saw males carry immature animals during 900 hours of observation. On only two occasions did he see play between adult males and infants. Lindburg did note that males occasionally defended infants from attack and males threatened nearby animals while sitting close to infants.

In Kaufmann's (1966) study of free-ranging rhesus monkeys in the island colony of Cayo Santiago, very similar types of interactions were observed. Adult males were never seen to approach infants. Infants several weeks of age, however, occasionally approached, contacted, and even climbed on males. On 76% of such occasions the males' response was to ignore, withdraw from, threaten, hit, or grab the infants. On the remaining 24% of those occasions, Kaufmann reported that the males held the infants gently in their arms.

Breuggeman (1973), who also studied the Cayo Santiago colony, found that age of caretaker and frequency of parental care were positively related. However, 3-year-old males also exhibited high levels of caretaking activity relative to other age groups of males. Males exhibited more frequent caretaking during the mating than during the birth season. In addition males showed more frequent care toward male than female young, and this difference was much more prominent in the mating season than in the birth season.

In summary, if one were to characterize adult males in their relations with infants in free-ranging rhesus groups, one would describe them as generally indifferent, somewhat sensitive to approach and contact, occasionally aggressive, and rarely affiliative.

Captive group-living adult males also tend to show relatively little interest in neonates (Rowell, Hinde, & Spencer-Booth, 1964). In a study of four species of captive macaques, Brandt, Irons, and Mitchell (1970) found that rhesus males showed the lowest total frequency of huddling, proximity, and passive contact with infants. Unlike Breuggeman's (1973) findings, in the studies of both Spencer-Booth (1968) and Brandt et al. (1970), younger males showed more interest in infants than fully mature adult males did. In the former study males 2 years older than the infants interacted most frequently with infants; in the latter study the ages of the young and fully adult males were not specified.

Interestingly, in Spencer-Booth and Hinde's (1967) colony at Madingley, when several mothers were removed from the group, there was an enhanced degree of male–infant interaction. One adult male frequently played with these infants, and other males sat with and carried them in a ventral-ventral position. (The ventrum is an animal's chest or stomach.) When Bucher (1970) removed the temporal neocortex of rhesus mothers in captive groups, caretaking behaviors such as retrieval were found to be impaired. The adult males in the groups became active in carrying, grooming, and playing with infants—a finding quite similar to Spencer-Booth and Hinde's.

Male care by adult rhesus males in a laboratory environment has received relatively little attention. M. K. Harlow, Suomi, and associates have established triadic ("nuclear family") social groups, each composed of a father, mother, and infant rhesus monkey (Harlow et al., in preparation; Suomi, 1972; Suomi et al., 1973). In social preference tests, infants raised in triads preferred their mothers to other adult females, their fathers to other adult males, and their mothers to their fathers. Fathers initiated few play sessions but responded to most of the infants' initiations, playing with male infants more frequently than with female infants. However, infants spent less than 5% of their time interacting with all adult males, including their fathers. (Infants were allowed access to members of other triads.) This was at a rate only slightly higher than that reported for free-ranging animals.

This writer recently completed a long-term laboratory study of male–infant interaction in wild-born rhesus monkeys (Redican, 1975), preliminary results of which were presented in papers by Redican and Mitchell (1973, 1974). Four pairs of fully mature male and infant rhesus monkeys were observed for 7 months, after which their responses to a 2-day period of separation were studied. Comparable data for a control group of four mother–infant pairs were available from studies by Baysinger, Brandt, and Mitchell (1972) and Brandt, Baysinger, and Mitchell (1972).

Mothers were found to be more consistently contact oriented toward infants than adult males were. Mother–infant pairs were in more frequent and longer contact (especially ventral contact), particularly during early months. Both mothers and their infants made contact as often as they broke it. In contrast adult males consistently broke contact more often than they established it, and the converse was true for their infants. Adult males restrained or retrieved infants extremely rarely but actively protected them by directly attacking the source of danger and/or interposing themselves between it and the infant. However, distress vocalizations and facial expressions were far more frequent in male-reared infants, and it was argued that they were aggressed to a greater extent than mother-reared infants were. Play between adult males and infants was far more intense and reciprocal than that between mothers and infants. Adult males were found to groom infants to the same extent as mothers did (see Fig. 2). There was evidence that measures of attachment increased over time in male–infant pairs, unlike previous reports for mother–infant pairs.

The magnitude of sex differences in many attachment behaviors was greater in male–infant pairs. For example, sex differences were not prominent in measures of mother–infant physical contact; where evident, there was more often greater contact with female infants. In adult male–infant pairs, sex differences in contact were more pronounced, and more extensive contact with male infants was observed. Mothers tended to play with female infants, whereas adult males did so with male infants. In general,

**Figure 2.**    An adult male rhesus monkey grooming a male infant. In the absence of mothers who actively restrict contact between infants and other animals, adult males and infants in dyads developed close filial attachments (Redican, 1975).

mothers interacted more positively with female infants, and adult males with male infants.

Infants responded to separation from mothers and adult males with comparable frequencies of distress vocalizations. During separation both groups of infants showed decreases in solitary play and exploration but increases in self-directed behaviors. It was inferred that mothers and adult males were comparably potent objects of attachment for infants, at least as measured by response to short-term separation. Mothers showed external signs of far greater distress at separation than adult males did, but as in previous studies these indications waned much more quickly than those of infants.

In general the results of the longitudinal and separation studies were interpreted as indicating a significant potential both for adult males to form attachments with infants and for infants to form attachments with adult males. Clearly the dimensions of parental caretaking reflect the opportunities available to the individual. In the absence of restrictive mothers, adult males were often seen to interact with infants in a highly affiliative manner very rarely observed in groups in the wild. If such an aggressive and inflexible creature as the rhesus monkey male is capable of such positive interactions with infants, there is reason to expect at least comparable potential in less sexually dimorphic, relatively monogamous, more flexible creatures such as *Homo sapiens*.

A similar study by Gomber (1975) compared male–infant interaction in isolate-reared adult males and the adult males described above. She found that deficits from early isolation were not as extensive as previous studies had suggested. The isolates were not hyperaggressive toward the infants and were capable of appropriately using communicative cues such as nonvocal expressions and gestures. In general isolate males showed less positive social behavior toward infants than wild-born males did, but the greatest differences were in nonsocial behaviors (e.g., self-directed activities). Gomber's principal conclusion was that

> The design of this study placed isolation-reared monkeys in a situation which minimized fear, disturbance, and socially disruptive behaviors, and maximized opportunities and stimuli for positive social interaction; under such conditions, the isolate males were capable of forming effective social relationships. The findings point to a need for re-evalution of certain commonly held conceptions about the social capabilities of isolation-reared monkeys (p. iii).

**Japanese Macaques**

One of the earliest instances in which attention was drawn to male care among Old World monkeys was Itani's (1959) study of Japanese monkeys

(*Macaca fuscata*) at Takasakiyama. Except for a lack of suckling, male care of infants was described as being similar to maternal care:

Males hug the infants, carry them on their loins, or accompany them when walking. They keep them from wandering away, and, when sitting, take them to their bosom or make them lie down just in front of their feet and groom them, or, sometimes, play with them for hours (p. 62).

Males also displayed the common macaque characteristic of defense of threatened infants. As Alexander (1970) found in a captive troop of this species, "Whenever a neonate has been handled by a human being . . . the dominant males have reacted with an intense rage and have attempted repeatedly to attack the human kidnapper" (p. 284). The extent of potential attachment between adult males and infants is illustrated by Kawai's (1960) observation that infants gathered around and played near the body of a troop leader for several days after the male's death.

In Itani's study male care was directed almost exclusively toward 1- and 2-year-old individuals (not neonates); yearlings accounted for 74% of such interactions. In contrast to Breuggeman's (1973) findings for rhesus monkeys, male care in Japanese macaques was seen only during the *birth* (not mating) season: "In the society of the wild Japanese Monkey [male care] . . . begins like the breaking of a dam" (Itani, 1959, p. 73). Male care thus appeared when mothers were devoting considerable energy and attention to their neonates. Adults showing male care were restricted to "leader" and "subleader" classes, approximately 20 and 15 years of age, respectively. Nearly all members of these classes engaged in male care.

## Bonnet Macaques

Observations of captive and wild bonnet macaques (*Macaca radiata*) suggest that adult males interact relatively frequently with immature troop members in an affiliative manner. In a laboratory colony in which the mothers had been experimentally removed, adult males became solicitous toward infants and cradled, carried, and held them on a number of occasions (Kaufman & Rosenblum, 1969).

In the groups studied in the wild by Simonds (1965, 1974) and Sugiyama (1971), play emerged as a prominent feature of social activity. Adult males played not only with infants and juveniles but with adults as well. Protection of infants was again an aspect of male–infant relations:

When the troop crossed the road or open land, one or several babies were sometimes left behind, as they were absorbed in play. Usually, on hearing the high-pitched screams of the babies, a mother or mothers went back to pick them up, but on a few occasions even mothers hesitated to go back from fear of passing close to the observers. On such occasions, young adult males . . . by themselves or leading the mothers, went back to the other side and returned to the troop carrying the babies on their backs or running with them (Sugiyama, 1971, p. 261).

In general, positive interactions between adult males and juveniles were more often observed than between adult males and infants. Sugiyama (1971) noted that juveniles gathered around adult males when the troop rested, and "Sometimes an adult male pulls a juvenile male close to him and holds him in his arms, and at other times juvenile males come to an adult male and cling to and embraced [sic] him" (p. 258). These types of interactions were not reported for infants. Simonds (1974) recently found that adult males consistently avoided contact with young infants with the coat color characteristic of neonates. Adult males interacted more frequently with infants as the latter's color changed, until by the infants' 6th week of age adult males and infants established regular contact. Juvenile females remained in close contact with their mothers and nearby females, whereas juvenile males turned toward play groups of older juveniles, subadults, and occasionally, adult males.

### Pigtail Macaques

Observations on male care of infants in pigtail macaques (*Macaca nemestrina*) are very limited. Kaufman and Rosenblum (1969) did not observe holding, carrying, or cradling of infants by adult males under any circumstances in any of their laboratory groups. However, when mothers were removed from one group, the adult male threatened animals that aggressed the infants and interposed himself between the infants and antagonists. No male care was directed specifically at the infants.

### Barbary Macaques

Among those species of macaque (if not Old World monkey) studied thus far, the Barbary macaque (*Macaca sylvana*) clearly shows the greatest degree of male caretaking activity (see Fig. 3). Deag and Crook (1971), studying free-ranging troops in Morocco, observed holding, grooming, carrying, and protecting of infants by adult males. For example, "Occasionally males invited babies [up to 6 months of age] to get onto their backs when the group was traversing difficult ground, or when a predator (dog or jackal) was attacking the group" (p. 171), an event that frequently occurred. Males were seen to have sole care of young infants for up to 20 minutes or more. A distinction can thus be made

**Figure 3.** An adult male Barbary macaque sitting with a young infant in the Middle Atlas Mountains of Morocco. This species was the subject of a recent field study by David M. Taub, University of California, Davis. The male assumes a posture that Taub considered to be structurally identical to that of a mother, with legs and arms forming a protective "bowl" around the infant. (Photographs courtesy of David M. Taub.)

between the pattern of male care in Barbary and Japanese macaques, insofar as males of the former species direct care toward neonates and infants, rather than exclusively toward yearlings and 2-year-olds.

Detailed observations have been made on the colony of Barbary macaques maintained at Gibraltar by the British army. Patterns of male care are generally similar to those found in Morocco. However, the Gibraltar groups were established with only one adult male in each, unlike the multimale groups in Africa. MacRoberts (1970) described retrieval and play behaviors involving adult males and infants. Burton and Bick (1972, p. 37) noted that leader and subadult males regularly held infants for "periods much exceeding 15 minutes."

Burton (1972) made a careful study of the socialization processes in the Gibraltar colony and distinguished four major roles of adult males in the socialization of immature conspecifics:

1. Adult males "encourage the infant to develop motor abilities that permit social interaction" (p. 55). For example, Burton observed the following extraordinary sequences:

> On four occasions, the . . . head male was the initiator of the infant's beginning to walk: he placed the animal on the ground, moving backward away from it to a distance of approximately two feet, lowering his head, looking at the infant and chattering to it. The infant would return the chatter and make crawling motions toward him. . . . As the infant approached within six inches to a foot, and if no other animal except the mother was nearby, the head male would again move away and repeat the chatter. If other animals began to close in, he would pick up the infant, and move away from the crowd, making a mild threat gesture to them (p. 35).

These interactions occurred during the infant's first week of life, before it had developed skilled motor coordination. Infants maturing in the troop in which these interactions took place were more skilled at locomotor activities at $1\frac{1}{2}$ months of age than were infants of another troop in which the adult males did not engage infants in these activities. It is also instructive to note that infants in the latter troop "began to walk largely on their own initiative, undoubtedly largely because their mothers often removed them from contact with [the leader male]" (p. 55).

2. Adult males reorient maturing young infants away from themselves and toward other troop members. For example, a leader male might return an infant to its mother after it had approached the male. Eventually the infant shifts its patterns of association away from adult and subadult males toward peer groups.

3. Adult males "reinforce socially acceptable behaviors appropriate to the age group by not interfering, or by giving positive reward (chatter, embrace, and so on)" (p. 55). An example is the shaping of the infant's sucking movements until the teeth-chattering facial expression emerges: each time the infant makes a sucking movement, both mother and father chatter to it and eventually the infant returns a facial chatter expression.

4. Adult males "extinguish or negate inappropriate behaviors by punishment (threat, chase, and so forth)" (p. 55). For example, aggressive interactions were disrupted by adult males.

These observations by Burton are extraordinary, since they document behaviors that involve not only highly affiliative contact between adult males and infants but also interactions that are virtually didactic as well. Whether or not such behaviors are evident in troops with more than one mature male is a question for future research. As to why such extensive caretaking has developed in adult males with a promiscuous mating system, this writer has no ready answer. Factors that bear consideration in the search for one are the extent of maternal restrictiveness and male–male antagonism among adults, both of which may influence patterns of male caretaking activity.

As mentioned above, Deag and Crook (1971) distinguished two forms of male–infant interaction in Barbary macaques: male care and agonistic buffering. We have been discussing the former throughout this paper, and it is now an opportune time to examine the latter. Deag and Crook used the term *agonistic buffering* to describe complex sequences in which a low-ranking individual interacts with a high-ranking one in the presence of a young infant. The presence of the infant is said to reduce the likelihood of attack by the higher ranking individual. For example, an adult male might hold a young infant to his chest and run up to a second adult male. The two males then interact with each other and the infant in an affiliative way. Adults both approach while carrying infants and are themselves approached while sitting with one. Further study is needed to explicate more precisely the functions of these interactions. It is not clear that an advantage is typically conferred to the "subordinate" animal, and there is evidence that such interactions do not necessarily take place in an agonistic context (Taub, personal communication). Thus the dichotomy between male caretaking and buffering may not be rigorous, particularly in light of the fact that "caretaking" behaviors such as holding, grooming, and carrying clearly take place during "buffering" sequences (see Fig. 4, page 366).

We stray across taxonomic lines at this point to examine similar sorts of interactions in three other species. In the first, the Japanese macaque, Itani (1959) described instances in which subleader and peripheral males carried or associated with infants. Infants were carried by these males when entering the central zone of the troop, in which the leader males and adult females were located. In Itani's view, "the infant was, as it were, playing the part of a passport for the central part of the troop" (p. 85).

---

[2] Although there is some dispute over classification, there are two principal groups of baboons: cynocephalus ("dog-headed ones") and hamadryas ("nymphs that live in the woods"). Etymology aside, the former occupy savannahs and forests south of the Sahara, and the latter occupy the semideserts of Ethiopia. Cynocephalus baboons have multimale groups, whereas hamadryas baboons have one-male groups.

In the case of the hamadryas baboon,[2] Kummer (1967) referred to a class of behaviors as "tripartite" (i.e., those simultaneously involving three individuals in different roles, with each individual interacting with both of the other members of the triad). As discussed in greater detail below, hamadryas baboons are organized in bands of one adult male, several adult females, and young. Surplus adult and subadult males form independent unisexual groups. The adult male of each band is somewhat of an autocrat: He is sought for protection but is also a source of intense fear. When subadult males approached leader males, an infant was occasionally used in a triadic interaction. An example follows (Kummer, 1967):

> When a subadult hamadryas male flees *toward* a dominant male . . . [he] will not dare to groom the male or to cling to him as a female would, nor will he present. He is trapped in front of the male, looking at his face and screaming more intensively every second until finally he may draw a bite from the adult male. If, however, he manages to invite a nearby infant to jump onto his back in this situation, he will at once run off with it (p. 69).

Subadults may also carry the infant in front of the adult male. Kummer found that adult males attack adult-infant pairs only half as frequently as they attack individuals, and so the buffering role of the infant in this species seems likely.

Ransom and Ransom (1971) observed buffering interactions in cynocephalus (anubis) baboons. Under stress adult males were seen to establish proximity or to carry infants on the ventrum or the back. One adult male frequently carried the young infant of a high-ranking female during a period of conflict with another adult male. In another case, in the presence of a particular adult male, another adult male often approached and displaced the former after picking up a young infant.

There thus appears to be a reliable body of observations indicating that adult and subadult males modulate interactions between themselves by associating with infants. Primate (if not most mammalian) infants are relatively immune from aggression, and this particular characteristic seems to promote their use in agonistic interactions between more mature animals.

### Cynocephalus Baboons

Male care of infants has been frequently documented for cynocephalus baboons. DeVore (1963, p. 322) stated that "the relationship of the infant to the adult males is important at every stage of the infant's maturation." He reported that juvenile and young adult males showed little interest in infants (a trend contrary to that seen in macaques). Fully mature

**Figure 4.** An "agonistic buffering" sequence in Barbary macaques. Two subadult males interact via a male 9- to 10-month-old infant. (*a*) One male carried the infant on his back up to the second male, and here both males sit in a characteristic ventral–ventral posture, grasping the infant, bending over it, and giving an affiliative teeth-chattering facial expression (often directed at the penis or anogenital area of

the infant). (*b*) Teeth chattering and manipulation of the infant by both males continues for about 15 seconds. (*c*) The infant begins to transfer from one male to the other. (*d*) Both males sit quietly next to each other as the infant climbs and explores. (*e*) The infant manipulates and sucks the penis of one male. (*f*) The sequence terminates as one male walks off, leaving the infant with the other male. Taub found that this form of male–infant interaction is common among Barbary macaques, although there is variation in its components, depending on social context and the identity of participants. (Photographs courtesy of David M. Taub.)

males of the central dominance hierarchy, in contrast, frequently approached and manipulated infants. Dominant males also carried young infants ventrally on some occasions.

Based primarily on DeVore's (1963) observations, the ontogeny of cynocephalus baboon male–infant interactions can be outlined as follows:

1. *Month 1–4.* Mature dominant males frequently approach mother–infant dyads. During the 1st month the infant rarely leaves its mother, but by the 3rd month infants crawl on males, leap on their shoulders, and sit upright on their backs. Interest in infants by adult males appears to peak from Month 2½ to 4. (Rowell [cited in Hinde, 1971] estimated this period to be Month 1½ to 3½.)

2. *Month 5–6.* Interest in the infant by the adult females declines rapidly during this period, and by the time the infant is solid brown, is negligible. Jealous protection by the adult males continues unabated, however, and the older infants and young juveniles increase their efforts to entice the young infants into a play group (p. 320).

3. *Month 8.* It is the oldest males of the central hierarchy, who have been near the infants since birth, who are the most active males in breaking up . . . squabbles and protecting the infants. The mother continues to intercede for her infant until it is 2 years old, that is, until her next infant is born, but males usually protect infants well into the infants' third year (p. 321).

4. *Month 10.* Infants now associate most frequently with peers but run to adult males for protection.

5. *Month 30.* By approximately this period the individual is no longer tolerantly protected, and it has entered into dominance–subordination relationships with other animals.

Contrary to DeVore's observations, Ransom and Ransom (1971) found that young (4- to 10-year-old) males do take an interest in infants—in this case the offspring of low-ranking females. Of particular value is their observation that:

An important factor in this type of relationship seemed to be the availability of the infant. Young mothers were more likely than older ones to allow the males to take their infants, probably for reasons which included inexperience as mothers and a comparative lack of well-established pair and subgroup bonds (p. 186).

Protective responses toward infants are very prominent among baboons. All the adult males of a troop respond to infant distress vocalizations and will intensely attack a human being who comes between an infant and the rest of the troop (DeVore, 1963). They also intervene in conspecific interactions:

Any sign of fear or frustration by the black infant causes an adult male to stare toward the play group, sometimes grunting softly, and the offending juvenile releases the infant immediately. Should the black infant cry out, the adult males leap to their feet and the juveniles scatter in terror while the young infant returns to its mother (DeVore, 1963, p. 319).

Adult males have been seen to carry off an infant after the sudden appearance of a human being, and play groups often form around dominant males (Tayler & Saayman, 1972). Ransom and Ransom (1971), who studied baboons in a deciduous forest, observed an enhancement of protective behaviors that coincided with the presence of predatory chimpanzees. Altmann and Altmann (1970) reported seeing an infant run to an adult male and be carried ventrally by him after a strong earthquake. Moreover, females with young infants tend to associate closely with adult males during troop movements (Tayler & Saayman, 1972).

There have been several reported cases of "adoption" of infants by adult males. Bolwig (1959) suggested that two cynocephalus (chacma) baboon infants had been adopted by adult males. Two large male infants in Nairobi National Park were also seen in constant association with two adult males (Dolhinow & Bishop, 1970). One 6- to 12-month-old infant, whose mother had died, was a constant associate of the second-ranking adult male: the infant groomed the male and walked next to him during troop movements in the day and slept next to him at night (DeVore, 1963).

After surveying male and female parental care in the above five species of macaque and one species of baboon, one can find support for the hypothesis that the extent of adult male parental care correlates positively with more relaxed, permissive maternal–infant interactions. A suggested ordinal ranking of the six species in terms of maternal restrictiveness and male care follows:

| *Extent of maternal restrictiveness (in ascending order)* | *Extent of parental care by adult males (in descending order)* |
|---|---|
| Barbary macaque | Barbary macaque |
| Bonnet macaque | Cynocephalus baboon |
| Cynocephalus baboon | Japanese macaque |
| Japanese macaque | Bonnet macaque |
| Pigtail macaque | Pigtail macaque |
| Rhesus macaque | Rhesus macaque |

(*Note:* A vertical line indicates approximate equality.)

Since this is an ordinal ranking, equal intervals between species are not necessarily implied. Specifically, the difference between baboons and Japanese macaques on the maternal scale, and the difference between bonnet and pigtail or rhesus macaques on the male scale, are greater than other interspecific differences.

One may tentatively conclude that the hypothesis stated above is supported, at least in the extremes of the scales. That is, Barbary macaques exhibit both low maternal restrictiveness and high male care of infants; the converse applies to pigtail and rhesus macaques. There is some lack of agreement in the middle of the scales. In part the lack of uniformity in the degree to which the various species have been studied contributes to this imperfect correlation.

Other sources of supporting evidence for the hypothesis are the observations of the consequences of removal of the mothers and the reports of variability in maternal restrictiveness. Specifically, there were the reports that: (1) rhesus male–infant contact in groups increased after the removal of the mother; (2) adult male and infant rhesus monkeys paired without the mother present were seen to develop extensive attachments; (3) some baboon mothers tolerate male–infant interaction to a greater degree than other mothers; and (4) Barbary macaque mothers in one troop allowed early male–infant contact, but in another troop they did not (to the same extent), and the consequences were evident in the infant's psychomotor development. It thus appears likely that the extent to which adult males in several macaque and baboon groups interact with infants is inversely proportional to the extent of restrictiveness of infants by mothers.[3] The simple point to be made is that the analysis of behavioral interactions between individuals of two classes cannot be done *in vacuo*; these relationships are inextricably bound in a complex system of social interactions with many individuals.

## Chimpanzees

There are only scattered references to male–infant interaction in chimpanzees (*Pan*). Infant chimpanzees are in virtually unbroken contact with

---

[3] Sarah Blaffer Hrdy (personal communication) has pointed out that this correlation may not hold for other groups of monkeys such as colobines. I agree, but my intentions were to control for other factors by surveying a selected number of species with relatively closely related phylogenies and habitats. Within such a highly selected sample, the correlation seems to withstand scrutiny; it must be generalized with care. In the case of several colobines, mothers are nonrestrictive in the sense that they freely pass infants among each other, but they often actively prohibit close contact between infants and adult males.

their mothers until 3½ to 5½ months, and it is thus not surprising that early male–infant contact is rarely observed in this promiscuous genus (van Lawick-Goodall, 1967, 1968). Adult males were said to be tolerant of infants while copulating with their mothers (van Lawick-Goodall, 1967), but under the circumstances that is not too surprising. Adult male chimpanzees have also been seen to be quite aggressive toward infants. Hamburg (cited in Maccoby & Jacklin, 1974, p. 372) observed an adult male smash an infant against a rock. Afterward he severely aggressed the mother trying to protect it. Indeed, Suzuki (1971) has even documented an instance in which several mature adult males in the Budongo Forest ate a newborn chimpanzee!

## ONE-MALE, MULTIFEMALE GROUPS

The remaining major classification of group organization to be considered here is one in which a single mature male is present, together with females and young. Additional males close to maturity are excluded from the primary group and either live solitarily or form all-male "bachelor" groups. Since the degree of kinship between the single adult male and the offspring in the group is greater than that between adult males and infants in multimale, multifemale promiscuous groups, and yet lower than that in monogamous groups, one would expect to find that the extent of male involvement in caretaking in one-male groups is intermediate between the other two types. Although it is difficult to put such a diffuse hypothesis to a rigorous test, evidence suggests that it is a reasonably viable one.

There are relatively few nonhuman primate groups with a one-male, multifemale organization. Most species considered in this section are Old World monkeys, and most are semiterrestrial. Whether one-male groups have evolved from multimale groups (e.g., Crook & Gartlan, 1966; Kummer, 1971, p. 94) or, conversely, have given rise to them (Eisenberg et al., 1972) is a question beyond the scope of this undertaking. It seems reasonable, however, that one-male reproductive groups are economical in the arid, impoverished habitats typical of these species (Gartlan & Brain, 1968). As stated by Crook and Gartlan (1966), "less food per reproductive unit goes to individuals not involved in rearing young" (p. 1202). More specifically Kummer (1971, p. 70) has suggested that, in areas where there is an extreme seasonal variability of food resources, such that a population must depend on a high reproductive potential of adults to replace seasonal losses, the number of females relative to males will be at a maximum. Sexual dimorphism is extremely pronounced in these species, presumably reflecting a high degree of sexual selection.

## Hamadryas Baboons

Undoubtedly the most well-known primate species exhibiting this form of group organization is the hamadryas baboon (*Papio hamadryas*). As shown in Figure 5, sexual dimorphism in this species is considerable. Males are at least twice as large as females and have a spectacular cape of fur.

The behavior of this species has been documented primarily through the intensive efforts of Hans Kummer, who has studied hamadryas baboons since 1955 (see, e.g., Kummer, 1968, 1971). Hamadryas form stable and cohesive units usually composed of one adult male, a "harem" of approximately four adult or subadult females, and several infants. The male tirelessly maintains the cohesion of the unit by threatening, neck-biting, or aggressively clasping females who either stray too far away or associate too closely with strangers. Approximately 20% of adult males

**Figure 5.** An adult male, infant, and adult female hamadryas baboon. The female is one of several who form a harem closely regulated by the adult male. (Photograph by Ron Garrison of the San Diego Zoo.)

in the troop as a whole do not form a harem, and instead typically associate in all-male groups.

A variety of male–infant interactions has been documented. Adult males frequently carry infants on their back while traveling. In addition,

> During rest periods, infants actively seek out certain young adult males who then hug and fondle them. Males, too, can adopt an infant. A motherless hamadryas infant is usually taken over by a young adult male that as yet owns no females. He then carries it en route . . . , allows it to sleep huddled against his belly at night, and prevents it from moving too far away (Kummer, 1971, pp. 80–82).

The key to understanding these sorts of interactions is the process of harem formation. Yearling baboons often play near a subadult or young adult male, out of sight of mothers. Frightened infants or young juveniles occasionally run to the arms of the male, who threatens the antagonist in much the same way as a mother might. The infant or young juvenile gradually establishes a protégé relationship with the older male. As they mature, female infants appear to transfer filial attachment from the mother to a subadult or adult male. Attraction to the male may be enhanced by the appearance of the male's cape of fur, possibly a "supernormal stimulus" for the infant (Jolly, 1963; Kummer, 1967). The process of male–infant attraction is actively supported by the male, of course, through the "adoption" behaviors described above. Such behaviors were not observed in females (exclusive of mothers), and they abruptly ended in males once they had formed a harem (Kummer, 1967). The use of infants by subadults in agonistic interactions, also discussed above, could also conceivably enhance the attraction of males to young.

## Gelada Monkeys

Gelada monkeys (*Theropithecus gelada*), which are more closely related to macaques than to baboons (e.g., Rowell, 1972, p. 56), are also organized in one-male, multifemale groups similar in many ways to those of hamadryas baboons. Harem units, all-male groups, and loose aggregations of juveniles are evident in free-ranging troops in their arid, mountainous Ethiopian habitat (Crook, 1966). Gelada females are not, however, strictly herded by males and are more likely to disperse throughout the troop. Moreover, one-male groups are formed and/or maintained not only by the male but also by the females (Crook, 1966; Kummer, 1971, p. 109).

Male–infant interaction has not been extensively documented in this genus. However, Bernstein (1975) recently reported observations of a captive group of geladas that reveal an interesting parallel with hamadryas baboons. He found that the bachelor male, but not the leaders of one-male groups, carried infants ventrally and dorsally (on the back), played with infants, and was the center of their play activities until he became leader of his own group of females. Moreover, on the day following his removal as group leader, an adult male was seen to carry and play with infants, apparently for the first time since becoming leader. Bachelor males aided immature individuals in distress, even during weaning struggles with the mother. It will be recalled that, in Kummer's hamadryas baboons, close affiliative interactions between adult males and infants abruptly terminated when the former formed a harem. It seems likely, therefore, that male–infant affiliative interactions in species with a harem sort of social organization are closely or almost exclusively related to the formation of one-male reproductive units.

## Patas Monkeys

Patas monkeys (*Erythrocebus patas*) also live in an arid habitat (sub-Saharan Africa), are primarily terrestrial, and show marked sexual dimorphism. Surplus adult males are solitary or form all-male bands. The number of adult females in the reproductive unit is, however, greater than that of geladas and hamadryas, ranging from 4 to 12. Moreover, males show relatively little aggressiveness toward females, probably because groups are widely dispersed and there is little likelihood of females' straying to another group (Hall, 1965).

The role of the adult male in patas groups is unique among primates in certain respects. Hall (1965) repeatedly observed instances in which adult males engaged in conspicuously watchful and diversionary behavior relative to potential antagonists or predators. For example, as Hall approached a group, the adult male descended noisily to the ground from a tree, crashed around in the brush, and ran off in the direction opposite from the one the group was taking. During such diversionary tactics the females and young often lie flat in the grass and hide, running at great speed from predators only as a last resort (Hall, 1965; Kummer, 1971, p. 53).

Hall found that the adult male often stays near the periphery of the group, and mothers with young infants were rarely close to the adult male at all. Kummer (1971, p. 55), however, reported an incident in which a patas male chased a jackal that was carrying an infant patas in its jaws. Such direct protective behavior is apparently rare, and adult males in patas groups benefit infants chiefly through their watchful and diversionary roles.

## Langurs

The langur genus (*Presbytis*) is of interest for several reasons. Troops of the same species—the hanuman langur, *Presbytis entellus*—are organized in both one-male and multimale patterns. Factors associated with these differences offer support for the correlation between habitat and group organization discussed earlier. Where hanuman langurs are found in a dry deciduous forest, with severe summer conditions and a high population density, they form one-male, multifemale groups with many extraneous males. In more temperate, less densely populated areas they are organized in more homogenous multimale, multifemale groups (Hrdy, 1974; Jay, 1965; Sugiyama, 1967; Yoshiba, 1968).

Of particular interest is the phenomenon of infanticide in langurs. There have been at least seven reported instances in which infants in one-male groups have been killed by an adult male, with approximately five infants being killed on each occasion (Hrdy, 1974; Mohnot, 1971; Sugiyama, 1965, 1966, 1967). In the purple-faced langur (*Presbytis senex*), Rudran (1973) reported eight probable deaths of infants and juveniles as a result of male aggression.

In all of the above cases (most of which were reviewed by Hrdy, 1974), attacks on langur infants by adult males followed the entry of an alien male into the one-male group. Typically the resident male was deposed by the newcomer, and the latter carried out the infanticide.

Given the exceptional care and attention devoted to immature individuals by most mammals, these reports of infanticide are exceptional indeed. In attempting to account for them, we once again have use for the concept of kinship selection. After the deaths of their infants, female langurs resumed being sexually receptive and copulated with the newcomer. Thus usurper males killed the progeny of another male and ultimately populated the group with their own offspring. Any defensive or generalized caretaking activities would be restricted to infants carrying the male's own genes and not those of another male. Invading males either ignore infants or are hostile toward them (Hrdy, 1974); however, established troop leaders are tolerant of infants (Yoshiba, 1968), actively defend the troop in general and infants in particular (Hrdy, 1974; Yoshiba, 1968), and have even been observed to play with infants (Yoshiba, 1968).

In my understanding of kinship selection, it is more suited to account for positive or caretaking behaviors—those most likely to enhance the survival of kin and therefore ultimately the agent's own genes. In this case, however, an application is being made for destructive interactions such as infanticide.

Is there any evidence that comparable behavioral systems are operative in other animals? In the case of the lion (*Panthera leo*), there is. To date, Schaller (1972) and Bertram (1975) have studied free-ranging lions in the Serengeti National Park, Tanzania, for a total of 7 years. Recently Bertram (1975) described a lion pride as consisting of a nucleus of 3 to 12 mature females, 1 to 6 (usually 2) mature males, and cubs of various ages. The group of females is a closed unit; that is, alien females were never observed to join a foreign pride. All the females in a pride are thus likely to be relatively closely related and are born and raised in their natal pride. Male lions, however, leave the natal pride when approximately 3 years old in small bands of up to 6 members. After approximately 2 years of nomadic existence they often take over a pride by expelling the resident males or finding a pride without males. These males, who are closely related, are unlikely to take over their natal pride, and so they are thus unlikely to be related to the females of the new pride.

Bertram found that the mortality rate of cubs rose steeply immediately after new males took over prides, and it remained high for about 3 months thereafter. The available evidence suggests that incoming males killed cubs of the former resident males. As was the case for langurs, female lions whose infants had died came into estrus and gave birth sooner than those whose offspring survived, and their offspring were almost certainly sired by the incoming male or males.

## Gorillas

The ongoing field study of free-ranging mountain gorillas by Dian Fossey (1976, personal communication) has provided particularly interesting information on male–infant interactions in this species. The group structure of mountain gorillas diverges from those of other species considered in this section insofar as more than one sexually mature male is typically present in a group. However, only the highest-ranking silverback male in each group is reproductively active. Thus the mating system of gorillas may be functionally similar to the one-male, multifemale groups typical of other species.

A striking parallel between langur and gorilla groups was documented by Fossey. In June of 1971, an adult female transferred from Group 4 to Group 8. Almost three years later, the highest-ranking silverback male of Group 8 died, leaving the group with no effective leader male. The transferred female had given birth to an infant 8 months previously. Shortly after the death of Group 8's leader male, the males of Group 4 began following Group 8 closely, and the highest-ranking silverback of Group 4 killed the infant. Its mother returned to Group 4 and subsequently gave birth to an infant sired by Group 4's leader. Once again we see one male eliminating genes of another male and ultimately caring for his own genetic investment. Two other infanticides were documented by Fossey, and in at least one case it is possible that a similar outcome will develop.

Happily, most male–infant interactions among gorillas are far from deadly. The same male that killed the infant of Group 8 had earlier adopted and reared an infant female. After her mother's death, the 3-year-old female made pitiful attempts at constructing nests next to the leading silverback male. On the 2nd or 3rd night, the male took the infant into his sleeping nest. Thereafter the infant traveled behind him constantly, but she walked, as he never carried her. The male groomed her more than a mother would typically groom her infant, and he remained in contact with her during rest periods. He was very protective of the infant, to the extent of not even allowing others to play with her.

Typically, very young individuals have little contact with silverback males. Mature and experienced mothers keep away from silverback males, and mothers with newborns stay on the periphery of the group. Only siblings are allowed nearby for 1–2 weeks, and the last to be allowed in close proximity are the silverback males (when infants are a few months old). Infants begin to approach silverback males by 2–3 years of age, and favorite play sites are the males' nests. Silverback males are typically very tolerant of infants, and low-intensity play sessions have been occasionally observed (e.g., a silverback walks up to an infant and pats it). This is generally responded to favorably by infants, since attention from silverbacks appears to be constantly sought.

## CONCLUSION AND SUMMARY

I have surveyed a wide range of species, habitats, behaviors, and social organizations. The variability of male–infant interaction within the primate order is impressive, but some constancies are evident. Concepts such as kinship and sexual selection are useful in approaching these relationships, but they cannot be expected to bear the full burden of explanation. Nonhuman primates have remarkably intricate systems of social interaction sufficiently complex to produce, for example, much closer affiliative male caretaking in promiscuous Barbary macaques than in one-male groups of gelada monkeys. What can emerge from a survey such as the present one is some idea of the variables affecting male caretaking activity, some indication of consistencies across divergent taxonomic groups, and some appreciation of the many dimensions of such behaviors. Male nonhuman primates have been observed to assist during the births of neonates; to premasticate food for infants; to carry, sleep with, groom, and play with young; to defend young virtually without exception; to provide a refuge during periods of high emotional arousal; to interact with young in a quasi-didactic fashion; to promote motor development; and to interrupt potentially destructive agonistic interactions among young. Less directly they may ultimately contribute to an infant's welfare by defending a territory from conspecifics or the troop itself from predators, and their activities as group leaders may promote the general welfare of the troop. At quite an opposite extreme they may also threaten, attack, kill, and eat infants, but these behaviors have been observed relatively rarely. There is evidence that, to the extent that adult males interact with infants, they respond to sex differences more clearly than mothers do. The degree of male–infant interaction in several species appears to be inversely related to the degree of maternal restrictiveness toward infants. I have also considered findings suggesting that typically hostile or indifferent males can form close attachments with infants and that the expression of behavioral potential for caretaking activity in males is a dimension that bears attention in nonhuman and, to be sure, in human primates.

## REFERENCES

Altmann, S. A., & Altmann, J. Baboon ecology: African field research. *Bibliotheca Primatologica*, 1970, No. 12, pp. 1–220.

Alexander, B. K. Parental behavior of adult male Japanese monkeys. *Behaviour*, 1970, **36**, 270–285.

Baysinger, C. M., Brandt, E. M., & Mitchell, G. Development of infant social isolate monkeys (*Macaca mulatta*) in their isolation environments. *Primates*, 1972, **13**, 257–270.

Berkson, G. Development of an infant in a captive gibbon group. *Journal of Genetic Psychology*, 1966, **108**, 311–325.

Bernstein, I. S. Activity patterns in a gelada monkey group. *Folia Primatologica*, 1975, **23**, 50–71.

Bertram, B. C. R. The social system of lions. *Scientific American*, 1975, **232**(5), 54–60, 65, 122.

Blaffer, Hrdy, S. Personal communication, March 12, 1976.

Blaffer, Hrdy, S. Care and exploitation of nonhuman primate infants by conspecifics other than the mother. In J. S. Rosenblatt, R. A. Hinde, E. Shaw, & C. Beer (Eds.), *Advances in the study of behavior* (Vol. 6). New York: Academic Press, 1976. Pp. 101–158.

Bolwig, N. A study of the behaviour of the chacma baboon, *Papio ursinus*. *Behaviour*, 1959, **14**, 136–163.

Box, H. O. A social developmental study of young monkeys (*Callithrix jacchus*) within a captive family group. *Primates,* 1975, **16**, 419–435.

Brandt, E. M., Baysinger, C., & Mitchell, G. Separation from rearing environment in mother-reared and isolation-reared rhesus monkeys (*Macaca mulatta*). *International Journal of Psychobiology,* 1972, **2**, 193–204.

Brandt, E. M., Irons, R., & Mitchell, G. Paternalistic behavior in four species of macaques. *Brain, Behavior and Evolution,* 1970, **3**, 415–420.

Breuggeman, J. A. Parental care in a group of free-ranging rhesus monkeys (*Macaca mulatta*). *Folia Primatologica,* 1973, **20**, 178–210.

Bucher, K. L. Temporal lobe neocortex and maternal behavior in rhesus monkeys. Unpublished doctoral dissertation, The Johns Hopkins University, Baltimore, Md., 1970.

Burton, F. D. The integration of biology and behavior in the socialization of *Macaca sylvana* of Gibraltar. In F. E. Poirier (Ed.), *Primate socialization.* New York: Random House, 1972. Pp. 29–62.

Burton, F. D., & Bick, M. J. A. A drift in time can define a deme: The implications of tradition drift in primate societies for hominid evolution. *Journal of Human Evolution,* 1972, **1**, 53–59.

Carpenter, C. R. A field study in Siam of the behavior and social relations of the gibbon (*Hylobates lar*). *Comparative Psychology Monographs,* 1940, **16**, 1–212.

Chance, M. R. A., & Jolly, C. J. *Social groups of monkeys, apes, and men.* London: Jonathan Cape, 1970.

Chivers, D. J. Spatial relations within the siamang group. *Proceedings of the Third International Congress of Primatology,* Zurich, 1970, **3**, 14–21. Basel: S. Karger, 1971.

Chivers, D. J. The siamang and the gibbon in the Malay Peninsula. *Gibbon and Siamang,* 1972, **1**, 103–135.

Crook, J. H. The evolution of social organisation and visual communication in the weaver birds (Ploceinae). *Behaviour,* 1964, Supplement 10, pp. 1–178.

Crook, J. H. The adaptive significance of avian social organizations. *Symposia of the Zoological Society of London,* 1965, **14**, 181–218.

Crook, J. H. Gelada baboon herd structure and movement: A comparative report. *Symposia of the Zoological Society of London,* 1966, **18**, 237–258.

Crook, J. H., & Gartlan, J. S. Evolution of primate societies. *Nature,* 1966, **210**, 1200–1203.

Crook, J. H., & Goss-Custard, J. D. Social ethology. *Annual Review of Psychology,* 1972, **23**, 277–312.

Darwin, C. [*On the origin of species by means of natural selection, or the preservation of favoured races in the struggle for life.*] Facsimile reproduction of 1st ed. edited by E. Mayr. New York: Atheneum, 1967. (Originally published, 1859.)

Darwin, C. [*The descent of man, and selection in relation to sex.*] (2 vols.). New York: International Publications Service, 1969. (Originally published, 1871.)

Dawson, G. A. Composition and stability of social groups of the tamarin, *Saguinus oedipus geoffroyi,* in Panama. *Proceedings of the Conference on the Biology and Conservation of the Callitrichidae,* August 18–20, 1975, Washington, D.C., in press.

Deag, J. M., & Crook, J. H. Social behavior and 'agonistic buffering' in the wild barbary macaque *Macaca sylvana* L. *Folia Primatologica,* 1971, **15,** 183–200.

DeVore, I. Mother–infant relations in free-ranging baboons. In H. L. Rheingold (Ed.), *Maternal behavior in mammals.* New York: Wiley, 1963. Pp. 305–335.

Dolhinow, P. J., & Bishop, N. The development of motor skills and social relationships among primates through play. In J. P. Hill (Ed.), *Minnesota symposia on child psychology* (Vol. 4). Minneapolis: University of Minnesota Press, 1970. Pp. 141–196.

Eisenberg, J. F. The social organizations of mammals. *Handbuch der Zoologie: Eine Naturgeschichte der Stamme des Tierreiches,* 1966, **8**(39), 1–92.

Eisenberg, J. F., Muckenhirn, N. A., & Rudran, R. The relation between ecology and social structure in primates. *Science,* 1972, **176,** 863–874.

Ellefson, J. O. Territorial behavior in the common white-handed gibbon, *Hylobates lar* Linn. In P. C. Jay (Ed.), *Primates: Studies in adaptation and variability.* New York: Holt, 1968. Pp. 180–199.

Epple, G. Vergleichende Untersuchungen uber Sexual- und Sozialverhalten der Krallenaffen (Hapalidae). *Folia Primatologica,* 1967, **7,** 37–65.

Epple, G. Maintenance, breeding, and development of marmoset monkeys (Callithricidae) in captivity. *Folia Primatologica,* 1970, **12,** 56–76.

Epple, G. Parental behavior in *Saguinus fuscicollis* ssp. [sic] (Callithricidae). *Folia Primatologica,* 1975, **24,** 221–238.

Epple, G. Pair formation and reproductive success in *Saguinus fuscicollis. Proceedings of the Conference on the Biology and Conservation of the Callitrichidae,* August 18–20, 1975, Washington, D.C., in press.

Evans, R. I. A conversation with Konrad Lorenz. *Psychology Today,* 1974, **8**(6), 82–93.

Fitzgerald, A. Rearing marmosets in captivity. *Journal of Mammalogy,* 1935, **16,** 181–188.

Forbes, H. O. *A handbook to the primates.* London: Edward Arnold, 1897.

Fossey, D. The behavior of mountain gorillas. Lecture presented at Stanford University, May 11, 1976.

Fossey, D. Personal communication, May 14, 1976.

Fox, G. J. Some comparisons between siamang and gibbon behaviour. *Folia Primatologica,* 1972, **18,** 122–139.

Fox, G. J. Peripheralization behavior in a captive siamang family. *American Journal of Physical Anthropology*, 1974, **41**, 479.

Gartlan, J. S., & Brain, C. K. Ecology and social variability in *Cercopithecus aethiops* and *C. mitis*. In P. C. Jay (Ed.), *Primates: Studies in adaptation and variability*. New York: Holt, 1968. Pp. 253–292.

Gomber, J. M. Caging adult male isolation-reared rhesus monkeys (*Macaca mulatta*) with infant conspecifics. Unpublished doctoral dissertation University of California, Davis, 1975.

Hall, K. R. L. Behaviour and ecology of the wild patas monkey, *Erythrocebus patas*, in Uganda. *The Journal of Zoology*, 1965, **148**, 15–87.

Hamilton, W. D. The genetical evolution of social behaviour. I, II. *Journal of Theoretical Biology*, 1964, **7**, 1–52.

Hamilton, W. J., III. *Life's color code*. New York: McGraw-Hill, 1973.

Hampton, J. K. Laboratory requirements and observations of *Oedipomidas oedipus*. *American Journal of Physical Anthropology*, 1964, **22**, 239–244.

Hampton, J. K., Hampton, S. H., & Landwehr, B. J. Observations on a successful breeding colony of the marmoset *Oedipomidas oedipus*. *Folia Primatologica*, 1966, **4**, 265–287.

Hanif, M. Notes on the breeding of the white-headed saki monkey (*Pithecia pithecia*) at Georgetown Zoo. *International Zoo Yearbook*, 1967, **7**, 81–82.

Harlow, M. K., Harlow, H. F., Eisele, C. D., & Ruppenthal, G. C. Rhesus macaque paternal behavior in a nuclear family situation. In preparation: Cited in Suomi et al., 1973.

Hearn, J. P., & Lunn, S. F. The reproductive biology of the marmoset monkey, *Callithrix jacchus*. *Laboratory Animal Handbooks*, 1975, **6**, 191–204.

Hinde, R. A. Development of social behavior. In A. M. Schrier & F. Stollnitz (Eds.), *Behavior of nonhuman primates* (Vol. 3). New York: Academic Press, 1971. Pp. 1–68.

Hoage, R. Parental care in *Leontopithecus r. rosalia*: Carrying behavior. *Proceedings of the Conference on the Biology and Conservation of the Callitrichidae, August 18–20, 1975, Washington, D.C.*, in press.

Horn, H. S. The adaptive significance of colonial nesting in the Brewer's blackbird (*Euphagus cyanocephalus*). *Ecology*, 1968, **49**, 682–694.

Hrdy, S. B. See also Blaffer Hrdy, S.

Hrdy, S. B. Male–male competition and infanticide among the langurs (*Presbytis entellus*) of Abu, Rajasthan. *Folia Primatologica*, 1974, **22**, 19–58.

Ingram, J. C. Husbandry and observation methods of a breeding colony of marmosets (*Callithrix jacchus*) for behavioural research. *Laboratory Animals*, 1975, **9**, 249–259.

Itani, J. Paternal care in the wild Japanese monkey, *Macaca fuscata fuscata*. *Primates*, 1959, **2**, 61–93.

Jay, P. C. The common langur of North India. In I. DeVore (Ed.), *Primate *behavior: Field studies of monkeys and apes.* New York: Holt, 1965. Pp. 197–249.

Jolly, A. *The evolution of primate behavior.* New York: Macmillan, 1972.

Jolly, C. A suggested case of evolution by sexual selection in Primates. *Man,* 1963, **63**, 177–178.

Kaufman, I. C., & Rosenblum, L. A. The waning of the mother–infant bond in two species of macaque. In B. M. Foss (Ed.), *Determinants of infant behaviour* (Vol. 4). London: Methuen, 1969. Pp. 41–59.

Kaufmann, J. H. Behavior of infant rhesus monkeys and their mothers in a free-ranging band. *Zoologica,* 1966, **51**, 17–27.

Kawai, M. A field experiment in the process of group formation in the Japanese monkey (*Macaca fuscata*) and the releasing of the group at Chirayama. *Primates,* 1960, **2**, 181–253.

Kummer, H. Tripartite relations in hamadryas baboons. In S. A. Altmann (Ed.), *Social communication among primates.* Chicago: University of Chicago, 1967. Pp. 63–71.

Kummer, H. Social organization of hamadryas baboons. *Bibliotheca Primatologica,* 1968, No. 6, pp. 1–189.

Kummer, H. *Primate societies.* Chicago: Aldine-Atherton, 1971.

Lack, D. *Ecological adaptations for breeding in birds.* London: Methuen, 1968.

Langford, J. B. Breeding behavior of *Hapale jacchus* (Common marmoset). *South African Journal of Science,* 1963, **59**, 299–300.

Lindburg, D. G. The rhesus monkey in North India: An ecological and behavioral study. In L. A. Rosenblum (Ed.), *Primate behavior: Developments in field and laboratory research* (Vol. 2). New York: Academic Press, 1971. Pp. 1–106.

Lucas, N. S., Hume, E. M., & Henderson Smith, H. On the breeding of the common marmoset (*Hapale jacchus* Linn.) in captivity when irradiated with ultra-violet rays. *Proceedings of the Zoological Society of London,* 1927, **30**, 447–451.

Lucas, N. S., Hume, E. M., & Henderson Smith, H. On the breeding of the common marmoset (*Hapale jacchus* Linn.) in captivity when irradiated with ultra-violet rays. II. A ten years' family history. *Proceedings of the Zoological Society of London,* Series A, 1937, **107**, 205–211.

Maccoby, E. E., & Jacklin, C. N. *The psychology of sex differences.* Stanford, Calif.: Stanford University Press, 1974.

MacRoberts, M. H. The social organization of Barbary apes (*Macaca sylvana*) on Gibraltar. *American Journal of Physical Anthropology,* 1970, **33**, 83–99.

Mallinson, J. J. C. The breeding and maintenance of marmosets at Jersey Zoo. *International Zoo Yearbook,* 1971, **11**, 79–83 (a).

Mallinson, J. J. C. Observations on the breeding of Red-handed Tamarin,

*Saguinus* ( = Tamarin) *midas* (Linnaeus, 1758) with comparative notes on other species of Callithricidae ( = Hapalidae) breeding in captivity. *Annual Review of the Jersey Wildlife Preservation Trust*, 1971, **8**, 19–31 (b).

Mason, W. A. Social organization of the South American monkey *Callicebus moloch*: A preliminary report. *Tulane Studies in Zoology*, 1966, **13**, 23–28.

McCann, C. Notes on the colouration and habits of the white-browed gibbon or hoolock (*Hylobates hoolock* Harl.) *Journal of the Bombay Natural History Society*, 1933, **36**, 395–405.

McClure, H. E. Some observations of primates in climax diptocarp forest near Kuala Lumpur, Malaya. *Primates*, 1964, **3–4**, 39–58.

Mitchell, G. D. Paternalistic behavior in primates. *Psychological Bulletin*, 1969, **71**, 399–417.

Mitchell, G., & Brandt, E. M. Paternal behavior in primates. In F. Poirier (Ed.), *Primate socialization*. New York: Random House, 1972. Pp. 173–206.

Mohnot, S. M. Some aspects of social changes and infant-killing in the hanuman langur, *Presbytis entellus* (Primates: Cercopithecidae) in Western India. *Mammalia*, 1971, **35**, 175–198.

Moynihan, M. Some behavior patterns of Platyrrhine monkeys. I. The night monkey (*Aotus trivirgatus*). *Smithsonian Miscellaneous Collections*, 1964, **146**, No. 5.

Napier, J. R., & Napier, P. H. *A handbook of living primates*. New York: Academic Press, 1967.

Neyman, P. F. Some aspects of the ecology of free-ranging cotton-top tamarins (*Saguinus o. oedipus*) and the conservation status of the species. *Proceedings of the Conference on the Biology and Conservation of the Callitrichidae*, August 18–20, 1975, Washington, D.C., in press.

Neyman, P. F. Personal communication, January 30, 1976.

Ochs, K. Pygmies in my drawing-room. *Animals,* 1964, **3**(6), 142–145.

Orians, G. H. On the evolution of mating systems in birds and mammals. *The American Naturalist*, 1969, **103**, 589–603.

Potter, S., & Sargent, L. *Pedigree: The origins of words from nature*. New York: Taplinger, 1973.

Ransom, T. W., & Ransom, B. S. Adult male–infant relations among baboons (*Papio anubis*). *Folia Primatologica*, 1971, **16**, 179–195.

Raphael, D. Uncle rhesus, auntie pachyderm, and mom: All sorts and kinds of mothering. *Perspectives in Biology and Medicine*, 1969, **12**, 290–297.

Redican, W. K. A longitudinal study of behavioral interactions between adult male and infant rhesus monkeys (*Macaca mulatta*). Unpublished doctoral dissertation, University of California, Davis, 1975.

Redican, W. K., & Mitchell, G. A longitudinal study of parental behavior in adult male rhesus monkeys. I. Observations on the first dyad. *Develop-*

*mental Psychology*, 1973, **8**, 135–136.

Redican, W. K., & Mitchell, G. Play between adult male and infant rhesus monkeys. *American Zoologist*, 1974, **14**, 295–302.

Rothe, H. Some aspects of sexuality and reproduction in groups of captive marmosets *(Callithrix jacchus). Zeitschrift für Tierpsychologie*, 1975, **37**, 255–273.

Rowell, T. *The social behaviour of monkeys*. Baltimore: Penguin, 1972.

Rowell, T. E., Hinde, R. A., & Spencer-Booth, Y. "Aunt"–infant interaction in captive rhesus monkeys. *Animal Behaviour*, 1964, **12**, 219–226.

Rudran, R. The reproductive cycles of two subspecies of purple-faced langurs *(Presbytis senex)* with relation to environmental factors. *Folia Primatologica*, 1973, **19**, 41–60.

Schaller, G. B. *The Serengeti lion: A study of predator–prey relations*. Chicago: University of Chicago, 1972.

Selander, R. K. Sexual selection and dimorphism in birds. In B. G. Campbell (Ed.), *Sexual selection and the descent of man: 1871–1971*. Chicago: Aldine, 1972. Pp. 180–230.

Simonds, P. E. The bonnet macaque in South India. In I. DeVore (Ed.), *Primate behavior: Field studies of monkeys and apes*. New York: Holt, 1965. Pp. 175–195.

Simonds, P. E. Sex differences in bonnet macaque networks and social structure. *Archives of Sexual Behavior*, 1974, **3**, 151–166.

Snyder, P. A. Behavior of *Leontopithecus rosalia* (Golden-lion marmoset) and related species: A review. *Journal of Human Evolution*, 1974, **3**, 109–122.

Southwick, C. H., Beg, M. A., & Siddiqi, M. R. Rhesus monkeys in North India. In I. DeVore (Ed.), *Primate behavior*. New York: Holt, 1965. Pp. 111–159.

Spencer-Booth, Y. The behaviour of group companions towards rhesus monkey infants. *Animal Behaviour*, 1968, **16**, 541–557.

Spencer-Booth, Y. The relationship between mammalian young and conspecifics other than mothers and peers: A review. In D. S. Lehrman, R. A. Hinde, & E. Shaw (Eds.), *Advances in the study of behavior* (Vol. 3). New York: Academic Press, 1970. Pp. 119–194.

Spencer-Booth, Y., & Hinde, R. A. The effects of separating rhesus monkey infants from their mothers for six days. *Journal of Child Psychology and Psychiatry and Allied Disciplines*, 1967, **7**, 179–197.

Stellar, E. The marmoset as a laboratory animal: Maintenance, general observations of behavior, and simple learning. *Journal of Comparative and Physiological Psychology*, 1960, **53**, 1–10.

Sugiyama, Y. On the social change of hanuman langurs *(Presbytis entellus)* in their natural conditions. *Primates*, 1965, **6**, 381–418.

Sugiyama, Y. An artificial social change in a hanuman langur troop. *Primates*, 1966, **7**, 41–72.

Sugiyama, Y. Social organization of hanuman langurs. In S. A. Altmann (Ed.), *Social communication among primates.* Chicago: University of Chicago, 1967. Pp. 221–236.

Sugiyama, Y. Characteristics of the social life of bonnet macaques (*Macaca radiata*). *Primates*, 1971, **12**, 247–266.

Suomi, S. J. Social development of rhesus monkeys reared in an enriched laboratory environment. Presented at the 20th International Congress of Psychology, Tokyo, Japan, August 13–19, 1972.

Suomi, S. J., Eisele, C. D., Grady, S. A., & Tripp, R. L. Social preferences of monkeys reared in an enriched laboratory environment. *Child Development*, 1973, **44**, 451–460.

Suzuki, A. Carnivority and cannibalism observed among forest-living chimpanzees. *Journal of the Anthropological Society of Nippon*, 1971, **79**, 30–48.

Taub, D. M. Personal communication, September 10, 1975.

Tayler, C. K., & Saayman, G. S. The social organisation and behaviour of dolphins (*Tursiops aduncus*) and baboons (*Papio anubis*): Some comparisons and assessments. *Annals of the Cape Provincial Museum*, 1972, **9**, 11–49.

Tenaza, R. R., & Hamilton, W. J., III. Preliminary observations of the Mentawai Islands gibbon, *Hylobates klossii*. *Folia Primatologica*, 1971, **15**, 201–211.

Trivers, R. L. Parental investment and sexual selection. In B. G. Campbell (Ed.), *Sexual selection and the descent of man: 1871–1971*. Chicago: Aldine, 1972. Pp. 136–179.

van Lawick-Goodall, J. Mother–offspring relationships in free-ranging chimpanzees. In D. Morris (Ed.), *Primate ethology*. Chicago: Aldine, 1967. Pp. 365–436.

van Lawick-Goodall, J. The behaviour of free-living chimpanzees in the Gombe Stream Reserve. *Animal Behaviour Monographs*, 1968, **1**, 161–311.

Wilson, E. O. *Sociobiology: The new synthesis*. Cambridge, Mass.: Belknap Press, Harvard University, 1975.

Yoshiba, K. Local and intertroop variability in ecology and social behavior of common Indian langurs. In P. C. Jay (Ed.), *Primates: Studies in adaptation and variability*. New York: Holt, 1968. Pp. 217–242.

# Subject Index

Ability, 19, 89, 101, 237, 238, 247, 256, 263, 266
  mathematical, 245, 250, 255, 256, 263, 264, 267
  verbal, 245, 255, 256
Acceptance, 247
Accessibility, paternal, 5, 9, 25, 29, 78, 96, 105, 250. *See also* Deprivation, paternal
Achievement, 19, 244, 248, 263
  arithmetic, 257
  high, 246
  low, 246
  motivation, 248
  *see also* Underachievement
Adjustment, 16, 21, 89, 104, 124. *See also* Heterosexual adjustment
Adolescence, 9, 94, 227, 243. *See also* Age
Adoption by males, 369, 373, 377
Affection, 76, 220
  fathers, 93, 253, 255, 283, 298
  mothers, 169, 175
  *see also* Love; Nurturance; Quality of relationship; *and* Warmth
Affiliative behaviors, 6, 309, 311, 312, 313
Affluence, 266. *See also* Economic context; Socioeconomic status
Age, of children, 233, 256, 360, 365, 368. *See also* Infancy; Juveniles
Aggression, 94, 129, 228, 230, 250, 350, 352, 355, 356, 359, 360, 361, 363, 364, 365, 368, 369, 371, 372, 373, 374, 375, 377. *See also* Defense; Hostility; Territoriality; *and* Warfare
Ambiguity, paternal intolerance of, 247
Ambivalence, paternal, 252, 288
Androgens, 208, 209, 210. *See*

*also* Hormones
Anthropoids, 348. *See also* Primates
Antisocial behavior, 107. *See also* Delinquency; Gang delinquency; Immorality; *and* Morality
Anxiety, 104, 105
Apes, 348
Assertiveness, 94
Attachment, 3, 4, 5, 159, 208, 287, 307-327, 358, 359, 370, 373, 377
  behavior, 3, 6, 308, 309, 311, 312, 313, 315-319
  father-infant, 77, 253, 292, 307-327
  mother-infant, 282, 285, 286, 288, 289, 294, 307-327
  theory, 164
  *see also* Infancy; Quality of relationships
Attitudes, 242
Authority, 110, 179, 246, 301
Autism, 121
Autonomy, 248, 253, 291

Baboons, 345, 355, 364, 369. *See also* Cynocephalus baboons; Hamadryas baboon; Primates
Barbary monkeys, 361, 362, 363, 364, 366, 367, 369, 370, 377. *See also* Primates
Bayley, I.Q., 178, 243. *See also* Intellectual development
Bedouin, Rwala, 193, 196
Berkeley Growth study, 238, 239, 260
Big Brothers, 137
Biological influences, 90, 102, 103, 237, 238, 245
Birds, 187, 188, 209, 353, 354
Birth, 291, 349, 360, 377

Subject Index 407

Time Perception, 110
Titi monkeys, 350. *See also* Primates
Transitivity, 178
Transport, 190, 191. *See also* Caretaking
Tupaia, 66
Twinning, 349, 353. *See also* Birth

Underachievement, 244, 246, 249, 255.
   *See also* Achievement
Unemployment, 211, 240. *See also* Occupation; Socioeconomic status

Values, 242
Verbal ability, *see* Ability
Vervet monkeys, 354. *See also* Primates
Vulnerability, 166, 256, 264, 265. *See also*
   Age; Critical periods; Father absence;

Femininity; Masculinity; *and* Sex
roles

Warfare, 194, 196, 198, 203, 204, 207.
   *See also* Aggression; Defense; *and*
   Territoriality
Warmth, 29, 104, 122, 253. *See also*
   Affection; Nurturance; *and* Quality of
   relationship
Whites, 246, 264
Wolves, 354. *See also* Canids
Women, 282
   liberation of, 81
   *see also* Feminity; Daughters; Mothers
Work, 73

Y.M.C.A., 137